U.S. COURT CASES
Revised Edition

Post abortive women say,

ABORTION
HURTS
WOMEN

U.S. COURT CASES

Revised Edition

Volume 3

Court Cases:

Roberts v. United States Jaycees —
Zurcher v. The Stanford Daily

Appendixes

Indexes

Edited by
Thomas Tandy Lewis
St. Cloud State University

SALEM PRESS
Pasadena, California   Hackensack, New Jersey

∞ The paper used in these volumes conforms to the American National Standard for Permanence of Paper for Printed Library Materials, Z39.48-1992 (R1997).

Some of the essays in this work originally appeared in the following Salem Press sets: *Criminal Justice* (2006), *Encyclopedia of the U.S. Supreme Court* (2001), *Great Events from History: The Nineteenth Century* (2007), *Great Events from History: The Twentieth Century* (2008), *U.S. Court Cases* (1999), and *U.S. Supreme Court* (2007). New material has been added.

Library of Congress Cataloging-in-Publication Data
U.S. court cases / editor, Thomas Tandy Lewis. — Rev. ed.
    p. cm. — (Magill's choice)
  Includes bibliographical references and index.
  ISBN 978-1-58765-672-9 (set : alk. paper)
  ISBN 978-1-58765-673-6 (vol. 1 : alk. paper)
  ISBN 978-1-58765-674-3 (vol. 2 : alk. paper)
  ISBN 978-1-58765-675-0 (vol. 3 : alk. paper)
    1. Law—United States—Cases. 2. Courts—United States. I. Lewis, Thomas
T. (Thomas Tandy) II. Title: US court cases. III. Title: United States court cases.
  KF385.A4U15 2010
  347.73'1—dc22
                                                                           2010019782

CONTENTS

CONTENTS

Appendixes

U.S. SUPREME COURT
CITATION NUMBERS

Since the year 1876, official versions of U.S. Supreme Court decisions and opinions have appeared in volumes titled *United States Reports*, published by the federal government. Each standard citation listed in these volumes usually includes this information:

- names of the parties involved in the case, in italics
- volume number of *United States Reports* containing the case
- abbreviation "U.S."
- page number on which the case begins
- page number of quoted passage (where relevant)
- year in which the decision was made, in parentheses

This is a typical example: "*Brown v. Board of Education of Topeka*, 349 U.S. 294, at 342 (1954)."

For Supreme Court rulings earlier than 1876, each official government volume was published under the last name of the Court reporter who supervised its editing and publication. Standard citations to pre-1876 cases include the names of the reporters preceded by the numbers of the volumes within the series the reporters edited. The citations then give the volume numbers used by *United States Reports* in parentheses. This is a typical example: "*Marbury v. Madison*, 1 Cranch (5 U.S.) 137, at 146 (1803)."

Through 1875, the volumes were edited by seven different Court reporters whose names (Dallas, Cranch, Wheaton, Peters, Howard, Black, and Wallace) appear in citations. Howard (abbreviated How.) supervised the publication of the most volumes (twenty-four); Black the fewest (two).

The names given to U.S. Supreme Court decisions sometimes are different from the standard forms discussed above. For example, petitions for habeas corpus frequently do not include two parties; names of such cases typically include the Latin expression *Ex parte*, which means "in behalf of" or "for one party," as in "*Ex parte Milligan*, 71 U.S. 2 (1866)." Also, the Latin expression *In re*, which means "concerning" or "in the matter of" is frequently employed in judicial proceedings when there are no adversarial parties, as in "*In Re Gault*, 387 U.S. 1 (1967)."

After the Supreme Court hands down a ruling, its official version is generally not published until one or two years later. Consequently, until the decision is officially published, its page number in *United States Reports* cannot be known. Early publications of such cases are known as "slip opinions," and their citations utilize an underscore line to substitute for the volume number, as in "*Ricci v. DeStefano*, 555 U.S. ____ (2009)."

Although the vast majority of lawyers and legal writers refer to the federal government's official publications, some prefer to utilize one of the privately published and unofficial compilations, such as *Supreme Court Reporter* or *United States Supreme Court Reports, Lawyers' Edition*. Until the Court's official opinions are published in *United States Reports*, many writers cite numbers from these unofficial compilations. This is an example of a citation from the former publication: "*Reno v. American Civil Liberties Union*, 117 S.Ct. 2329 (1997)." In *United States Reports*, the same case is cited as "*Reno v. American Civil Liberties Union*, 521 U.S. 824 (1997)."

For more detailed information on citing court cases, one of the best resources is *The Bluebook: A Uniform System of Citation* (19 ed., 2010), an annually updated publication of the *Harvard Law Review*. Another useful publication is *ALWD Citation Manual: A Professional System of Citation* (2005) by Darby Dickerson and the Association of Legal Writing Directors.

COMPLETE LIST OF CONTENTS

Volume 1

Law and the Courts

Court Cases

Volume 2

Volume 3

Contents lxxxv

Appendixes

U.S. COURT CASES
Revised Edition

ROBERTS V. UNITED STATES JAYCEES

Court: U.S. Supreme Court
Citation: 468 U.S. 609
Date: July 3, 1984
Issues: Freedom of assembly and association; Sex discrimination

- *Jaycees* was a landmark U.S. Supreme Court decision that held that the state's interest in combating sex discrimination was sufficiently compelling to justify application of an antidiscrimination statute to some private organizations.

The Minnesota Human Rights Act prohibited sex discrimination in a place of public accommodation. The state's enforcement agency applied the statute to the Jaycees, a private service club that restricted membership to men. The Jaycees brought a lawsuit, claiming that requiring the organization to accept women as members violated its right of free association guaranteed by the First and Fourteenth Amendments.

By a 7-0 vote, the Supreme Court rejected the claim. Writing for a majority, Justice William J. Brennan, Jr., recognized constitutional protection for two varieties of freedom of association: the right to choose "intimate human relationships" and the right to engage in expressive activities. Brennan noted that the Jaycees was "neither small nor selective," and that the presence of women in the organization would require no change in its announced creed. Such a small limit on the free association rights of the Jaycees was justified by the state's interest in eradicating discrimination. In a more narrow concurrence, Justice Sandra Day O'Connor argued that the Jaycees operated more like a commercial organization than a private club.

Subsequent to the *Jaycees* decision, the Court ruled that public accommodation laws apply to many other private organizations. In *New York State Club Association v. City of New York* (1988), for example, the Court held that certain all-male social clubs must admit women. However, in the case of *Hurley v. Irish-American Gay, Lesbian, and Bisexual Group of Boston* (1995), the Court held that the principle of free association permitted a private group to exclude a gay rights group from participating in its annual St. Patrick's Day parade.

Thomas Tandy Lewis

Further Reading

Gold, Susan Dudley. *Roberts v. Jaycees: Women's Rights.* Tarrytown, N.Y.: Marshall Cavendish Benchmark, 2009. Part of its publisher's Supreme Court Milestones series designed for young-adult readers, this volume offers an accessible history and analysis of the *Jaycees* case that examines opposing sides in the case, the people involved, and the case's lasting impact. Includes bibliography and index.

See also *Hurley v. Irish-American Gay, Lesbian, and Bisexual Group of Boston*; *New York State Club Association v. City of New York*; *Rotary International v. Duarte*.

ROBINSON V. CALIFORNIA

Court: U.S. Supreme Court
Citation: 370 U.S. 660
Date: June 25, 1962
Issues: Cruel and unusual punishment; Illegal drugs; Incarceration

- *Robinson v. California* which held that it was cruel and unusual punishment to incarcerate drug addicts simply because of their addictions, was for some critics emblematic of the Warren Court's "softness" on crime.

Robinson was convicted under a California statute making it a crime to be a drug addict and was sentenced to ninety days in jail. The statute did not require the state to prove that the accused had either bought or purchased drugs or that he or she possessed them—the mere status of being a drug addict was enough to convict a defendant. Robinson appealed, and the U.S. Supreme Court overturned the conviction on grounds that incarceration for ninety days for what amounts to an illness constitutes cruel and unusual punishment.

Because of such rulings as *Mapp v. Ohio* (1961), which extended guarantees against unreasonable search and seizure to state defendants, the Court overseen by Chief Justice Earl Warren was criticized for "coddling" criminals. *Robinson* was doubly controversial because it is based on the assumption that drug addiction is an illness over which the addict has no control. Indeed, six years later the Court declined to follow its own precedent in *Powell v. Texas*

(1968), in which it upheld the criminal conviction of a chronic alcoholic, declaring that the state of knowledge regarding alcoholism was inadequate to permit the enunciation of a new constitutional principle.

Still, *Robinson* is important for making the cruel and unusual punishment clause of the Eighth Amendment applicable at the state as well as the federal level. The case was a continuation of the "due process revolution," championed initially by Justice Hugo Black, that reached its high-water mark during Earl Warren's tenure as chief justice. By means of the due process clause of the Fourteenth Amendment, the guarantees of the Bill of Rights limiting federal action were "incorporated" into the Fourteenth Amendment, thus becoming applicable to state governments.

The Fourteenth Amendment, passed in the wake of the Civil War, makes all persons born in the United States citizens whose privileges and immunities cannot be restricted and whose rights of due process and equal protection cannot be denied. Some framers of the amendment indicated that the privileges and immunities extended therein included the guarantees of the Bill of Rights, but this point was left ambiguous. In *Palko v. Connecticut* (1937), the Court explicitly addressed the issue for the first time, stating that some of the rights embodied in the first ten amendments to the Constitution were so fundamental that the Fourteenth Amendment obligated states to observe them.

Writing in dissent in *Adamson v. California* (1947), Justice Black argued that the Fourteenth Amendment obligated states to honor all aspects of the Bill of Rights. The Court has never quite adopted this view, but by the time Earl Warren's leadership ended in 1969, most of the Bill of Rights had been applied to the states.

Lisa Paddock

See also *Adamson v. California; Furman v. Georgia; Hudson v. Palmer; Hutto v. Davis; Mapp v. Ohio; Palko v. Connecticut; Rummel v. Estelle; Solem v. Helm; Trop v. Dulles.*

Rochin v. California

Court: U.S. Supreme Court
Citation: 342 U.S. 165
Date: January 2, 1952
Issues: Due process of law; Evidence; Incorporation doctrine

- Although the U.S. Supreme Court did not make the Fifth Amendment or the exclusionary rule binding on the states, it held that evidence obtained in a shocking and grossly unfair manner cannot be used in a criminal trial.

Based on information that Antonio Rochin was selling drugs, the police entered his home without obtaining a search warrant. After observing Rochin swallow two capsules, the police rushed him to a hospital, where a doctor used an emetic solution and a stomach pump to force him to vomit the pills into a pail. The pills, which contained morphine, were used as evidence in his trial. He was found guilty and sentenced to sixty days in jail.

By an 8-0 vote, the Supreme Court overturned Rochin's conviction. Speaking for a majority, Justice Felix Frankfurter declared that breaking into the defendant's house and then forcibly extracting his stomach's content was "conduct that shocks the conscience." Quoting *Palko v. Connecticut* (1937), Frankfurter interpreted the due process clause as protecting those personal immunities that "are implicit in the concept of ordered liberty." In concurring opinions, Justices Hugo L. Black and William O. Douglas argued in favor of deciding the case on the basis of the Fifth Amendment, which should have been made binding on the states through the Fourteenth Amendment. Black criticized Frankfurter for using a subjective natural law approach.

The Court finally ruled that the Fifth Amendment applied to the states in *Malloy v. Hogan* (1964), and it ruled that in Fourth Amendment cases, the exclusionary rule is binding on the states in *Mapp v. Ohio* (1961). Even though states are now required to respect most of the principles in the Bill of Rights, the subjective "shock the conscience" standard reappears from time to time in a variety of different contexts.

Thomas Tandy Lewis

See also *Escobedo v. Illinois; Malloy v. Hogan; Mapp v. Ohio; Palko v. Connecticut.*

ROE V. WADE

Court: U.S. Supreme Court
Citation: 410 U.S. 113
Date: January 22, 1973
Issues: Reproductive rights; Right to privacy; Women's issues

• The decision in *Roe v. Wade* struck down states' restrictions on a woman's ability to obtain an abortion and generated an ongoing controversy concerning reproductive choice.

Restrictions on a woman's decision to terminate a pregnancy emerged in the mid-nineteenth century in the United States. Prior to that time, English common law attitudes, which prohibited abortion after "quickening," the point at which the pregnant woman could feel fetal movement, were occasionally and irregularly enforced. The growing organized medical profession began a campaign to criminalize abortion at any point after conception and to discourage home remedies and midwives, who, despite a lack of formal medical training, usually assisted at abortions.

The rhetoric of the antiabortion campaign expanded during the second half of the nineteenth century. The initial calls for restrictions on abortion to safeguard maternal health were buttressed, eventually, by moral condemnations of abortion as a threat to marriage, the institution of the family, and the proper role of women in society, since readily available abortions might encourage promiscuity and lead to a decline in the white middle class. Many of the early proponents of women's rights supported these justifications for restrictions on reproductive choice. Early opponents of abortion rarely argued the position that the fetus was a person, entitled to rights. In any event, the campaign ultimately succeeded, and by 1890 antiabortion statutes had been enacted throughout the United States.

A reaction to this trend began to emerge in the 1960's. Women and physicians again joined forces, this time to call for the reform of the restrictive laws and, ultimately, for their repeal. An effective birth control pill became widely available as women began to join the workforce in large numbers and to become politicized through participation in civil rights actions, the antiwar movement, and early women's organizations. Physicians played a role in publicizing the physical danger faced by women who resorted to "back alley" abortions. Estimates of the number of illegal abortions during the 1960's range from 200,000 to 1,200,000 annually. These developments, in conjunction with worries about a potential population explosion, began to change public attitudes. For many years, abortion had been a "dirty secret," unworthy of public discussion and debate. By 1970, 60 percent of the American public believed that the choice to abort ought to be private. These attitudinal changes led to abortion rights reform in a number of states, including New York, California, Colorado, and Hawaii. It is against this background that the U.S. Supreme Court took up the issues presented in the 1973 *Roe v. Wade* case.

The Court's Ruling

It is useful to view the majority opinion of the *Roe* case, authorized by Associate Justice Harry A. Blackmun and supported by six other Supreme Court justices, as an attempt to strike a balance between a woman's unfettered choice to terminate a pregnancy (the "abortion on demand" position) and the state's interest in regulations protecting the health of the mother and the well-being of the fetus. The *Roe* case came to the Supreme Court as a challenge to an 1859 Texas law which made it illegal to "procure an abortion" except when a physician certified that the abortion was necessary to save the life of the woman. Jane Roe, the appellant, challenged the Texas statute through a class-action suit in which she represented the interests of similarly situated women in Texas.

In *Roe*, Blackmun held that the choice to abort is a "fundamental right" of the woman. That right is anchored in the Fourteenth Amendment's due process clause, which had been interpreted in earlier cases to establish a right of privacy in matters relating to marriage and childbearing. The Court considered the right to reproductive control to be fundamental, but not absolute. In instances involving a compelling state interest, legislatures may restrict the woman's choice. Blackmun isolated two compelling state interests: the woman's health and the well-being of potential life. The Court superimposed these competing interests—the woman's fundamental right to choose and the state's compelling interests in maternal health and the well-being of the fetus—on a trimester scheme, which divided pregnancy into three roughly equal time periods. During the first three months of pregnancy, the first trimester, choices concerning reproduction must be left to the woman, in consultation with a licensed physician. In months four through six, the state was given a very limited ability to restrict the woman's choice: It could do so only to protect maternal health. As the fetus becomes viable, that is, can survive outside the womb, the state's interest in regulating abortion becomes compelling. During the viability stage, the state may regulate or prohibit abortion entirely, except where the abortion procedure is necessary to preserve the life or health of the mother.

As a corollary matter, the Court also decided that a fetus is not a "person" under the Constitution. The tension, then, in *Roe*, as articulated by the Court, was not between fetus and mother. Rather, a balance was struck between the mother and the interests of the state in the later stages of pregnancy.

A strong dissent, penned by Justice William H. Rehnquist, took issue with several of the basic propositions of the majority opinion. It rejected the notion that the choice to abort is a privacy right, since a doctor and the fetus are involved, and accused the Court of ignoring the wishes of the states in striking down local restrictions on abortion.

On the same day that *Roe* was decided, the Court handed down its decision in the related *Doe v. Bolton* case, which challenged abortion laws in Georgia. In the latter and less well-known case, the Court, again speaking through Justice Blackmun, declared unconstitutional aspects of a Georgia law that regulated the procedures involved in procuring an abortion. Requirements as to the place where abortions might be performed, residency requirements for the woman requesting an abortion, and approval by two physicians other than the pregnant woman's doctor were all struck down.

Significance

State laws restricting abortions in ways prohibited by *Roe* and its companion case, *Doe*, were constitutionally invalid after 1973. The laws of some thirty-three states were affected.

The most immediate impact of the 1973 decisions was on the availability of legal abortions in the United States. About 500,000 abortions were performed in 1972 in states that had liberalized restrictions on abortion; by 1978, that number had more than doubled; by the late 1980's, approximately 1.6

While an associate justice, William H. Rehnquist wrote a strong dissent in Roe v. Wade. (Library of Congress)

million legal abortions were performed in the United States annually; by the early twenty-first century, that number had dropped to about 1.3 million.

Public opinion on the abortion question had begun to change before *Roe*. By 1973, polls indicated that the majority of Americans approved of abortion in several circumstances: when the pregnancy results from rape, when the pregnancy seriously compromises the health of the mother, and when the fetus is defective. Those attitudes remained relatively consistent in the years after *Roe*. Support for abortion where the pregnant woman is poor, working, or unmarried, however, has been less strong. In such cases (which, in fact, represent the most common reasons given for the decision to abort a pregnancy), a smaller majority of Americans is in favor of reproductive choice.

Scholarly reaction to *Roe* has been mixed. Many conservative critics have disputed the morality of abortion, arguing that it is tantamount to murder. Others have objected to what they believe to be federal interference with state autonomy in the legislative process and have found unconvincing the privacy argument that undergirds the majority's opinion.

Diverse Criticisms

More surprising, perhaps, is the criticism of the Court that has come from the other side of the political spectrum. Many who applaud the outcome of the *Roe* case in its protection of reproductive choice for women have been uneasy with the Court's legal justification for that outcome. Some have commented on the legislative nature of the Court's trimester scheme in the case. Others, exemplified by lawyer Catharine A. MacKinnon, have noted the problems of grounding questions of reproductive choice in a rhetoric of "privacy," rather than equality. The equality approach would necessarily account for existing social inequities between men and women and the special relationship between the pregnant woman and her fetus. "Women were granted the abortion right as a private privilege, not as a public right," MacKinnon argued.

The impact of *Roe* in the political arena has been equally divisive. Antiabortion forces quickly grouped in the wake of the 1973 decision. The Roman Catholic Church has been prominent in condemning *Roe*, and some bishops prohibited members of pro-choice organizations from participating in religious ceremonies, while others opposed the decision in the pulpit or in legislative hearings. Activists staged confrontations with women at clinics, and a significant number of bombings of abortion clinics have been attributed to the antiabortion groups.

Pro-life groups have been extremely effective politically. These groups have been given a sympathetic hearing in some quarters in Congress. Since 1973, Congress enacted some twenty-five laws restricting federal funding for abortion procedures. Efforts have also been made to create a constitutional amendment reversing *Roe* and to remove abortion rights cases from the federal courts.

Similar organizational efforts in the pro-choice camp have occurred, notably under the auspices of the Planned Parenthood Federation of America, the National Abortion Rights Action League, and the National Organization for Women. An important consequence of these activities was the establishment of clinics where women could obtain safe, inexpensive abortions and counseling concerning reproductive matters.

Later Abortion Issues

The Supreme Court continued to wrestle with abortion matters after its *Roe* decision. Routinely since 1973, the Court affirmed its commitment to reproductive choice. Some two hundred bills were introduced in state legislatures in the year after *Roe*; inevitably, some of these measures restricting and limiting abortions gained legislative support and became the basis for continuing litigation in the Supreme Court. Restrictions requiring "informed consent," waiting periods, the consent of the father, parental consent requirements for teenage girls, hospital reporting, and regulations concerning the location where second trimester abortions could be legally performed created indirect but powerful barriers to reproductive choice. When several conservative appointees joined the Court after *Roe v. Wade*, pro-choice activists feared that the Court now harbored a group willing to overturn *Roe*.

Roe, then, is likely to continue to serve as a lightning rod for controversy over abortion in the legal and political arenas. The case has figured prominently in scrutiny of Supreme Court nominees, indicating the strength of ongoing controversy over the abortion issue. More women are the sole breadwinners for their families; many others must take their places in the workforce to maintain an acceptable standard of living for the two-salary family. For women in these situations, an unwanted pregnancy can be disastrous financially and emotionally. Sexual patterns are also changing, with teenagers more sexually active than in the past. It is also the case that new technological developments are likely to intrude on the legal, political, and ethical arguments concerning abortion which have been heard since 1973.

Robert J. Janosik

Further Reading

Balkin, Jack M., ed. *What Roe v. Wade Should Have Said: The Nation's Top Legal Experts Rewrite America's Most Controversial Decision.* New York: New York University Press, 2005. Eleven constitutional scholars rewrite the opinions in the landmark case using sources available at the time its decision. Authors take positions for and against the right to abortion.

Butler, J. Douglas, and David F. Walbert, eds. *Abortion, Medicine, and the Law.* 4th rev. ed. New York: Facts On File, 1992. Good collection of essays explores the legal, medical, and ethical aspects of abortion. Includes selections by several prominent opponents of *Roe,* including Ronald Reagan and John T. Noonan, Jr. Also helpful is Tushnet's survey of post-*Roe* legal developments. Includes full text of the *Roe* decision and index.

Faux, Marian. *Roe v. Wade: The Untold Story of the Landmark Supreme Court Decision That Made Abortion Legal.* New York: Macmillan, 1988. Detailed, nontechnical narrative of the events surrounding the *Roe* litigation. Follows the case through the court system. Includes bibliography and index.

Greenhouse, Linda, and Reva Siegel. *Before Roe v. Wade: Voices That Shaped the Abortion Debate Before the Supreme Court's Ruling.* New York: Kaplan, 2010. Most thorough study of the Supreme Court's 1973 *Roe v. Wade* decision on abortion rights. Written by a Pulitzer Prize-winning journalist with thirty years of experience following the Court and a law professor, this book examines the background to the case, the process leading to the Court's decision, and the impact the decision has since had.

Hull, N. E. H., and Peter Charles Hoffer. *Roe v. Wade: The Abortion Rights Controversy in American History.* Lawrence: University Press of Kansas, 2001. Provides a complete legal history of abortion in the United States from colonial times to the early twenty-first century.

Jaffe, Frederick S., Barbara L. Lindheim, and Philip R. Lee. *Abortion Politics: Private Morality and Public Policy.* New York: McGraw-Hill, 1981. Study of public policy developments related to abortion notes the failure of the U.S. health care system to respond to the need for abortion services, especially among the poor. Summarizes the views of assorted interest groups and public opinion on aspects of the abortion controversy. References and index.

Mohr, James C. *Abortion in America: The Origins and Evolution of National Policy, 1800-1900.* New York: Oxford University Press, 1978. Standard scholarly study of the status of abortion in the nineteenth century in the United States traces the century-long process of the criminalization of abortion in state law back to efforts by American physicians to establish a monopoly over family medicine, to changing political currents, and to emerging class and ethnic biases. References, appendixes, and index.

Rhode, Deborah L. *Justice and Gender: Sex Discrimination and the Law.* Cambridge, Mass.: Harvard University Press, 1989. Chapter 9, "Reproductive Freedom," includes a brief discussion of responses to the reasoning of *Roe* and places the question of abortion in the context of legal attitudes toward women. References and index.

Rodman, Hyman, Betty Sarvis, and Joy Walker Bonar. *The Abortion Question.*

New York: Columbia University Press, 1987. An effort to provide a balanced review of the "moral positions" that shape pro-life and pro-choice arguments. Also describes the legal dimensions of the abortion debate. Includes appendix of state laws regulating abortion in 1973 and index.

Tribe, Laurence H. *Abortion: The Clash of Absolutes.* Rev. ed. New York: W. W. Norton, 1992. One of the best volumes on the *Roe* decision and its aftermath for the general reader. The author, an eminent liberal constitutional scholar, includes a brief, enlightening discussion of the cases after 1973 and a survey of abortion practice in the United States and worldwide. Summarizes attempts to find a compromise position in the debate over abortion. References and index.

See also *Adamson v. California; Bigelow v. Virginia; Doe v. Bolton; Griswold v. Connecticut; Maher v. Roe; Planned Parenthood of Central Missouri v. Danforth; Thornburgh v. American College of Obstetricians and Gynecologists; Webster v. Reproductive Health Services.*

ROMER V. EVANS

Court: U.S. Supreme Court
Citation: 517 U.S. 620
Date: May 20, 1996
Issues: Equal protection of the law; Gay and lesbian rights;
Right to privacy

• In 1992, Colorado citizens voted in favor of a state constitutional amendment that would have imposed a statewide prohibition against protection from discrimination based on sexual orientation. The U.S. Supreme Court declared the amendment unconstitutional, setting the stage for later decisions that would find laws prohibiting consensual homosexual sodomy to be unconstitutional.

After the gay and lesbian revolution of the 1970's faded, antigay backlash swept across the United States in the form of the Christian Right in the 1980's, with conservative politicians supporting the trend. By the 1990's, debates about individual issues, most related to some specific questions, began to dominate the news. Some of the most prominent issues addressed questions of employment, marriage, and sexual privacy. Many political battles were fought at the local level, not a few of which were swept into the national debate. Gay, lesbian, bisexual, and transgender (GLBT) rights activists argued that sexual orientation should not affect a person's ability to marry or to secure housing and employment. Opponents advanced arguments against GLBT rights: that only a heterosexual orientation is moral and that supporting GLBT goals promotes immoral behavior; that sexual orientation should be kept private, and that those who choose to publicize a GLBT orientation do not deserve special treatment because of it; and that the rights the GLBT community expects go beyond the protections offered to other citizens, and it is unfair to protect one group more than others.

Anti-Gay Rights Amendment

In the early 1990's in Colorado, voters, by a narrow margin (53.4 percent), accepted an anti-gay rights amendment to the state constitution, designed to rebuff laws in Aspen, Denver, and Boulder that already existed to protect gay rights. Amendment 2 to the Colorado state constitution was designed to prevent anyone from claiming minority status based on sexual orientation and to prevent government (state or local) from offering protections based on sexual orientation.

GLBT groups throughout the state immediately protested that the amendment would bring Colorado's constitution into conflict with the U.S. Constitution and filed suit to prevent the amendment from being enacted. Colorado governor Roy Romer was named as the primary defendant. The fight against Amendment 2 was led by eight individuals, including Richard G. Evans, in addition to the Boulder Valley School District, the city and county of Denver, the cities of Boulder and Aspen, and Aspen's city council. These groups opposed the Colorado amendment based on several factors in the First and Fourteenth Amendments to the U.S. Constitution. The largest part of their argument came from the Fourteenth Amendment, which requires governments to provide all citizens equal protection under the law. They believed that, in addition to lacking rational governmental interest, the amendment placed an unfair burden on the GLBT community to gain protection from discrimination.

They also believed that Amendment 2, because it was directed at all levels of government, hampered the ability of gays, lesbians, and bisexuals (transgender individuals were not named specifically in the amendment) to seek redress from the government, a violation of the First Amendment to the U.S. Constitution. Finally, because it would have prevented governments from enforcing policies prohibiting discrimination based on sexual orientation, the plaintiffs argued the law violated the due process clauses of both the U.S. and Colorado constitutions.

On January 15, 1993, Colorado district court judge Jeffrey Bayless issued an injunction against Amendment 2's becoming part of the Colorado constitution. The state immediately appealed Bayless's injunction to Colorado's supreme court, which, on July 19, 1993, upheld the injunction. The opinion, authored by Colorado's chief justice, Luis Rovera, found that Amendment 2 denied gays, lesbians, and bisexuals equal protection under the law—specifically, equal access to the normal political process. He stated that Amendment 2 would prevent gays, lesbians, and bisexuals from seeking protection from discrimination without entering into the process of seeking a constitutional amendment.

Rovera thus required the amendment to face the "strict scrutiny" test. Under this test, a law must advance a compelling state interest in order to be allowable. He returned the case to the district court, where Judge Bayless ruled on December 14, 1994, that the law did not advance any such compelling state interest and that it was therefore unconstitutional. When the state appealed once more to the state supreme court, that group upheld the district court ruling, declaring Amendment 2 unconstitutional on October 11, 1994. The state of Colorado, therefore, had no further option but to appeal the case to the U.S. Supreme Court.

The oral arguments were presented to the Court on October 10, 1995, nearly a year to the day after the Colorado state supreme court ruling. During the questioning of the state's counsel, the justices asked some very pointed questions about the amendment's vague language and its singling out a specific group of people and preventing them from having redress from prejudice except through constitutional amendment. The verdict was rendered on May 20, 1996, with the court voting 6-3 to strike the amendment. In the Supreme Court's decision, Justice Anthony Kennedy took a slightly different tack from that of Colorado. Whereas Colorado's supreme court had required the amendment to meet the strict scrutiny test, Justice Kennedy declared that the amendment failed to demonstrate a rational relationship to a genuine government interest. Kennedy stated that the amendment did indeed single out homosexuals and denied them the same protections of law enjoyed by other persons. Although Justice Antonin Scalia wrote a dissent, he was joined by only a minority of the Court, and Amendment 2 was prohibited from being enacted.

Significance

The *Romer* case is significant for both legal and social reasons. Legally, it set a precedent that Cincinnati activists attempted to use to overturn a similar ordinance. However, because the Cincinnati ordinance was local, the Sixth Circuit Court of Appeals ruled it to be unaffected by the *Romer* decision, and the Supreme Court refused to hear the case. Nationally, *Romer* set a precedent discussed in a later Supreme Court decision. In his dissent, Scalia observed that the decision in *Romer* was entirely contrary to the Court's decision in the 1986 *Bowers v. Hardwick* case, which had upheld a Georgia law prohibiting consensual sodomy. Thus when the 2003 case of *Lawrence and Garner v. Texas* came before the Supreme Court some seven years after the *Romer* decision, *Romer* was again discussed. *Lawrence* overturned the *Bowers* decision, forbidding states to make laws that render consensual homosexual sodomy illegal. The precedent the Court set in *Romer* by going against *Bowers* thus helped fuel the arguments in *Lawrence and Garner.*

At the social level, *Romer v. Evans* was significant for entirely different reasons. The language of both Kennedy's majority opinion and Scalia's dissent demonstrated that the real argument over Amendment 2 was over the perceived morality of homosexuality. Although the state framed its case in terms of preventing homosexuals from having what it dubbed special rights, Kennedy bluntly stated that the amendment would have effectively singled out homosexuals for discrimination. Moreover, Scalia supported the amendment not on the grounds that it allowed the state to prevent itself from giving special rights to one group but because he felt it was acceptable for Colorado voters to use legal means to protect what he deemed traditional sexual social behavior. Thus the Supreme Court's decision, even the dissent, affirmed the activists' position that the amendment was aimed at allowing antigay discrimination.

Jessie Bishop Powell

Further Reading

Badgett, M. V. Lee. *When Gay People Get Married: What Happens When Societies Legalize Same-Sex Marriage.* New York: New York University Press, 2009. Concludes that legal recognition has not harmed heterosexual marriage and that some same-sex couples have benefited.

Chauncey, George. *Why Marriage? The History Shaping Today's Debate over Gay Equality.* New York: Basic Books, 2004. Examines the reasons for the GLBT rights debate to center on gay marriage, from the perspective of a gay rights activist.

Gallagher, John, and Chris Bull. *Perfect Enemies: The Religious Right, the Gay Movement, and the Politics of the 1990's.* New York: Crown, 1996. Examines the contrasting perspectives in conservative religious movements and the GLBT rights movements in the context of the unique political situation of the 1990's.

Gerstmann, Evan. *Same-Sex Marriage and the Constitution.* New York: Cambridge University Press, 2007. Clear and fair-minded analysis of the strengths and weaknesses of the major arguments in favor and against the legal recognition of same-sex marriage.

Kahn, Karen, Patracia Gozemba, and Marilyn Humphries. *Courting Equality: A Documentary History of America's First Legal Same-Sex Marriages.* Boston: Beacon, 2007. The authors chronicle the path to the *Goodridge* decision, argue that it has had entirely positive results for everyone in Massachusetts, and celebrate the marriages that have occurred.

Keen, Lisa, and Suzanne B. Goldberg. *Strangers to the Law: Gay People on Trial.* Ann Arbor: University of Michigan Press, 1998. Discusses the politics behind gay rights struggles, with a focus on the law. Includes a section regarding the debate comparing legal rights against "special" rights as well as the *Romer v. Evans* case.

Phy-Olsen, Allene. *Same-Sex Marriage.* Westport, Conn.: Greenwood Press, 2006. Examines historical attitudes toward homosexuality and marriage throughout history and presents the strongest arguments on both sides.

Pinello, Daniel R. *Gay Rights and American Law.* New York: Cambridge University Press, 2003. Examines the development of gay rights throughout the American legal system, including both the Supreme Court and appellate courts. Covers nearly four hundred court decisions between 1980 and 2000.

See also *Bowers v. Hardwick*; *Davis v. Beason*; *Lawrence v. Texas.*

Rompilla v. Beard

Court: U.S. Supreme Court
Citation: 545 U.S. 374
Date: June 20, 2005
Issues: Right to counsel

• The U.S. Supreme Court reaffirmed that criminal defendants have a right to effective assistance of counsel and also provided additional clarification about practices that constitute ineffectiveness.

Rompilla v. Beard expanded and clarified the principles of *Strickland v. Washington* (1984), recognizing that the Sixth Amendment's right to counsel can be infringed by an incompetent lawyer. In overturning a verdict, *Strickland* required that a defendant must demonstrate a "reasonable probability" that except for the deficiency the outcome would have been different. Although it was difficult for defendants to meet this standard, one defendant had his conviction overturned in *Wiggins v. Smith* (2003), which held that a defense attorney's failure to investigate his troubled background as mitigating evidence amounted to ineffective assistance of counsel.

A Pennsylvania jury found Ronald Rompilla guilty of first-degree murder. At the sentencing phase, the prosecutor informed the jury of Rompilla's previous convictions of assault and rape, which were aggravating factors. The jury sentenced him to death. Rompilla then obtained a new lawyer, who appealed the verdict with the argument that the earlier defense attorney had failed to present mitigating evidence that might have produced a different sentence. Although a district court rejected the argument, the Third Circuit Court of Appeals ruled in Rompilla's favor.

The Supreme Court agreed with the Third Circuit's decision. Speaking for a 5-4 majority, Justice David H. Souter argued that Pompilla's trial attorney had acted ineffectively when not looking for mitigating circumstances, especially his early life experiences with mental illness, alcoholism, and abuse. The attorney had even failed to read the file on Rompilla's criminal record, which contained evidence of these mitigating considerations. In conclusion, Souter noted that knowledge of this evidence might have influenced the jury's perception of culpability, so that there existed a "likelihood of a different result" with effective counsel.

Thomas Tandy Lewis

See also *Argersinger v. Hamlin; Betts v. Brady; Escobedo v. Illinois; Faretta v. California; Gideon v. Wainwright; Johnson v. Zerbst; Minnick v. Mississippi; Powell v. Alabama.*

ROPER V. SIMMONS

Court: U.S. Supreme Court
Citation: 543 U.S. 551
Date: March 1, 2005
Issues: Capital punishment; Cruel and unusual punishment

• In this controversial decision, the U.S. Supreme Court ruled that the Eighth Amendment's prohibition against cruel and unusual punishment forbade the execution of an offender who was younger than eighteen when he committed a capital crime.

When ruling in *Gregg v. Georgia* (1976) that capital punishment per se does not violate the Eighth Amendment's cruel and unusual punishment clause, the majority of justices on the Supreme Court had accepted the premise that the prohibition against "cruel and unusual punishment" should be assessed according to society's "evolving sense of decency." Such a standard is rather subjective. In *Ford v. Wainwright* (1986), the justices voted five to four to disallow the execution of insane persons. Although the Court in *Thompson v. Oklahoma* (1988) had disallowed the execution of someone younger than sixteen, in the case of *Stanford v. Kentucky* (1988) it had upheld the execution of persons of age seventeen and older. In 1989, the Court allowed the execution of mentally retarded murderers, but it overturned this decision in *Atkins v. Virginia* (2002). The Court's reasoning in the *Atkins* case led many informed observers to expect the Court to disallow the execution of anyone classified as a minor in the near future.

In 1993, Christopher Simmons was seventeen years old when he formulated a plan to murder Shirley Crook, and he persuaded two younger friends, Charles Benjamin and John Tessmer, to participate in his crime. Although Tessmer decided not to participate, Simmons and Benjamin broke into the victim's house, murdered her, and then drove to a state park, where they threw their victim's body off a bridge. Simmons afterward boasted about the act to Tessmer and others, and he confessed shortly after his arrest. At trial, based on the overwhelming evidence and the shocking nature of the murder, Simmons was found guilty of murder and sentenced to death. In 2003, Missouri's supreme court, referring to the recent *Atkins* precedent, declared that a "national consensus has developed against the execution of juvenile offenders" and reduced Simmons's sentence to life imprisonment without parole. The state of Missouri then appealed the decision to the U.S. Supreme Court, which reviewed the case and then upheld the ruling by a 5-4 margin.

U.S. Supreme Court's Ruling

Speaking for the majority, Justice Anthony Kennedy declared that under the "evolving standards of decency" test it is unconstitutional to execute a person under the age of eighteen at the time of the crime. Kennedy wrote that the ultimate punishment should be reserved to only the "worst offenders," and he observed that only three states had carried out executions of juvenile offenders during the previous decade. He further pointed to parental experiences and "scientific and sociological studies" that tend to confirm that young persons often manifest "a lack of maturity and an underdeveloped sense of responsibility"—which meant that young murderers were "not as reprehensible" as adults murderers. Defending such a double standard, he noted that almost every state prohibited persons under the age of eighteen from voting, serving on juries, or marrying without parental consent. Drawing the line at eighteen, moreover, was not arbitrary in view of the fact that many laws referred to this age as the demarcation line between minority and adulthood.

The most controversial portion of the opinion was its reference to world opinion and laws of foreign nations. Referring to the United Nations Convention on the Rights of the Child, ratified by all countries except the United States and Somalia, Kennedy wrote that "the United States now stands alone in a world that has turned its face against the juvenile death penalty."

Dissenting Opinions

Two justices, Antonin Scalia and Sandra Day O'Connor, wrote dissenting opinions. Challenging the majority's view on the existence of a "national consensus," both justices pointed out that only eighteen states, fewer than half of those having the death penalty, prohibited the imposition of the penalty on minors. Scalia registered other strong disagreements with Kennedy's opinion. Objecting to his method of constitutional interpretation, Scalia argued that instead of inquiring about society's current standards of decency, the Court should investigate dominant ideas about those eligible for the death penalty when the Eighth Amendment had been ratified during the late eighteenth century. Elected legislatures should be allowed to decide which public policies violate current standards, for it is undemocratic for unelected courts to substitute their judgments for those of the legislatures. In addition, Scalia strongly objected to the majority's reference to foreign laws in interpreting the U.S. Constitution, and he accused the liberal members of the Court of inconsistency because they ignored the laws of other countries when they disagreed with them.

Because it is not unusual for juveniles to commit horrendous crimes, numerous people throughout the country believed that the Court's judgment in *Simmons* was a unwise decision. The impact of the decision was immediately felt in the state of Virginia, where Lee Boyd Malvo, one of the two participants in the notorious Beltway sniper attacks, was no longer eligible to receive a death sentence.

Thomas Tandy Lewis

See also *Atkins v. Virginia; Ford v. Wainwright; Gregg v. Georgia; McCleskey v. Kemp; Stanford v. Kentucky; Thompson v. Oklahoma.*

Rosenberg v. United States

Court: U.S. Supreme Court
Citation: 346 U.S. 273
Date: June 19, 1953
Issues: Capital punishment; Foreign policy

• The U.S. Supreme Court's denial of this appeal on behalf of the Rosenbergs, a couple convicted of espionage, led to their execution.

Julius Rosenberg and his wife, Ethel Rosenberg, were convicted in 1951 of giving atomic and other military secrets to the Soviets in violation of the Espionage Act of 1917. The federal appeals court affirmed their conviction, and the Supreme Court initially refused to hear the case. However, legal counsel for the "next friend" of the Rosenbergs filed an appeal asserting that the 1946 Atomic Energy Act had superseded the 1917 act in requiring a jury determination before a capital punishment sentence could be imposed. Justice William O. Douglas found this a substantial legal question and granted a stay, but the Court's majority vacated the stay two days later without hearing the case in full.

Chief Justice Fred M. Vinson wrote the opinion for the 6-3 majority in upholding the convictions and death sentences of the Rosenbergs for conspiring to violate the 1917 act. The majority held that most of the activities occurred before the 1946 act was adopted and further that the 1946 act did not actually supersede the penalty section of the 1917 act. Subsequent discoveries in the files of the former Soviet Union cast grave doubt on whether Julius was ever more than a very minor spy and whether his wife was a spy at all.

Richard L. Wilson

See also *American Communications Association v. Douds; Scales v. United States; Schenck v. United States; United States v. Lovett; Watkins v. United States.*

Rosenfeld v. Southern Pacific

Court: U.S. Court of Appeals for the Ninth Circuit
Citation: 293 F.Supp. 1219
Date: June 1, 1971
Issues: Civil rights and liberties; Employment discrimination; Labor law;
Sex discrimination; Women's issues

• This U.S. Court of Appeals Ninth Circuit opinion strictly interpreted the Civil Rights Act of 1964 with regard to the prohibition of discrimination in employment based on sex, thus striking down a California law permitting sex discrimination in employment.

In 1966, Leah Rosenfeld applied for the job of sole agent-telegrapher in Thermal, California. Her employer refused to consider her application, stating that the decision had been made that women would not be employed in such a position. Rosenfeld responded by filing a complaint with the Equal Employment Opportunity Commission (EEOC) claiming that the refusal to hire women as agent-telegraphers violated the Civil Rights Act of 1964.

Southern Pacific argued that it could not hire women for the sole agent-telegrapher position under a California law that prohibited the employment of women in jobs involving lifting more than a certain amount of weight. The job, as defined by Southern Pacific, required the lifting of objects weighing as much as fifty pounds and extraordinarily long workdays during the harvest season. The Court responded by striking down the California law, ruling that prospective employees should be considered regardless of sex and "on the basis of individual capacity."

Donald C. Simmons, Jr.

See also *Bowe v. Colgate-Palmolive; County of Washington v. Gunther; Lorance v. AT&T Technologies; Meritor Savings Bank v. Vinson; Weeks v. Southern Bell.*

Ross, United States v. *See* United States v.
Ross

Rostker v. Goldberg

Court: U.S. Supreme Court
Citation: 453 U.S. 57
Date: June 25, 1981
Issues: Sex discrimination; Women's issues

• The U.S. Supreme Court held that Congress's decision to authorize the president to require registration of males but not females for possible military service did not constitute gender discrimination in violation of the due process clause of the Fifth Amendment.

The Military Selective Service Act authorizes the president to require male citizens and male resident aliens between the ages of eighteen and twenty-six to register for the draft. Registration was discontinued in 1975. In 1980, President Jimmy Carter recommended that Congress reactivate the registration process and that Congress amend the act to permit the registration and possible conscription of women. Congress considered the president's recommendations at length and decided to reactivate the registration process but declined to permit the registration of women. A three-judge federal district court ruled that the challenged gender-based distinction violated the due process clause of the Fifth Amendment. By a 6-3 vote, the U.S. Supreme Court reversed that decision on direct appeal.

Justice William H. Rehnquist, joined by Chief Justice Warren Burger and Justices Potter Stewart, Harry Blackmun, Lewis Powell, and John Paul Stevens, wrote the majority opinion. Rehnquist emphasized the Court's traditional deference to Congress in cases involving the national defense and military affairs. Registering women had been "extensively considered" by Congress, and its decision to register only males was not an "accidental by-product of a traditional way of thinking about females." Congress's purpose was to prepare a draft of "combat troops," and since women were ineligible for combat, Congress exempted them.

Rehnquist noted that the gender classification was "not invidious." He reasoned that Congress was not choosing arbitrarily to burden one of two similarly situated groups, "such as would be the case with an all-black or all-white, or an all-Roman Catholic or all-Lutheran, or an all-Republican or all-Democratic registration." He found that men and women are not "similarly situated" for purposes of a draft or draft registration "because of the combat restrictions on women."

Justice Byron White, joined by Justice William Brennan, dissented, noting that not all positions in the military must be filled by combat-ready men and that women could be registered to fill noncombat positions "without sacrificing combat-readiness." Justice Thurgood Marshall, joined by Justice Brennan, also dissented on grounds that the government had failed to show that registering women would "seriously impede" its efforts to achieve "a concededly important governmental interest in maintaining an effective defense."

This decision continues to be important because female military personnel who are ineligible for combat find themselves disadvantaged when they compete with combat-eligible male personnel for positions and promotion. In the 1990's, combat restrictions on women were eased. Such developments speak directly to Rehnquist's premise that male-only draft registration is not discriminatory because only males are eligible for combat.

Joseph A. Melusky

See also *County of Washington v. Gunther; Frontiero v. Richardson; Geduldig v. Aiello; Grove City College v. Bell; Hoyt v. Florida; Meritor Savings Bank v. Vinson; Phillips v. Martin Marietta Corp.; Rosenfeld v. Southern Pacific; Stanton v. Stanton.*

ROTARY INTERNATIONAL V. DUARTE

Court: U.S. Supreme Court
Citation: 481 U.S. 537
Date: May 4, 1987
Issues: Civil rights and liberties; Desegregation;
First Amendment guarantees; Private discrimination;
Racial discrimination

- The U.S. Supreme Court attempted to reconcile competing values of the law with its ruling that states and communities could enforce antidiscrimination regulations of nonintimate private clubs so long as First Amendment rights are respected.

In 1958, the U.S. Supreme Court explicitly ruled that the First Amendment implies a "freedom of association" in *National Association for the Advancement of Colored People v. Alabama ex rel. Patterson*. The Court prohibited the state of Alabama from requiring that the National Association for the Advancement of Colored People provide a list of its members, on the grounds that this would discourage people from joining the civil rights group. Six years later, in *Bell v. Maryland*, Justice Arthur J. Goldberg made a distinction between a public business and a private club, declaring that for the latter the U.S. Constitution gives each person the right "to choose his social intimates and business partners solely on the basis of personal prejudices including race." Likewise, in *Evans v. Newton* (1966), Justice William O. Douglas wrote that in a group such as a private golf club, membership based on race or sex was a protected "expression of freedom of association."

Title II of the Civil Rights Act of 1964 made it illegal to discriminate on the basis of race, religion, or national origin in public accommodations (meaning businesses open to the public). Title II expressly exempted private clubs not open to the public, and, in contrast to other parts of the 1964 law, it did not prohibit discrimination based on gender. Within a few years, the Court was faced with the complex task of deciding when a club should be treated as a business establishment and, even more complicated, deciding at what point a state's involvement with a club would constitute "state action" that should be regulated by the equal protection clause of the Fourteenth Amendment to the Constitution.

In 1969, the Court examined the Lake Nixon recreation club of Arkansas, where as many as 100,000 white patrons purchased services each year after paying a "membership fee" of twenty-five cents. The majority of the Court decided that this was a place of "public entertainment" that could not exclude African Americans. In 1972, however, the Court decided that the Loyal Order of Moose in Pennsylvania was indeed a private club that might refuse to serve African Americans. In this controversial opinion, the majority ruled six to three that the issuance of a liquor license did not constitute the kind of state action that would come under the Fourteenth Amendment.

Meanwhile, those dissatisfied with Title II were able to convince many states and communities to pass public accommodations acts (PAAs) that went beyond federal standards. By 1983, twenty-eight states had passed PAAs that did not make exemptions for most private clubs, and twenty-six PAAs prohibited sex discrimination. Minnesota was one of the states with a broad PAA, and when the national organization of the United States Jaycees threatened to expel two chapters in Minnesota because they had defied the organization's national bylaws by allowing women full membership, the local groups sought legal relief, arguing that the U.S. Jaycees bylaws were in violation of Minnesota's law. The national organization prevailed in the U.S. Court of Appeals on the grounds that associational freedom outweighed a state law and that the law was excessively vague in reference to public accommodations.

Roberts v. United States Jaycees

On July 3, 1984, however, the U.S. Supreme Court reversed the lower court in *Roberts v. United States Jaycees*, deciding by a vote of seven to zero that the law's application did not violate the freedom of association in this particular instance. In the official opinion, Justice William J. Brennan recognized that the Fourteenth Amendment gave Minnesota "a compelling interest in eradicating discrimination against female citizens," justifying state regulations of private clubs so long as there was no "serious burden" on their rights to "intimate association" or "expressive association." The first principle referred to characteristics such as "relative smallness" and selectivity in membership; the second principle referred to the promotion of ideas and other activities protected by the First Amendment.

Brennan noted that the two Minnesota chapters had about 400 members each, that there were some 300,000 members nationwide, and that the requirements for membership were minimal. The organization, moreover, was for business and community-service training; it was not concerned with the promotion of any political or religious ideas. Given that the Jaycees allowed women to join as associate members, the group had failed to demonstrate that full membership for women would force the organization to change its mission or character. Justice Sandra Day O'Connor agreed with the outcome of the decision but disagreed with Brennan's stress on intimacy. She argued that the key point was that the U.S. Jaycees had more of the characteristics of a "commercial association" than of a private association and that the former could claim "only minimal constitutional protection."

The *Roberts* decision failed to answer a number of important questions. Some observers believed that a private club might have a better case if it totally excluded women from membership, in contrast to the Jaycees' policy of partial exclusion. More important, Brennan wrote in the Court's decision that a smaller group such as the Kiwanis might enjoy constitutional exemption from state regulations, but he presented few guidelines about the degree of intimacy required for such protection.

In 1974, California amended its statutes to outlaw gender-based discrimination in "all business establishments of every kind whatsoever," giving no exemption to nonprofit groups. Rotary International was a nonprofit corporation that at that time had 19,788 local clubs in 157 countries, with local clubs having from twenty to four hundred members. The organization was moderately selective in membership requirements. Although the Rotary bylaws did not allow women to be members, in 1977 the local Rotary chapter in Duarte, California, because of declining membership, voted to admit three women— Mary Lou Elliott, Dona Bogard, and Rosemary Freitag. As a result, the international organization's board of directors terminated the charter of the Duarte club.

The local group filed a complaint in the California Superior Court of Los Angeles, which ruled that Rotary International was not a business establishment. The Duarte club, however, won the decision in the state court of appeals, giving Rotary International the choice of readmitting the club or ceasing operations in California. After the California Supreme Court denied a petition for review, the U.S. Supreme Court accepted the petition in order to decide whether the appellate court's decision was a violation of Rotary International's First Amendment rights.

U.S. Supreme Court's Ruling

On March 30, 1987, the Supreme Court heard the opposing arguments. The attorney who spoke for the Duarte chapter argued that Rotary International was a "business-like organization" and that "the message to women is that we're second-class citizens, not part of the business community's leadership." The attorney representing the Rotarians stressed that the organization's goal was community service rather than career advancement and that the club was more selective than the Jaycees. On May 4, 1987, the Court, in a 7-0 decision, upheld the application of the California statute to the Rotarians (Justices Harry A. Blackmun and Sandra Day O'Connor did not take part in the decision because of conflicts of interest).

Justice Lewis F. Powell, Jr., wrote the opinion for the Court, using the theoretical framework that Brennan had presented in the *Roberts* case. First, Powell argued that individuals enjoy a "zone of privacy" that allows them to exclude people from many kinds of "intimate or private relationships," but that the Rotarians did not constitute one of these relationships. Second, individuals enjoy the freedom to form associations that have the goal of expressing political or religious ideas, a freedom that must be respected. States, however, could regulate private clubs when necessary to serve a compelling state interest as long as they did not violate the two rights of intimate association and expressive association. In a footnote, Powell wrote that he was not making any judgment about the possible protection of other clubs and that each club's privileges would depend on such factors as its size, selectivity, and purposes. Powell did not refer directly to O'Connor's theory about the special limits of business-related clubs, although her perspective appears to have colored the logic of his opinion.

Significance

Very often, Supreme Court justices must attempt to reconcile competing values of the law, and this was certainly the challenge in the *Roberts* and *Rotary* decisions. The First Amendment freedom of association implies that an individual can decide to exclude some people in private relationships, whereas the Fourteenth Amendment and laws concerning public accommodations create governmental interests in providing equal opportunities for commercial and professional activities. The conflict is especially apparent in private clubs, for it is generally recognized that these institutions present important opportunities for making business contacts and for professional training. In 1975, the New York City Commission on Human Rights published a report on a survey of businesspeople in which two-thirds of the respondents said that participation in private clubs was important to their success. In addition to such considerations, feminists maintained that women's exclusion from such organizations tended to perpetuate stereotypes of gender inequality.

After the *Roberts* and *Rotary* decisions, observers expected that in the majority of states most business-related clubs would soon be forced to include women. In 1988, women who wanted to join private clubs won another victory in the case of *New York State Club Association v. City of New York*. This decision of the U.S. Supreme Court upheld a New York City ordinance that prohibited sex-based discrimination in social clubs of more than four hundred members when nonmembers were allowed to purchase meals. Because this case dealt with social clubs that had very limited connections to the business world, it appeared that few significant limitations remained on the ways in which states and communities might apply their antidiscrimination laws to private clubs. Almost half of U.S. states did not have such laws, but these were mostly smaller states that historically tended to follow the examples of larger concentrations of population.

Some libertarians were unhappy with the *Roberts* and *Rotary* decisions, protesting that they were overly broad and interfered unjustly with the personal liberty of individuals to form associations of their own choosing. Supporters of the decisions responded by noting that the Supreme Court had not taken away the rights of intimate association and expressive association. Groups of men or women might form single-sex clubs when their goals presented reasonable justification for a policy of exclusion. The Connecticut Supreme

Court in 1987 ruled that the Boy Scouts of America had the right to bar women from leadership roles because the purposes of the organization included a need for male role models, although after the decision the Boy Scouts changed the policy, in part to avoid costly legal battles. Not many women wanted to join such groups of special purpose anyway, but a growing number of professional women did want to have the right to join those private clubs that might help them to advance their businesses and careers.

Thomas Tandy Lewis

Further Reading

Abraham, Henry J., and Barbara A. Perry. *Freedom and the Court: Civil Rights and Liberties in the United States.* 8th ed. Lawrence: University Press of Kansas, 2003. Standard text provides a broad perspective on how the Court has interpreted issues of freedom and equality over time. Presents a good summary of the topic of private clubs. Includes bibliographic references and index.

Burns, Michael. "The Exclusion of Women from Influential Clubs: The Inner Sanctum and the Myth of Full Equality." *Harvard Civil Rights-Civil Liberties Law Review* 18 (1983): 321-409. Presents a well-documented treatment of how single-sex clubs prevent women from advancement and business opportunities. Attacks a narrow view of "state action" and argues that state and local laws should not exempt private clubs.

Marshall, William. "Discrimination and the Right of Association." *Northwestern University Law Review* 81 (Fall, 1988): 68-107. Theoretical discussion addresses how the freedom of association might conflict with the goal of equality in the public realm. Proposes a solution that allows freedom of expression but prohibits discriminatory actions.

Pavchinski, Alexa. "Social Clubs as Public Accommodations: Expressive and Intimate Association v. State Anti-discrimination Legislation." *University of Florida Law Review* 40 (Fall, 1988): 1035-1077. Provides excellent short summaries of the major cases that relate to the topic and argues that although the Supreme Court has allowed some infringement on association freedoms, First Amendment rights have been respected.

Pompa, Lisa Tarin. "*Rotary International v. Duarte*: Limiting Association Rights to Protect Equal Access to California Business Establishments." *Pacific Law Journal* 19 (January, 1988): 339-426. One of the best and most detailed analyses available of the issues and facts of the *Rotary* case. Argues that the case reflected the changing roles of women in the United States.

Rhode, Deborah. *Justice and Gender: Sex Discrimination and the Law.* Cambridge, Mass.: Harvard University Press, 1989. Excellent treatment of all legal issues relating to gender equality takes a strong feminist point of view. On the issue of private clubs, supports the views of Justice O'Connor and criticizes the emphasis on intimate rights. Includes a very useful bibliography. Varela, Paul. "A Scout Is Friendly: Freedom of Association and the State Effort to End Private Discrimination." *William and Mary Law Review* 30 (Summer, 1989): 919-955. Argues that zealous reformers have produced vague laws and have gone too far in limiting the freedom of association. Provides a good summary of public accommodation acts in various states. The libertarian viewpoint expressed here can be contrasted with the perspectives in the Pavchinski and Rhode works cited above.

See also *National Association for the Advancement of Colored People v. Alabama; New York State Club Association v. City of New York; Roberts v. United States Jaycees.*

ROTH V. UNITED STATES

Court: U.S. Supreme Court
Citation: 354 U.S. 476
Date: June 24, 1957
Issues: Censorship; Freedom of speech; Pornography and obscenity

• Ruling that obscene material is not protected by the First Amendment in this case and in its companion case, *Alberts v. California*, the Supreme Court defined obscenity narrowly and put strict limits on the kinds of obscenity that might be proscribed by law.

Samuel Roth conducted a business in New York in the publishing and sale of books, magazines, and photographs. A federal statute made it a crime to send "obscene, lewd, lascivious, or filthy" materials or advertisements through the U.S. mail, and Roth was found guilty in district court for violating four counts of the statute. Contemporary with Roth's conviction, David Alberts was convicted in California of advertising obscenity in violation of the state's penal code. When Roth and Alberts each petitioned the U.S. Supreme Court for review, the Court accepted both cases and consolidated them into one decision. The major issue was whether the federal and state statutes, as interpreted, were consistent with the First Amendment's freedom of speech and press.

Historically, both the federal government and the states had long criminalized most forms of pornography, and in numerous cases the Court had

One of the most distinguished American jurists never to sit on the U.S. Supreme Court, Learned Hand served more than thirty years on federal appeals courts and wrote more than three thousand opinions. (Library of Congress)

recognized such laws as a reasonable means to promote the state's legitimate interest in "decency."

Between 1842 and 1956 the U.S. Congress had enacted twenty antiobscenity laws, and at least six times the Supreme Court had approved prosecutions under these laws. Some American courts continued to follow *Regina v. Hicklin* (1868), which looked at the effects of isolated passages on the most susceptible persons in society. Roth and Alberts had been convicted under a less restrictive standard, endorsed by Judge Learned Hand and many liberals, that considered the work as a whole and its impact on the average adult. Still, given the precedents, few observers considered that the Supreme Court would strike down antiobscenity statutes.

The Court ruled six to three to uphold Roth's federal conviction and seven to two to uphold Alberts's state convictions. Writing for the majority, Justice William Brennan summarized the Anglo-American tradition of proscribing obscenity, and he concluded that obscenity enjoyed no constitutional protection because it had been historically recognized as "utterly without redeeming social importance." Making a distinction between sex and obscenity, Brennan rejected the *Hicklin* test as "unconstitutionally restrictive." He endorsed the alternative test of "whether to the average person, applying contemporary community standards, the dominant theme of the material taken as a whole appeals to the prurient interest."

Two liberal members of the Court, Justices William O. Douglas and Hugo L. Black, dissented and argued that the First Amendment protected all forms of expression. One member of the Court, John M. Harlan, distinguished between federal and state prosecution of obscenity, allowing the states greater power in the area.

The *Roth* decision was a landmark case because the Court for the first time limited government's prerogative to criminalize obscene material, and because it insisted on a narrow definition of obscenity. While allowing the continuation of antiobscenity laws, *Roth* recognized that all ideas were protected unless they were "utterly without redeeming social importance." Equally important was the explicit rejection of the *Hicklin* test, so that subsequent prosecutions had to be based on the influence of a work in its entirety on an average person of the community. In post-*Roth* cases, the Court would continue to be divided over the definition and protection of obscenity, a controversy that culminated in the three-pronged compromise of *Miller v. California* (1973).

Thomas Tandy Lewis

See also *Burstyn v. Wilson; Memoirs v. Massachusetts; Miller v. California; Stanley v. Georgia.*

ROWAN V. U.S. POST OFFICE DEPARTMENT

Court: U.S. Supreme Court
Citation: 397 U.S. 728
Date: May 4, 1970
Issues: Freedom of expression; Regulation of commerce; Right to privacy

- In a case originating in a mail-order company's complaint that its constitutional right to free speech was violated by a federal postal law empowering people to stop unsolicited mailings, the U.S. Supreme Court issued a ruling favoring protection of individual rights to privacy over free speech.

Section 4009 of the 1967 U.S. Postal Revenue and Federal Salary Act, Title III, empowers individuals to order companies engaged in mass mailings to stop sending them unsolicited advertisements for material that they regard as "erotically arousing or sexually provocative." The law also permits individuals to order their names deleted from all mailing lists in the mail-order companies' possession. *Rowan v. U.S. Post Office Department* originated in a case brought by the owner of a mail-order company who claimed that the 1967 law violated his First and Fifth Amendment rights of free speech and due process. He also asserted that the law's section 4009 was "unconstitutionally vague, without standards, and ambiguous."

In deciding *Rowan*, the Court examined the subsections of section 4009 that outline the procedures for ordering the cessation of mailings to individual households. One subsection states that mailers can be ordered by private individuals "to refrain from further mailings . . . to designated addressees." Another subsection assigns the postmaster general the duty of issuing requested cessation orders to specified mailers. A third subsection requires mailers to remove the names of complainants from their mailing lists and prohibits the sale, transfer, or exchange of lists bearing their names. Upon determination of a violation, the postmaster general can ask the attorney general to issue a compliance order against the mailer.

The Court decision affirmed the right of private individuals to direct the cessation of mailings and the deletion of their names from mailing lists used in the distribution of unsolicited advertisements. Explaining the Court's opinion, Chief Justice Warren Burger wrote: "Weighing the highly important right to communicate . . . against the very basic right to be free of sights, sounds, and tangible matter we do not want, it seems to us that a mailer's right to communicate must stop at the mailbox of an unreceptive addressee." Burger added that "a mailer's right to communicate is circumscribed only by an affirmative act of the addressee." In sum, the Court ruled that a mailer's right to communicate is not significantly infringed upon when balanced by a recipient's right to be free from unwanted communications.

The Court also held that the appellant's due process was not violated, and that section 4009 of the law was not unconstitutionally vague. Burger noted that "the only administrative action not preceded by a full hearing is the initial issuance of the prohibitory order. Since the sender risks no immediate sanction by failing to comply with that order . . . it cannot be said that this aspect of the procedure denies due process." Furthermore, Burger reasoned that because "appellants know precisely what they must do on receipt of a prohibitory order," the appellant's vagueness argument was ruled invalid.

Thomas Aaron Wyrick

See also *Ashcroft v. Free Speech Coalition; Bates v. State Bar of Arizona; Bigelow v. Virginia; 44 Liquormart, Inc. v. Rhode Island.*

RUMMEL V. ESTELLE

Court: U.S. Supreme Court
Citation: 445 U.S. 263
Date: March 18, 1980
Issues: Cruel and unusual punishment; Incarceration

- The Court found no cruel and unusual punishment in a state's mandatory life-imprisonment statute as applied to a man convicted of three fraudulent offenses involving only $229.11.

In 1973, William Rummel was convicted under the Texas recidivist statute, which required a mandatory life sentence after three felony convictions, even for nonviolent offenses. In 1964 Rummel had been convicted of his first felony, the fraudulent use of a credit card to obtain goods worth eighty dollars. Four years later he had been found guilty of passing a forged check for $28.36.

Finally, in 1973 Rummel was charged with a third felony of receiving $120.75 by false pretenses. Rummel might have avoided the life sentence if he had yielded to the state's pressure to accept a plea bargain without a jury trial, but he insisted on a trial. Rummel sought relief in federal court, with the argument that his life sentence was "cruel and unusual" because it was grossly excessive and disproportionate to the penalties for more serious crimes. The district court and court of appeals rejected the argument, and Rummel appealed to the U.S. Supreme Court.

The Court voted five to four to affirm the constitutionality of Rummel's punishment. Writing for the majority, Justice William H. Rehnquist maintained that the doctrine that the Eighth Amendment prohibited sentences disproportionate to the severity of the crime was relevant only in death-penalty cases, because this penalty was unique in its total irrevocability. Rehnquist found that the Texas statute had two legitimate goals: to deter repeat offenders and to isolate recidivists from society as long as necessary after they had demonstrated their incapacity to obey the law. The states generally had the authority to determine the length of isolation deemed necessary for such recidivists. Rehnquist also made much of the fact that the Texas statute allowed the possibility of parole.

In an important dissent, Justice Lewis F. Powell, Jr., argued that the doctrine of disproportionality also applied to penalties in noncapital cases. He pointed to precedents that could be interpreted as prohibiting grossly excessive penalties, especially *Weems v. United States* (1910) and *Robinson v. California* (1962). Powell observed that in Texas, even those convicted of murder or aggravated kidnapping were not subject to a mandatory life sentence. In addition, he maintained that the possibility of parole should not be considered in assessing whether the penalty was grossly disproportionate.

The *Rummel* decision would prove to be limited and uncertain in its application as a precedent. In 1983, when the Court encountered a life sentence without any chance of parole based on a recidivist statute in *Solem v. Helm,* Justice Powell would write the majority opinion while Rehnquist would write a dissent. While *Solem* did not directly overturn *Rummel,* the *Solem* majority did endorse the idea that a prison sentence might be unconstitutional if it was disproportionate to punishments for other crimes. However, in upholding a life sentence for the possession of 650 grams of cocaine in *Harmelin v. Michigan* (1991), the Court would indicate its continued reluctance to apply the doctrine of disproportionality in noncapital cases.

Thomas Tandy Lewis

See also *Harmelin v. Michigan; Hutto v. Davis; Robinson v. California; Solem v. Helm; Weems v. United States.*

RUNYON V. MCCRARY

Court: U.S. Supreme Court
Citation: 427 U.S. 160
Date: June 25, 1976
Issues: Civil rights and liberties; Desegregation; Education; Employment discrimination; Right to privacy

• In this case, the U.S. Supreme Court broadened the meaning of Title 42, section 1981 of the 1866 Civil Rights Act to outlaw discrimination in all contracts.

Parents of African American children brought suit in federal court against private schools in Virginia that had denied their children admission. Disregarding the defendant schools' argument that a government-imposed obligation to admit black students to their unintegrated student bodies would violate constitutionally protected rights of free association and privacy, the district and appellate courts both ruled in the parents' favor, enjoining the schools from discriminating on the basis of race.

The parents had based their case on a section of the 1866 Civil Rights Act that was still in effect. In 1968, the Supreme Court had held in *Jones v. Alfred H. Mayer Co.* that section 1982 of the act prohibited racial discrimination among private parties in housing. In *Runyon*, the Court broadened this holding to imply that section 1981, the act's right-to-contract provision, outlawed all discriminatory contracts, whether involving public or private parties—including one between private schools and the parents of student applicants.

In the wake of *Runyon*, lower federal courts employed section 1981 to outlaw racial discrimination in a wide variety of areas, including banking, security deposit regulations, admissions to amusement parks, insurance, and mortuaries. The breadth of the Court's interpretation in *Runyon* of section 1981 also caused it to overlap with Title VII of the Civil Rights Act of 1964, governing employment contracts.

This overlap, together with ongoing concern about the extensiveness of the interpretation of section 1981, caused the Court to consider overruling *Runyon* in *Patterson v. McLean Credit Union* (1989). Instead, *Patterson* severely restricted *Runyon* by declaring that section 1981 did not apply to postcontractual employer discrimination. *Patterson* went so far as to declare that although section 1981 protected the right to enter into employment contracts, it did not extend to future breaches of that contract or to the imposition of discriminatory working conditions. Congress in turn overruled this narrow reading of section 1981 in the Civil Rights Act of 1991, which includes explicit language permitting courts to prohibit employment discrimination that takes place after hiring.

The reason for the Court's about-face with regard to section 1981 can be found in its changing political composition. *Runyon* was decided midway through Chief Justice Warren Burger's tenure, when the Court was dominated by justices who occupied the middle of the political spectrum. In 1986, however, one of two dissenters in *Runyon*, the conservative Justice William H. Rehnquist, succeeded Burger. Rehnquist, who had always been outspoken in his criticism of what he regarded as the Court's excess of liberalism under Chief Justice Earl Warren, dissented in *Runyon* on grounds that the Warren-era *Jones* case had been improperly decided. By 1989, when the Court handed down its decision in *Patterson*, Rehnquist had been joined by enough fellow conservative thinkers to overrule *Runyon*'s interpretation of section 1981 by one vote.

Lisa Paddock

See also *Adarand Constructors v. Peña*; *Jones v. Alfred H. Mayer Co.*; *Patterson v. McLean Credit Union.*

RUST V. SULLIVAN

Court: U.S. Supreme Court
Citation: 500 U.S. 173
Date: May 23, 1991
Issues: Reproductive rights; Right to privacy; Women's issues

- This case is one of a series of decisions dating back to *Maher v. Roe* (1977) authorizing the government to make access to, and information about, abortion dependent on a woman's ability to pay for it.

Section 1008 of the Public Health Service Act prohibits the use of federal funds in family planning programs "where abortion is a method of family planning." Prior to 1988, the regulations implementing this provision prohibited family planning programs which received federal funds from performing abortions. In 1988, new regulations also prohibited such programs from abortion counseling and from mentioning abortion when referring pregnant women to other services or facilities. The new regulations were commonly referred to as the "gag rules" because they forbade family planning health care programs to mention abortion and required them, if asked about abortion, to respond only that it was not considered an appropriate method of family planning.

Health care providers that offered family planning services and doctors filed suit, challenging the constitutionality of the gag rules. They raised three arguments. First, they claimed that the Department of Health and Human Services was acting beyond the scope of its authority. Second, they said, the rules violated the free speech rights of family planning programs under the First Amendment. Third, they argued that the rules violated the right to privacy (upheld in *Roe v. Wade*, 1973) of individuals using the services of family planning programs. The U.S. Supreme Court, by a 5-4 vote, rejected all three arguments and held that the rules were constitutional.

The Court's Ruling

In an opinion written by William Rehnquist, the Court stated that the statutory language was broad in scope and ambiguous. In such cases the Court defers to the interpretation adopted by the agency charged with administering the statute as long as it reflects a plausible construction of the statute's plain language and does not otherwise conflict with Congress's expressed intent. Nothing in the language of the statute or its legislative history prohibited the Department of Health and Human Services from adopting a more restrictive view concerning abortion as a method of family planning. The gag rules were supported by a reasoned analysis demonstrating that the new restrictions assure federal funds are spent on only authorized purposes and avoid creating the appearance of governmental support for abortion-related activities.

Second, the Court held that the regulations do not violate the First Amendment free speech rights of family planning programs, their staffs, or their patients. The government may make a value judgment favoring childbirth over abortion and implement that judgment via the allocation of public funds. Such a preference is not discriminating on the basis of viewpoint, but ensuring that government funds are being spent for a chosen activity rather than another which the government has chosen not to support. The gag rules do not force clinic personnel or patients to give up all abortion-related speech. Rather, they require that certain speech must occur outside the government-funded family planning program. When the government chooses to subsidize one activity, nothing in the First Amendment requires it also to subsidize the presentation of an alternative point of view or service.

Third, the Court found that the gag rules do not violate a woman's right to choose whether to terminate her pregnancy. The government has no constitutional duty to subsidize an activity merely because it is constitutionally protected, and it may validly allocate public funds for services relating to childbirth but not to abortion. This allocation, according to the Court, places no insurmountable obstacle in the path of a woman wishing to terminate her pregnancy, and it leaves her with the same choices as if the government had chosen not to fund any family planning programs.

The gag rules do not place impermissible restrictions on patient/doctor discussions concerning a woman's right to make an informed and voluntary choice on whether to carry her pregnancy to term, because this information remains available through private health care providers not receiving funds under the Public Health Service Act. The Court decided that the fact that most women participating in family planning programs funded by the act are too poor to obtain private health care services was irrelevant. Such financial constraints on a woman's ability to enjoy the full range of constitutionally protected choices, the Court said, are the product not of governmental restrictions but rather of her personal financial circumstances.

Johnny C. Burris

See also *Akron v. Akron Center for Reproductive Health; Bigelow v. Virginia; Doe v. Bolton; Harris v. McRae; Maher v. Roe; Planned Parenthood of Central Missouri v. Danforth; Roe v. Wade; Webster v. Reproductive Health Services.*

RUTAN V. REPUBLICAN PARTY OF ILLINOIS

Court: U.S. Supreme Court
Citation: 110 S.Ct. 2729
Date: January 16, 1990
Issues: Freedom of speech

• The U.S. Supreme Court concluded that patronage hiring and firing of low-level government employees violates their free speech rights.

An Illinois Republican governor issued an order prohibiting state hiring without his approval, which required adherence to Republican Party beliefs. By a 5-4 vote, the Supreme Court extended First Amendment protection to low-level government employees denied jobs or promotions through patronage politics. In his opinion for the Court, Justice William J. Brennan, Jr., followed the Court's decisions in *Elrod v. Burns* (1976) and *Branti v. Finkel* (1980). The Court was badly split, with Justice Antonin Scalia writing a dissent longer than the Court's opinion defending traditional patronage politics for its party-enhancing characteristics. Scalia argued that *Elrod* and *Branti* should both be overturned and that a legislature—not the Court—should decide whether patronage had values that should be balanced against any loss of free speech that resulted from the patronage system. The Scalia dissent was joined by Justices Anthony M. Kennedy and Sandra Day O'Connor and Chief Justice William H. Rehnquist. Justice John Paul Stevens concurred with Brennan, giving a point-by-point rebuttal of Scalia's arguments.

Richard L. Wilson

See also *Buckley v. Valeo; Elrod v. Burns; United Public Workers v. Mitchell.*

SAFFORD UNIFIED SCHOOL DISTRICT V. REDDING

Court: U.S. Supreme Court
Citation: 557 U.S. ___
Date: June 25, 2009
Issues: Education; Immunity from prosecution; Right to privacy;
Search and seizure

- The U.S. Supreme Court unanimously held that school officials violated the Fourth Amendment when conducting a strip search of a middle school student without any reason to suspect either that the alleged drugs were dangerous or that they were concealed in her underwear. In addition, the majority of the Court held that the officials had qualified immunity against civil suit because the law on the matter was not clearly established before the present decision.

During the 1970's, the U.S. Supreme Court began making a series of decisions concerning the due process protections of public school students when faced with possible disciplinary sanctions. Because of the Fourth Amendment's prohibition of unreasonable searches and seizures, the Court has limited the methods that school officials may use in gathering evidence of misbehavior. However, in *New Jersey v. T.L.O.* (1985) it authorized school searches of students' notebooks or purses based on "reasonable suspicion," a less demanding standard than "probable cause," which is usually required for a police search. School officials, in other words, may conduct searches based on a "moderate chance" of discovering evidence of wrongdoing, in contrast to the police, who must show a "fair probability" of finding evidence of criminal conduct. When school officials must decide whether to conduct a search, moreover, they are expected to follow a "rule of reasonableness," which requires them to take into account a number of considerations, including the nature of the infraction, the threat to students' safety, and the extent to which the search invades a student's zone of privacy.

The Safford Case

In 2003, at the Safford Middle School in Arizona, Assistant Principal Wilson discovered that a young female student possessed five nonprescription pills commonly used for menstrual cramps. The girl informed Wilson that another student, thirteen-year-old Savana Redding, had given her the pills. Although the pills were not considered dangerous, school rules banned such medications, unless used with advance permission. Wilson escorted Redding, who had the reputation of being somewhat rowdy, into his office. When asked whether the allegations were true, she claimed to have no knowledge of the matter. After she gave Wilson permission to search her backpack and notebook, Wilson examined them but found nothing. Wilson then instructed a female assistant and the school nurse to search the girl's outer clothing and underwear. Although Redding did not agree to this search, she cooperated with the women's instructions. After she stripped to her underwear, the two women had her pull out and shake her bra as well as the elastic of her panties, exposing parts of her breasts and pelvic area to the two women. The search did not produce any evidence of contraband.

Later, Savana Redding's mother filed a civil lawsuit against the Safford school district and the three school officials responsible for the strip search, which she claimed was contrary to the Fourth Amendment. Savana Redding asserted in an affidavit that she never consented to the intrusive search but had not protested because of fear that she would be in greater trouble if she did not cooperate. She further declared that she had felt violated by the search, which she described as "the most humiliating experience" of her life.

The defendants denied that any violation of a constitutional right had occurred, and the three officials also argued that they were entitled to qualified immunity from such a suit. The district court ruled in favor of the defendants, but the court of appeals reversed, holding that the search was unreasonable and therefore unconstitutional. They rejected Wilson's claim of qualified immunity, but recognized the immunity of the two administrative assistants because they were not independent decision makers. Wilson and the school district appealed to the U.S. Supreme Court, which granted *certiorari.*

The Court's Ruling

The justices of the Court voted eight to one that a violation of the Fourth Amendment had occurred, but they voted seven to two that the school officials were entitled to qualified immunity. Writing the opinion for the Court, Justice David Souter evaluated the strip search from the perspective of the "rule of reasonableness" enunciated in the *T.L.O.* decision. Although the evidence of Redding's distribution of pills was "sufficiently plausible" to justify a search of her backpack and outer clothing, Souter emphasized the "indignity" of a strip search on such a young girl and concluded that "the content of the suspicion failed to match the degree of intrusion." The officials did not have any evidence suggesting that the medication threatened the safety of students.

Moreover, their information provided no reason to suppose that Redding was carrying pills in her underwear. Souter conceded, however, that *T.L.O.* and other Court rulings had not provided clear notice that a strip search would be unwarranted in the conditions of the case, as demonstrated by the great differences in judges' ruling. He concluded that a school official cannot be sued when clearly established law does not show that a search has violated the Fourth Amendment.

Justices John Paul Stevens and Ruth Bader Ginsburg disagreed with the majority on the question of qualified immunity, and each wrote dissenting opinions. Stevens believed that the conduct of the school officials was obviously "outrageous"; that it did not require a constitutional scholar to conclude that a strip search of a thirteen-year-old child is an "invasion of constitutional rights of some magnitude." He was particularly unhappy that Justice Souter had referred to disagreement by different judges as evidence that the Court's precedent was not clear on such an intrusive search.

Justice Ginsburg recalled that the *T.L.O.* ruling had mandated that searches be reasonably related to the objectives of the search and not excessively intrusive, taking into account the age and sex of the student and the nature of the infraction. According to these standards, she thought, the assistant principal's order for a strip search was "abusive" and it was not reasonable for him to believe that the law permitted it.

Justice Clarence Thomas concurred that the school officials were entitled to immunity, but he dissented from the other eight justices on the issue of a constitutional violation. He noted that all of the justices agreed that the initial search of the girl's belongings was justified in view of the reasonable suspicion that Redding was in possession of drugs in violation of school policies. After officials had adequate evidence to initiate a search, Thomas argued that they were justified in extending the search to "any area where small pills could be concealed." Observing that it is not unusual for persons to conceal pills in their undergarments, he warned that the Court's *Redding* decision "announces the safest place to conceal contraband in school."

Thomas Tandy Lewis

Further Reading

Alexander, Kern, and M. David Alexander. *American Public School Law.* Belmont, Calif.: Cengage Learning, 2009. Comprehensive guide to the many laws applicable to schools, including privacy rights under the Fourth Amendment.

Essex, Nathan. *School Law and the Public Schools: A Practical Guide for Educational Leaders.* Boston: Allyn & Bacon, 2008. Provides practical information about legal issues faced by teachers and school administrators.

Thomas, Stephen, Martha McCarthy, and Nelda Cambron-McCabe. *Public School Law: Teachers' and Students' Rights.* 6th ed. Boston: Allyn & Bacon, 2008. Comprehensive and well-documented text on the evolution and current status of laws governing the public schools.

See also *New Jersey v. T.L.O.*; *Vernonia School District 47J v. Acton.*

SAN ANTONIO INDEPENDENT SCHOOL DISTRICT V. RODRIGUEZ

Court: U.S. Supreme Court
Citation: 411 U.S. 1
Date: March 21, 1973
Issues: Education

• The U.S. Supreme Court held that wealth was not a suspect classification and that education was not a fundamental right. Therefore, the Court used the minimal scrutiny test and concluded that the U.S. Constitution did not require states to provide school districts with equal funding for public education.

Like many other states, Texas financed its public schools largely through local property taxes. As a result, wealthy school districts were able to spend significantly more money on public education than poor districts. Demetrio Rodriguez lived in a relatively poor district in San Antonio, where per capita expenditures were about half those in the city's most affluent district. Filing a class-action suit, Rodriguez claimed that the Texas system of school finance discriminated on the basis of wealth and that education was a fundamental interest that the state should provide to all its citizens without regard to their ability to pay for it.

By a 5-4 vote, the Supreme Court upheld the Texas system of finance. Justice Lewis F. Powell, Jr.'s majority opinion employed the minimal scrutiny test, inquiring whether the system bore "some rational relationship to legitimate state purposes." Powell noted that no claim was being made that poor children were being denied a free public education and that the state provided enhancement funds to maintain minimum standards for each school district.

Taking all relevant facts into account, he reasoned that a system using local taxation promoted the state's legitimate interest in encouraging local participation in public education.

In a long and memorable dissent, Justice Thurgood Marshall insisted that the Court had previously recognized that certain unenumerated rights were fundamental and that Texas's system had a discriminatory impact on an identifiable "class." In addition, Marshall argued that the use of a two-tier approach to judicial scrutiny was too rigid, and he advocated an alternative sliding-scale approach.

The Court expanded the *Rodriguez* decision in *Kadrmas v. Dickinson Public Schools* (1988), rejecting a poor family's challenge to a North Dakota school district policy that required parents to pay for bus transportation to and from school. Critics of *Rodriguez* sometimes had more success at the state level. In 1989 the Texas supreme court declared that the state's constitution required the legislature to provide relatively equal revenues per student for the financing of public education. Previous to this decision, nine other state supreme courts had issued similar rulings.

Thomas Tandy Lewis

See also *Dandridge v. Williams; Edgewood Independent School District v. Kirby.*

SANTA CLARA COUNTY V. SOUTHERN PACIFIC RAILROAD CO.

Court: U.S. Supreme Court
Citation: 118 U.S. 394
Date: May 10, 1886
Issues: Regulation of commerce

• The U.S. Supreme Court announced that corporations were "persons" within the meaning of the Fourteenth Amendment.

In a relatively unimportant ruling, the Supreme Court unanimously decided that the fences on railroad property could not be taxed under California law.

However, the case was of constitutional importance because of Chief Justice Morrison R. Waite's statement, without argument, that the equal protection clause of the Fourteenth Amendment applied to corporations as well as to natural persons. The idea logically extended to the due process clause. Waite's statement helped lay the foundation for the court's later protection of economic liberties under the doctrine of substantive due process.

Thomas Tandy Lewis

See also *Bank of Augusta v. Earle; Citizens United v. Federal Election Commission; Louisville, Cincinnati, and Charleston Railroad Co. v. Letson; Northern Securities Co. v. United States; Paul v. Virginia.*

SANTA CLARA PUEBLO V. MARTINEZ

Court: U.S. Supreme Court
Citation: 436 U.S. 49
Date: May 15, 1978
Issues: Native American sovereignty

• The U.S. Supreme Court essentially gutted the 1968 Indian Civil Rights Act that applied most of the U.S. Bill of Rights to Native American tribal governments.

The 1968 Indian Bill of Rights applied most of the U.S. Bill of Rights to Native American tribal governments. The lower federal courts gradually expanded the jurisdiction of the federal courts over Native American affairs, but *Martinez* reversed much of that expansion. In *Martinez*, a woman tribe member charged that a tribal membership rule violated the equal protection clause by favoring men. In his opinion for the 7-1 majority, Justice Thurgood Marshall said a federal cause of action was unnecessary and urged aggrieved Native Americans to appeal to their tribal courts for satisfaction as a way of increasing tribal self-determination. Justice Byron R. White dissented, arguing that the Supreme Court was forcing aggrieved Native Americans to appeal any grievance directly back to the authorities who had violated their rights.

The decision had a profound effect in reducing the number of appeals regarding Native Americans to reach the Court.

Richard L. Wilson

See also *California v. Cabazon Band of Mission Indians; Cherokee Cases; Employment Division, Department of Human Resources of Oregon v. Smith; Ex parte Crow Dog; Lone Wolf v. Hitchcock; Muskrat v. United States; Talton v. Mayes; Worcester v. Georgia.*

SANTOBELLO V. NEW YORK

Court: U.S. Supreme Court
Citation: 404 U.S. 257
Date: December 20, 1971
Issues: Immunity from prosecution

• In this case, which granted the petitioner the right to either a resentencing or a new trial, the U.S. Supreme Court confirmed the binding nature of plea-bargaining agreements made by prosecutors with defendants in criminal proceedings.

In 1969, in New York, Rudolph Santobello was arraigned on two criminal counts of violating state antigambling statutes. At first, Santobello entered a plea of not guilty, but later, after negotiations with his prosecutors, he changed his plea to guilty to a lesser-included charge, which carried a maximum penalty of one year in prison. Between the entering of the new guilty plea and the sentencing there was a delay of several months, and in the interim Santobello obtained a new defense attorney, who immediately attempted to have the guilty plea removed and certain evidence suppressed. Both motions were denied.

At Santobello's sentencing, a new prosecutor recommended the maximum penalty of one year in prison. The defense quickly objected, using the argument that the petitioner's plea-bargaining agreement had stipulated that the prosecution would make no recommendation regarding sentencing. The judge, rejecting the relevancy of what prosecutors claimed they would do, sentenced Santobello to the full one-year term on the grounds that he was a seasoned and habitual offender. Subsequently, the Appellate Division of the Supreme Court of the State of New York unanimously upheld the conviction.

The U.S. Supreme Court found that the prosecution had breached the plea-bargaining agreement and remanded the case to the state court to determine whether the circumstances required only resentencing before a different judge or whether the petitioner should be allowed to withdraw his guilty plea and be granted a new trial on the two counts as originally charged. The fact that the breach in the plea-bargaining agreement was inadvertent was deemed irrelevant, as was the sentencing judge's claim that he was not influenced by the prosecutor's recommendation. Chief Justice Warren E. Burger, in the Court ruling, argued that the plea-bargaining procedure in criminal justice "must be attended by safeguards to ensure the defendant what is reasonably due in the circumstances." Therefore, any agreement made in the plea-bargaining process, because it is part of the inducement used to encourage a plea of guilty, constitutes "a promise that must be fulfilled."

In its decision in *Santobello*, the Supreme Court both confirmed its formal recognition of plea bargaining, first granted in *Brady v. United States* (1970), and established its binding nature. Although in later decisions it would review and somewhat modify its position, as, for example, in *Mabry v. Johnson* (1984), it established an extremely important principle: that prosecutors and courts could not unilaterally renege on promises made in plea-bargaining agreements. The *Santobello* decision had the effect of encouraging wider use of the plea-bargaining process, an important aid in expediting justice.

John W. Fiero

See also *Brady v. United States.*

SCALES V. UNITED STATES

Court: U.S. Supreme Court
Citation: 367 U.S. 203
Date: June 5, 1961
Issues: Antigovernment subversion; Freedom of assembly and association; Freedom of expression

- In this case, the U.S. Supreme Court found that laws providing penalties for active membership in organizations advocating overthrow of the government do not necessarily violate the Constitution's guarantees of due process and freedom of speech.

Scales, a member of the Communist Party of the United States, was convicted under the membership clause of the Smith Act of 1940, making it a crime knowingly to belong to an organization whose aim is overthrow of the federal government by force or violence. The Smith Act was one of several antisubversive measures Congress passed after the outbreak of World War II. Although its first section addressed attempts to subvert the military, in fact the act was seldom invoked during World War II.

Afterward it became one of the government's primary methods of combating domestic communism during the Cold War. In *Dennis v. United States* (1951), the Supreme Court upheld the convictions of eleven Communist Party leaders under the conspiracy provisions of the act, a decision that led to the indictment of 141 state party leaders throughout the country. *Scales v. United States* resulted from those indictments, as did the earlier *Yates v. United States* (1957).

In *Yates*, the Court by a vote of six to one reversed the convictions of fourteen party leaders involved. The opinion of the Court, written by Justice John M. Harlan and emphasizing the distinction between advocacy of a subversive ideology and advocacy of subversive action, found the conspiracy provisions of the Smith Act defective, thus rendering them worthless. No further prosecutions were undertaken under them.

Between the time the Supreme Court handed down its decision in *Dennis* and that in *Yates*, personnel changes on the Court as well as an easing of Cold War tensions resulted in a reorientation. *Yates* produced a backlash in Congress, however, and by the time the Court decided *Scales*, it had again changed its attitude. Justice Harlan, joined by Justice Felix Frankfurter, changed sides, with the result that Scales's conviction was upheld by a vote of five to four.

In a companion case, *Noto v. United States*, decided the same day as *Scales*, the Court dismissed the conviction of a Communist Party member under the membership clause of the Smith Act. Justice Harlan's opinions in the two cases were careful to distinguish between mere membership in organizations such as the Communist Party and "not only knowing membership, but purposive membership, purposive that is as to the organization's criminal ends." Construed in this fashion, the Smith Act membership clause violated neither the due process clause of the Fifth Amendment nor the free speech guarantee embodied in the First Amendment.

In both *Yates* and *Scales*, the Court interpreted the Smith Act more narrowly than it had in *Dennis*, with the result that finally only twenty-nine of the individuals indicted under the act served time in jail for their convictions.

Lisa Paddock

See also *Dennis v. United States; Elfbrandt v. Russell; Lovell v. City of Griffin; Noto v. United States; Whitney v. California; Yates v. United States.*

Schall v. Martin

Court: U.S. Supreme Court
Citation: 467 U.S. 253
Date: June 4, 1984
Issues: Children's rights; Due process of law; Incarceration;
Juvenile justice

- In agreeing with a New York State family court in this preventive detention case, the U.S. Supreme Court limited the application of the Fourteenth Amendment's due process clause.

Schall v. Martin was a preventive detention case involving juveniles. New York State had enacted a Family Court Act pertaining to juvenile delinquents and to juveniles arrested and remanded to the family court prior to trial. If the family court determined that pretrial release of juveniles might result in their disappearance or place them or the general public at risk, it was authorized to detain them. Detention occurred only after notice was given to parents and other authorities, a hearing was held, a statement of facts and reasons was presented, and the "probable cause" that release might be harmful was established.

Juvenile detainees Gregory Martin, Luis Rosario, and Kenneth Morgan (along with thirty-three other juveniles introduced into the case) faced serious charges. Martin had been arrested in 1977, charged with first-degree robbery, second-degree assault, and criminal possession of a gun after he and two others struck another youth on the head with a loaded gun and beat him in order to steal his jacket and sneakers. He was found guilty of these crimes by a family court judge and placed on two years' probation. Martin was fourteen. Rosario, also fourteen, was charged with robbery and second-degree assault for trying to rob two men by putting a gun to their heads and beating them. He previously had been detained for knifing a student. Morgan, fourteen, had four previous arrests and had been charged with attempted robbery, assault, and grand larceny for robbing and threatening to shoot a fourteen-year-old girl and her brother.

Martin and the others brought suit claiming that their detention deprived them of a writ of habeas corpus and violated the due process clause of the Fourteenth Amendment. The federal district appeals court agreed that their detention "served as punishment without proof of guilt according to requisite constitutional standards." Gregory Schall, commissioner of the New York City Department of Juvenile Justice, appealed to the Supreme Court. The case reached the Supreme Court at a time when polls showed that crime was a major fear of the American public and when a relatively conservative Court was exercising judicial restraint and limiting the expansion of civil liberties.

Reading the majority 7-2 decision, Justice William Rehnquist acknowledged that the due process clause of the Fourteenth Amendment indeed applied to the pretrial detention of juveniles. He agreed with Schall, however, that when, as in these cases, there was "serious risk" involved to both the juveniles and the public by their release, the New York law was compatible with the "fundamental fairness" demanded by the due process clause.

Clifton K. Yearley

See also *Boumediene v. Bush*; *Hamdan v. Rumsfeld*; *Ozawa v. United States*; *Zadvydas v. Davis*.

SCHECHTER POULTRY CORP. V. UNITED STATES

Court: U.S. Supreme Court
Citation: 295 U.S. 495
Date: May 27, 1935
Issues: Separation of powers

• Of the three U.S. Supreme Court cases voiding vague delegations of power to executive branch agencies, this ruling regarding the constitutionality of the National Industrial Recovery Act (1933) was the broadest.

The Schechter Poultry Corporation was charged with violating wage and hour provisions of the slaughterhouse industry and selling an "unfit chicken" under the 1933 National Industrial Recovery Act (NIRA). The act was designed to stimulate business recovery and end unemployment, largely through codes of fair competition and other regulations. The Supreme Court unanimously held that the NIRA was essentially unconstitutional because Congress delegated its lawmaking power to the executive branch through excessively vague legislation.

Schechter should be considered along with two other cases: *Panama Refining Co. v. Ryan* (1935) and *Carter v. Carter Coal Co.* (1936). In these three cases, the Court attempted to limit the later widespread congressional practice of transferring its lawmaking responsibility by delegating the hard decisions or the actual wording to executive branch agencies. In *Schechter,* the Court addressed the essence of the NIRA, unlike its narrow holding in the other cases. In his dissent in *Panama,* Justice Benjamin N. Cardozo argued that the national economic emergency of the Great Depression justified this vague delegation of power, but in *Schechter* he found that the delegation was so extensive that it had "run riot."

Carter, the last Court decision attempting to limit vague delegations of congressional lawmaking power, was supported by only a 5-4 majority. The opinion, written by Justice George Sutherland, used the Tenth Amendment and the indirect-direct commerce distinction as an additional basis for rejecting the NIRA but ended up losing support on the Court. The four dissenters in *Carter* objected to this direct-indirect distinction. The Court never overturned its holdings in these cases but simply ignored them. *Schechter* is currently valid only on the narrow issues of the case.

Richard L. Wilson

See also *Bowsher v. Synar, Carter v. Carter Coal Co.; Mistretta v. United States, Morrison v. Olson, Panama Refining Co. v. Ryan.*

SCHENCK V. UNITED STATES

Court: U.S Supreme Court
Citation: 249 U.S. 47
Date: March 3, 1919
Issues: First Amendment guarantees; Freedom of expression

- The U.S. Supreme Court promulgated the "clear and present danger" doctrine as a guideline in freedom of speech cases.

The Schenck case involved the constitutionality of the Espionage Act. Passed by Congress on June 15, 1917, that wartime measure provided severe penalties for individuals convicted of such treasonable offenses as aiding the enemy, obstructing recruiting, instigating disloyalty among American troops, or mailing seditious material. The passage of the statute reopened the old conflict between military necessity and the Bill of Rights.

Charles T. Schenck, the general secretary of the Socialist Party, strongly opposed American participation in World War I. He expressed his resistance to the "capitalist" war by distributing about fifteen thousand leaflets that urged noncompliance with the 1917 Selective Service Act. He was indicted under the Espionage Act for plotting to obstruct the draft and for using the mails to circulate his leaflets. After a federal court convicted him and sentenced him to prison, Schenck appealed to the U.S. Supreme Court on the grounds that he had been deprived of his freedom of speech and press guaranteed by the First Amendment to the Constitution.

The nation's highest court was thus confronted with the challenge of reconciling the Espionage Act with the First Amendment. After hearing arguments in 1919, the Court upheld the constitutionality of the 1917 law. Justice Oliver Wendell Holmes, Jr., speaking for a unanimous Court, maintained that the First Amendment guarantee of freedom of speech and press is not absolute. "The most stringent protection of Free speech," he said, "would not protect a man in falsely shouting fire in a theater and causing a panic." Freedom of expression is always under restraint, particularly in wartime.

In his decision, Holmes formulated the clear and present danger doctrine as a criterion for judging between permissible and illicit speech: "The question . . . is whether the words are used in such circumstances and are of such a nature as to create a clear and present danger that they will bring about the substantive evil that Congress has a right to prevent." Applying the test to Schenck's distribution of antidraft circulars during World War I, Holmes ruled that the defendant's activities did pose an immediate danger to the nation's war effort. Schenck's conviction was upheld.

The major legacy of the case to American justice has been the clear and present danger precept. The test subsequently became an influential yardstick in freedom of speech cases. A version of Holmes's criterion permits advocacy to be punished only if its objective is to incite lawless behavior and if such behavior is likely to occur. If the perceived danger is not imminent or its likelihood is minimal, the government may not restrict freedom of speech.

Ronald W. Long

See also *Abrams v. United States; DeJonge v. Oregon; Dennis v. United States; Gompers v. Buck's Stove and Range Co.; Kunz v. New York; Rosenberg v. United States; Stromberg v. California; Terminiello v. Chicago; Whitney v. California.*

SCOTT V. HARRIS

Court: U.S. Supreme Court
Citation: 550 U.S. 372
Date: April 30, 2007
Issues: Immunity from prosecution; Police powers

• The U.S. Supreme Court held that when a police officer ended a dangerous high-speed automobile chase by causing the fleeing car to crash, the officer's action did not violate the Fourth Amendment rights of the driver, even though the maneuver resulted in his becoming seriously disabled for the remainder of his life.

In 2001, when a police officer near Peachtree City, Georgia, attempted to pull over a nineteen-year-old driver, Victor Harris, for traveling eighteen miles faster than the speed limit, the young man fled away in his vehicle, thereby initiating a high-speed car chase. During the middle of the chase, Harris drove into a shopping center and was briefly trapped by police cars, but he escaped by colliding into an officer's car before speeding away. A sheriff's deputy, Timothy Scott, then took the leading role in the chase. Harris reached a speed of over eighty-five miles an hour on a two-lane highway.

Although Scott had never been trained in stopping cars with the precision intervention technique (PIT), he radioed a supervisor for permission to perform the maneuver. The supervisor replied, "Take him out." Scott decided that he was traveling too fast for the PIT, so he instead applied his push bumper to the rear of Harris's vehicle, causing it to leave the road and crash into an embankment. Harris survived but was rendered quadriplegic. He filed suit in federal court, alleging that Deputy Scott had used excessive force, constituting an unreasonable seizure under the Fourth Amendment. Both the chase and the accident were recorded on a videotape.

Scott claimed qualified immunity as a government official acting in his official capacity, arguing that the law was not sufficiently clear at the time of the incident to put him on notice that his actions were possibly illegal. The district court rejected the claim. The Eleventh Circuit Court of Appeals affirmed the ruling for two reasons: first, a jury might find that Scott's action was unreasonable in the circumstances of the chase, and second, that the law of the circuit was sufficiently clear to give the police "fair notice" that it was unlawful to ram a vehicle under such circumstances. The circuit court even suggested that a jury might conclude that Scott's action constituted an inappropriate use of "deadly force" under *Tennessee v. Garner* (1985). According to the court's analysis in the written opinion, the traffic at the time was relatively light, Harris remained in control of his vehicle, and innocent bystanders were in no immediate danger. Scott appealed the decision to the U.S. Supreme Court, which granted *certiorari*.

The Court's Ruling

The Supreme Court overturned the rulings of the two lower courts and held that Scott was entitled to a summary judgment recognizing his qualified immunity. Speaking for an 8-1 majority, Justice Antonin Scalia observed that the threshold question for a denial of qualified immunity was whether the facts showed that the officer's actions had violated the constitutional rights of the injured person. In defending a negative answer, Scalia maintained that the high-speed chase posed an immediate and substantial risk of serious injury or even death to other persons; therefore, the police officer's decision to terminate the chase by forcing the fleeing driver off the road was entirely reasonable. In reaching this conclusion, Scalia balanced the dangers that the speeding and reckless driver intentionally posed to innocent bystanders against the risk posed to the driver by Scott's action.

Drawing the evidence of the videotape of the chase, Scalia took strong issue with the Eleventh Circuit's analysis and concluded that no reasonable jury could possibly conclude that the police officer had violated the Fourth Amendment rights of the fleeing driver. To allow a speeding driver to escape would encourage other drivers to flee the police, and it was impossible for the officers to know that the driver was not a dangerous criminal. Denying that the *Garner* precedent was relevant, Scalia asserted that the issue in the case under consideration was not whether or nor Scott's actions constituted "deadly force," but "what mattered is whether those actions were reasonable."

Justice John Paul Stevens agreed with the analysis of the two lower courts and filed the lone dissenting opinion. Observing that there was no indication that the driver had committed a crime before the chase, Stevens found that the videotape did not show that he had created any great danger to other vehicles on the road. Based on all of the circumstances, he concluded that a jury should be allowed to decide if the police officer had violated the young man's constitutional rights.

Police departments throughout the country took a keen interest in the *Scott* ruling. During the years that followed, the number of high-speed chases appears to have increased, in part because of dramatic television broadcasting of the events. Many critics of such chases have argued that they endanger innocent bystanders to the extent that the police should not pursue them except in extraordinary circumstances, such as when the fleeing drivers are known to be dangerous criminals. Although the ruling supported the right of law-enforcement officers to apprehend fleeing vehicles, it also emphasized that officers must conduct chases in a reasonable way. Some observers worried that police agencies might take the decision as a green light to engage in dangerous chases and tactical maneuvers without proper training.

Thomas Tandy Lewis

Further Reading

Adams, Thomas F. *Police Operations.* Upper Saddle River, N.J.: Prentice Hall, 2006. Written from the perspective of police officers, this handbook provides guidelines on the use of force, including deadly force.

May, David A., and James E. Headley. *Reasonable Use of Force by Police: Seizures, Firearms, and High-Speed.* New York: Peter Lang, 2008. Analysis of reasonableness standards that police officers must make split-second decisions about the use of force.

See also *Brandenburg v. Ohio; Gitlow v. New York; Noto v. United States; Tennessee v. Garner; Whitney v. California.*

SCOTT V. SANDFORD

Court: U.S. Supreme Court
Citation: 19 How. (60 U.S.) 39
Date: March 6, 1857
Issues: Citizenship; Congressional powers;
Racial discrimination; Slavery

- In one of the most reviled decisions in its history, the U.S. Supreme Court ruled that Congress could not limit slavery in the territories, nullifying the Missouri Compromise, and also that African Americans could not be U.S. citizens.

Few decisions of the U.S. Supreme Court have had the political repercussions of *Scott v. Sandford*. The decision supplied the infant Republican Party with new issues to use against the Democrats, who were already divided by the disturbances in Kansas that historians have called Bleeding Kansas. The decision also was an embarrassment to the Republicans, for in denying the authority of Congress to legislate on slavery in the territories, the ruling destroyed the major platform of the Republican Party. The Supreme Court's opinion also damaged, if not destroyed, the practicability of Stephen A. Douglas's doctrine of popular sovereignty, for if Congress had no authority to regulate slavery in the territories, then territorial legislatures had no authority either, as they were inferior bodies created by Congress. The Court had thus entered completely into the political issues tearing at the union, and the reputation of Chief Justice Roger Brooke Taney was shattered in the North.

The Issues

Two pertinent questions were raised by the Scott case. First, could an African American, whose ancestors were imported into the United States and sold as slaves, become a member of the political community created by the U.S. Constitution and thereby enjoy the rights and privileges of a U.S. citizen? Second, did the Constitution regard African Americans as a separate class of persons distinct from the class known as citizens?

Dred Scott, the plaintiff in *Scott v. Sandford*, was a slave of African descent. In 1834, he had been taken by his owner, John Emerson, an army surgeon, to

Chief Justice Roger Brooke Taney's opinion in Scott v. Sandford *ranks as one of the worst in Supreme Court history.* (Mathew Brady/Collection of the Supreme Court of the United States)

the free state of Illinois and then to Wisconsin Territory, which was free by the provisions of the Missouri Compromise of 1820. Emerson returned to Missouri with Scott in 1838. After Emerson's death in 1846, Scott sued his widow in the Missouri courts for his freedom, on the grounds that his residence in a free state and in a free territory had made him free. Although he won in the lower court, Missouri's supreme court reversed the decision in 1852 and declared that Scott was still a slave because of his voluntary return to Missouri.

While Scott's litigation was in progress, Emerson's widow remarried. Under Missouri law, administration of her first husband's estate passed to her brother, John F. A. Sanford. Because Sanford was a citizen of New York, Scott's lawyer, Montgomery Blair, acting on the grounds that the litigants in the case were residents of different states, sued for Scott's freedom in the United States circuit court in Missouri. The verdict there also went against Scott.

As expected, the case was appealed to the U.S. Supreme Court, where it was argued in February, 1856, and reargued in January, 1857. At first, the justices of the Supreme Court agreed to decide against Scott on the grounds that Scott was a slave under Missouri law, as it was interpreted by its supreme court, despite his residence on free soil. However, for a variety of reasons, the justices changed their minds and determined to deal with the controversial questions of African American citizenship and congressional power over slavery in the territories. One of the justices confidentially informed President-Elect James Buchanan of the Court's intention. Buchanan supported the Court's plan and even persuaded one justice to concur in the majority opinion. The Supreme Court announced its decision on March 6, 1857, two days after Buchanan's inauguration as president.

The Court's Ruling

Although each of the nine justices issued a separate opinion, a majority of them held that African Americans who were descendants of slaves could not belong to the political community created by the Constitution and enjoy the right of federal citizenship. They also agreed that the Missouri Compromise of 1820, forbidding slavery in the part of the Louisiana Purchase territory north of $36°30'$ north latitude, was unconstitutional.

According to the opinion of Chief Justice Taney, African Americans were "beings of an inferior order" who "had no rights which the white man was bound to respect." The significance of Taney's comments lies in the fact that they established a perception of African Americans that transcended their status as slaves. In considering the issue of equality, Taney did not limit his assessment of African Americans to those who were slaves but also included African Americans who were free. His opinion raises questions about the extent to which his public pronouncement on the alleged inferiority of African Americans helped to establish conditions for the future of race relations in the United States.

Although individual states could grant citizenship to African Americans, state action did not give them U.S. citizenship under the U.S. Constitution. Therefore, concluded Taney, "Dred Scott was not a citizen of Missouri within the meaning of the Constitution of the United States, and not entitled as such to sue in its courts." There is considerable evidence that African Americans were not considered citizens and guaranteed rights and privileges by the U.S. Constitution. One of these rights, the ability to sue, was critical to the opinion of the Court.

The Constitution granted each of the original thirteen states the authority to continue the importation of slaves until 1808. In so doing, the Constitution supported an enterprise that relegated African Americans to the status of chattel. In effect, extending the trading of slaves by the states for more than twenty years after the signing of the Constitution shows that African Americans were not included as a class granted citizenship. The Constitution also indicated that states were to make a commitment to each other to assist slave owners in retaining their property. Because slaves were defined as chattel, this applied directly to them as a class. Finally, the intent of the Constitution to exclude African Americans as citizens was revealed in the congruence between the stated ideas and the conduct that was prescribed. That is, the authors of the Constitution expected the language and the actual practices and conventions during that time period to be consistent.

On the second point, Taney declared that, since slaves were property, under the Fifth Amendment to the Constitution—which prohibited Congress from taking property without due process of law—Congress had only the power and duty to protect the slaveholders' rights. Therefore, the Missouri Compromise law was unconstitutional. This part of Taney's opinion was unnecessary, an *obiter dictum*, for, having decided that no African American could become a citizen within the meaning of the Constitution, there was no need for the Supreme Court to consider the question of whether Congress could exclude slavery from the territories of the United States. The Court's decision was consistent with earlier decisions regarding slavery. Historically, the Court's opinions had protected slave owners' rights to their property, even when the chattel was slaves.

The two antislavery justices on the Court, John McLean and Benjamin Curtis, wrote dissenting opinions. They stated that before the adoption of the U.S. Constitution, free African Americans were citizens of several states and were, therefore, also citizens of the United States. Consequently, the United States circuit court had jurisdiction in the Scott case. Because the Constitution gave Congress full power to legislate for the federal territories, it could act as it pleased regarding slavery, as on all other subjects.

Newspaper article describing the writer's visit to Dred Scott's home and the outcome of the *Scott v. Sandford* case. (Library of Congress)

Significance

The nation reacted strongly to the Supreme Court's decision. White slaveholders in the South were delighted, for a majority of the justices had supported the extreme southern position. Under the Court's ruling, all federal territories were now legally opened to slavery, and Congress was obliged to protect the slaveholders' possession of their chattel. The free-soil platform of the Republicans was unconstitutional. The Republicans denounced the decision in the most violent terms, as the product of an incompetent and partisan body. They declared that when they obtained control of the national government, they would change the membership of the Supreme Court and secure reversal of the decision. Northern Democrats, while not attacking the Supreme Court, were discouraged by the decision, for if Congress could not prohibit slavery in any territory, neither could a territorial legislature. Therefore, popular sovereignty also would cease to be a valid way of deciding whether a federal territory should be slave or free.

The Supreme Court's decision in this case and many subsequent opinions of the Court would have an adverse impact upon African Americans seeking legal rights as citizens of the United States. Moreover, as the first decision since *Marbury v. Madison* (1803) to reverse an act of Congress as unconstitutional, it generated lower esteem for the Court among northerners, widening the growing rift between North and South.

John G. Clark, updated by K. Sue Jewell

Further Reading

Abraham, Henry J. *Freedom and the Court: Civil Rights and Liberties in the United States.* New York: Oxford University Press, 1967. Focuses on civil rights and liberties for African Americans in the United States.

Bell, Derrick. *Race, Racism and American Law.* 2d ed. Boston: Little, Brown, 1980. Presents a comprehensive analysis of U.S. law that asserts that racial inequality is integrated into the legislative and judicial system in the United States.

Blue, Rose, and Corinne Naden. *Dred Scott: Person or Property?* Tarrytown, N.Y.: Marshall Cavendish Benchmark, 2005. Part of its publisher's Supreme Court Milestones series designed for young-adult readers, this volume offers an accessible history and analysis of the *Scott* case that examines opposing sides in the case, the people involved, and the case's lasting impact. Includes bibliography and index.

Fehrenbacher, Don E. *The Dred Scott Case: Its Significance in American Law and Politics.* New York: Oxford University Press, 1978. Excellent scholarly account of the *Dred Scott* case, with considerable attention given to the various issues facing the United States on the eve of the Civil War.

Finkelman, Paul. *Dred Scott v. Sandford: A Brief History with Documents.* Boston: Bedford, 1997. Useful casebook on the *Dred Scott* decision that contains detailed and useful documentation.

Herda, D. J. *The Dred Scott Case: Slavery and Citizenship.* Berkeley Heights, N.J.: Enslow, 2010. Designed for young-adult readers, this volume examines the issues leading up to the *Scott* case, people involved in the case, the legal development of the case, and the historical impact of the ruling. Includes chapter notes, further reading list, and index.

Huebner, Timothy S. *The Taney Court: Justices, Rulings, and Legacy.* Santa Barbara, Calif.: ABC-CLIO, 2003. Study of Taney's twenty-eight-year tenure on the Supreme Court, including historical background, biographical sketches of the justices, and analyses of the court's major decisions and legacy.

Kaufman, Kenneth C. *Dred Scott's Advocate: A Biography of Roswell M. Field.* Columbia: University of Missouri Press, 1996. Biography covering the personal and professional life of Field, a St. Louis-based attorney who pled Scott's case before the U.S. Supreme Court.

Lewis, Thomas T., and Richard L. Wilson, eds. *Encyclopedia of the U.S. Supreme Court.* 3 vols. Pasadena, Calif.: Salem Press, 2001. Comprehensive reference work on the Supreme Court that contains substantial discussions of *Dred Scott v. Sandford,* Roger B. Taney, and other related subjects.

Paul, Arnold, ed. *Black Americans and the Supreme Court Since Emancipation: Betrayal or Protection?* New York: Holt, Rinehart and Winston, 1972. Explores various precedent-setting Supreme Court cases that reveal the Court's failure to ensure equal rights for African Americans.

See also *Civil Rights Cases; Marbury v. Madison; Plyler v. Doe.*

SELECTIVE DRAFT LAW CASES

Court: U.S. Supreme Court
Citation: 245 U.S. 366
Date: January 7, 1918
Issues: Military law

• The U.S. Supreme Court unanimously upheld the constitutionality of the Selective Service Act of 1917.

Several persons convicted of draft evasion asserted that compulsory military conscription was inconsistent with both the Thirteenth Amendment's prohibition against involuntary servitude and the religious clauses of the First Amendment. Speaking for the Supreme Court, Chief Justice Edward D. White responded that congressional authority for imposing the draft was firmly grounded in the authorization of Congress to declare war and "to raise and support armies." Conscription was entirely consistent with Anglo-American traditions, and it was a necessary corollary to federal sovereignty and the power to wage war. White found no reason to conclude that the draft, which contained an exemption for conscientious objectors, infringed on any rights under the First Amendment. In addition, he wrote that the obligations of citizenship included the "supreme and noble duty of contributing to the defense of the rights and honor of the nation." Although many people objected to White's patriotic tone, the Court never overturned any of his rulings.

Thomas Tandy Lewis

See also *Cohen v. California; Rostker v. Goldberg; United States v. O'Brien.*

SEMINOLE TRIBE V. FLORIDA

Court: U.S. Supreme Court
Citation: 517 U.S. 44
Date: March 27, 1997
Issues: States' rights

- The U.S. Supreme Court held that the Eleventh Amendment prevents Congress from authorizing suits by Native American tribes to enforce federal statutes.

The Indian Gaming Regulatory Act of 1988 required states to negotiate gaming compacts with Indian tribes located in their states. The act authorized the tribes to bring suit in federal court against a state failing to negotiate a compact "in good faith." Based on the statute, the Seminole Tribe sued the state of Florida.

By a 5-4 vote, the Court held that Congress had exceeded its constitutional authority in the gaming legislation. Speaking for the majority, Chief Justice William H. Rehnquist argued that the Eleventh Amendment presupposes that each state is a sovereign entity and that an inherent principle of sovereignty is that a state may not be sued without its consent. Neither the Indian commerce clause nor the commerce clause provided Congress with the power to abrogate the sovereign immunity of the states. The immunity of states, however, did not extend to local governments or to state officials. The *Seminole Tribe* decision overruled *Pennsylvania v. Union Gas Co.* (1989). The decision did not involve suits to enforce treaty rights. Justice David H. Souter dissented in a vigorous and lengthy opinion.

Thomas Tandy Lewis

See also *California v. Cabazon Band of Mission Indians; Cherokee Cases; Ex parte Crow Dog; Johnson and Graham's Lessee v. McIntosh; Lone Wolf v. Hitchcock; Santa Clara Pueblo v. Martinez; Talton v. Mayes; United States v. Kagama.*

SHAPIRO V. THOMPSON

Court: U.S. Supreme Court
Citation: 394 U.S. 618
Date: April 21, 1969
Issues: Equal protection of the law; Right to travel;
Welfare rights

- Ruling that one-year residence requirements for receiving welfare benefits were unconstitutional, the Court defended a broad right to establish residence in the state of one's choice and to enjoy equal rights with other residents.

After living in Connecticut for two months, Vivian Thompson applied for public assistance under the Aid to Families with Dependent Children (AFDC) program. Thompson, pregnant and a mother of one child, was denied assistance because she did not meet the state's one-year residency requirement. She then sued the welfare commissioner, Bernard Shapiro, in federal district court. The district court ruled in her favor based on two principles: that the residency requirement had a "chilling effect on the right to travel" and that it denied Thompson's guarantee of equal protection under the Fourteenth Amendment. Connecticut appealed the ruling to the U.S. Supreme Court, which accepted review and consolidated the case with others dealing with the same requirement to receive welfare.

The Supreme Court decided by a 6-3 vote to strike down the durational residency requirements, with Justice William Brennan delivering the opinion of the majority. Brennan observed that the right to migrate from state to state, implied in several places in the Constitution, was well established in the precedents of the Court. Concerning the second issue, the equal protection clause of the Fourteenth Amendment, Brennan wrote that the residency requirement created two classes of needy residents, with the two classes receiving unequal benefits. Since this classification restricted "the fundamental right of interstate movement," it could only be justified by a "compelling state interest." Although a state had a valid interest in restricting its expenditures, it could not promote this interest "by invidious discrimination between classes of its citizens."

The dissenters in the case accepted the constitutional principle of a right to travel, but they believed that the impact of residency requirements were indirect and quite insubstantial. Justice John M. Harlan attacked the expansion of judicial power that occurred when courts arbitrarily decided that fundamental rights required a more rigorous standard of review.

Shapiro was an important step in the Warren Court's development of "strict scrutiny" doctrine, which required states to show a compelling state interest to justify laws limiting fundamental rights or laws based upon "suspect classifications" such as race. Since the right to interstate migration was recognized as fundamental, *Shapiro* made it difficult for states to justify durational residency requirements for most services. Later the Court would invalidate residency requirements for voting, indigent medical care, and other basic services but would allow them for less basic services, upholding requirements for seeking divorce and for exemption from paying out-of-state tuition at public universities. Contrary to some expectations, *Shapiro* did not mark the beginning of a new governmental obligation to provide the economic necessities of life.

Thomas Tandy Lewis

See also *Dandridge v. Williams; Goldberg v. Kelly; Gomez v. Perez; Graham v. Richardson.*

SHAW V. HUNT

Court: U.S. Supreme Court
Citation: 517 U.S. 899
Date: June 13, 1996
Issues: Equal protection of the law; Reapportionment and redistricting; Voting rights

• The U.S. Supreme Court held that the equal protection clause of the Fourteenth Amendment prohibits the drawing of irregularly shaped congressional districts designed to produce electoral majorities of racial and ethnic minorities.

One of the purposes of the Voting Rights Act of 1982 was to protect racial and ethnic minorities from vote dilution. After the census of 1990, the Department of Justice interpreted the act to mean that legislatures must adopt reapportionment plans that included, whenever possible, congressional districts with heavy concentrations of racial and ethnic minorities. Some of the resulting race-conscious districts were spread out and highly irregular in shape. In the election of 1992, these new districts helped elect an unprecedented number of African Americans to Congress.

In North Carolina, there were two race-based districts, with one following a narrow strip of land for 160 miles. Ruth Shaw and other white voters of North Carolina filed suit, claiming that these two voting districts violated their rights under the equal protection clause. In *Reno v. Shaw* (1993), the Supreme Court directed the federal district court to reconsider the reapportionment plan according to the strict scrutiny standard. This decision, often called *Shaw I*, clearly indicated that a majority of the justices did not approve of racial gerrymandering. The lower court, nevertheless, approved the districts.

In *Shaw v. Hunt* (also known as *Shaw II*), the Supreme Court reversed the lower court's judgment. Speaking for a majority of five, Chief Justice William H. Rehnquist noted that any law that classifies citizens on the basis of race is constitutionally suspect and concluded that the drawing of the two contested districts had not been narrowly tailored to further a compelling state interest. He insisted that the state's interest in remedying the effects of past or present racial discrimination must be justified by an "identified past discrimination" rather than simply a generalized assertion of such discrimination. Also, he argued that the Justice Department's policy of maximizing majority-black districts was not authorized by the Voting Rights Act, which said nothing about subordinating the traditional districting factors of compactness, contiguity, and respect for political subdivisions. Justice John Paul Stevens wrote a strong dissent, arguing that the white plaintiffs' claims of harm were "rooted in speculative and stereotypical assumptions."

In two closely related decisions, *Bush v. Vera* (1996) and *Abrams v. Johnson* (1997), the Court struck down race-based congressional districts in Texas and Georgia respectively. Each of these decisions was decided by a 5-4 vote, which meant that a future change in Court personnel could result in a different judgment about the controversial issue of racial gerrymandering.

Thomas Tandy Lewis

See also *Colegrove v. Green; Davis v. Bandemer; Reapportionment Cases; Shaw v. Reno; Wesberry v. Sanders.*

SHAW V. RENO

Court: U.S. Supreme Court
Citation: 509 U.S. 630
Date: June 28, 1993
Issues: Reapportionment and redistricting; Voting rights

- By calling for close scrutiny of a predominantly black congressional district whose shape it considered "bizarre," the U.S. Supreme Court struck a blow against the practice of drawing district boundaries to create "majority-minority" electoral districts.

After the 1990 census, the state legislature of North Carolina began the task of "reapportionment," or redrawing its electoral districts. Although about 22 percent of the state's population was African American, no blacks had been elected to Congress for almost a century. To remedy this, and ostensibly to meet provisions of the Voting Rights Act, the legislature created two majority-nonwhite districts. In order to avoid disturbing incumbents' districts, the legislature drew one of the two districts largely along an interstate highway, snaking 160 miles through the north-central part of the state. The resulting district was 53 percent black.

Five voters filed suit against the reapportionment plan, objecting that the race-based district violated their right to participate in a nonracial electoral process. The case reached the Supreme Court, whose 5-4 majority instructed the lower courts to reconsider the constitutionality of such a district in light of its "bizarre" shape and its "uncomfortable resemblance to political apartheid." In essence, the majority expressed its concern about the practice of creating districts on the basis of race and of establishing contorted geographical boundaries. The coupling of the two practices presumably could result in districts that patently violated the Constitution's equal protection clause, unless a compelling state interest could be demonstrated.

When the *Shaw* case was subsequently returned to North Carolina, a federal panel upheld the reapportionment plan after finding that the state did indeed have a compelling interest in complying with the VRA. Nevertheless, the Supreme Court's *Shaw* decision has been the basis for other important decisions concerning racially defined districts. In 1994, for example, a majority-black district in Louisiana was rejected by a federal district court invoking *Shaw.* The court expressed particular concern that the district was intentionally created on the basis of the voters' race. More significant, in 1995 the U.S. Supreme Court extended *Shaw*'s admonitions about racial reapportionment to argue that voters' rights are violated whenever "race was the predominant factor motivating the legislature's decision to place a significant number of voters within or without a particular district," irrespective of shape.

Shaw served as a watershed in the contest between advocates of racial representation and those who champion a "color-blind" electoral system. It came at a time when various racial issues that had for years remained largely outside of sharp political debate—affirmative action, welfare reform, and so forth— had been thrust into the center stage of American political discourse. Although *Shaw* by no means resolved these debates, it helped to clarify the battle lines.

Steve D. Boilard

See also *Colegrove v. Green; Davis v. Bandemer; Reapportionment Cases; Shaw v. Hunt; Wesberry v. Sanders.*

SHELLEY V. KRAEMER

Court: U.S. Supreme Court
Citation: 344 U.S. 1
Date: May 3, 1948
Issues: Equal protection of the law; Housing discrimination; Racial discrimination; Right to privacy

• Although the U.S. Supreme Court acknowledged the right of private individuals to make racially restrictive covenants, the Court ruled that state action to enforce such covenants was a violation of the Fourteenth Amendment.

After J. D. Shelley, an African American, purchased a house in a predominantly white neighborhood of St. Louis, Missouri, one of the neighbors, Louis Kraemer, sought and obtained an injunction preventing Shelley from taking possession of the property. Unknown to Shelley, the neighboring landowners had signed a contractual agreement barring owners from selling their property to members of "the Negro or Mongolian race." Supported by the National Association for the Advancement of Colored

Chief Justice Fred M. Vinson. (James Whitmore/Collection of the Supreme Court of the United States)

People (NAACP), Shelley challenged the constitutionality of the contract in state court, but the Missouri Supreme Court upheld its legality. Appealing to the U.S. Supreme Court, Shelley's case was argued by the NAACP's leading counsel, Charles Houston and Thurgood Marshall. President Harry S. Truman put the weight of the executive branch in favor of the NAACP's position.

This was not the first time that the issue of residential segregation had appeared before the Court. In *Buchanan v. Warley* (1917), the Court had struck down state statutes that limited the right of property owners to sell property to a person of another race, but in *Corrigan v. Buckley* (1926) the Court upheld the right of individuals to make "private" contracts to maintain segregation. *Corrigan* was based on the establishment principle that the first section of the Fourteenth Amendment inhibited the actions of state governments, not those of individuals.

The Court refused to declare restrictive contracts unconstitutional, but it held 6-0 that the Fourteenth Amendment's equal protection clause prohibited state courts from enforcing the contracts, meaning that the contracts were not enforceable. The decision, written by Chief Justice Fred Vinson, emphasized that one of the basic objectives of the Fourteenth Amendment was to prohibit the states from using race to discriminate "in the enjoyment of property rights." The decision did not directly overturn *Corrigan*, but it interpreted the precedent as involving only the validity of private contracts, not their legal enforcement. In a companion case five years later, *Barrows v. Jackson* (1953), Chief Justice Vinson dissented when the majority used the *Shelley* rationale to block enforcement of restrictive covenants through private damage suits against covenant violators.

Eliminating the last direct method for legally barring African Americans from neighborhoods, *Shelley* was an important early victory in the struggle against state-supported segregation. Civil rights proponents hoped that a logical extension of the case would lead to an abolition of the distinction between private and state action in matters of equal protection, but in later decisions such as *Moose Lodge v. Irvis* (1972), the majority of judges were not ready to rule against private conduct that was simply tolerated by the state.

Thomas Tandy Lewis

See also *Buchanan v. Warley*; *Corrigan v. Buckley*; *Jones v. Alfred H. Mayer Co.*; *Moose Lodge v. Irvis*.

Sheppard v. Maxwell

Court: U.S. Supreme Court
Citation: 384 U.S. 333
Date: June 6, 1966
Issues: Freedom of the press

- In *Sheppard v. Maxwell*, the U.S. Supreme Court for the first time provided guidelines for trial courts on how to balance the interests of the media in reporting information about a criminal trial and the rights of a criminal defendant.

Problems related to too much media publicity about a criminal trial extend back to the nineteenth century, but it was not until the 1960's that the Supreme Court discussed the effects of publicity in criminal trials. Between 1959 and 1966, the Court reversed five convictions on the grounds that the amount of publicity had affected the defendant's right to a fair trial. It was not until 1966, when it decided *Sheppard v. Maxwell*, that it actually provided practical suggestions to the trial courts on how to solve the issues related to prejudicial publicity.

Sheppard involved the murder conviction of Sam Sheppard, a well-known physician in Cleveland accused of murdering his wife. Even before the arrest of the defendant in this case, the media published countless stories about him, accentuating his alleged failure to cooperate with the investigation and strongly arguing for his arrest. After an article demanded to know why there had been no public inquest, a three-day inquest took place where Sheppard's questioning was covered by television and radio.

Another article also seemed to influence the decision to arrest Sheppard, since he was arrested hours after the headline "Why Isn't Sam Sheppard in Jail?" was run. Many articles and editorials implied his guilt and discussed allegedly incriminating evidence that was never introduced at trial. During the trial itself, the media filled the courtroom, and the constant movement of reporters made it difficult for some witnesses to be heard. A special table for media representatives was set in the courtroom, and twenty people were assigned to it.

The court also reserved four rows of seats behind the bar railing for television and radio reporters and for representatives of out-of-town newspapers and magazines. A radio station was allowed to broadcast from a room adjacent to the room where the jury rested and deliberated. Because of his proximity to reporters in the courtroom, it was almost impossible for the defendant to speak privately with his attorney during the proceedings. Despite this situation, the trial judge did not take steps to limit the effects of the publicity or the behavior of the press during the trial. The Supreme Court reversed the murder conviction, holding that the publicity surrounding the trial had deprived the defendant of his right to a fair trial.

In criticizing the trial court for allowing a "carnival atmosphere in the courtroom" and for failing to control the flow of publicity, the Supreme Court ordered lower courts to take an affirmative role in protecting the rights of the defendants from undue interference by the press. The Court enumerated some ways in which courts could make sure the publicity did not affect the defendant's right to a fair trial. For example, courts could regulate the conduct of reporters in the courtroom, change venue, order a continuance of the trial, isolate witnesses, and control the release of information to the media by law-enforcement personnel and counsel.

Alberto Bernabe-Riefkohl

See also *Nebraska Press Association v. Stuart; Richmond Newspapers v. Virginia.*

Sherbert v. Verner

Court: U.S. Supreme Court
Citation: 374 U.S. 398
Date: June 17, 1963
Issues: Freedom of religion

- The U.S. Supreme Court allowed individuals to make First Amendment claims against governmental policies that indirectly burdened their free exercise of religion and required government to show that any such burdens were justified by a compelling state interest.

Adell Sherbert, a member of the Seventh-day Adventist church, worked in a textile mill in South Carolina, and in 1959 her employer informed her that henceforth she would be required to work on Saturdays. Since it was against her religious beliefs to work on the Sabbath, she refused the new conditions, and she was fired. Not able to find employment consistent with her beliefs, she filed for state unemployment benefits. South Carolina law did not allow benefits for applicants who refused to accept work without good cause, and the unemployment office rejected her religious scruples as a justification.

Sherbert and her lawyers filed suit against the unemployment office at state court, but the South Carolina Supreme Court ruled in favor of the state agency. The state court relied on the recent precedent of *Braunfeld v. Brown* (1961), in which the U.S. Supreme Court had allowed for Sunday closing laws (blue laws) even if such laws disadvantaged Jewish merchants whose religious convictions prevented them from working on Saturdays. The state court concluded that the burdens on Sherbert were essentially the same as the economic hardships accepted in *Braunfeld*.

The U.S. Supreme Court, however, voted seven to two that South Carolina's policy was in violation of the religious exercise clause of the First Amendment, made applicable to the states by the Fourteenth Amendment. Writing for the majority, Justice William Brennan began with the premise that religious exercise was a fundamental right and that any governmental burden on this right must be justified by a compelling state interest. In addition, Brennan wrote that the state had the obligation to adopt the alternative which was the least restrictive on religious practice, a test that had previously been used in free speech cases. The state was violating the First Amendment when it presented Sherbert with the "cruel choice" of either forfeiting an economic benefit or abandoning one of the precepts of her religion.

The two dissenters, supported by many informed observers, argued that Brennan's opinion contradicted the reasoning in *Braunfeld*, but Brennan maintained that the two cases were quite different. In the earlier case, he wrote, the state had demonstrated a compelling interest to provide a uniform day of rest for all workers, while in Sherbert the state had no compelling reason to refuse to modify its requirements for unemployment benefits.

Sherbert required governments to make exceptions in enforcing laws to accommodate religious practices unless the normal application of the law could be defended according to the tests that it served a compelling state interest and was the least restrictive alternative. The result was a maximum of protection for unpopular religious practices. In *Employment Division, Department of Human Resources of Oregon v. Smith* (1990), however, the Court ruled that indirect burdens were acceptable when state policies had a secular basis and were equally applicable to all citizens.

Thomas Tandy Lewis

See also *Boerne v. Flores; Church of Lukumi Babalu Aye v. Hialeah; Employment Division, Department of Human Resources of Oregon v. Smith; Wisconsin v. Yoder.*

SHIPP, UNITED STATES V. *See* UNITED STATES V. SHIPP

SHREVEPORT RATE CASES

Court: U.S. Supreme Court
Citation: 234 U.S. 342
Date: June 8, 1914
Issues: Regulation of commerce

• The U.S. Supreme Court, in these railroad cases, strengthened the Interstate Commerce Commission (ICC) during the early twentieth century.

Two cases, *Houston, East, and West Texas Railway Co. v. United States* and *Texas and Pacific Railway Co. v. United States*, were decided together and are known as the *Shreveport Rate Cases*. A state railroad commission had authorized Texas railroads to charge significantly lower rates for intrastate versus interstate rail shipments. The Interstate Commerce Commission (ICC) issued an order that overruled that state railroad commission's authorization. The railroads argued that Congress lacked the right to set rates for intrastate transport under the Constitution's commerce clause, but the Supreme Court found that intrastate and interstate commerce were so intertwined that the Texas intrastate rates had a harmful effect on interstate commerce. By a 7-2 vote, the Supreme Court upheld the ICC order, significantly strengthening the ICC. Justice Charles Evans Hughes wrote the opinion for the majority.

Richard L. Wilson

See also *Champion v. Ames; Cooley v. Board of Wardens of the Port of Philadelphia; Hall v. DeCuir; License Cases.*

SIEBOLD, EX PARTE. *See* EX PARTE SIEBOLD

SIERRA CLUB V. MORTON

Court: U.S. Supreme Court
Citation: 405 U.S. 727
Date: April 19, 1972
Issues: Environmental issues and animal rights; Standing

• In a decision that rejected the Sierra Club's suit to block the construction of a ski resort on public land, the U.S. Supreme Court defined the role judges were thereafter to play in environmental issues, providing guidelines for how environmental groups would continue to pursue their goals.

On April 19, 1972, the U.S. Supreme Court decided in the case *Sierra Club v. Morton* that the Sierra Club, the large national environmental organization founded in 1892 by John Muir, could not file suit to stop the U.S. Forest Service from granting permission to Walt Disney Enterprises to construct a ski resort in Sequoia National Forest. The Court decided the case by a 4-3 margin, with two members of the nine-member Court not participating. At issue were critical questions about who was entitled to make decisions about the use of national property, how such decisions were to be made, and who, if anyone, could legally represent the interests of the environment.

The 1970's are sometimes referred to as the environmental decade because at no previous time had more sweeping environmental legislation been implemented. The decade began with such developments as the passage of the National Environmental Policy Act of 1969 (signed into law on January 1, 1970), which mandated environmental impact statements, and the first Earth Day on April 22, 1970. The 1970's ended with the creation in 1980 of the so-called Superfund, which coordinated the cleanup of toxic-waste sites. *Sierra Club v. Morton* was one of several key cases that defined the role judges were thereafter to play in environmental issues.

As is often true of Supreme Court cases, the actual ruling was less important than the direction set by it. In rejecting the Sierra Club's initial presentation, the Supreme Court had also given guidelines for how the environmental group could continue to pursue its goals. In accordance with these guidelines, the Sierra Club used legislation to delay the construction project until Congress put an end to further plans for commercial development.

Mineral King Valley

Mineral King Valley, a beautiful region in the Sierra Nevada adjacent to Sequoia National Park, had become a national game refuge and part of the Sequoia National Forest by a special act of Congress in 1926. The region, which had once been extensively mined, was relatively inaccessible and therefore attracted only a limited number of visitors.

The U.S. Forest Service, the agency that administers all national forests, was created in the early twentieth century after information about the misuse of government forests became known. The Forest Service had first considered Mineral King a potential site for recreational development in the late 1940's, but the idea was shelved at the time. In the mid-1960's, the service invited bids from private developers for the construction of a year-round ski and entertainment resort. In 1969, a plan proposed by Walt Disney Enterprises was approved for the area. The proposal, which was designed to accommodate fourteen thousand visitors per day, included a complex of motels, restaurants, swimming pools, ski lifts, a cog-assisted railway, and a twenty-mile access highway to the facility. When J. Michael McCloskey, the Sierra Club's executive director, was unsuccessful in seeking a public hearing on the proposal, the organization decided to file suit in federal court to prevent the construction of the resort in Mineral King.

This decision marked the beginning of the Sierra Club's use of the legal system to combat threats to the environment. Until 1966, conservationist suits had not been regarded as legally admissible. In 1966, however, the Scenic Hudson Preservation Conference had won a precedent-setting ruling in its effort to stop construction of a power plant in New York State, giving environmental groups renewed hope.

Federal Court Rulings

The district court in San Francisco that was the first to hear the Sierra Club's case sided with the organization and granted a preliminary injunction blocking construction. The Ninth Circuit Court of Appeals, however, reversed that opinion on the grounds that the Sierra Club had no "standing"—in other words, that the group was not legally qualified to file suit on behalf of the environment. When the Supreme Court reviewed the decision of the two lower courts in 1972, the justices agreed with that opinion. Writing for the majority, Justice Potter Stewart emphasized that the Sierra Club had failed to demonstrate clear injury to either itself or its members.

William O. Douglas, then the strongest environmentalist on the Court, strongly dissented from the majority decision. He alone took the view that it should be possible legally to represent trees and rocks, citing the land ethic set forth in Aldo Leopold's *A Sand County Almanac, and Sketches Here and There* (1949). Leopold maintained that trees, wildlife, rivers, and soil have intrinsic value that ought to be widely recognized. He embraced the land and its inhabitants as part of the ethical community and feared the threats posed by so-called progress and development.

Douglas also used legal arguments from a 1972 article by law professor Christopher Stone titled "Should Trees Have Standing?" Stone noted that the law vigorously protected the rights of some nonhuman things such as corporations and trusts, as well as legally incompetent individuals for whom the courts appoint a guardian. Stone suggested that organizations such as the Sierra Club and the National Audubon Society should be regarded as legal guardians of the environment and empowered to file suit on its behalf. In his dissenting opinion, Justice Harry A. Blackmun asked, "Must our law be so rigid and our procedural concepts so inflexible that we render ourselves helpless when the existing methods and the traditional concepts do not quite fit and do not prove to be entirely adequate to new issues?"

What should be regarded as harm deserving judicial attention is an issue that has continued to change over the years. Justice Stewart in his majority opinion cited Alexis de Tocqueville's astute observation, written in the 1830's, that "scarcely any political question arises in the United States that is not resolved, sooner or later, into a judicial question." Tocqueville's point unquestionably applies to environmental issues, which have repeatedly led to litigation in which the courts are asked to determine the precise definition of terms such as "clean" and "safe." The upsurge in environmental laws and litigation of the 1970's required legislators and judges to redefine who had the right to litigate which alleged harms. This greatly increased involvement of the courts was in itself controversial in the legal community.

Significance

There had been a few important earlier legal cases involving environmental issues, but only in the 1970's did environmental litigation become common. After that, virtually no major construction project—highway, dam, nuclear power plant, incinerator, airport, or sports complex—would go unchallenged in court. In the 1970's, the Sierra Club brought more cases to court than any other conservationist organization, filing 93 out of the decade's 351 U.S. environmental cases.

Courts have complex rules about who has standing to bring suit. Private citizens and taxpayers are, for example, not allowed to challenge congressional appropriations. In *Sierra Club v. Morton*, the Court ruled that the Sierra Club "lacked standing to maintain the action." At the same time, however, the Court outlined the steps the organization could take in order to pursue the action more successfully, for example by including the allegation that a ski resort would harm specific members by destroying their hiking trails, campsites, and vistas. Court decisions on subsequent cases generally granted environmental groups such as the Sierra Club the right to voice their objections in court.

The basic structure of American government is biased against environmental values in three important ways. First, the U.S. Constitution favors individual rights, particularly property rights, over environmental concerns. Second, environmental goals have to be pursued through legislation that is far more likely to prohibit unecological behavior than to reward ecologically desirable actions. Electric companies, for example, are punished if they release too much pollution but are not rewarded when they succeed in reducing pollution. The emphasis on violations ensures frequent litigation by wealthy alleged violators. Third, the legal system is inherently slow to act and conservative in its concern for procedure and precedent. Moreover, there are many roadblocks to successful litigation, not the least of which is the cost.

In general, the courts have steered a middle course between environmentalists and proponents of rapid economic growth, permitting a broad range of environmental cases to be heard but frequently siding against environmentalists. Although the Supreme Court has sometimes been accused of letting political events dictate its decisions, this charge was not true of the Court's rulings on environmental law. The Court's rulings during the 1970's did not reflect the popular bias in favor of protecting the environment.

Sierra Club v. Morton came at the beginning of the modern era of environmental legislation and litigation. The deeply divided decision and the Court's focus on legalities set the tone for the ensuing decades.

Drew Christie

Further Reading

Breyer, Stephen G. *Breaking the Vicious Circle: Toward Effective Risk Regulation.* 1993. Reprint. Cambridge, Mass.: Harvard University Press, 2006. Discussion of the difficulties of effective environmental law by a jurist who was appointed to the Supreme Court in 1994.

Buck, Susan J. *Understanding Environmental Administration and Law.* 3d ed. Washington, D.C.: Island Press, 2006. An especially useful source for non-lawyers that explains complex legal and regulatory issues.

Findley, Roger W., and Daniel A. Farber. *Environmental Law in a Nutshell.* 6th ed. St. Paul, Minn.: West Group, 2004. A short and readable, though dry, summary of environmental law. Part of an excellent and frequently updated series.

Stone, Christopher D. *Should Trees Have Standing? Toward Legal Rights for Natural Objects.* Los Altos, Calif.: W. Kaufmann, 1974. An expanded version of the influential and widely anthologized article, "Should Trees Have Standing? Toward Legal Rights for Natural Objects," which first appeared in 1972 in the *California Legal Review.*

Turner, Tom. *Sierra Club: One Hundred Years of Protecting Nature.* New York: Harry N. Abrams, 1991. A beautifully produced history of the Sierra Club, which includes a useful summary of the events leading up to *Sierra Club v. Morton.*

See also *Bryant v. Yellen; Oregon Waste Systems v. Department of Environmental Quality; Tennessee Valley Authority v. Hill.*

SKINNER V. OKLAHOMA

Court: U.S. Supreme Court
Citation: 316 U.S. 535
Date: June 1, 1942
Issues: Medical ethics; Reproductive rights; Right to privacy

• The U.S. Supreme Court ruled that states could not require sterilization because of criminality or moral turpitude.

Oklahoma, as well as other states in 1942, authorized sterilization of "habitual criminals" after multiple convictions for enumerated crimes of "moral turpitude." The Oklahoma law did not apply to those persons guilty of embezzlement and other white-collar crimes. The justification for the law, inspired by the eugenics movement, was the theory that some traits of criminality and mental defect were biologically inherited. Skinner, who had been convicted once for stealing chickens and twice for armed robbery, was ordered to submit to a vasectomy.

By a 9-0 vote, the Supreme Court ruled that the law was unconstitutional, but two justices disagreed with the majority's constitutional reasoning in the decision. Speaking for the majority, Justice William O. Douglas found that the law violated the equal protection clause of the Fourteenth Amendment. The state had presented no evidence that the tendency to engage in larceny was more likely to be inheritable than the tendency to commit embezzlement. Although Douglas did not base the decision on substantive due process, he nevertheless emphasized that the liberty of procreation was "one of the basic civil rights of man." For this reason, *Skinner* helped prepare the foundation for a later constitutional right of privacy.

Thomas Tandy Lewis

See also *Buck v. Bell*; *Griswold v. Connecticut.*

SKINNER V. RAILWAY LABOR EXECUTIVES' ASSOCIATION

Court: U.S. Supreme Court
Citation: 489 U.S. 602
Date: March 21, 1989
Issues: Illegal drugs; Right to privacy; Search and seizure

- In this case the U.S. Supreme Court ruled that drug and alcohol testing in the workplace was not a violation of the Fourth Amendment.

The Fourth Amendment to the U.S. Constitution protects not only against unreasonable search and seizure of persons and places but also against the issuance of warrants for search and seizure unless just cause is demonstrated.

The Federal Railroad Administration (FRA), in response to evidence that drug and alcohol abuse was becoming a problem in the nation's railways, established regulations to address the problem. These regulations required blood and urine samples from employees to test for drugs or alcohol after train accidents where deaths, injuries, or property damage occurred. Employees also had to submit to breath or urine tests if there was reasonable suspicion that they were under the influence of drugs or alcohol, even if no accident had occurred.

Railway labor organizations filed suit in the U.S. District Court for the Northern District of California. The court held the regulations to be constitutional. The railway organizations then appealed in the U.S. Court of Appeals for the Ninth Circuit. The appeals court reversed the lower trial court's decision, holding that such tests were search and seizure without warrant and constituted a violation of an employee's Fourth Amendment rights.

The U.S. Supreme Court, on *certiorari*, reversed the court of appeals ruling and upheld the original decision, finding that Fourth Amendment rights had not been violated. In addition, the Court noted that the FRA regulations were well known to, and understood by, the railway workers subject to them.

The Court found that the tests were not unconstitutional even when a warrant had not been issued. The justices cited the need to ensure the safety of the public using the railways. Because evidence of drug or alcohol use could disappear from a person's body within a brief period of time, timely testing was essential for accurate results. Obtaining a warrant would take too long. Furthermore, they said that the railway did not need to prove that there was particular reason to suspect drug or alcohol use before testing employees who had not been involved in accidents. The justices pointed out the need to discourage all employees from using drugs or alcohol during working hours or shortly before. In general, the Court held that the greater good of protecting the public outweighed the private rights of individuals responsible for ensuring travel safety.

The opinion was written by Justice Anthony Kennedy with Chief Justice William H. Rehnquist and Justices Byron R. White, Harry A. Blackmun, Sandra Day O'Connor, and Antonin Scalia concurring. Justice John Paul Stevens concurred in part and concurred in the judgment. Justices Thurgood Marshall and William J. Brennan dissented.

Elizabeth Algren Shaw

See also *National Treasury Employees Union v. Von Raab*; *Vernonia School District 47J v. Acton*.

SLAUGHTERHOUSE CASES

Court: U.S. Supreme Court
Citation: 83 U.S. 36
Date: April 14, 1873
Issues: Due process of law

• In this case, the U.S. Supreme Court largely eliminated the Fourteenth Amendment's due process clause as a protection of individuals from actions of the state in which they resided.

Hundreds of butchers in New Orleans, operating as small individual businesses typical of nineteenth century America, were thrown out of business by what is widely regarded as the corrupt passage of a law in the Louisiana legislature granting a single state franchise (monopoly) to one company. Having been deprived of their livelihood (their property rights), the butchers sued, arguing they had been deprived of their property by the state without due process of law or just compensation.

Justice Samuel F. Miller wrote the opinion for the 5-4 majority, holding that the Fourteenth Amendment sought only to make African American citizens equal with white citizens and did not affect the relationships between white persons and other white persons (that is, butchers and butchers), and the butchers lost. This view that the Bill of Rights protected citizens only from actions by the federal government continued until the incorporation doctrine began to be applied in the twentieth century. Justices Stephen J. Field, Noah H. Swayne, Joseph P. Bradley, and Chief Justice Salmon P. Chase dissented.

Richard L. Wilson

See also *Bradwell v. Illinois; Civil Rights Cases; Maxwell v. Dow; Plessy v. Ferguson; Schechter Poultry Corp. v. United States.*

SLOCHOWER V. BOARD OF EDUCATION OF NEW YORK CITY

Court: U.S. Supreme Court
Citation: 350 U.S. 551
Date: April 9, 1956
Issues: Antigovernment subversion; Loyalty oaths

• The U.S. Supreme Court overturned a summary dismissal of a public school teacher for refusing to answer questions before a congressional committee.

Justice Tom C. Clark wrote the opinion for the 5-4 majority, voiding a summary dismissal of a tenured college professor who cooperated substantially with a congressional inquiry into "communist" subversion in college education but who asserted his right against self-incrimination for a brief period before World War II. The New York Charter provided for termination if an employee refused to answer questions about official conduct. The Supreme Court found that provision of the Charter unconstitutional and declared that the dismissal of the teacher without a hearing violated the due process clause of the Fourteenth Amendment. Justices Sherman Minton, Harold H. Burton, Stanley F. Reed, and John M. Harlan II dissented.

Richard L. Wilson

See also *Aptheker v. Secretary of State; Communist Party v. Subversive Activities Control Board; Dennis v. United States; Keyishian v. Board of Regents; Scales v. United States; Yates v. United States.*

SMITH V. ALLWRIGHT

Court: U.S. Supreme Court
Citation: 321 U.S. 649
Date: April 3, 1944
Issues: Civil rights and liberties; Equal protection of the law; Racial discrimination; Voting rights

• The U.S. Supreme Court ruled that disenfranchisement of African Americans in state primary elections was unconstitutional. Although a significant victory for civil rights, the decision did not end attempts by Texans to disenfranchise African American voters, especially in county elections.

In 1923, the Texas legislature sought to disenfranchise African American voters in the state by passing a resolution that "in no event shall a Negro be eligible to participate in a Democratic primary. . . ." Since the 1890's, in Texas as in all other Southern states, nomination in the Democratic primary was tantamount to election; therefore, while African Americans would be permitted to vote in the general election, they would have no meaningful role in the political process.

Almost immediately after the Texas legislature barred African Americans from participating in the Democratic primary, the National Association for the Advancement of Colored People (NAACP) secured a plaintiff, Dr. Lawrence Aaron Nixon, to test the constitutionality of the law. In *Nixon v. Herndon* (1927), the United States Supreme Court, in an opinion written by Justice Oliver Wendell Holmes, Jr., held that the Texas statute violated the equal protection clause of the Fourteenth Amendment to the U.S. Constitution by discriminating against African Americans on the basis of race. He also ruled, however, that it was unnecessary to strike down the white primary as a denial of suffrage "on account of race [or] color" repugnant to the Fifteenth Amendment.

The Texas legislature reacted defiantly to the Supreme Court decision. On June 7, 1927, the legislature passed a new resolution granting to the state executive committees of every political party the authority to establish the qualifications of their members and to determine who was qualified to vote or otherwise participate in the party. In turn, the Democratic Party State Executive Committee limited participation in its primary to white voters in Texas.

Once again Nixon filed suit, this time against James Condon, the election officer who refused to give him a ballot in the 1928 Democratic primary. In *Nixon v. Condon* (1932), the Supreme Court struck down this new Texas statute as a violation of the equal protection clause. The vote was five to four.

The Democratic Party State Executive Committee immediately rescinded its resolution prohibiting African Americans from voting in its primary, but the state party convention voted to limit participation in its deliberations to whites, and Nixon and the NAACP, after two Supreme Court cases and an expenditure of six thousand dollars, were once more back at the beginning. In July, 1934, Richard Randolph Grovey in Houston, Texas, was refused a ballot to vote in the Democratic primary. On April 1, 1935, in *Grovey v. Townsend*, Justice Owen J. Roberts ruled that the Democratic Party was a private organization, and that its primary, although held under state law, was a party matter paid for by the Democrats. Since Roberts could find no state action in the process by which Democrats nominated their candidates, there was, he said, no violation of the Fourteenth Amendment.

There the matter rested. The primary was held not to be part of the general election, so there was presumably no relationship to the Fifteenth Amendment's protection of suffrage. Because the Democratic Party was a private organization, it was free to establish membership qualifications, and there was not sufficient state involvement to invoke the guarantees of the Fourteenth Amendment.

United States v. Classic

It seemed there was no way to contest the validity of the Texas white primary. In 1941, however, in *United States v. Classic*, a case that ostensibly had nothing to do with African Americans or the white primary, the Supreme Court held for the first time that the right to vote was protected in a primary as well as in the general election, "where the state law has made the primary an integral part of the process of choice or where in fact the primary effectively controls the choice."

United States v. Classic dealt with a Louisiana primary in which there had been fraudulent returns, but otherwise there was no way to distinguish the Texas primary from the one held in the neighboring Southern state. In Texas, as in Louisiana, in 1941 as in 1923, Democratic Party nomination was a virtual guarantee of election, and the general election was a mere formality. The NAACP took immediate advantage of the ruling: Lonnie E. Smith, a Houston dentist and NAACP member, sued a Texas election official for five thousand dollars for refusing to give him a ballot to vote in the 1940 Democratic congressional primaries. The NAACP's legal counsel, Thurgood Marshall, and William Henry Hastie, dean of the Howard Law School, brought *Smith v. Allwright* to the U.S. Supreme Court.

In April, 1944, mindful of Southern sensibilities but intent upon overruling the nine-year-old precedent in *Grovey*, the Court chose Stanley F. Reed, a Democrat from Kentucky, to write its opinion. Justice Reed's opinion made it clear that the Court, except for Justice Roberts (the author of the *Grovey* decision), had concluded that the primary was an integral part of a general election, particularly in the Southern states. The *Classic* decision, wrote Justice Reed, raised the issue of whether excluding African Americans from participation in the Democratic Party primary in Texas violated the Fifteenth Amendment. The answer was in the affirmative, and *Grovey v. Townsend* was expressly overruled.

Significance

The long litigative battle against the Texas white primary seemed to be over—but it was not. In Fort Bend County, Texas, the Jaybird Democratic Party, organized after the Civil War, held primaries closed to African American voters; its candidates consistently won county offices. In spite of *Smith v. Allwright*, the Jaybirds refused to open their primary to African Americans, ar-

Stanley F. Reed being photographed and grilled by the news media shortly after his nomination to the Supreme Court in early 1938. (Harris & Ewing Collection/Library of Congress)

guing that they did not operate under state law or use state officers or funds. Nevertheless, in *Terry v. Adams* (1953), the Supreme Court held that the Jaybird primary violated the Fifteenth Amendment, because it controlled the electoral process in Fort Bend County.

It took twenty-one years for the United States Supreme Court to rule that the Texas white primary violated the right to vote guaranteed by the Fifteenth Amendment. It would take another twenty-one years before the Voting Rights Act of 1965 finally secured the ballot for African Americans in the South. In the interim, the fall of the white primary had the practical effect of increasing African American registrants in the Southern states from approximately 250,000 in 1940 to 775,000 seven years later. African Americans were still intimidated and defrauded of their suffrage rights, but *Smith v. Allwright* was an important landmark on the road to uninhibited enfranchisement. It also was a symbol that the Supreme Court would examine the reality behind the subterfuge engaged in by antisuffrage lawmakers and act to protect African Americans in the enjoyment of their civil rights.

David L. Sterling

Further Reading

Fassett, John D. *New Deal Justice: The Life of Stanley Reed of Kentucky.* New York: Vantage Press, 1994. Biography of the conservative Democratic justice who wrote the majority opinion in *Smith v. Allwright.*

Hine, Darlene Clark. *Black Victory: The Rise and Fall of the White Primary in Texas.* Millwood, N.Y.: KTO Press, 1979. Examination of the background of the white primary and the struggle to bring about its demise.

Kluger, Richard. *Simple Justice: The History of Brown v. Board of Education and Black America's Struggle for Equality.* New York: Alfred A. Knopf, 1976. Eminently readable analysis of another landmark Supreme Court case in African American history.

Lawson, Steven F. *Black Ballots: Voting Rights in the South, 1944-1969.* New York: Columbia University Press, 1976. Traces the development of African American enfranchisement from *Smith v. Allwright* to the Voting Rights Act of 1965 and its aftermath. Includes a chapter on the white primary.

Powledge, Fred. *Free at Last: The Civil Rights Movement and the People Who Made It.* Boston: Little, Brown, 1991. Popular account of the struggle for equality during the 1960's, with numerous human interest stories.

Zelden, Charles L. *The Battle for the Black Ballot: Smith v. Allwright and the Defeat of the Texas All-White Primary.* Lawrence: University Press of Kansas, 2004. Book-length study of the case, its intricacies, and its consequences. Bibliographic references and index.

_____. *The Supreme Court and Elections: Into the Political Thicket.* Washington,

D.C.: CQ Press, 2010. Collection of historical essays and documents tracing the U.S. Supreme Court's rulings on voting rights issues throughout U.S. history.

See also *Grovey v. Townsend; Newberry v. United States; Nixon v. Condon; Nixon v. Herndon; Terry v. Adams; United States v. Classic.*

SMYTH V. AMES

Court: U.S. Supreme Court
Citation: 169 U.S. 466
Date: March 7, 1898
Issues: Regulation of business

- The U.S. Supreme Court ruled that a state law setting unreasonably low rates for certain businesses violated the Fourteenth Amendment, and it prescribed a complex method for determining reasonable rates.

During the 1890's the Supreme Court overruled a number of state laws regulating railroads and utilities. Among other things, it held that regulated businesses were constitutionally entitled to charge a reasonable rate and that the determination of reasonableness was a judiciary question. In *Smyth v. Ames,* the Court unanimously agreed that the low railroad charges set by the Nebraska legislature amounted to a deprivation of property without due process of law. In addition, the Court held that a regulated business was entitled to a "fair return" on its current value and even prescribed a specific formula to ascertain the value. Critics argued that the Court's reasoning was illogical because the value of a business was determined in part by the rates it charged. Reflecting the Court's commitment to property rights during the late nineteenth century, the *Smyth* decision was based on a substantive due process reading of the Fourteenth Amendment. The Court finally abandoned *Smyth*'s fair-value standard for calculating charges in *Federal Power Commission v. Hope Natural Gas Co.* (1944).

Thomas Tandy Lewis

See also *Chicago, Milwaukee, and St. Paul Railway Co. v. Minnesota; Munn v. Illinois; Shreveport Rate Cases; Wabash, St. Louis, and Pacific Railway Co. v. Illinois.*

Snepp v. United States

Court: U.S. Supreme Court
Citation: 444 U.S. 507
Date: February 19, 1980
Issues: Censorship; First Amendment guarantees;
Freedom of speech

• This decision held that agreements requiring government employees to submit their writings for review prior to publication did not violate their First Amendment rights.

As a condition of employment, agents of the Central Intelligence Agency (CIA) are required to sign an agreement that they will not publish any information during or after employment without prepublication clearance by the agency. In 1977 former CIA employee Frank W. Snepp III published a book, *Decent Interval*, that described CIA activities in Vietnam, without first submitting his manuscript for prepublication review. The government then sued him for breach of contract, requesting that an injunction be imposed requiring him to submit all future publications for prepublication review. The government also sought to control all profits earned from the sale of Snepp's book. A federal district court in Virginia sided with the government in 1978. Two years later the U.S. Supreme Court upheld the district court ruling in *Snepp v. United States.*

Snepp argued that the prepublication agreement constituted an unconstitutional prior restraint upon his freedom of expression. The Supreme Court ruled, however, that such agreements are reasonable and appropriate to prevent unauthorized disclosure of CIA sources and methods, because the government has a "compelling interest" in protecting both national security secrets and the appearance of agency confidentiality.

This ruling reaffirmed a previous decision of the Fourth Circuit Court of Appeals in *United States v. Marchetti* (1972), which had enjoined publication of *The CIA and the Cult of Intelligence* (1974) by Victor Marchetti and John Marks, until the manuscript was purged of classified information. A federal appeals court subsequently ruled that both secrecy agreements and prepublication agreements did not violate the First Amendment in *McGehee v. Casey* (1983).

The CIA cases involved government efforts to impose censorship upon massive quantities of information regarding government activities because of potential danger to national security. The government and the courts have routinely viewed these cases as matters of contract law. To defenders of free speech, however, these attempts to censor writings critical of the government raise several concerns. First, questions of whether material might endanger national security is left entirely to government agencies; the courts have been reluctant to intercede in these determinations. Therefore, the authority to weigh the arguments for and against censorship has been delegated to the censor. Second, because the information is relevant to government policies and decisions, opponents of censorship fear that both the right of authors to criticize the government and the people's right to know may be jeopardized by agency decisions. Third, these regulations constitute prior restraints upon publication. With few exceptions, the courts have overturned prior restraints because they impose direct burdens upon authors and publishers and because they deter critics from engaging in expression that might be deemed seditious. However, the CIA prepublication and secrecy agreements constitute one area where prior restraints have been upheld by the courts.

Richard A. Parker

See also *Hazelwood School District v. Kuhlmeier; National Treasury Employees Union v. Von Raab; New York Times Co. v. United States.*

SOLEM V. HELM

Court: U.S. Supreme Court
Citation: 463 U.S. 277
Date: June 28, 1983
Issues: Cruel and unusual punishment; Incarceration

• In this case, the U.S. Supreme Court interpreted the Eighth Amendment's prohibition on cruel and unusual punishments to limit the ability of states to impose life sentences for multiple convictions on nonviolent felony charges.

In 1979, Jerry Helm was convicted of issuing a "no account" check for one hundred dollars. This was his seventh felony conviction in South Dakota. In 1964, 1966, and 1969, he had been convicted of third-degree burglary. He had been convicted of obtaining money under false pretenses in 1972, and in

1973 he was convicted of grand larceny. Moreover, his third drunk-driving conviction in 1975 counted as a felony offense.

All the offenses were nonviolent, none involved personal, physical victimization of another person, and alcohol was a contributing factor in each case. Although the maximum penalty for writing a "no account" check would have been five years in prison and a five-thousand-dollar fine, Helm was sentenced to life imprisonment without possibility of parole because anyone convicted of four felonies under South Dakota law may be given the maximum penalty for a class 1 felony—even if he or she has never committed any class 1 felonies. The purpose of the tough sentencing law was to put habitual offenders away forever so that they could not commit additional offenses.

On appeal, the South Dakota Supreme Court rejected Helm's claim that the sentence of life without parole for a nonviolent offense constituted cruel and unusual punishment in violation of the Eighth Amendment. The U.S. court of appeals disagreed and invalidated Helm's sentence. When the U.S. Supreme Court reviewed the case, a narrow five-member majority agreed with Helm's argument.

In a prior decision (*Rummel v. Estelle*, 1980), the U.S. Supreme Court had permitted Texas to impose a life sentence on a man who, over the course of a decade, was convicted of three separate theft offenses in which he stole less than $250. The Supreme Court regarded the *Helm* case as different because South Dakota, unlike Texas, did not permit people with life sentences to become eligible for parole. Thus the realistic impact of Helm's sentence was much harsher than that of life sentences imposed in other states where prisoners typically earn an eventual parole release if they exhibit good behavior. The Court decided that Helm's punishment was disproportionate to his crimes because sentences of life without parole are typically reserved for people convicted of first-degree murder, kidnapping, or treason—not for people who commit nonviolent offenses involving modest amounts of money.

The importance of *Solem v. Helm* is that the Supreme Court placed limitations on the ability of the states to impose severe sentences on people convicted of multiple nonviolent felonies. The case also reinforced the Court's view that the Eighth Amendment contains an implicit requirement that sentences cannot be disproportionate to the crimes committed.

Christopher E. Smith

See also *Furman v. Georgia; Harmelin v. Michigan; Hudson v. Palmer; Hutto v. Davis; Rhodes v. Chapman; Robinson v. California; Rummel v. Estelle; Stanford v. Kentucky; Weems v. United States.*

SOUTH CAROLINA V. KATZENBACH

Court: U.S. Supreme Court
Citation: 383 U.S. 301
Date: March 7, 1966
Issues: Voting rights

• The U.S. Supreme Court upheld the constitutionality of the 1965 Voting Rights Act.

The Voting Rights Act of 1965 prescribed remedies for states that had practiced racial discrimination in voting. Under the act, South Carolina was prevented from enforcing literacy tests and property requirements for voting, and federal officials were appointed to oversee the registration of voters in the state and ensure that racial discrimination did not take place. By an 8-1 vote, the Supreme Court upheld the constitutionality of the 1965 act, including the appointing of federal voting registrars in states with a record of discrimination against minorities in registering to vote. The decision was unanimous except for a partial dissent from Justice Hugo L. Black. Chief Justice Earl Warren wrote the opinion for this landmark case, which became a benchmark in congressional enforcement of the Civil War amendments by allowing Congress to proscribe a class of suspect practices without specifying in every case that the judiciary would hear evidence that the practices were unconstitutional.

Richard L. Wilson

See also *Breedlove v. Suttles; Colegrove v. Green; Dunn v. Blumstein; Ex parte Yarbrough; Harper v. Virginia State Board of Elections; Lassiter v. Northampton County Board of Elections; Oregon v. Mitchell; United States v. Reese.*

SOUTH DAKOTA V. DOLE

Court: U.S. Supreme Court
Citation: 483 U.S. 203
Date: June 23, 1987
Issues: Federal supremacy

• The U.S. Supreme Court upheld congressional legislation mandating that states impose a minimum drinking age of twenty-one as a condition for receiving their full complement of federal highway funds.

By a 7-2 vote, the Supreme Court upheld congressional legislation mandating that states impose a minimum drinking age of twenty-one as a condition for receiving their full complement of federal highway funds. South Dakota had long had a minimum drinking age lower than twenty-one and argued that states had the right to govern rules over alcoholic beverages after the repeal of Prohibition. South Dakota further argued that the federal law violated federal power under the taxing and spending clause in the Constitution. The Court ruled against the state, holding that four conditions must be met for congressional restrictions on grants to states. First, the spending must be within the general welfare; second, the restriction must be unambiguous; third, the restriction must be related to a federal interest in the project; and fourth, other constitutional provisions may not be violated. Justice William J. Brennan, Jr., dissented as did Justice Sandra Day O'Connor, who found that the third item—the federal government's interest in highway construction—was insufficiently related to the minimum drinking age to merit federal interference in a traditionally state activity.

Richard L. Wilson

See also *United States v. Butler; Vernonia School District 47J v. Acton.*

SOUTH-EASTERN UNDERWRITERS ASSOCIATION, UNITED STATES V. *See* UNITED STATES V. SOUTH-EASTERN UNDERWRITERS ASSOCIATION

SPALLONE V. UNITED STATES

Court: U.S. Supreme Court
Citation: 493 U.S. 265
Date: January 10, 1990
Issues: Federal supremacy; Housing discrimination; Local government

- The U.S. Supreme Court limited the lower federal courts' ability to impose fines on local governing bodies.

The Yonkers, New York, city council reneged on a consent decree in which it agreed to stop using federal public housing funds to promote segregated public housing. The federal district court imposed daily increasing fines for contempt both on the city and on the individual council members. By a 5-4 vote, the Supreme Court overturned the district court's ruling, effectively placing limits on the ability of lower courts to impose fines on local government. The Court criticized the fines on the individual council members, maintaining that the members should have been given more time to comply. Justice William J. Brennan, Jr., dissented, arguing that the local federal judge knew the situation better than the Court did and should be granted the discretion to handle the case.

Richard L. Wilson

See also *Ex parte Young; Missouri v. Jenkins.*

SPRINGER V. UNITED STATES

Court: U.S. Supreme Court
Citation: 102 U.S. 586
Date: January 24, 1881
Issues: Taxation; Warfare and terrorism

- The U.S. Supreme Court upheld the 1862 income tax used to finance the Civil War, holding that it was not a direct tax.

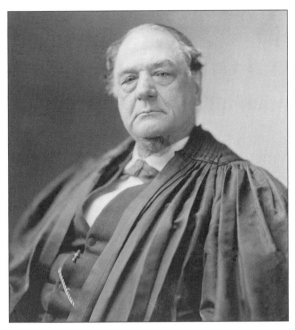

Justice Noah H. Swayne.
(Brady-Handy Collection/
Library of Congress)

In 1862 an income tax was enacted to help pay for the Civil War. Attorney William Springer refused to pay the income tax on his earnings, arguing that the tax was an invalid direct tax. Justice Noah H. Swayne wrote the opinion for the 7-0 majority on the Supreme Court in a case in which Justices Nathan Clifford and Ward Hunt did not participate. Relying on *Hylton v. United States* (1796) and a uniform practical construction of the U.S. Constitution, Swayne ruled the 1862 income tax to be constitutional. It was not, he stated, a direct tax not apportioned among the states in contravention of the Constitution. This case was not the last word, for the Court in *Pollock v. Farmers' Loan and Trust Co.* (1895) carefully and narrowly construed *Springer* so that this later Court majority could find the 1894 income tax to be an unconstitutional direct tax. The Sixteenth Amendment authorizing an income tax finally settled this issue.

Richard L. Wilson

See also *Collector v. Day; Dobbins v. Erie County; Graves v. New York ex rel. O'Keefe; Hylton v. United States; Pollock v. Farmers' Loan and Trust Co.*

STANDARD OIL V. UNITED STATES

Court: U.S. Supreme Court
Citation: 221 U.S. 1
Date: May 15, 1911
Issues: Antitrust law; Regulation of commerce

• In its decision to break up the Standard Oil Company, the U.S. Supreme Court established the principle of the "rule of reason" in relation to the violation of antitrust laws.

Founded in 1870, Standard Oil Company became one of the largest companies in the United States by the end of the nineteenth century. In *Standard Oil v. United States*, decided on May 15, 1911, the U.S. Supreme Court found the company guilty of violating the Sherman Antitrust Act of 1890 based on alleged "unreasonable" restraints of trade, including buying out small independent oil companies and cutting prices in selected areas to force out rivals. The Court's decision resulted in the separation of the parent Standard Oil from its thirty-three affiliates.

Eleven years after the historic oil discovery in Titusville, Pennsylvania, that marked the beginning of the modern oil refining industry, the Standard Oil Company was incorporated by John D. Rockefeller in Cleveland, Ohio, on January 10, 1870. At the time of the company's formation, the oil refining industry was decentralized. Standard Oil's share of refined oil production in the United States was less than 4 percent, and Rockefeller had to compete with more than 250 other independent refineries.

During the last quarter of the nineteenth century, deflation and oversupply of oil brought down oil prices, causing fierce competition among oil refineries. The price for refined oil fell from more than thirty cents a gallon in 1870 to ten cents a gallon in 1874 and to eight cents in 1885. Compared with other oil refineries, Standard Oil was managed efficiently under Rockefeller and his associates; this enabled it to survive while many competitors failed.

During the post-Civil War deflationary period, the railroad industry became very competitive. Rockefeller took advantage of Standard Oil's increasing size to secure secret rebates from shipping companies, thus reducing transportation costs and overall operating costs. Rockefeller further reduced

Standard Oil's operating costs by vertically integrating the company, acquiring oil wells, railroads, pipelines, tank cars, and retail outlets. Vertical integration gave the company more control at all stages of production.

Meanwhile, because of declining market conditions, many small and nonintegrated oil companies that were unable to reduce their operating costs became unprofitable to operate. In addition, the method of destructive distillation introduced in 1875 increased the minimum efficient size of a refinery to more than one thousand barrels per day, making smaller companies even less competitive. Rockefeller began to take advantage of the situation, buying out many of the independent refineries in Pittsburgh, Philadelphia, New York, and New Jersey at low prices, often below their original cost. Standard Oil soon refined about 25 percent of the U.S. industry output. In 1882, Rockefeller and his associates formed the Standard Oil Trust in New York, the first major "trust" form of business combination in U.S. history. The company held "in trust" all assets of the many regional Standard Oil subsidiary companies, one of which was Standard Oil of New Jersey, the third-largest U.S. refinery in the 1880's. Despite the substantial drop in oil prices, Standard Oil was able to increase its profits by reducing costs from about three cents per gallon in 1870 to less than one-half cent per gallon in 1885. By 1900, the oil trust controlled more than 90 percent of the petroleum refining capacity in the United States.

Sherman Antitrust Act

The size and power of Standard Oil led to public hostility against the company and against monopolies in general, prompting the U.S. Congress to pass the Sherman Antitrust Act in 1890. During the same year, immediately after New York State's action against the "sugar trust," the state of Ohio brought a lawsuit against Standard Oil for illegal monopolization of the oil industry. On March 2, 1892, the Ohio Supreme Court found that Standard Oil had violated the Sherman Act by forming a holding company and forbade the company to operate Standard Oil of Ohio in that state.

The Ohio court decision led to dissolution of the Standard Oil Trust back into its independent parts. The New Jersey unit took advantage of favorable state laws to become the Standard Oil Company of New Jersey, later known as Jersey Standard, as the trust's parent holding company. Rockefeller remained president, and management of the trust was consolidated through interlocking directorates of the more than thirty subsidiary companies. The supposedly separate companies thus were able to act as a single entity.

In 1901, the discovery of the Spindletop oil field created a boom in oil production on the Gulf coast of Texas. The formation of new oil companies, such as Texaco and Gulf, increased the competition faced by Standard Oil. Standard Oil responded by continuing to buy out independent oil refineries. The Standard Oil Trust's market share in the oil industry continued to expand.

Meanwhile, the commissioner of the U.S. Bureau of Corporations, James Rudolph Garfield, investigated Standard Oil for violations of antitrust law. As a result of his studies, the federal government, led by Attorney General George Woodward Wickersham, brought charges in November, 1906, in the Federal Circuit Court of the Eastern District of Missouri against Standard Oil for monopoly and restraint of trade in violation of the Sherman Antitrust Act.

In 1909, the Missouri court found Jersey Standard guilty of violating section 1 of the Sherman Act by forming a holding company and of violating section 2 by restraining competition among merged firms by fixing transportation rates, supply costs, and output prices. Standard Oil appealed the decision to the U.S. Supreme Court, and on May 15, 1911, the Court upheld the Missouri decision. The Court later entered a dissolution decree to dismember the Standard Oil trust and divest the parent holding company, Jersey Standard, of its thirty-three major subsidiaries. Many of its offspring still bore the name Standard Oil. These new companies included the Standard Oil Company of Indiana (later American), the Standard Oil Company (Ohio), Standard Oil Company of California (later Chevron), Standard Oil of New Jersey (later Exxon), and Standard Oil of New York (later Mobil).

Significance

The Standard Oil case marked the beginning of a new direction in U.S. antitrust legislation and prosecution. Along with the Supreme Court's decision in the American Tobacco case in 1911, the Court's ruling, led by Chief Justice Edward D. White, departed from rulings in earlier cases. The new interpretation of section 2 of the Sherman Act was that only "unreasonable," instead of all, restraints of trade were illegal. The Standard Oil decision, followed closely by the American Tobacco case, gave birth to a new doctrine in U.S. antitrust policy known as the rule of reason.

The allegedly "unreasonable" practices by Standard Oil that were ruled illegal under sections 1 and 2 of the Sherman Act included forcing smaller independent companies to be bought on unfavorable terms and selectively cutting prices in market areas where rivals operated, with the intent of bankrupting those rivals, while maintaining higher prices in other markets. Chief Justice White maintained that it was mainly Standard Oil's merger practices in an attempt to monopolize the oil refining industry that constituted illegal restraint of trade.

The Standard Oil case of 1911 significantly altered the course of American business history as well as the development of U.S. antitrust laws. The victory of the government against a powerful trust provided an important lesson in the early history of antitrust. The dissolution of Standard Oil into many independent companies effectively increased competition in the oil industry. In addition, the case provides a classic study of the development of American big business at the beginning of the twentieth century.

The first major antitrust law was the Sherman Antitrust Act of 1890, which emerged largely from public dissatisfaction with the monopoly power gained by Standard Oil in the oil refining market. The Sherman Act prohibits conspiracies or combinations in restraint of trade (section 1) and any attempts to create them, known as monopolization (section 2). The limits of the law regarding what constitutes unlawful practices were not precisely defined in the act, leading to different judicial interpretations of the act.

In the first decade following passage of the Sherman Act, only sixteen antitrust cases were brought to court. Even though the courts began to establish that actions such as formal agreements to fix prices or limit output were definitely illegal, judges were equivocal in their treatments of the existing large trusts in industries such as oil (Standard Oil), tobacco (American Tobacco), and steel (United States Steel).

New Antitrust Legislation

The Supreme Court's decision against Standard Oil marked the beginning of a new era in antitrust legislation and prosecution. It established the "rule of reason" approach, by which Chief Justice White maintained that it was not the history or the relative size of a monopoly such as Standard Oil in its market that was an offense against the law, but rather its "unreasonable" business practices. This new doctrine set a precedent for cases involving antitrust laws that was not broken until the Alcoa case in 1945.

The Supreme Court decision in the Standard Oil case highlighted the need for additional legislation to define specific business practices that constitute "unreasonable," and thus illegal, conduct. That need led to passage of the Clayton Antitrust Act and the Federal Trade Commission Act in 1914. The Clayton Act declared illegal specific "unfair" business practices, including price discrimination, exclusive dealing and tying contracts, acquisitions of competing firms, and interlocking directorates. The Federal Trade Commission Act gave birth to a new government authority, the Federal Trade Commission, to enforce compliance of the modified antitrust law.

The government's victory in its prosecution of Standard Oil, together with passage of the Clayton Act, led to more vigorous enforcement of the antitrust laws. The U.S. Justice Department filed suit in the 1910's and early 1920's against many trusts in other industries, including American Can Company (tin cans), United Shoe Machinery Company (shoe machinery), International Harvester Company (farm machinery), and United States Steel Corporation (steel). The Supreme Court decision against Standard Oil also signi-fied the government's attitude toward mergers. Mergers and acquisitions subsided briefly, until the government's failure in prosecuting the merger practices of the United States Steel Corporation in 1920.

The dissolution of the oil monopoly, Standard Oil, effectively changed the structure of the oil industry. On one hand, its successor companies, partic-ularly the New Jersey unit, maintained considerable market power in their regional territories. The retail price of gasoline increased sharply in 1915, leading to government investigation of the extent of competition in the oil industry. On the other hand, the government apparently succeeded in en-forcing competition among the separated units. As a result of the dissolution, Standard Oil's successor companies were allowed to operate only in the oil re-fining business. They began to confront competition from other companies, such as Shell, Gulf, and Sun, which operated with the advantage of vertical integration.

In an attempt to battle the rising competition, two of Standard Oil's succes-sor companies, Standard Oil of New York and the Vacuum Oil Company, pro-posed a merger in 1930. The government filed suit in federal district court against the merger, asserting that it would violate the 1911 decree. The court's decision in favor of the merger began a new era of merger movement in the oil industry. Through mergers, the original thirty-four successor companies combined into nineteen companies during the 1930's.

In the 1920's, Standard Oil's successor companies began to expand their oil exploration overseas, particularly in the Middle East and Europe. That ex-ploration continued as American resources were exhausted. Increased im-ports of oil, notably from the Organization of Petroleum Exporting Countries (OPEC) after its formation in 1960, intensified competition in the U.S. oil market and reduced American companies' market shares. The oil refining in-dustry developed into one with companies operating worldwide, many of them large relative to the industry as a whole but none with the power for-merly held by Standard Oil.

Jim Lee

Further Reading
Adams, Walter, and James Brock, eds. *The Structure of American Industry.* 10th
   ed. Upper Saddle River, N.J.: Prentice Hall, 2000. Chapter 2 provides good
   coverage of the background and historical development of the petroleum
   industry as well as discussions of the industry's structure, price behavior,
   and performance. Valuable for undergraduate and graduate students in
   industrial organization.
Areeda, Phillip, Louis Kaplow, and Aaron Edlin. *Antitrust Analysis: Problems,*

Text, Cases. 6th ed. New York: Aspen, 2004. Textbook containing case studies of the major antitrust cases in American history. Bibliographic references and index.

Armentano, Dominick T. *Antitrust and Monopoly: Anatomy of a Policy Failure.* 2d ed. Oakland, Calif.: Independent Institute, 1990. Covers major antitrust lawsuits since the Sherman Act and the development of antitrust legislation. Chapter 4 covers the Standard Oil case. Includes an appendix of relevant sections of antitrust laws. Written for undergraduate business and economics students.

Bradley, Robert L. *Oil, Gas, and Government: The U.S. Experience.* Washington, D.C.: Cato Institute, 1996. The second section of this book presents a comprehensive account of the U.S. oil industry's history, including interventions in the industry by state and federal governments and the courts.

Destler, Chester McArthur. *Roger Sherman and the Independent Oil Men.* Ithaca, N.Y.: Cornell University Press, 1967. A biographical study of the author of the Sherman Antitrust Act, who fought for small independent oil refineries against the monopolization of the industry by Standard Oil in the northeastern region.

Gibb, George Sweet, and Evelyn H. Knowlton. *The Resurgent Years, 1911-1927.* Vol. 2 in *History of Standard Oil Company* (New Jersey), edited by Henrietta M. Larson. New York: Harper & Brothers, 1956. Discusses the evolutionary development of the New Jersey unit following the Standard Oil case in 1911, including operations overseas, increased competition with other Standard Oil successors, and labor relations.

Hall, Kermit L., ed. *Supreme Court Decisions.* New York: Oxford University Press, 1999. Multiauthored collection of essays on more than four hundred significant Court decisions, with supporting glossary and other aids.

Hidy, Ralph W., and Muriel E. Hidy. *Pioneering in Big Business, 1882-1911.* Vol. 1 in *History of Standard Oil Company* (New Jersey), edited by Henrietta M. Larson. New York: Harper & Brothers, 1955. Comprehensive documentation of the company's early history, particularly its administration and vertically integrated operations in the oil business. Good discussion of the dynamic development of a big corporation from the perspectives of business administration and business history. Valuable for business students.

Hylton, Keith N. *Antitrust Law: Economic Theory and Common Law Evolution.* New York: Cambridge University Press, 2003. Comprehensive text on economic principles behind antitrust and the development of American antitrust law over more than one hundred years of litigation. Includes a chapter on the Alcoa case. Bibliographic references and index.

McGee, John. "Predatory Price Cutting: The Standard Oil (N.J.) Case." *Journal of Law and Economics* 1 (October, 1958): 137-169. Controversial article provides arguments and evidence against accusations of predatory pricing practices by Standard Oil. This critique led to debates about the profitability of predatory price cutting and its violation of antitrust law.

Whitney, Simon N. *Antitrust Policies: American Experience in Twenty Industries.* 2 vols. New York: Twentieth Century Fund, 1958. Chapter 3 of volume 2 provides a case study of the petroleum industry until 1950. Good economic analysis of the impacts of the antitrust suit on development of the industry. Other chapters are case studies of other major industries. Appendix contains critiques of the studies of economists and government officials.

See also *Goldfarb v. Virginia State Bar; Northern Securities Co. v. United States; Swift and Co. v. United States; United States v. E. C. Knight Co.*

STANFORD V. KENTUCKY

Court: U.S. Supreme Court
Citation: 492 U.S. 391
Date: June 26, 1989
Issues: Capital punishment; Cruel and unusual punishment; Juvenile justice

• In this case, the U.S. Supreme Court held that the Eighth Amendment's prohibition against "cruel and unusual punishment" did not prevent the execution of individuals who were juveniles at the time they committed the crimes for which they were executed.

The Supreme Court's decision addressed two cases, one involving a seventeen-year-old male convicted of first-degree murder for having robbed a gas station, then raped, sodomized, and shot a station attendant to death, and the other involving a sixteen-year-old sentenced to death for having robbed a convenience store, stabbed the attendant, and left her to die. Both criminal defendants had been tried as adults.

The Supreme Court held that the Eighth Amendment's "cruel and unusual punishment" clause did not bar states from executing individuals who were sixteen and seventeen years of age at the time they committed the applicable crimes. The Court noted that such executions were not the kinds of punishment considered cruel and unusual at the time the Bill of Rights was adopted. Furthermore, the Court concluded that the executions at issue in the case were not contrary to "evolving standards of decency that mark the progress of a maturing society."

Justice Sandra Day O'Connor concurred in this holding but wrote separately to emphasize her belief that the Court had a constitutional obligation to assure in each case that a particular defendant's blameworthiness was proportional to the sentence imposed. Justice Antonin Scalia, who wrote the majority opinion and the opinion of four justices on this point, argued that the Court had never invalidated a punishment solely because of an asserted disproportion between the punishment and the defendant's blameworthiness.

Justices William J. Brennan, Thurgood Marshall, Harry A. Blackmun, and John Paul Stevens dissented. These justices stated that the "cruel and unusual punishment" clause of the Eighth Amendment bars the execution of any person for a crime committed while the person was under the age eighteen. Justice Brennan, writing for the dissenters, asserted that such executions violated contemporary standards of decency. He pointed out that the laws of a majority of states would not have permitted the executions at issue in this case and that in the vast majority of cases involving juvenile offenders, juries did not impose the death penalty. The justice concluded by arguing that the imposition of the death penalty for juvenile crimes served the interests of neither retribution nor deterrence.

Capital punishment in these cases did not serve the interests of retribution since, according to Justice Brennan, the penalty was disproportionate to the defendants' blameworthiness. The punishment did not advance the interests of deterrence since juveniles were not likely to make the kind of cost-benefit analysis that would dissuade them from committing a crime for fear of receiving the death penalty.

Timothy L. Hall

See also *In re Gault; In re Winship; Roper v. Simmons.*

STANLEY V. GEORGIA

Court: U.S. Supreme Court
Citation: 394 U.S. 557
Date: April 7, 1969
Issues: Pornography and obscenity; Right to privacy

• The U.S. Supreme Court broadly declared that adults have the right to possess pornographic materials in the privacy of their own homes.

The Supreme Court unanimously decided that a state could not convict adults for the mere possession of legally obscene materials in their own homes. In part, Thurgood Marshall's opinion rests on the Fourth Amendment protection of the home from search and seizure; in other parts, it relies on the First Amendment protection of freedom of expression. Still other parts of the opinion seem to rely on an expanded right of privacy, but this last conclusion was undercut by the Court's later decision in *Bowers v. Hardwick* (1986), which allowed the state to regulate private sexual behavior. After *Roth v. United States* (1957), the Court's rulings on obscenity had followed a tortuous path. For a time, some thought *Stanley* might represent a clear unanimous conclusion on the part of the Court on the question of possession of pornography in one's home. However, Justice Byron R. White, writing for the majority in *Osborne v. Ohio* (1990), banned the mere possession of child pornography in the home and cautioned that *Stanley* should not be read too broadly.

Richard L. Wilson

See also *Bowers v. Hardwick*; *Jacobellis v. Ohio*; *Memoirs v. Massachusetts*; *New York v. Ferber*; *Osborne v. Ohio*; *Roth v. United States*.

STANTON V. STANTON

Court: U.S. Supreme Court
Citation: 421 U.S. 7
Date: April 15, 1975
Issues: Equal protection of the law; Sex discrimination

• The U.S. Supreme Court voided a child support statute as a violation of the equal protection clause.

Utah's highest court of appeals upheld a state law setting the maximum age for child support for males at twenty-one and females at eighteen, finding women matured faster than men. Thelma Stanton sued her former husband after he stopped paying child support when their daughter turned eighteen.

By an 8-1 vote, the Supreme Court voided the statute as a violation of the equal protection clause of the Fourteenth Amendment. In the opinion for the Court, Justice Harry A. Blackmun claimed the Court had used the rational basis test in this sex discrimination case. Nonetheless, the Court found the statute lacking in a rational basis although other judges and legislators had found it rational. Justice William H. Rehnquist dissented saying that the issue was not properly before the Court because the age limit had been set voluntarily in the divorce decree.

Richard L. Wilson

See also *Craig v. Boren; Gomez v. Perez; Reed v. Reed; Zablocki v. Redhail.*

STEWARD MACHINE CO. V. DAVIS

Court: U.S. Supreme Court
Citation: 301 U.S. 548
Date: May 24, 1937
Issues: Taxation

• The U.S. Supreme Court upheld the portion of the 1935 Social Security Act that established unemployment compensation.

Justice Benjamin N. Cardozo wrote the opinion for the 5-4 majority sustaining the 1935 Social Security Act's provision for unemployment compensation. The Supreme Court clearly departed from its earlier decision in *United States v. Butler* (1936), which was decided before Justice Owen J. Roberts switched to a more liberal position. Justices Pierce Butler, James C. McReynolds, George Sutherland, and Willis Van Devanter dissented, asserting that the Tenth Amendment limited the federal government's taxing and spending power—a position clearly rejected by the Court's new majority.

Richard L. Wilson

See also *Helvering v. Davis; United States v. Butler.*

STONE V. MISSISSIPPI

Court: U.S. Supreme Court
Citation: 101 U.S. 814
Date: May 10, 1880
Issues: Freedom of contract

• The U.S. Supreme Court narrowed the scope of the application of the contracts clause to public contracts.

Early in U.S. history, the Supreme Court determined that both public and private contracts were covered by the Constitution's ban on the impairment of contracts. This proposition was harder to maintain for public contracts. John B. Stone's corporation was given a Mississippi charter to operate a lottery, but the next year, Mississippi adopted a constitution banning all lotteries. The state ordered Stone to cease operating his lottery, and the Mississippi high court upheld the order. The Supreme Court unanimously held for Mississippi, distinguishing this abrogation of contract by arguing that a state's police power controlled lotteries and that no state could contract away its police power, generally following the logic of *West River Bridge Co. v. Dix* (1848). It also ruled that state charters authorizing lotteries were either licenses or privileges but not contracts. Justice Morrison R. Waite wrote the unanimous opinion for the Court, and Justice Ward Hunt did not participate.

Richard L. Wilson

See also *Green v. Biddle; Keystone Bituminous Coal Association v. DeBenedictis; Providence Bank v. Billings; West River Bridge Co. v. Dix.*

STONE V. POWELL

Court: U.S. Supreme Court
Citation: 428 U.S. 465
Date: July 6, 1976
Issues: Habeas corpus

- The U.S. Supreme Court limited the habeas corpus appeals that could be made to it.

Justice Lewis F. Powell, Jr., wrote the opinion for the 6-3 majority. Congress had allowed state convicts to petition for a writ of habeas corpus challenging their state convictions, despite the general legal presumption that a matter once decided cannot be relitigated. In *Brown v. Allen* (1953), the Supreme Court had ruled that a state convict could obtain a federal court hearing on any federal constitutional issue. Powell's opinion reinterpreted *Brown v. Allen* and held that it did not apply to Fourth Amendment (search and seizure) questions if the state had provided a full, fair hearing on the issue. Justice William J. Brennan, Jr., joined by Justice Thurgood Marshall, dissented as did Justice Byron R. White separately. Critics' fears that habeas corpus would be placed in jeopardy because of this decision were not realized because this ruling was not expanded.

Richard L. Wilson

See also *Boumediene v. Bush; Frank v. Mangum; McCleskey v. Zant; Mapp v. Ohio; Maryland v. Buie; Moore v. Dempsey.*

HABEAS CORPUS IN THE U.S. CONSTITUTION

The common-law principle of habeas corpus is clearly acknowledged in Article I, section 9 of the Constitution:

> The Privilege of the Writ of Habeas Corpus shall not be suspended, unless when in Cases of Rebellion or Invasion the public Safety may require it.

STRAUDER V. WEST VIRGINIA

Court: U.S. Supreme Court
Citation: 100 U.S. 303
Date: March 1, 1880
Issues: Equal protection of the law; Juries

• The U.S. Supreme Court declared that exclusion of African Americans from juries was a violation of the equal protection clause of the Fourteenth Amendment.

During the late nineteenth century, West Virginia had a statute that explicitly limited jury service to "white male persons." Strauder, a black man convicted of murder, claimed that he had not received a fair trial because of the statute. The Supreme Court agreed. Writing for a 7-2 majority, Justice William Strong explained that such a law constituted precisely the kind of discrimination that the Fourteenth Amendment was designed to prevent. Also in 1880, the Court decided three other important cases dealing with racial exclusion from juries. In *Neal v. Delaware* and *Ex parte Virginia*, it held that even if the

Justice William Strong during the 1870's.
(Brady-Handy Collection/ Library of Congress)

state's laws did not exclude blacks, the actual practice of exclusion was a denial of equal protection. In *Virginia v. Rives*, however, the Court ruled that the mere absence of African Americans from juries was not in itself a violation of the Fourteenth Amendment. In effect, *Rives* allowed local officials to use their discretionary authority to exclude blacks from juries. Although *Strauder, Ex parte Virginia*, and *Neal* had limited impact during the Jim Crow era, they nevertheless helped prepare a constitutional foundation for the Civil Rights movement of the mid-twentieth century.

Thomas Tandy Lewis

See also *Batson v. Kentucky; Edmonson v. Leesville Concrete Co.; Williams v. Mississippi.*

STRAWBRIDGE V. CURTISS

Court: U.S. Supreme Court
Citation: 7 U.S. 267
Date: February 13, 1806
Issues: Diversity jurisdiction

- The U.S. Supreme Court established the rule of complete diversity in federal courts.

Chief Justice John Marshall wrote the opinion for the 6-0 majority, interpreting the command in Article III of the Constitution that the federal judiciary shall cover controversies "between the citizens of different states." This case raised the question of diversity jurisdiction for the first time. Marshall relied on the 1789 Judiciary Act—rather than the Constitution—in deciding that all parties to a lawsuit must have an adequate basis for jurisdiction to enter federal court. This still-valid judgment means that all parties on one side must be diverse from all parties on the other side (or completely diverse) in federal courts as a practical matter.

Richard L. Wilson

See also *Bank of the United States v. Deveaux; Erie Railroad Co. v. Tompkins; Louisville, Cincinnati, and Charleston Railroad Co. v. Letson; Pennoyer v. Neff.*

STROMBERG V. CALIFORNIA

Court: U.S. Supreme Court
Citation: 283 U.S. 359
Date: May 18, 1931
Issues: Symbolic speech

• The U.S. Supreme Court first used the Fourteenth Amendment's incorporation of the First Amendment to strike a state law limiting freedom of speech.

During the Red Scare (anticommunist hysteria) after World War I, California banned the display of a red flag but did not enforce the law until a right-wing group, Better American Federation, persuaded a local sheriff to raid a working-class children's youth camp, where they found instructor Yetta Stromberg's red flag. Chief Justice Charles Evans Hughes, who wrote the landmark opinion for the 7-2 majority, stated that citizens might have had many uses for a red flag and that the California statute was simply too vague to pass constitutional muster. The California statute could, he argued, be used to suppress a wide range of constitutionally protected opposition to those in power. The Supreme Court's ruling was the first to extend the Fourteenth Amendment to protect a First Amendment right (symbolic speech) from state action. Justices Pierce Butler and James C. McReynolds dissented.

Richard L. Wilson

See also *Brandenburg v. Ohio; Schenck v. United States; Texas v. Johnson; Tinker v. Des Moines Independent Community School District; United States v. O'Brien; Whitney v. California.*

STUART V. LAIRD

Court: U.S. Supreme Court
Citation: 5 U.S. 299
Date: March 2, 1803
Issues: Judicial review

• The U.S. Supreme Court upheld a congressional modification of the federal court structure.

In 1802 Congress repealed the 1801 Judiciary Act, abolishing previously established circuit courts and depriving sitting judges of their positions, despite the Article III, section 1, lifetime term protections. Congress also required Supreme Court justices to ride the circuits as judges. Declaring yet another congressional enactment unconstitutional only six days after the Supreme Court overruled Congress on *Marbury v. Madison* (1803) would have left the Court in a difficult position. Justice William Paterson, who wrote the unanimous opinion for the Court, avoided this potential constitutional crisis by narrowly focusing on the question of whether Congress could act to move a case from the old circuit court to a new one. The Court found that it could and also found that the Court had already accepted the practice of riding circuit and was not able to withdraw from the practice at this late date. Chief Justice John Marshall did not participate.

Richard L. Wilson

See also *Budd v. New York; Calder v. Bull; Chicago, Milwaukee, and St. Paul Railway Co. v. Minnesota; Fletcher v. Peck; Hayburn's Case; Hylton v. United States; Marbury v. Madison; Yakus v. United States.*

STURGES V. CROWNINSHIELD

Court: U.S. Supreme Court
Citation: 17 U.S. 122
Date: February 17, 1819
Issues: Bankruptcy law

- In this case, the U.S. Supreme Court provided its first evaluation of the constitutionality of state bankruptcy statutes.

Sturges and Crowninshield were parties to two contracts involving promissory notes dated March 22, 1811. When the defendant in the case, the maker of the notes, could not repay them, he was sued in federal court. The court relieved him from repaying his debts on the basis of the New York bankruptcy statute, passed April 3, 1811. The plaintiff, who had lent money in good faith and prior to enactment of the New York law, appealed this decision, basing his case on two arguments: first, that individual states did not have the power to pass bankruptcy laws, which were the exclusive province of Congress, and second, that even if states were vested with such power under the Constitution, the New York law was invalid because, in permitting discharge of debts incurred before the statute was passed, it violated the contract clause (Article I, section 10) of the Constitution, which prohibits states from passing laws that impair the obligations of contracts. The judges of the circuit court were divided as to whether the ruling in favor of the defendant should be overturned, thus obliging the Supreme Court to decide the appeal.

The Supreme Court, by a vote of six to none, voided the New York statute. Although Chief Justice John Marshall, writing for the Court, rejected the argument that the federal government had exclusive jurisdiction over insolvency laws, he did find the New York law an unconstitutional state interference with contracts.

Although Article I, section 8 of the Constitution empowers Congress to establish "uniform Laws on the subject of Bankruptcies throughout the United States," in 1819, there was no national bankruptcy law. In the absence of a comprehensive national scheme, Marshall declared, states were free to create their own systems of bankruptcy relief—so long as they did not discharge contracts involving debt. Since this is the very point of bankruptcy laws, *Sturges v. Crowninshield* left states in confusion until the Court again addressed the question in *Ogden v. Saunders* (1827), holding that states could pass insolvency laws so long as they did not permit discharge of debts that predated the laws.

Ogden, however, did not resolve the bankruptcy problem. Although various states, primarily northern ones, did attempt schemes for discharging insolvent debtors, they found they had difficulty meeting the needs of both debtors and creditors. Some states, fearful that bankruptcy laws would discourage lending altogether, did not even enter the field. Finally, in 1898, Congress put the controversy to rest by passing national bankruptcy legislation which preempted state insolvency laws. Flaws in the administration of the system were further addressed with the Bankruptcy Reform Act of 1978, which created a separate system of bankruptcy courts to enforce the new legislation.

Lisa Paddock

See also *Adair v. United States; Bronson v. Kinzie; Ogden v. Saunders.*

SWANN V. CHARLOTTE-MECKLENBURG BOARD OF EDUCATION

Court: U.S. Supreme Court
Citation: 402 U.S. 1
Date: April 20, 1971
Issues: Civil rights and liberties; Desegregation; Education; Equal protection of the law

- In its decision in the case of *Swann v. Charlotte-Mecklenburg Board of Education,* the U.S. Supreme Court endorsed the use of busing to desegregate the public schools of Charlotte, North Carolina, opening the way for federal judges throughout the United States to impose busing as a means of racial desegregation in public schools.

Although the Fourteenth Amendment to the U.S. Constitution, enacted in 1868, required that states provide equal protection of the laws for all persons, African Americans continued to suffer from severe discrimination in education, employment, housing, and other aspects of American life. In 1896, in

Plessy v. Ferguson, the Supreme Court formally endorsed racial segregation as an acceptable practice that did not violate the equal protection clause of the Constitution. Cities and states were permitted to create laws that forced blacks to attend separate schools, ride on separate train cars, and even drink from separate drinking fountains in public buildings.

Many kinds of local facilities, such as municipal swimming pools and golf courses, were reserved for whites only. The facilities provided for blacks, if there were any at all, were often shabby and grossly inferior to those provided by the government for whites. For example, African American students were frequently forced to receive their education in unheated, one-room shacks with virtually no funding for paper, pencils, desks, or other supplies. Meanwhile, white students in the same districts attended well-equipped schools with superior resources.

During the twentieth century, civil rights lawyers filed lawsuits seeking judicial decisions that would outlaw racial segregation in schools. The lawyers wanted to stop state and local governments from providing inferior educational resources to African Americans. Because most black children had access only to inferior educational resources, they had little hope of attending college in the future or of competing with whites for good jobs. The inferior schooling provided to African American children helped to ensure that many of them would spend their lives as poor laborers in the employ of whites.

Brown v. Board of Education

The Supreme Court finally gave meaning to the constitutional right of equal protection by declaring, in the 1954 landmark case of *Brown v. Board of Education of Topeka, Kansas,* that segregated public schools violated the U.S. Constitution. The Court declared that racial discrimination in public schools caused damage to the personal development and life prospects of black children. The Court's opinion in *Brown,* delivered in 1955, was supposed to tell the nation how to dismantle school segregation. The Supreme Court said only that desegregation should proceed with "all deliberate speed."

Federal district judges were instructed to examine school systems on a city-by-city basis in order to develop individual remedies that would correct illegal segregation. Because the Supreme Court did not provide clear guidance on how and when schools were to end racial segregation, many school systems remained segregated for years after the *Brown* decision. Black students continued to be barred from attending the well-equipped, all-white public schools. In many cities, government officials intentionally delayed making any changes in the schools because they did not agree with the judicial decisions mandating desegregation.

As a result of widespread resistance to the Supreme Court's decision against racial segregation, civil rights lawyers filed new lawsuits on behalf of black parents and children seeking judicial orders that would mandate specific desegregation plans for individual cities. Frequently, the parents and children were represented in court by lawyers from the National Association for the Advancement of Colored People (NAACP), a public-interest organization that had pursued school desegregation cases since the 1930's. In a 1969 decision, *Alexander v. Holmes County Board of Education*, the Supreme Court indicated that it would no longer tolerate delays in implementing school desegregation. The Court said that "every school district is to terminate dual school systems at once," but it did not say how schools should achieve desegregation.

Julius LeVonne Chambers, a lawyer for the NAACP, initiated a lawsuit in 1965 that sought to end racial segregation in the Charlotte, North Carolina, public schools. The preliminary court decision in *Swann v. Charlotte-Mecklenburg Board of Education* did not require significant changes in the school system. Initially, the school district purported to eliminate segregation by permitting students to transfer between schools voluntarily if there were open places available. This freedom of choice plan did little to change the fact that schools were essentially either all-white or all-black. Only 490 of the 20,000 black students attended schools that contained any white students, and most of these students were in one school that happened to have only 7 white students. The few black students who attempted to attend all-white schools were often attacked by mobs of angry whites.

Federal Court Ruling

Chambers filed a legal action in 1969 to ask the court to force the schools to end segregation. After hearing evidence during a trial, Judge James B. McMillan, the federal district judge in Charlotte, found that the Charlotte schools were illegally segregated. Judge McMillan gave the Charlotte-Mecklenburg Board of Education an opportunity to develop a plan for desegregating the schools, but he subsequently rejected the board's proposals as inadequate. With the assistance of education consultants, McMillan developed and imposed a desegregation plan in the public schools that involved transporting white children to previously all-black schools and black children to previously all-white schools in order to achieve desegregation. By mixing black children and white children in every school building, the school officials would no longer be able to provide adequate educational resources only for white students.

Many white residents did not want their children to attend schools with black children. Judge McMillan received threatening telephone calls and was ostracized by the community. Chambers was victimized by more specific attacks, with his office, car, and home damaged by firebombs and dynamite.

Amid the controversy, the school board still sought to avoid implementing desegregation. The school system asked the Supreme Court to overturn Judge McMillan's busing plan.

Since 1954, even with changes in the composition of the Supreme Court, the justices had always unanimously supported desegregation whenever school districts challenged court orders against racial segregation. In the *Swann* case, however, many people expected at least some of the justices to be critical of busing as a tool for desegregating schools. The use of busing had become a controversial political issue, and President Richard M. Nixon had campaigned against the forced busing of schoolchildren. Nixon's two appointees to the Supreme Court, Chief Justice Warren E. Burger and Associate Justice Harry A. Blackmun, were presumed to agree with the president's view that courts should be less active in forcing school districts to desegregate.

When the Supreme Court considered the *Swann* case, Chief Justice Burger and Associate Justice Hugo L. Black initially disagreed with Judge McMillan's busing order. Burger circulated several draft opinions that were critical of busing. Associate Justice William J. Brennan and other justices made repeated suggestions for revisions in the opinion that would support Judge McMillan's order. Ultimately, because a majority of justices supported the busing order, Burger accommodated the other justices and wrote an opinion supporting the use of busing. On April 20, 1971, the Court announced that judges could order school districts to use busing as a means to desegregate schools. Because all nine justices supported the opinion, the Court gave busing the full weight of its authoritative endorsement. The unanimous decision was regarded as a political defeat for the Nixon administration, which urged the Court to invalidate Judge McMillan's busing order.

Significance

The Court's decision opened the way for federal judges throughout the United States to impose busing as a means of ending racial segregation in public schools. The use of busing spread as federal judges began to hear more lawsuits challenging discriminatory conditions in school systems. A 1973 case in which Denver, Colorado, was ordered to implement a busing plan demonstrated that the judges were willing to examine segregation in northern school systems. The results of busing plans have been mixed. Initially, there were highly publicized protests against busing by many white people. In Boston, Massachusetts, for example, residents of several white neighborhoods threw rocks at buses and attacked black passersby. As schools in many cities became integrated after decades of operation as single-race institutions, there were sometimes fights between black and white students.

Eventually, however, most schools adjusted, and desegregation became an accepted component of normal school operations. In smaller cities and countywide systems, such as Charlotte-Mecklenburg County, transportation of students to desegregated schools gave black students the opportunity to receive educational benefits that had previously been denied to them. Black students were no longer trapped in inferior schools with limited resources. Public opinion research indicated that, especially in southern states, the implementation of desegregation orders was accompanied by an increase in racial tolerance. Fewer people expressed the racial prejudice that had once been a component of many Americans' attitudes. In many large metropolitan areas, however, schools failed to become racially mixed. They would have had to mix their schools with neighboring suburban schools in order to desegregate.

In 1974, however, after President Nixon had appointed a total of four justices to the Supreme Court, the Court issued a divided 5-4 decision in *Milliken v. Bradley* that prevented most busing plans from crossing school district boundaries. As large cities experienced economic decline and shrinking tax bases, deteriorating central city schools often contained predominantly poor, minority student bodies that resembled those in illegally segregated schools. Many big-city school systems had significantly fewer resources than neighboring suburbs for maintaining school buildings and for providing quality educational programs. Black students thus continued to receive inferior educational resources in many large cities.

Christopher E. Smith

Further Reading

Clotfelter, Charles T. *After Brown: The Rise and Retreat of School Desegregation.* Princeton, N.J.: Princeton University Press, 2004. Historical account of the attempts to promote racial segregation in the public schools since the landmark decision, *Brown v. Board of Education.*

Dimond, Paul R. *Beyond Busing: Inside the Challenge to Urban Education.* Ann Arbor: University of Michigan Press, 2005. A detailed description of several school desegregation cases, including cases concerning Detroit, Michigan; Dayton and Columbus, Ohio; and Wilmington, Delaware. Contains good descriptions of the individual lawyers, judges, and school officials involved in litigation concerning busing. Provides useful descriptions of evidence and courtroom testimony that affected the judicial decisions.

Gaillard, Frye. *The Dream Long Deferred: The Landmark Struggle for Desegregation in Charlotte, North Carolina.* Columbia: University of South Carolina Press, 2006. Argues that the Supreme Court's *Swann* decision ordering busing in 1971 successfully promoted desegregation, but that neighborhood schools returned because of a judicial reversal in 1999.

Kluger, Richard. *Simple Justice: The History of Brown v. Board of Education and Black America's Struggle for Equality.* Rev. ed. New York: Vintage Books, 2004. Thorough, readable history of racial segregation in American schools and the various lawsuits in the early twentieth century that attacked discrimination. The most detailed description available of the litigants, lawyers, and judges who shaped the landmark decision in *Brown v. Board of Education.* Considered the definitive work on the history of school desegregation.

Orfield, Gary. *Must We Bus? Segregated Schools and National Policy.* Washington, D.C.: Brookings Institution, 1989. Comprehensive review of the implications and consequences of busing plans to achieve desegregation. Examines the costs and benefits of busing and discusses alternative policies for achieving desegregation. Discusses actions by presidents, Congress, and government agencies that affected desegregation. Includes coverage of the effects of school segregation on Hispanic children.

Rossell, Christine H. *The Carrot or the Stick for School Desegregation Policy: Magnet Schools or Forced Busing.* Philadelphia: Temple University Press, 1990. A study of problems that occur when white parents remove their children from city school systems. Presents evidence supporting magnet schools as effective tools to achieve desegregation. Asserts that white and black parents will voluntarily send their children to the same schools if schools present special programs to attract students.

Rossell, Christine H., David J. Armor, and Herbert J. Walberg, eds. *School Desegregation in the Twenty-first Century.* Westport, Conn.: Praeger, 2002. Arguing that mandatory busing and racial quotas had too many costs and too few benefits, the essays advocate compensatory programs and school choice plans that do not use racial criteria.

Rossell, Christine H., and Willis D. Hawley, eds. *The Consequences of School Desegregation.* Philadelphia: Temple University Press, 1983. Contains several studies on the consequences of school desegregation. Examines the effects of desegregation on intergroup relations, students' academic achievement, and whites' departures from the public schools. Provides a useful review of academic research on busing and its effects.

Schwartz, Bernard. *Swann's Way: The School Busing Case and the Supreme Court.* New York: Oxford University Press, 1986. Detailed description of people, events, and court decisions that affected the Supreme Court's endorsement of busing in *Swann v. Charlotte-Mecklenburg Board of Education.* Provides an excellent portrait of Supreme Court justices as human beings who must persuade each other as they make, rather than follow, the law when confronted with new issues.

See also *Alexander v. Holmes County Board of Education*; *Board of Education of Oklahoma City v. Dowell*; *Brown v. Board of Education*; *Columbus Board of Education v. Penick*; *Keyes v. Denver School District No. 1*; *Lemon v. Kurtzman*; *Milliken v. Bradley*; *Parents Involved in Community Schools v. Seattle School District No. 1*; *Plessy v. Ferguson*.

SWEATT V. PAINTER

Court: U.S. Supreme Court
Citation: 339 U.S. 629
Date: June 5, 1950
Issues: Civil rights and liberties; Education; Racial discrimination

• This unanimous U.S. Supreme Court declared that the "separate but equal" standard established in *Plessy v. Ferguson* was unattainable in higher education.

Plessy v. Ferguson (1896) established the "separate but equal" doctrine that provided the legal justification for segregation. Civil rights organizations, including the National Association for the Advancement of Colored People (NAACP), although opposed to "separate but equal," decided to use the courts in an attempt to make sure that the "equal" part of the "separate but equal" doctrine was being enforced. In a series of cases running from 1936 to the *Sweatt* decision in 1950, the NAACP attacked the lack of law schools and graduate programs for blacks throughout the South.

If no professional schools existed, clearly the "separate but equal" doctrine was not being met. When African Americans started seeking admission to professional schools throughout the South, many states established "overnight" law schools and professional schools in order to comply with *Plessy*. These schools were certainly separate, but were they equal? Herman Sweatt, a Houston, Texas, postal worker, applied to admission to the University of Texas Law School in 1946. He was denied admission on the grounds that Texas had just created a law school for blacks. To avoid integration, Texas had rented a few rooms in Houston and hired two black lawyers as its faculty.

Sweatt refused to attend the "black law school," saying that it was inferior and he would be deprived of the "equal protection of the law." A unanimous Supreme Court sided with Sweatt, whose case was argued by Thurgood Marshall of the NAACP. Even if the facilities at the two Texas schools were equal, the Court concluded that inequality might exist with respect to other factors "which make for greatness in a law school." Such factors include the reputation of the faculty and administration and the prestige of the alumni. "It is difficult to believe," said Chief Justice Fred M. Vinson, "that one who had a free choice between these law schools would consider the question close."

The Court ordered that Sweatt be admitted to the University of Texas Law School. The *Sweatt* case marked the first time the Supreme Court found a black professional school to be unequal in quality. Although the Court refused to reexamine *Plessy v. Ferguson*, the decision in *Sweatt* paved the way for the NAACP to launch a direct assault in overturning *Plessy* in *Brown v. Board of Education* only four years later.

Darryl Paulson

See also *Brown v. Board of Education; Cumming v. Richmond County Board of Education; Hall v. DeCuir; Louisville, New Orleans, and Texas Railway Co. v. Mississippi; McLaurin v. Oklahoma State Regents for Higher Education; Missouri ex rel. Gaines v. Canada; Plessy v. Ferguson.*

SWIFT AND CO. V. UNITED STATES

Court: U.S. Supreme Court
Citation: 196 U.S. 375
Date: January 30, 1905
Issues: Antitrust law; Interstate commerce

• The U.S. government's successful prosecution of the beef trust represented an early and notable antitrust victory from which sprang an important new legal concept concerning interstate commerce.

Still new in his presidency, Theodore Roosevelt wrote to a U.S. senator in 1902 that he was fully aware that the American people were "very bitter" about operations of the "beef trust." Roosevelt was accurate. Independent butchers, businesspeople, farmers, and consumers had complained since the 1880's that the large packinghouses, led by Gustavus F. Swift, Nelson Morris, Philip Danforth Armour, Jonathan Ogden Armour, and the Cudahy family, were preserving their meats with poisons. In the decade following passage

President
Theodore Roosevelt.
(Library of Congress)

of the Sherman Antitrust Act of 1890, two federal indictments had been brought against the "pooling" arrangements of meat exchanges, commission dealers, and stockyard operators. Each indictment was overruled by the U.S. Supreme Court on grounds that pooling—a practice in which businesses strike agreements not to compete—comported with current business philosophy and that stockyard transactions, which were local, formed no part of interstate commerce. Although the Supreme Court had ruled against legal arguments of federal attorneys, those rulings had neither resulted in a slackening of press campaigns against the beef trust nor allayed the public's disquiet about prospects of a monopoly or exercise of monopoly power.

From his service in the Spanish-American War, Roosevelt had firsthand knowledge of the scandal about the "embalmed beef" supplied to American forces. Complaints from businesses and consumers continued to pour into the office of Philander C. Knox, the U.S. attorney general, about the rising prices of beef trust products and about the big packers' collusion with railroads. More directly, Knox was bombarded by demands from influential members of the House of Representatives to reveal the government's intentions in regard to actions against this trust.

The "Big Six"

By 1902, therefore, at Roosevelt's initiative, Knox launched antitrust inquiries concerning activities in the meatpacking industry. The evidence subsequently amassed showed the six leading meatpackers (the "big six") to be engaged in price fixing, conspiracies to divide markets in regard to purchases of livestock and meat sales, blacklisting of competitors or of businesses failing to conform to trust practices, false bidding in dealings with public institutions, and acceptance of rebates from railroads. The six companies brought under federal scrutiny were Swift, Armour, Morris, Cudahy, Wilson, and Schwartz-child, all of which consorted in pooling agreements.

Together, the big six controlled about half of the American beef-packing industry, a proportion that rose in the eastern United States to as much as 60 percent in Pittsburgh and Philadelphia, 75 percent in New York City, and 85 percent in Boston. The overall industrial reach was far more extensive, and the industrial importance of these meatpackers was much greater than their substantial trade in beef, because they also handled calves, hogs, and sheep. They drew significant parts of their $700 million yearly business from the purchase, storage, and sales of dairy and poultry products. Furthermore, in most major cities they owned packing plants, stockyards, and grain elevators. They all had subsidiaries that dealt in or manufactured by-products such as hides, fats, animal foods, fertilizers, glue, soap, and canned fruits, and they owned refrigeration plants as well as railroad refrigerator cars for transporting their wares.

Capitalized in the aggregate at $93 million in 1903, these industry leaders could boast impressive achievements for their firms as well as for consumers. Philip Armour, originally based in Milwaukee, Wisconsin, and Nelson Morris, nearby in Chicago, Illinois, had profited from government Civil War contracts. With the postwar projection of railways into the prairies, they had stimulated the great cattle drives from Texas to the transcontinental railroads. In so doing, they contributed to the existence and prosperity of many prairie communities. Gustavus Swift, arriving in Chicago from Massachusetts in 1875, revolutionized the industry through the regular employment of refrigerator cars and through efforts, soon followed by other packers, to attain the efficiencies of vertical integration. He played a large part in making Chicago famous as the world's greatest meatpacking and meat-processing center. The meatpackers' outraged response to government action, typified by Jonathan Ogden Armour's *Saturday Evening Post* articles defending his industry, was predictable if not commendably accurate.

Saddled with Sherman Act injunctions in May, 1902, for pooling agreements and for taking railroad rebates, Swift, Armour, and Morris dissolved their pool, destroyed its records, and contracted to merge their firms into one. Cudahy and Schwartzchild quickly consented to join, and many other meatpacking companies were rapidly purchased by these three companies. Failing to secure adequate financing from Wall Street to expand their merger, they formed the National Packing Company in 1903. National's leaders were the same figures who had dominated the previous pool, and they continued meeting to regulate their trade. In response, the federal injunctions were made permanent. The government's equity proceeding was heard by the U.S. Supreme Court in 1905, shortly after the Roosevelt administration's much-heralded victory in the Northern Securities case of 1904. The Court's decision in that case had broadened the meaning of interstate commerce and provided a favorable context for a decision against the beef trust.

In *Swift and Co. v. United States,* Justice Oliver Wendell Holmes, Jr., spoke for the Court. Holmes took his cues from the narrow interpretation of interstate commerce propounded in *United States v. E. C. Knight Company* (1895) as modified by the Northern Securities decision and broadened the concept of interstate commerce. Granting that many sales and transactions by the enjoined meatpackers occurred as local ones, Holmes emphasized the steady movement of animals and meat products in and out of stockyards and localities to and from all parts of the nation. The reality was that they were actually a part of the "stream of commerce." Having concluded that this was true, Holmes asserted that activities of the beef trust fell under federal jurisdiction, as did all matters pertaining to interstate commerce, and were therefore in violation of the Sherman Act. The Supreme Court's decision was unanimous.

Significance

The Swift decision had several ramifications. The Roosevelt administration clearly had won a political victory against an unpopular trust, even though the trust's leaders were heavy Republican contributors. Roosevelt, who was basically a moderate conservative, earned respectful enmity in corporate circles while gaining a reputation as an ardent reformer in many other quarters. His action in the beef trust prosecution, strengthened by forty more antitrust suits during his tenure in office, also contributed to the public's impression that the federal government was becoming an effective umpire of the nation's economic affairs. Roosevelt's position on trusts, which constituted a significant step toward a stronger, more interventionist federal government, helped establish precedents for later presidencies.

The Supreme Court also contributed to foundations of the modern state in advancing Holmes's "stream of commerce" doctrine. In the short run, this doctrine encouraged the federal government to pursue other antitrust cases, many of which were prosecuted successfully. Over the long term, the "stream of commerce" doctrine became a working concept basic to expanded understandings of the federal government's control of commerce. During the late 1930's, judicial applications of the doctrine served to break down earlier Supreme Court decisions that had isolated manufacturing from commerce. In so doing, they allowed federal authorities to initiate a vast array of economic legislation and a broad spectrum of social programs.

Government prosecution of the beef trust focused on the trust's business practices, their effects on competition, and restraints of trade. Health and working conditions within the industry lay beyond the scope of these government inquiries. Such limitations, however, did not inhibit journalists ("muckrakers") and writers whose attention was directed to the beef trust by government injunctions or by judicial decisions. A series of articles written by Charles Edward Russell, appearing in *Everybody's Magazine* during 1904 and 1905, condemned the trust as greedy while impugning a number of public officials as its dupes. More impressive and influential was novelist Upton Sinclair's dramatic exposé of specific sanitary and working conditions in Chicago packing plants in his 1906 book *The Jungle*. Forced to address the public alarm generated by Sinclair's novel, government officials characterized its depictions as misleading and false. These and similar exposures of practices of the meatpacking industry led to the passage of both the Pure Food and Drug Act and the Meat Inspection Act in 1906. These acts greatly augmented federal inspection powers, and both came to be ranked, less for immediate effectiveness than for precedents set, among the most memorable legislation of Theodore Roosevelt's presidency.

Ongoing Government Investigations

Because its products were items of daily consumption in the nation's households, the meatpacking industry remained under government investigation and attack long after the Swift decision was rendered and reform legislation had been passed. Federal criminal and civil charges, for example, were filed against officials of the National Packing Company and additional companies in 1910. The companies were charged with infractions ranging from rigged agreements on livestock purchases to use of uniform accounting practices and the establishment of market quotas by trust members. National's officers won acquittal, but they were defeated by the firm's own inefficiencies and dissolved it in 1912.

A Federal Trade Commission (FTC) investigation into the meatpacking industry initiated by President Woodrow Wilson in 1917 gathered a mass of evidence on unfair competition, and the FTC subsequently recommended government ownership. By 1920, after their purchase of thirty-one smaller companies, the industry's leaders were confronted once more by FTC and Justice Department charges that they had violated antitrust provisions of the

Sherman Act and the Clayton Antitrust Act of 1914. Responding to what became a famous antitrust consent decree, the companies disposed of substantial holdings in stockyard companies, stockyard railroads, and trade newspapers. They also agreed to abandon dealing in 114 nonmeat and dairy products as well as to give up their retail outlets. Authorities on the industry, in concert with its spokespersons, later acknowledged that these federal antitrust measures had redounded to the ultimate benefit of the industry.

The principal result of the FTC's investigation and the consent decree was the passage of the Packers and Stockyards Act of 1921, which brought the meatpacking and related industries under federal regulation. The act placed stockyard markets and those operating with them under federal rules and supervision by the U.S. secretary of agriculture. In effect, the industry could thereafter be perceived as a kind of public utility. The act also comprehensively forbade anyone manufacturing or preparing meats to engage in price fixing, price discrimination, or the apportionment of markets. On balance, the federal investigations and antitrust suits, and the judicial decisions arising from them, left the meatpacking industry with an oligopolistic concentration of leading firms but with access to the industry much more open to smaller competing firms. Antitrust proceedings beginning in 1902 destroyed the industry leaders' pool and helped prevent the evolution of such agreements into something approximating a genuine monopoly.

Clifton K. Yearley

Further Reading

Areeda, Phillip, Louis Kaplow, and Aaron Edlin. *Antitrust Analysis: Problems, Text, Cases.* 6th ed. New York: Aspen, 2004. Textbook containing case studies of the major antitrust cases in American history. Bibliographic references and index.

Crunden, Robert M. *Ministers of Reform: The Progressives' Achievement in American Civilization, 1889-1920.* New York: Basic Books, 1982. Clear, informative reading. Chapter 6 is excellent on muckraking journalists and especially on Upton Sinclair and his influence on the Pure Food and Drug Act. Includes a useful index.

Hovenkamp, Herbert. *Federal Antitrust Policy: The Law of Competition and Its Practice.* 2d ed. Eagan, Minn.: West, 1999. Covers nearly all aspects of U.S. antitrust policy in a manner understandable to people with no background in economics. Chapter 2 discusses "history and ideology in antitrust policy."

Hylton, Keith N. *Antitrust Law: Economic Theory and Common Law Evolution.* New York: Cambridge University Press, 2003. Comprehensive text on economic principles behind antitrust and the development of American antitrust law over more than one hundred years of litigation. Includes a chapter on the Alcoa case. Bibliographic references and index.

Purdy, Harry L., Martin L. Lindahl, and William A. Carter. *Corporate Concentration and Public Policy.* New York: Prentice-Hall, 1942. Good survey filled with specifics. Chapter 23 deals with the meat industry and provides good background material in a balanced account that takes note of the industry's problems. No bibliography, but ample page notes.

Sinclair, Upton. *The Jungle.* New York: New American Library, 1906. A classic of literary realism. Sinclair had firsthand experience in Chicago packing plants. This graphic and engaging novel is stronger on conditions in the meatpacking industry than on character development.

Thorelli, Hans B. *The Federal Antitrust Policy: Origination of an American Tradition.* Baltimore: Johns Hopkins University Press, 1955. Scholarly and dense but very valuable. Chapter 7 is excellent on the development of Theodore Roosevelt as a trust buster and his decision to pursue the beef trust. Many page notes, bibliography, table of cases, and good index. Good for context on the antitrust movement in general.

Whitney, Simon N. *Antitrust Policies: American Experience in Twenty Industries.* 2 vols. New York: Twentieth Century Fund, 1958. Clear and authoritative treatment written by a scholar and FTC official. Concentrates on meatpacking in chapter 1. Superb on post-1920 developments. Includes page notes and a table of cases.

Wiebe, Robert H. *The Search for Order, 1877-1920.* New York: Hill & Wang, 1967. A fine interpretive history, well written and informative. Offers perspectives on the antitrust and antimonopoly movement throughout. Excellent for explanations of concepts and context on trusts. Bibliographical essay for each chapter. Index.

See also *Alcoa v. Federal Trade Commission; Loewe v. Lawlor; Northern Securities Co. v. United States; Standard Oil v. United States; United States v. American Tobacco Co.; United States v. E. C. Knight Co.; United States v. United States Steel Corp.*

Swift v. Tyson

Court: U.S. Supreme Court
Citation: 16 Pet. (41 U.S.) 1
Date: January 25, 1842
Issues: Federalism; Regulation of commerce

- In suits arising from diversity citizenship, the U.S. Supreme Court held that federal courts were free to exercise an independent judgment in principles of general commercial law, even if the principles were inconsistent with decisions of state courts.

Section 34 of the Judiciary Act of 1789 required federal courts to follow state "laws" whenever applicable. Before 1842, the requirement was usually assumed to extend to decisions of state courts, which blocked any serious attempt to establish a uniform commercial law. In *Swift v. Tyson*, two litigants living in different states had a conflict over the validity of a bill of exchange. In New York, where the trial took place, state courts would have voided the bill of exchange because it was corrupted by original fraud. However, the plaintiff argued that general interstate commercial law required that the bill must be paid.

By a 9-0 vote, the Supreme Court supported the plaintiff. Speaking for the Court, Justice Joseph Story held that section 34 referred only to state statutes and not to decisions of state courts. Federal courts, therefore, were free to resolve interstate commercial disputes according to their own interpretations of "the general principles and doctrines of commercial jurisprudence." Although Story hoped that the decision would encourage national uniformity, it actually resulted in separate bodies of state and federal commercial common law, which was the source of much confusion. A century later, *Swift* was overruled in *Erie Railroad Co. v. Tompkins* (1938), the only time in history that the Court ever held that the decision of a previous Court had been unconstitutional.

Thomas Tandy Lewis

See also *Bank of the United States v. Deveaux; Erie Railroad Co. v. Tompkins; Strawbridge v. Curtiss.*

TALTON V. MAYES

Court: U.S. Supreme Court
Citation: 163 U.S. 376
Date: May 18, 1896
Issues: Native American sovereignty

- The U.S. Supreme Court held that Native Americans in tribal courts were not protected in the same way as other U.S. citizens.

A Native American convicted of murder in a Cherokee nation court maintained that his trial was unfair because the indicting grand jury had only five members, contrary to the Fifth Amendment. However, by an 8-1 vote, the Supreme Court found that the Fifth Amendment did not apply because the Cherokee nation retained its sovereignty. In the opinion for the Court, Chief Justice Edward D. White held that the U.S. Bill of Rights did not apply to Native Americans in tribal courts. Federal law would not apply unless tribal law conflicted with a specific national law applied to Native American tribal governments. Justice John Marshall Harlan dissented.

Richard L. Wilson

See also *California v. Cabazon Band of Mission Indians; Cherokee Cases; Employment Division, Department of Human Resources of Oregon v. Smith; Ex parte Crow Dog; Lone Wolf v. Hitchcock; Muskrat v. United States; Santa Clara Pueblo v. Martinez; United States v. Kagama.*

TAYLOR V. LOUISIANA

Court: U.S. Supreme Court
Citation: 419 U.S. 522
Date: January 21, 1975
Issues: Trial by jury

- The U.S. Supreme Court held that women could not be excluded from juries, even indirectly.

A Louisiana man charged with rape argued that the state's volunteer jury service provision violated his Sixth Amendment right to a jury that represented a cross section of the local population. The volunteer method often created juries that were composed mainly of men. Justice Byron R. White wrote the opinion for the 8-1 majority, striking Louisiana laws that formed juries by a volunteer method. Departing from *Hoyt v. Florida* (1961), the Supreme Court found that the Sixth Amendment was violated by juries on which very few women (less than 15 percent of all jurors) were seated if the states excused or avoided seating women in various ways. *Hoyt* was not directly overturned because it was not decided on Sixth Amendment grounds. Chief Justice Warren E. Burger concurred, and Justice William H. Rehnquist dissented.

Richard L. Wilson

See also *Ballard v. United States*; *Hoyt v. Florida.*

TENNESSEE V. GARNER

Court: U.S. Supreme Court
Citation: 471 U.S. 1
Date: March 27, 1985
Issues: Common law; Police powers

- This case significantly limited the power of police officers to use deadly force in effecting an arrest.

Most arrests do not entail problems, but occasionally the accused will resist arrest or flee. There are also occasions when law-enforcement officers must make an instantaneous decision on the severity of any threat posed to the officers. The common law developed the rule that law-enforcement officers could use all necessary and reasonable force, including deadly force, to arrest a suspected felon, regardless of whether the suspect committed an act of violence or posed a threat to the arresting officers.

The common-law rule became increasingly controversial during the 1960's and 1970's, but courts adhered to it. There were numerous objections of a constitutional, legal, and humanistic nature. The main objection was that, in essence, the rule allowed police officers to become judge, jury, and even executioner. Indeed, many jurisdictions which did not use capital punishment allowed officers to use deadly force through "fleeing felon" statutes modeled after the common law.

In *Tennessee v. Garner*, a fifteen-year-old boy, Edward Garner, broke a window and entered an unoccupied residence in suburban Memphis on the night of October 3, 1974. A neighbor called the police. Two police officers responded and intercepted the minor as he ran from the back of the house to a six-foot cyclone fence in the backyard. By shining a flashlight on the suspect, the officers could tell that the suspect was a youth and apparently unarmed. There was therefore no indication that the boy had committed a felony involving violence, nor did he pose an apparent threat to the officers' safety.

The suspect ignored the officers' directive to stop. Instead, he tried to escape. One officer took aim and fatally shot the suspect in the back as he climbed over the fence. The officer had acted in accordance with his training, the Tennessee fleeing felon statute, and police department policy. The deceased had ten dollars worth of money and jewelry in his possession stolen from the house.

The decedent's father brought suit against the officers, their superiors, and the city under the federal civil rights statute to recover damages for wrongful death caused by violation of the decedent's constitutional rights. The lawsuit was filed in federal court in a successful attempt to circumvent the common law. The U.S. Supreme Court overturned the common-law rule in a 6-3 decision. Justice Byron White delivered the majority opinion, which held that deadly force may be used to effectuate an arrest only in cases where it is necessary to prevent the escape of the suspect and the officer has probable cause to believe that the suspect poses a significant threat of death or serious physical injury to the officer or others.

The Court noted that most major police departments have forbidden the use of deadly force against nonviolent suspects. The practical effect of *Tennessee v. Garner* was that lawsuits involving wrongful death causes of action against state law-enforcement officers will be brought in federal courts and will invoke federal constitutional law.

Denis Binder

See also *Miranda v. Arizona; Scott v. Harris.*

Tennessee Valley Authority v. Hill

Court: U.S. Supreme Court
Citation: 437 U.S. 153
Date: June 15, 1978
Issues: Environmental issues and animal rights

• The U.S. Supreme Court affirmed an appeals court decision protecting a three-inch fish, the snail darter, which had been listed as an endangered species. Despite the Court's ruling, Howard Baker and other Tennessee lawmakers successfully engineered legislation exempting Tellico Dam from the provisions of the Endangered Species Act, which protected the fish.

On June 15, 1978, the U.S. Supreme Court announced that it was affirming a lower court ruling that protected the snail darter's existence and habitat, thus bringing construction of the Tellico Dam in Tennessee to a halt. The battle over the construction of the dam had gone on for more than a decade.

As early as 1936, the Tennessee Valley Authority (TVA) considered building the Tellico Dam on the Little Tennessee River, an exceptionally clean, highly oxygenated river that was filled with fish. It was not until 1966, however, that Congress first appropriated funds for construction of the dam. From the start, various groups—including farmers whose land would be destroyed by the reservoir, fishermen and canoeists, and some Cherokee Indians to whom the river was sacred—opposed the dam. These groups, led by law professor Zygmunt Plater, opposed the dam's construction by invoking various environmental laws.

In 1971, the opponents of the dam succeeded in halting construction until the TVA submitted an acceptable environmental impact statement under the newly enacted National Environmental Policy Act. Two years later, just as the TVA produced an acceptable statement and the injunction was lifted, zoologist David Etnier discovered the existence of the snail darter. This three-inch fish, which lived in the shoals of the Little Tennessee River, took its name from the fact that its diet consisted solely of snails. The discovery of the fish coincided with the passage in 1973 of the Endangered Species Act; section 7 of the act prohibited any action that might jeopardize the existence of an endangered species or modify a critical habitat. By November, 1975, the snail darter had been listed as an endangered species, and by 1976, the Little Tennessee River had been designated its critical habitat.

At that point, construction of the dam was 80 percent complete and had cost $78 million. Opponents of the dam brought suit in a federal district court to prohibit the dam's completion. In the case *Hiram G. Hill, Jr., et al. v. Tennessee Valley Authority*, the court decided that although completion of the dam and the subsequent creation of a reservoir might destroy the snail darter, a court order requiring that construction cease at such a late date would be unreasonable, given the fact that the project had been under way for seven years before the act was passed. The court dismissed the suit, and the plaintiffs appealed.

The appeals court established two facts in reaching its decision: Completion of the Tellico Dam would violate the Endangered Species Act of 1973 because it would jeopardize the continued existence of the snail darter; and there were no grounds to exempt the dam from the act. The court therefore decided that an injunction on further construction was appropriate. This time, the TVA appealed the decision to the U.S. Supreme Court, in *Tennessee Valley Authority v. Hill*. Plater argued the case for the opponents of the dam.

U.S. Supreme Court Ruling

The Supreme Court, in a 6-3 decision, affirmed the appeals court opinion, stating that section 7 of the Endangered Species Act allowed for no exceptions to projects under way when the act was passed, even if, as with the Tellico Dam, a project was nearly completed. Furthermore, the Court decided that in spite of the fact that Congress had appropriated funds for the dam's completion during the various court proceedings since 1976, this did not mean that Congress intended to repeal the Endangered Species Act; the Court believed that Congress had authorized the funds under the assumption that the act did not apply to the dam's construction. Finally, the Court stated that by underscoring the importance of the act, the Court was merely upholding the separation of powers as it was required to do by the Constitution: The role of Congress was to enact laws; that of the court to interpret them.

This decision did not guarantee victory for the environmentalists or the snail darter. At the urging of Howard Baker, a senator from Tennessee with presidential aspirations, Congress passed an amendment to the Endangered Species Act that created a committee with the power to exempt certain organizations from the act. Baker and others hoped that this committee would exempt the Tellico Dam. A new obstacle appeared, however, with the appointment of S. David Freeman, who opposed the completion of the dam, as the director of the TVA. When Freeman testified before the committee, he proposed that no reservoir should be created, and on January 23, 1979, to the surprise of many, the committee denied exempt status to the dam. The committee stated what the opponents of the dam had always believed, that the project was ill conceived and uneconomical.

Baker and other Tennessee legislators thereupon raised the issue again in Congress, stating that the snail darter had been successfully transplanted to another river, where no harm would come to the species should the dam be completed. On a quiet afternoon in June, 1979, when few congressmen were present, a rider was attached to an appropriations bill that allowed the Tellico Dam to be finished in spite of any existing law. The bill passed the House of Representatives, and eventually Baker was able to force it through the Senate. Those who voted for it ignored the fact that Congress was doing precisely what the Supreme Court had said it could not do, authorizing funding while repealing one of its own laws by implication. President Jimmy Carter reluctantly signed the bill, and the dam was completed and the valley flooded on November 28, 1979.

Significance

Tennessee Valley Authority v. Hill, one of several environmental court cases during the 1970's, was perhaps the most notorious and eventually involved the TVA and its changing directorate, environmentalists, Congress, and the courts. The press simplified the complexities of the case by presenting it as a fight between a tiny fish and a mighty dam. This oversimplification notwithstanding, the case left several legacies.

The case strengthened the Endangered Species Act of 1973 by giving it the appearance of more flexibility. The case affirmed that federal agencies could not afford to ignore endangered species. Concurrent with the case passing through the court system, the list of endangered species was growing. By 1978, 228 domestic and 457 foreign endangered species had been included. Amendments added in 1982 strengthened the act still further.

Although the case gave rise to oversimplifications, it revealed how complex an environmental case could be. The resolution of the case involved finding a habitat, an ecosystem, that could provide the fish with the proper environment in which to grow. After this case, the term "ecosystem," with its implication of delicate balances between life-sustaining and life-threatening forces, became standard in analyzing environmental cases, as for example in the 1990's controversy involving the northern spotted owl and timberland in the northwestern United States.

Tennessee Valley Authority v. Hill also reinforced the doctrine of the separation of powers. The Court went to great lengths to state that laws could not be repealed by implication, as was the case when Congress appropriated funds for a project barred by a preexistent law. When Congress attached a rider to a bill, which stated that the Tellico Dam was to be completed in spite of all existing laws, Congress acted illegally and in circumvention of its own rules. The Court, however, did no more than point out the discrepancy. Subsequently, the Court continued to support the act, and in most instances Congress worked in tandem with the Court's dictates.

Zygmunt Plater said once that only in the United States could citizens with so little power and so few resources have taken such an issue so far—all the way to a victory in the Supreme Court—only to be crushed in the end by Congress and the TVA. The citizens proved in retrospect to be more accurate and more rational in their criticisms of the dam than the TVA authorities and Congress, for the dam once completed was a developmental debacle. Few developers were interested in it, and at one time it was even suggested that the area be turned into a toxic-waste site.

The snail darter case provided many lessons. Natural, economic, political, social, and even planetary issues had been at stake, but they were overwhelmed by media slogans and politics. The snail darter itself did survive, however, despite the media and politics. Before the valley was flooded, the fish had been moved from the Little Tennessee River to feeder streams of the larger Tennessee River, where it flourished. On August 6, 1984, the Department of the Interior was able to upgrade the condition of the species from endangered to threatened.

Jennifer Eastman

Further Reading

Gray, Aelred J., and David A. Johnson. *The TVA Regional Planning and Development Program: The Transformation of an Institution and Its Mission.* Burlington, Vt.: Ashgate, 2005. Study of institutional change within the TVA and its causes and effects in relation to its fundamental mission. Bibliographic references and index.

Lowry, William R. *Dam Politics: Restoring America's Rivers.* Washington, D.C.: Georgetown University Press, 2003. A study of American river restoration efforts and the policy changes that are taking place. Presents eight case studies.

Plater, Zygmunt J. B. "In the Wake of the Snail Darter: An Environmentalist Law Paradigm and Its Consequences." *University of Michigan Journal of Law Reform* 19 (1986): 805-862. Well-written, highly readable overview of the case. Lucid account of the issues and the groups involved and of the simplifications at the time.

_____. "Reflected in a River: Agency Accountability and the TVA Tellico

Dam Case." *Tennessee Law Review* 49 (Summer, 1982): 747-787. Account of the case by an opponent to the dam. Includes a discussion of the inner workings of the TVA.

Rohm, Kathryn A., ed. *Balancing on the Brink of Extinction: The Endangered Species Act and Lessons for the Future.* Washington, D.C.: Island Press, 1991. Twenty-two articles on the Endangered Species Act of 1973. Description of the snail darter case as the turning point.

Wheeler, William Bruce, and Michael J. McDonald. *TVA and the Tellico Dam, 1936-1979: A Bureaucratic Crisis in Post Industrial America.* Knoxville: University of Tennessee Press, 1986. Comprehensive account of the case with colorful descriptions of all the characters involved.

See also *Ashwander v. Tennessee Valley Authority; Oregon Waste Systems v. Department of Environmental Quality; Sierra Club v. Morton.*

TERMINIELLO V. CHICAGO

Court: U.S. Supreme Court
Citation: 337 U.S. 1
Date: May 16, 1949
Issues: Freedom of assembly and association;
Freedom of speech

• The U.S. Supreme Court strengthened freedom of speech rights when speakers draw hostile opposition.

Justice William O. Douglas wrote the opinion for the 5-4 majority, overturning the conviction of a profascist, anti-Semitic priest named Terminiello who spoke to a sympathetic audience while a hostile crowd gathered outside. Terminiello was arrested for disturbing the peace. The local court convicted him by simply finding that his speech made the audience outside the hall angry. The Supreme Court found that the fact that his speech had angered a group was inadequate grounds for a conviction because it did not show that the speaker incited actions that were a clear and present danger. The case featured strong dissents by Chief Justice Fred M. Vinson and Justices Felix Frankfurter and Robert H. Jackson, who argued that the case should have followed the fighting words limitation set out in *Chaplinsky v. New Hampshire*

(1942). The strength of the dissents is significant because the Court's 5-4 majority evaporated in similar cases such as *Feiner v. New York* (1951).

Richard L. Wilson

See also *Brandenburg v. Ohio*; *Chaplinsky v. New Hampshire*; *Feiner v. New York*; *Gitlow v. New York*; *Schenck v. United States*; *Whitney v. California.*

TERRY V. ADAMS

Court: U.S. Supreme Court
Citation: 345 U.S. 461
Date: May 4, 1953
Issues: Racial discrimination; Voting rights

• The U.S. Supreme Court clearly declared the white primary unconstitutional.

Beginning in 1889, the Jaybird Democratic Association in Texas started the practice of holding a primary election to select candidates for the Democratic Party in order to circumvent the Fifteenth Amendment. These candidates, often uncontested, usually were elected to office. Although white voters could participate in this process, black voters were excluded. The Supreme Court, by a vote of eight to one, declared the white primaries unconstitutional. Justice Hugo L. Black announced the decision for the 8-1 majority in this case, but there was no majority opinion. Instead, there were a series of opinions issued by various justices. Black emphasized that the government could not exclude African Americans from primaries, which were the only significant elections in most southern jurisdictions. Justice Felix Frankfurter criticized the complicity of southern election officials in excluding African Americans from the process. Justice Tom C. Clark focused on the fact that the white primary was an adjunct of the state-regulated Democratic Party. In general, eight justices believed that in some way, the white primary was a public institution in violation of the Fifteenth Amendment. Only Justice Sherman Minton dissented, finding that the white primary acted simply as an interest group.

Richard L. Wilson

See also *Smith v. Allwright.*

TERRY V. OHIO

Court: U.S. Supreme Court
Citation: 392 U.S. 1
Date: June 10, 1968
Issues: Police powers; Search and seizure

• In this case, the U.S. Supreme Court ruled that, if an officer had reasonable suspicion that he was dealing with an armed individual, he could subject that person to a limited search of the outer clothing, a procedure sometimes known as "stop and frisk."

In October, 1963, veteran detective Martin McFadden observed suspicious activity by two men in a Cleveland business district. Suspecting a daylight robbery, McFadden approached John Terry and Richard Chilton and identified himself as a police officer. When his attempts to question the men on their activities were ignored, McFadden seized the two and patted down their outer clothing. Feeling a weapon on each, McFadden removed the guns and arrested the men for carrying concealed weapons. In a pretrial motion, Terry and Chilton contended that the guns were seized during an illegal search. The Court of Common Pleas overruled the motion and sentenced the men to three years. Chilton died before the case was appealed.

In June, 1968, the Supreme Court ruled eight to one to uphold Terry's conviction. Writing for the majority, Chief Justice Earl Warren concluded that the issue at hand was "whether it is always unreasonable for a policeman to seize a person and subject him to a limited search for weapons unless there is probable cause for an arrest." In deciding this issue, the Court divided the case into the "seizure" and the "search." The decision defined a seizure as occurring any time a police officer restrains an individual's freedom to walk away.

Determining the constitutionality of the search required a balance between the Fourth Amendment's protection from unreasonable searches and seizures with the safety to the individuals involved. Warren concluded that a limited search was allowable if based on "specific reasonable inferences" drawn upon "the facts in the light of [the officer's] experience." In addition, the Court stipulated that "the issue is whether a reasonably prudent man in the circumstances would be warranted in the belief that his safety or that of others was in danger." Dissenting with the decision, Justice William O. Douglas looked to the legal differences between "probable cause" and "reasonable suspicion." Relying on the protection found in the Fourth Amendment, Douglas saw the search in question as an "infringement on personal liberty" because McFadden had no probable cause for arrest prior to the search.

Terry v. Ohio allowed a significant change in police procedures. It provided a police officer, once identified as such, with a legal right to perform a limited search of suspicious individuals by means of a protective pat-down. This provision helped to lower the number of injuries and deaths during initial confrontations between individuals and police officers. In addition, the police were authorized to seize any nonthreatening contraband, such as drugs or drug paraphernalia, found during a *Terry* search. Recognizing the potential for abuse in allowing "stop and frisk" actions by police, however, the Court was careful to outline the Fourth Amendment limitations that apply to stop and frisk searches. In *Sibron v. New York*, a companion case to *Terry*, the Court held that if the reason for the search is to find evidence rather than to check for weapons, then any evidence found is inadmissible.

Jennifer Davis

See also *Illinois v. Wardlow; Maryland v. Buie; Whren v. United States.*

TEXAS V. HOPWOOD

Court: U.S. Supreme Court
Citation: 116 S.Ct. 2581
Date: July 1, 1996
Issues: Affirmative action

- The U.S. Supreme Court denied review of a circuit court decision that prohibited almost all considerations of race in the admissions policies of educational institutions.

In the late 1990's there was a national movement against the use of racial preferences in education and employment. The Supreme Court in *Adarand Constructors v. Peña* (1995) held that all such programs must be justified by the compelling state interest test. Shortly thereafter, the Fifth Circuit Court of Appeals invalidated an affirmative action program of the University of Texas Law School. The court of appeals concluded that many of the ideas that Justice Lewis F. Powell, Jr., expressed in *Regents of the University of California v. Bakke* (1978) were not binding precedents. The court held that any racial preferences would have to be justified by proof of the continuing effects of past discrimination and that the goal of diversity would not pass constitutional scrutiny as a "compelling" justification. Because the Supreme Court refused to grant *certiorari*, the judgment was binding on the fifth circuit unless modified by a later decision. Justice Ruth Bader Ginsburg took the unusual step of writing that the denial of *certiorari* did not necessarily mean that the majority of the justices agreed with the circuit court's rationale.

Thomas Tandy Lewis

See also *Adarand Constructors v. Peña; Gratz v. Bollinger/Grutter v. Bollinger; Johnson v. Santa Clara County; Parents Involved in Community Schools v. Seattle School District No. 1; Regents of the University of California v. Bakke; Ricci v. DeStefano.*

TEXAS V. JOHNSON

Court: U.S. Supreme Court
Citation: 491 U.S. 397
Date: June 21, 1989
Issues: First Amendment guarantees; Freedom of expression; Symbolic speech

- The decision of the U.S. Supreme Court that flag burning as a form of political protest was protected under the First Amendment guarantee of freedom of speech sparked a continuing debate about flag desecration and civil liberties.

In 1984, the Republican National Convention was held in Dallas, Texas. As part of a political demonstration against the renomination of President Ronald Reagan and the policies of certain locally based corporations, Gregory Lee Johnson burned an American flag as protesters chanted, "America, the red, white, and blue, we spit on you." During the event, no one was physically harmed, although witnesses later declared that they were seriously offended by the action. Johnson was arrested and convicted under a Texas statute that prohibited desecration of a venerated object. The intermediate state court of appeals affirmed the conviction, but the Texas Court of Criminal Appeals (the highest appellate court for criminal cases in Texas) overturned it on the basis that Johnson's conduct was symbolic speech and protected by the First Amendment to the U.S. Constitution. The U.S. Supreme Court granted *certiorari* to consider Texas's appeal because of that constitutional issue.

U.S. Supreme Court Ruling

Justice William J. Brennan, joined by Justices Thurgood Marshall, Harry A. Blackmun, Antonin Scalia, and Anthony Kennedy in the majority opinion, held that the flag burning fell within the protection of the First Amendment as expressive conduct and overturned the conviction. The Court noted that the Texas statute controlled only physical conduct with the flag and not the written or spoken word, so Johnson was not convicted for his words. Although the First Amendment literally addresses only speech, in prior cases the Court had recognized that communicative or expressive elements of conduct might bring that conduct under the protection of the First Amendment. The Court's established two-pronged test for deciding whether the conduct fell under the First Amendment was, first, whether the actor had the specific intent to convey a message through the conduct and, second, whether the observers were likely to understand the message. Clearly, both prongs were met in that the spectators unequivocally understood Johnson's message of disdain, and, in fact, the state of Texas conceded in oral argument that Johnson's act was expressive conduct.

The state argued, however, that its independent and substantial governmental interest in preventing disorder and disturbances of the peace that could result from flag burning should override any expressive aspect of the conduct. Justice Brennan noted that the Court in prior decisions had decided that governments are freer to regulate expressive conduct than they are to regulate the oral or written word under the First Amendment and that when speech and nonspeech are combined into one act, important government objectives may allow limited regulation of expression. In the case of Johnson's action, however, no disorder did erupt, and other state statutes prohibited breaches of the peace, so the argument was not persuasive.

The state of Texas also asserted its interest in protecting the flag as a symbol. However, Brennan pointed out that an integral part of the symbolism of the flag is its representation of cherished freedoms such as speech and political dissent and that government may not suppress expression solely because the ideas are unpopular or even offensive. The First Amendment protections of political discourse and dissent trump the government's claim in this instance.

Chief Justice William H. Rehnquist, joined by Justices Byron White and Sandra Day O'Connor in dissent, drew heavily from history and literature to illustrate the flag's importance and its unique position as the principal symbol of the nation. Rehnquist stated, "Millions and millions of Americans regard it with an almost mystical reverence regardless of what sort of social, political, or philosophical beliefs they may have." Within that perspective, the dissent noted, flag burning is an egregiously offensive method of political expression and should not be protected, especially given that political dissidents such as Johnson have alternative means to express their opinions. Government has the right to proscribe conduct that is repugnant to the majority of people, Rehnquist argued; to protect flag burning as expressive conduct is an unjustified and inappropriate expansion of the First Amendment.

Justice John Paul Stevens, a World War II veteran, noted his staunch opposition to any and all forms of flag desecration, especially flag burning. Just as the government has the right to punish those who spray graffiti on public property or attach advertisements to national monuments, it has the obligation to take action against those who attack the corporal flag and the principles it represents, Stevens asserted. Johnson was punished for the physical act he committed, not the ideas he expressed, and Stevens would sustain the conviction.

Significance

The American flag did not achieve prominence as a preeminent symbol of the nation until after the Civil War. There were no restrictions on the use of the flag: Veterans' groups printed battle locations on the flag, politicians imprinted their images and slogans on the flag during campaigns, and commercial entities employed the flag in advertisements or as adornments on sundry merchandise. Following the Civil War, veterans' groups and patriotic-hereditary organizations initiated efforts to protect the flag from unseemly commercial uses, and a number of states enacted laws concerning flag desecration at the end of the nineteenth century. These statutes often were challenged successfully by the commercial interests on the basis that their private property rights were infringed. However, in 1907, the U.S. Supreme Court upheld the constitutionality of flag desecration laws when it decided *Halter v. Nebraska,* a case involving a bottle of beer with an American flag on the label.

During the same period, the employment of the American flag as a tool to force shows of loyalty or as a tool of political protests was becoming more common. Instances of prosecution for flag abuse were rare even during World Wars I and II, but protests against U.S. involvement in the Vietnam War that included physical abuse of the American flag reignited the controversy and resulted in the first national law forbidding such abuse, the federal Flag Desecration Act of 1968. However, court cases involving either state or federal statutes and the First Amendment's freedom of speech guarantee produced incongruous decisions, and it was not until *Texas v. Johnson* that the Supreme Court, previously having avoided the constitutional question, finally provided definitive guidelines.

The Court's decision in *Texas v. Johnson* generated a firestorm of controversy that continued into the twenty-first century. In response to the decision, Congress enacted the Flag Protection Act of 1989, which was subsequently struck down by the Court in *United States v. Eichman* (1990). That decision, in turn, spurred several attempts by Congress to pass the Flag Desecration Amendment. A by-product of the dispute was an increase in attacks on the legitimacy of the Supreme Court—that is, the confidence of the American people in the Court and the esteem in which the institution is held. Public opinion polls indicated that the Court's decisions concerning flag desecration negatively affected perceptions of the Court, an institution that is heavily dependent on public perceptions of its legitimacy because it lacks both the power of the purse and the power of the sword.

Susan Coleman

Further Reading

Gibson, James L., Gregory A. Calderia, and Lester Kenyatta Spence. "Measuring Attitudes Toward the United States Supreme Court." *American Journal of Political Science* 47 (April, 2003): 354-367. Presents the findings of a study of public opinion concerning the short-term and long-term attitudes of confidence toward the Supreme Court.

Goldstein, Robert Justin. *Flag Burning and Free Speech: The Case of Texas v. Johnson.* Lawrence: University Press of Kansas, 2000. Provides a thorough account of the facts of the case and the context of the decision, including public and political reactions. Written for a general audience.

_____. *Saving "Old Glory": The History of the American Flag Desecration Controversy.* Boulder, Colo.: Westview Press, 1995. Provides a detailed review of legislative, judicial, and other materials relating to flag desecration statutes and controversies.

Grosskopf, Anke, and Jeffery J. Mondak. "Do Attitudes Toward Specific Supreme Court Decisions Matter? The Impact of *Webster* and *Texas v. Johnson* on Public Confidence in the Supreme Court." *Political Research Quarterly* 51 (September, 1998): 633-654. Analyzes public opinion following two controversial Supreme Court decisions to examine the linkage between specific cases and support for the Court as an institution.

See also *Cohen v. California; R.A.V. v. City of St. Paul; Stromberg v. California; United States v. Eichman; United States v. O'Brien.*

TEXAS V. WHITE

Court: U.S. Supreme Court
Citation: 74 U.S. 700
Date: April 12, 1869
Issues: States' rights

- During the Reconstruction era, the U.S. Supreme Court declared that secession by a state was unconstitutional and that Congress, in cooperation with the president, had authority to determine policies for the reconstruction of the southern states.

Following the Civil War (1861-1865), the provisional government of Texas attempted to recover title to bonds that had been sold by the Confederate state government during the war. The defendants argued that the state had not yet been readmitted to the Union and thus had no authority to sue in federal court. Writing for a 5-3 majority, Chief Justice Salmon Chase based the Supreme Court's ruling on the powers of Congress and the president to decide political questions. He stated that because both Congress and the president had recognized the reconstructed government of Texas, it had the right to sue in court. Chase also wrote that the United States was "an indissoluble union of indissoluble states." The actions of the state's confederate government in support of the recent rebellion, therefore, were illegal and void. Chase carefully avoided any comments about the constitutionality of the Reconstruction Acts.

Thomas Tandy Lewis

See also *Ex parte McCardle; Hall v. DeCuir; Luther v. Borden; Mississippi v. Johnson.*

THOMPSON V. OKLAHOMA

Court: U.S. Supreme Court
Citation: 487 U.S. 815
Date: June 29, 1988
Issues: Capital punishment; Juvenile justice

• This U.S. Supreme Court ruling abolished the death penalty for convicts who were aged fifteen or younger at the time they committed their crimes. Capital punishment remained legal for minors older than fifteen.

When he was only fifteen years old, William W. Thompson participated in a brutal murder and was consequently sentenced to death by the State of Oklahoma. The Oklahoma Court of Criminal Appeals supported the trial court's decision, and the case was appealed to the U.S. Supreme Court. In a 5-3 decision (including a four-justice plurality and a separate concurring opinion), Thompson was spared the death penalty. The plurality opinion, written by John Paul Stevens, based its reasoning upon the "evolving standards of decency of society." The dissent, written by Antonin Scalia, could not dismiss the notion of a minor potentially being mature and responsible enough for a crime to warrant state execution. Sandra Day O'Connor cast the deciding vote: She wrote in her concurring opinion that Thompson could not be executed, because the Oklahoma law establishing the death penalty for murder did not specify a minimum age of eligibility for receiving that penalty.

The legal significance of the case was that capital punishment could no longer be applied to those criminals who were aged fifteen or younger during the commission of their crime. Opponents of the death penalty have historically pursued so-called death penalty exception cases. These are controversial cases in which a characteristic of the accused murderer could potentially negate the prosecution's attempt to seek death on behalf of the state. For example, the 2002 *Atkins v. Virginia* case established that mentally retarded offenders could not be executed. Typically these "exception" arguments are supported by the Eighth Amendment's ban on "cruel and unusual punishment." As in the *Atkins* case, *Thompson* was argued on Eighth Amendment grounds and Fourteenth Amendment grounds. Executing a fifteen-year-old was found to be cruel and unusual, and the Fourteenth Amendment applied this clause of the Eighth Amendment to the states.

The larger societal issue that the *Thompson* case raised was the appropriateness of the state-sanctioned execution of minors. Under the legal concept of *parens patriae*, juveniles have traditionally been treated with different rights and obligations than adults. Though this concept has been variously interpreted, it was not unusual for the American justice system to treat children as adults in cases of perpetrating murder. This practice met with both international disdain, as the United States was one of the few countries to permit the practice, and ire among the country's voters. The *Thompson* case was the first to limit the practice, hence saving minors fifteen years and younger from the death penalty. This finding was not only popular but also supported by contemporary psychiatric evidence on the reduced culpability of minors resulting from the incomplete maturation of the adolescent brain. However, the execution of sixteen- and seventeen-year-olds continued after *Thompson*.

Further Reading

Fagan, Jeffrey. "Atkins, Adolescences, and the Maturity Heuristic: Rationales for a Categorical Exemption for Juveniles from Capital Punishment." *New Mexico Law Review* 33 (Spring, 2003): 207-254.

Parrish, Michael E. *The Supreme Court and Capital Punishment: Judging Death.* Washington, D.C.: CQ Press, 2010.

Skovron, Sandra Evans, Joseph E. Scott, and Francis T. Cullen. "The Death Penalty for Juveniles: An Assessment of Public Support." *Crime and Delinquency* 35, no. 4 (1989): 546-561.

R. *Matthew Beverlin*

See also *Atkins v. Virginia; Ford v. Wainwright; Gregg v. Georgia; McCleskey v. Kemp; Roper v. Simmons; Stanford v. Kentucky.*

THORNBURGH V. AMERICAN COLLEGE OF OBSTETRICIANS AND GYNECOLOGISTS

Court: U.S. Supreme Court
Citation: 476 U.S. 747
Date: June 11, 1986
Issues: Reproductive rights; Right to privacy; Women's issues

- The Court upheld a woman's right to abortion, striking down a number of provisions that would have limited that right and placed restrictions on physicians.

In June, 1982, Pennsylvania enacted the Abortion Control Act, which placed severe restrictions on access to abortion. Before signing an abortion consent form, a woman had to read, or hear read, material about abortion alternatives, stages of fetal development, and psychological and physical harm that abortion might cause. Physicians were required to file extensive information about the women on whom they performed abortions and provide criteria by which fetal viability was determined in each case. A second physician was required to attest fetal viability. Additionally, physicians were required to use the abortion method that best protected the viability of the fetus. Failure to comply was a third-degree felony.

Following passage, a case was filed with the U.S. Court of Appeals, Third Circuit, by the American College of Obstetricians and Gynecologists against the state of Pennsylvania, represented by Governor Richard Thornburgh. This court ruled against all the major restrictions, citing earlier U.S. Supreme Court decisions. Pennsylvania then filed an appeal with the Supreme Court. Opponents of abortion were hopeful that an increasingly conservative Court would use this case to overturn the major provisions of *Roe v. Wade* (1973).

The Supreme Court, by a 5-4 majority, upheld the findings of the appeals court. The consent requirements were deemed an attempt to persuade women to change their minds, not to provide necessary information for informed consent. The restrictions placed on physicians were ruled as impinging on the doctor-patient relationship and limiting physicians' professional judgment. Restricting the method of abortion was viewed as giving fetal rights priority over the health and well-being of the mother. The Court did reaffirm the states' right to intervene on behalf of the fetus, but only during the last trimester of pregnancy. It also invoked the concept of *stare decisis* (let past decisions stand) in affirming a woman's right to abortion. It argued that constant reinterpretation of the law undermines societal stability.

The dissenting minority questioned the fundamental right to abortion, arguing that no such right is found in the Constitution. It declared its belief that *Roe v. Wade* had gone too far in affirming a woman's right to privacy, arguing that fetal rights should be strengthened. These issues have continued to be part of the public debate surrounding abortion and have reappeared in other state laws and cases brought before the Supreme Court. The narrow majority decision in this case continues to generate hope among abortion opponents that continued challenges will eventually result in strict and severe limitations being placed on abortion.

Charles L. Kammer

See also *Akron v. Akron Center for Reproductive Health; Bigelow v. Virginia; Doe v. Bolton; Harris v. McRae; Maher v. Roe; Planned Parenthood of Central Missouri v. Danforth; Roe v. Wade; Rust v. Sullivan; Webster v. Reproductive Health Services.*

Thornhill v. Alabama

Court: U.S. Supreme Court
Citation: 310 U.S. 88
Date: April 22, 1940
Issues: First Amendment guarantees; Freedom of assembly and association; Labor law

- The U.S. Supreme Court declared that peaceful labor union picketing was protected by the First Amendment.

Justice Frank Murphy wrote the opinion for the 8-1 majority, striking down an Alabama statute that prohibited all forms of labor union picketing. The Supreme Court clearly held that the First Amendment guarantee of the right "peaceably to assemble" would apply to labor union picketing. The qualifier "peaceably" meant states could enact specific limitations on the time, place, and manner of labor union picketing as they could for other demonstrations, but they could not simply ban all picketing as Alabama had. Justice James C. McReynolds dissented.

Richard L. Wilson

See also *Commonwealth v. Hunt; Hague v. Congress of Industrial Organizations; In re Debs; Truax v. Corrigan.*

TILTON V. RICHARDSON

Court: U.S. Supreme Court
Citation: 403 U.S. 672
Date: June 28, 1971
Issues: Education; Establishment of religion

- The Court held that it is constitutional for the federal government to provide grants to private sectarian colleges for the construction of academic buildings used solely for secular purposes.

The Higher Education Facilities Act of 1963 provided private colleges, both religious and secular, with federal grants and loans to construct academic buildings. The subsidized buildings were not to be used for religious instruction or worship for at least twenty years, but one section of the act allowed buildings to be used for any purpose after that period. The act was administered by the commissioner of education, and the commissioner required institutions receiving grants to provide assurances that the religious restrictions would be observed.

Eleanor Tilton and other taxpayers filed suit in a federal district court against the federal officials who administered the act, charging that grants to four church-related colleges in Connecticut were a violation of the establishment clause of the First Amendment. After the district court dismissed the complaint, the taxpayers appealed their suit to the U.S. Supreme Court.

The Court ruled five to four to uphold the provisions of the 1963 law that allowed religious colleges and universities to obtain federal funding for buildings used only for secular instruction, but the Court found that the part of the law ending the ban on religious practices after twenty years to be an unconstitutional contribution to a religious body. In defending the major portion of the law, Chief Justice Warren Burger wrote that the crucial question was not whether the law provided some benefit to a religious institution but whether the primary effect of the law was to advance religion.

In making a distinction between the 1963 law and cases in which the Court had ruled against state subsidies to primary and secondary schools, Burger argued that church-related colleges were not dealing with impressionable children, that the colleges under consideration did not have religious indoctrination as one of their substantial purposes, that buildings were themselves religiously neutral with little need for government surveillance, and that one-time grants required only minimal inspection. Cumulatively, Burger concluded that these factors lessened the potential for the grants to cause divisive religious fragmentation. He did acknowledge, however, that it might be unconstitutional for government to provide grants to a college which had religious indoctrination as one of its primary missions.

Since first dealing with the issue in *Everson v. Board of Education of Ewing Township* (1947), the Court has had a difficult time interpreting the establishment clause in its relationship to governmental assistance to students attending religious schools. Sometimes the Court has supported the strict separationist view, which is suspicious of even indirect aid to religious education, while in other cases the Court has tended to promote accommodation and emphasize neutrality. The *Tilton* decision indicated that the Court was willing to allow an extreme accommodationist position when the case involved religious colleges and universities.

Thomas Tandy Lewis

See also *Agostini v. Felton*; *Everson v. Board of Education of Ewing Township*; *Mueller v. Allen*; *Zelman v. Simmons-Harris*.

TIME V. HILL

Court: U.S. Supreme Court
Citation: 385 U.S. 374
Date: January 9, 1967
Issues: Right to privacy

• The U.S. Supreme Court extended the application of the actual malice rule in libel cases to false-light privacy actions.

An article in *Life* magazine contained inaccurate information about the Hill family, whose experiences while held in their own home by convicted criminals had been portrayed in a Broadway play. The Hill family sued the magazine's publisher, Time, Inc., for invasion of privacy under a New York law. Justice William J. Brennan, Jr., writing for a 5-4 member majority, held that the magazine and its publisher were not liable for a libel judgment because a public figure failed to prove the necessary condition that the magazine had acted out of actual malice or a reckless disregard of the truth. Justices Hugo L. Black and William O. Douglas concurred. Chief Justice Earl Warren and Justices Abe Fortas and Tom C. Clark dissented. Justice John Marshall Harlan dissented in part and concurred in part. In *Gertz v. Robert Welch* (1974), however, the Court ruled that private people did not have to prove actual malice to recover damages even if matters of public interest were involved. This ruling made the impact of *Time v. Hill* less clear.

Richard L. Wilson

See also *Garrison v. Louisiana; Gertz v. Robert Welch; Milkovich v. Lorain Journal Co.; New York Times Co. v. Sullivan.*

Times Film Corp. v. City of Chicago

Court: U.S. Supreme Court
Citation: 365 U.S. 43
Date: January 23, 1961
Issues: Censorship; Pornography and obscenity

- This case upheld the principle of prior restraint on films, thereby continuing a pattern of treating film differently than other media.

The controversy surrounding this court case arose after the Times Film Corporation, a foreign-film importer and distributor, applied for a permit to show the Austrian film *Don Juan* (1956), an adaptation of Wolfgang Amadeus Mozart's opera *Don Giovanni*. While the film contained no obscenities or sexual scenes, Chicago's municipal code required that films be submitted for censorship review along with applications before they could be publicly shown. The import company did not submit the film, claiming that the city's censorship statute was "null and void on constitutional grounds." They further stated that content of the film should not be subjected to censorship and if the city objected to the film, criminal process should not be brought against it until after *Don Juan* had been shown. The city denied them the permit because of the corporation's refusal to submit the film.

The film company filed suit in federal district court, asking that the film be permitted to be shown without prior censorship review, arguing that having a censor review films "amounted to a prior restraint on freedom of expression prohibited by the First and Fourteenth Amendments." The city argued that it could not protect the citizens of Chicago against "dangers of obscenity" if prior viewing and censorship were not permitted. The district court dismissed the case and an appeals court upheld the decision.

The Times Film Corporation's lawyers then petitioned the U.S. Supreme Court, which agreed to hear the case. The case was unusual in that most suits were filed because films submitted for review had been refused due to the content. The lawyers argued against permitting censorship prior to the film's viewing. In the Court's ensuing 5-4 decision, Justice Tom C. Clark said that the prior restraint in submitting a film did not violate the First Amendment. Chief Justice Earl Warren, one of the dissenting justices, warned that other forms of censorship on "newspapers, journals, books, magazines, television, radio or public speeches" might be invoked as a result of this decision. He also stated that the censor in offering judgment of the film's content does not have obligations to the public but to those who have hired him.

Marilyn Elizabeth Perry

See also *Burstyn v. Wilson; Freedman v. Maryland; Mutual Film Corp. v. Industrial Commission of Ohio; Near v. Minnesota.*

TINKER V. DES MOINES INDEPENDENT COMMUNITY SCHOOL DISTRICT

Court: U.S. Supreme Court
Citation: 393 U.S. 503
Date: February 24, 1969
Issues: Education; First Amendment guarantees;
Freedom of speech

• In this case, the U.S. Supreme Court decided that students attending public junior high and high school have a constitutional right to express their opinions on important public policy issues as long as they do not materially disrupt the school's educational program while doing so.

In December, 1965, several students met at one of their homes and agreed to wear black armbands to their respective schools to demonstrate their opposition to the war in Vietnam. School authorities, upon learning of the students' plans, adopted a policy requiring the suspension of any student who wore an armband to school and refused to remove it. Five students wore black armbands to school and were suspended from class and sent home when they refused to obey the school's policy. Three of these students and their parents filed suit in federal district court on the grounds that the suspension of the students violated their First Amendment rights to freedom of speech. The district court dismissed their complaint, and the Court of Appeals for the Eighth Circuit affirmed that decision.

The Court's Ruling

The Supreme Court by a vote of seven to two reversed the decision of the lower court. In ringing terms, the Court declared that students and teachers do not "shed their constitutional rights to freedom of speech or expression at the schoolhouse gate." The Court was particularly concerned that the school authorities permitted students to wear other political symbols to class without sanction but had determined to discipline only those students who wore armbands to protest the Vietnam War. This kind of regulatory discrimination against a specific viewpoint of speech directly challenged the most basic of free speech principles: Government cannot prohibit the expression of one opinion while allowing other points of view to be openly debated.

Despite its endorsement of the free speech rights of students in *Tinker*, the Court was careful not to undermine the legitimate authority of school officials. The majority opinion of Justice Abe Fortas made it clear that while students had a constitutionally protected right to express their beliefs at school, their freedom of speech was not unlimited in its scope. Student expressive activities could be appropriately regulated to prevent any disturbance of the school's educational programs.

The First Amendment did not protect disruptive speech or expression that impinged on the rights of other students. In the case before it, however, there was no evidence that the passive wearing of armbands caused disruption or interfered with school activities. The Court rejected the argument that the speculative concerns of school officials, who feared that a protest against the Vietnam War might prove disorderly, constituted a sufficient basis for forbidding the students' speech. "In our system," Justice Fortas wrote, "undifferentiated fear or apprehension of disturbance is not enough to overcome the right to freedom of expression."

The primary holding in *Tinker* is that bedrock principles of freedom of speech apply to public school students. No case prior to *Tinker* had stated this rule as forcefully or as clearly. The Court's decision in *Tinker* did not purport to resolve all the conflicts that might arise between student speakers and school authorities. Subsequent decisions have demonstrated, for example, that when student speech is part of the school's educational program and

Justice Abe Fortas.
(Library of Congress)

bears the imprimatur of the school, officials have the discretion to regulate nondisruptive expression on the grounds that it does not further the school's educational goals.

Alan E. Brownstein

Further Reading

Gold, Susan Dudley. *Tinker v. Des Moines: Free Speech for Students.* Tarrytown, N.Y.: Marshall Cavendish Benchmark, 2007. Part of its publisher's Supreme Court Milestones series designed for young-adult readers, this volume offers an accessible history and analysis of *Tinker v. Des Moines* that examines opposing sides in the case, the people involved, and the case's lasting impact. Includes bibliography and index.

Raskin, Jamin B. *We the Students: Supreme Court Cases for and About Students.* 2d ed. Washington, D.C.: CQ Press, 2003. Designed to help students achieve literacy on their constitutional rights as students. Includes learning exercises, case excerpts, and discussion prompts.

Thomas, Stephen, Martha McCarthy, and Nelda Cambron-McCabe. *Public School Law: Teachers' and Students' Rights.* 6th ed. Boston: Allyn & Bacon, 2008. Comprehensive and well-documented text on the evolution and current status of laws governing the public schools.

See also *Cohen v. California; Hazelwood School District v. Kuhlmeier.*

TISON V. ARIZONA

Court: U.S. Supreme Court
Citation: 481 U.S. 137
Date: April 21, 1987
Issues: Capital punishment

- In this case, the U.S. Supreme Court created a flexible standard for applying the death penalty to felony-murder accomplices who demonstrate reckless disregard for human life even though they do not directly participate in killing a victim.

On July 30, 1978, brothers Donny, age twenty-one, Ricky, age twenty, and Raymond Tison, age nineteen, smuggled guns into the Arizona State Prison and helped in the escape of their father Gary, a convicted murderer, and another convicted murderer. The group changed cars and made their escape on a desert highway. When they had a flat tire, they flagged down a passing car containing young parents, a baby, and a teenage cousin and held the family at gunpoint. Gary Tison ordered his sons to load their possessions into the young family's car. As the brothers loaded the car and pushed their own disabled car into the desert, their father and the other prison escapee brutally murdered the entire family, including the baby, with shotgun blasts at close range. The escaping group traveled for several more days before encountering a police roadblock. During the ensuing shootout, Donny was killed, Gary escaped into the desert but soon died from exposure, and Ricky, Raymond, and the other convict were captured.

As accomplices to the killing of the young family, Ricky and Raymond Tison were charged with felony murder. When they were sentenced to death, they appealed their sentences based on a Supreme Court decision (*Enmund v. Florida*, 1982) which had declared that felony-murder accomplices cannot be sentenced to death if they do not directly participate in the actual killing. After the Arizona Supreme Court upheld the sentences, the Tisons took their case to the U.S. Supreme Court.

In a 5-4 decision, the U.S. Supreme Court created a flexible standard for imposing the death penalty. The Court declared that felony-murder accomplices could receive the death penalty if they demonstrated "reckless disregard for human life," even if they did not directly participate in the killing. The justices used this new standard to uphold the capital sentences imposed on the Tisons because they viewed the brothers' active involvement in supplying weapons to convicted murderers and kidnapping the young family as a demonstration of "reckless disregard."

In *Tison v. Arizona* the Supreme Court gave state prosecutors greater flexibility to seek the death penalty against accomplices who participate in crimes that result in homicides. This new flexibility came at the price of greater inconsistency in the application of capital punishment. Under the prior rule, it was relatively clear which offenders were eligible for the death penalty, based on their direct participation in a killing. By contrast, under the *Tison* rule, jurors and judges applying the vague "reckless indifference" standard have broad opportunities to impose capital punishment based on their negative feelings toward the accomplice or their revulsion at the crime without precise consideration of the defendant's actual participation.

Christopher E. Smith

See also *Furman v. Georgia; Gregg v. Georgia; Woodson v. North Carolina.*

TROP V. DULLES

Court: U.S. Supreme Court
Citation: 356 U.S. 86
Date: March 31, 1958
Issues: Citizenship; Cruel and unusual punishment; Military law

• The U.S. Supreme Court held that Congress could not authorize the military to deprive a soldier of his citizenship. A plurality of four justices wanted to rule that expatriation was a cruel and unusual punishment, violating the Eighth Amendment.

Based on several acts of Congress, Albert Trop was sentenced to involuntary expatriation for the crime of wartime desertion. By a 5-4 vote, the Supreme Court overturned the sentence on narrow grounds. Speaking for a plurality, Chief Justice Earl Warren argued that the punishment violated the Eighth Amendment and that the amendment "must draw its meaning from the evolving standards of decency that mark the progress of a maturing society." Warren's opinion was accepted by a majority of the justices in 1967, and his dictum (individual, nonbinding statement) on the meaning of the Eighth Amendment has often been quoted in capital punishment cases.

On the same day that *Trop* was announced, the Court also issued a companion decision, *Perez v. Brownell* (1958), in which the justices voted five to four to uphold the revocation of a person's citizenship for voting in a foreign election. In a strong dissent, Chief Justice Warren repeated the arguments he used in his *Trop* opinion. In *Afroyim v. Rusk* (1967), the Court accepted Warren's point of view, reversed the *Perez* decision, and held that the expatriation provision of the Nationality Act of 1940 was unconstitutional.

Thomas Tandy Lewis

See also *Afroyim v. Rusk; Atkins v. Virginia; Furman v. Georgia.*

TRUAX V. CORRIGAN

Court: U.S. Supreme Court
Citation: 257 U.S. 312
Date: December 19, 1921
Issues: Labor law

• The U.S. Supreme Court, which typically took a conservative, pro-business, antilabor stance while William H. Taft was chief justice, struck down a state law protecting strikers against injunctions.

Chief Justice William H. Taft wrote the opinion for the 5-4 majority, striking down an Arizona law that protected labor union strikers from injunctions although not from suits for damages. Arizona and some other states sought to protect strikers from injunctions issued by conservative, probusiness courts. The Arizona courts upheld the statute in the face of a challenge from a business owner who lost half his customers while being picketed. The Supreme Court struck the Arizona statute on Fourteenth Amendment grounds. Taft held that the statute violated due process in that it deprived the owner of his property and equal protection in that it singled out employer-employee disputes for special treatment. Justice Oliver Wendell Holmes attacked the use of the Fourteenth Amendment to limit state experimentation. Justice Louis D. Brandeis dissented, setting out the legal and historical basis for the statute. Justice Mahlon Pitney was joined in a dissent by Justice John H. Clarke attacking all of the majority's conclusions.

Richard L. Wilson

See also *Commonwealth v. Hunt; Hague v. Congress of Industrial Organizations; In re Debs; Thornhill v. Alabama.*

TWINING V. NEW JERSEY

Court: U.S. Supreme Court
Citation: 211 U.S. 78
Date: November 9, 1908
Issues: Self-incrimination

- Reaffirming that the due process requirements of the Fourteenth Amendment did not include all the principles in the Bill of Rights, the U.S. Supreme Court ruled that the Fifth Amendment privilege against self-incrimination did not apply to the states.

In a criminal trial, the trial judge instructed the jury that the defendant's refusal to testify might be considered in reaching a verdict. Found guilty, Twining claimed that the judge's instructions were a violation of his Fifth Amendment right. The Supreme Court, however, rejected Twining's position by an 8-1 vote. Justice William H. Moody's opinion emphasized that many precedents had held that the states were not obligated to follow all the require-

Justice William H. Moody. (Library of Congress)

ments of the Bill of Rights. For the purposes of discussion, Moody acknowledged that the trial judge's comments constituted an infringement on Twining's privilege against self-incrimination. In dissent, John M. Harlan II argued that the privilege was a fundamental principle of the Anglo-American legal tradition, and he also spoke in favor of the full incorporation of the Bill of Rights into the Fourteenth Amendment. Although subsequent Courts never accepted Harlan's position on full incorporation, the *Twining* decision was finally reversed in *Malloy v. Hogan* (1964).

Thomas Tandy Lewis

See also *Adamson v. California*; *Albertson v. Subversive Activities Control Board*; *Counselman v. Hitchcock*; *Griffin v. California*; *Kilbourn v. Thompson*; *Malloy v. Hogan*; *Murphy v. Waterfront Commission of New York*; *Slochower v. Board of Education of New York City*.

TYSON V. BANTON

Court: U.S. Supreme Court
Citation: 273 U.S. 418
Date: February 28, 1927
Issues: Regulation of business

- Reaffirming that the states could regulate only "business affected with a public interest," the U.S. Supreme Court overturned a law restricting ticket scalping.

During the 1920's the New York State legislature passed a statute to protect the public against excessive charges in the resale of theater tickets. By a 5-4 vote, the Supreme Court ruled that the law violated a substantive freedom of enterprise, which was protected by the Fourteenth Amendment. Justice George Sutherland's opinion for the majority was based on the theory that government could use its police power only to regulate those businesses that were "affected with a public interest." Using the narrow definition of such businesses in *Wolff Packing Co. v. Court of Industrial Relations* (1923), Sutherland observed that only a small percentage of the public went to theaters and that the business of selling theater tickets was not an essential service in the economy. The dissenters rejected the idea that only some businesses were of interest to the public, and they argued that state legislatures should be able to use their police powers to regulate any private business to promote the welfare of their citizens. In 1934 the majority of the justices would accept the view of the dissenters in the landmark case of *Nebbia v. New York*.

Thomas Tandy Lewis

See also *Ferguson v. Skrupa; Legal Tender Cases; Nebbia v. New York; New State Ice Co. v. Liebmann; Wolff Packing Co. v. Court of Industrial Relations.*

ULLMANN V. UNITED STATES

Court: U.S. Supreme Court
Citation: 350 U.S. 422
Date: March 26, 1956
Issues: Congressional powers; Immunity from prosecution;
Self-incrimination

• The U.S. Supreme Court refused to protect those given limited immunity from prosecution in exchange for their testimony before a grand jury investigating communist activities.

Justice Felix Frankfurter wrote the opinion for the 7-2 majority, upholding the Immunity Act. A federal court acting under the Immunity Act ordered defendant Ullmann to testify before a grand jury investigating communist activities that potentially endangered national security. Despite having transactional immunity from state or federal prosecution for his compelled testimony, Ullmann refused to testify and was imprisoned for six months for contempt of court. On appeal, Ullmann said the immunity was incomplete because he still faced potential loss of a job or union membership and public contempt. Frankfurter rejected the argument, pointing out that the Fifth Amendment protected only against criminal prosecution. Justices Hugo L. Black and William O. Douglas dissented.

Richard L. Wilson

See also *Communist Party v. Subversive Activities Control Board; Counselman v. Hitchcock; Dennis v. United States; Scales v. United States; Wesberry v. Sanders; Yates v. United States.*

United Jewish Organizations of Williamsburgh v. Carey

Court: U.S. Supreme Court
Citation: 430 U.S. 144
Date: March 1, 1977
Issues: Reapportionment and redistricting

• The U.S. Supreme Court upheld a state reapportionment plan based on a strict racial quota.

Justice Byron R. White wrote the opinion for the 7-1 majority, upholding a New York state reapportionment scheme based explicitly on racial quotas. This scheme was required to obtain the U.S. attorney general's approval under the 1965 Voting Rights Act, but it required splitting a Hasidic Jewish community, which sued, alleging essentially reverse discrimination. The Supreme Court rejected its claim. Justice Thurgood Marshall did not participate, and Chief Justice Warren E. Burger dissented strongly, rejecting any use of racial quotas in reapportionment.

Richard L. Wilson

See also *Baker v. Carr; Colegrove v. Green; Gomillion v. Lightfoot; Gray v. Sanders; Kirkpatrick v. Preisler; Mahan v. Howell; Reynolds v. Sims.*

United Mine Workers, United States v. *See* United States v. United Mine Workers

UNITED PUBLIC WORKERS V. MITCHELL

Court: U.S. Supreme Court
Citation: 330 U.S. 75
Date: February 10, 1947
Issues: Freedom of speech; Political campaigning

- The U.S. Supreme Court ruled that Congress had the authority to limit political activities of public employees, notwithstanding their loss of freedom of speech.

Executive agency employees challenged the Hatch Act of 1939, which forbade executive branch officers and employees from exercising their freedom of speech by endorsing candidates and engaging in political campaigning. The Supreme Court reviewed precedents going back decades to establish that the individual right to freedom of speech needed to be balanced against the public's interest in having civil servants barred from direct political participation. Justice Stanley F. Reed wrote the opinion for the 4-3 majority in a case in which Justices Frank Murphy and Robert H. Jackson did not participate. Justice William O. Douglas concurred in part but found the statute was excessively vague. Justice Hugo L. Black wrote a strong dissent, arguing that the Hatch Act deprived millions of U.S. civil servants of their right to freedom of speech.

Richard L. Wilson

See also *Buckley v. Valeo; Elrod v. Burns; National Treasury Employees Union v. Von Raab; Rutan v. Republican Party of Illinois; Snepp v. United States.*

UNITED STATES TERM LIMITS V. THORNTON

Court: U.S. Supreme Court
Citation: 514 U.S. 779
Date: May 22, 1995
Issues: Federal supremacy

• The U.S. Supreme Court struck down an amendment to the Arkansas constitution that imposed term limits for members of both houses of Congress.

By 1995 Arkansas and twenty-two other states had adopted limits on the terms of office for members of Congress. By a 5-4 vote, the Supreme Court ruled that such limits were unconstitutional. In his sixty-one-page opinion for the Court, Justice John Paul Stevens observed that term limits were qualifications and that neither states nor Congress were authorized to add to the qualifications for representatives found in Article I of the U.S. Constitution. Allowing individual states to craft their own qualifications would "erode the structure envisioned by the framers." Therefore, a constitutional amendment was the only acceptable way to obtain the desired limits. The dissenters emphasized two points: states' rights and silence in the Constitution concerning the issue.

Thomas Tandy Lewis

See also *Hutchinson v. Proxmire*, *Palmer v. Thompson.*

UNITED STATES V. ALVAREZ-MACHAIN

Court: U.S. Supreme Court
Citation: 504 U.S. 655
Date: June 15, 1992
Issues: Foreign policy; International law; Treaties

• In this ruling, the U.S. Supreme Court held that nothing in the extradition treaty between the United States and Mexico and nothing in general international law prohibited the trial of a defendant whose arrest was the result of a forcible abduction from Mexico.

Humberto Alvarez-Machain, a physician and a citizen of Mexico, was believed by the U.S. Drug Enforcement Administration (DEA) to have been partly responsible for the torture and murder of a DEA agent. Alvarez-Machain was indicted by a federal court for kidnapping and murder. After U.S. negotiations with Mexico for his extradition failed, he was forcibly abducted from his office in Guadalajara, flown to the United States, and arrested on arrival. His abductors, though not employees of the federal government, had been solicited by the DEA and promised a reward.

When Alvarez-Machain was brought to trial, he moved to dismiss the indictment because his arrest had been illegal. The district court judge found that although the Drug Enforcement Administration did not directly participate in the kidnapping, it was responsible for it. The indictment was dismissed on the grounds that the extradition treaty between the United States and Mexico had been violated by the illegal arrest. The court of appeals upheld the district court, arguing that the abduction violated the purpose of the extradition treaty. The government appealed to the Supreme Court.

Chief Justice William Rehnquist wrote the opinion for a 6-3 majority. He held that the complicity of the U.S. government in Alvarez-Machain's abduction did not nullify the indictment. The case turned on a narrow question: Does the extradition treaty between the United States and Mexico provide the only means by which a defendant can legally be brought from one of the two countries to the other? As the majority saw the case, the extradition treaty does not establish an exclusive means of bringing potential defendants from Mexico to the United States. It does not specifically exclude kidnapping or unlawful arrest. Therefore the illegality of U.S. actions in Mexico did not affect the validity of the indictment. The case was remanded to the lower courts so that Alvarez-Machain's trial could go forward.

Justice John Paul Stevens wrote a strong dissenting opinion in which he argued that the extradition processes set out in the treaty are designed to provide an orderly means of dealing with cross-border crimes. The dissent argued that by substituting kidnapping for extradition, the United States had violated the treaty. Stevens also argued that the decision would encourage the government to engage in additional acts of international lawlessness.

Although the decision cleared the way for Alvarez-Machain to be put on trial in the United States, Mexican protests about U.S. violation of Mexican sovereignty resulted in an executive decision to return Alvarez-Machain to Mexico. He was repatriated within a few months of the Court's decision.

Robert Jacobs

Further Reading

Blakesley, Christopher L. *Terrorism, Drugs, International Law, and the Protection of Human Liberty.* Ardley-on-Hudson, N.Y.: Transnational, 1992.

Cassese, Antonio. *International Criminal Law.* New York: Oxford University Press, 2003.

See also *Goldwater v. Carter; Martin v. Hunter's Lessee; Missouri v. Holland; Ware v. Hylton.*

UNITED STATES V. AMERICAN TOBACCO CO.

Court: U.S. Supreme Court
Citation: 221 U.S. 106
Date: May 29, 1911
Issues: Antitrust law; Regulation of commerce

• The U.S. Supreme Court's ruling that the American Tobacco Company engaged in unreasonable anticompetitive business practices led to the company's dissolution.

Founded in 1890, the American Tobacco Company became one of the largest holding companies in the United States before its forced dissolution in 1911. In *United States v. American Tobacco Co.*, the company was found guilty under the Sherman Antitrust Act of 1890 of monopolizing the cigarette industry through "unreasonable" business practices, including buying out rivals, excluding rivals from access to wholesalers, and predatory pricing.

The market for tobacco products included smoking tobacco, chewing tobacco, cigars, snuff, and cigarettes. Developments in the cigarette market had had significant effects on other branches of trade. Early in the 1880's, the cigarette industry experienced increasing competition in prices. Innovations in production technology, including Bonsack cigarette-making machines that replaced hand labor, caused oversupply in the market. James Buchanan Duke, who first adopted the Bonsack machine for full-scale production, began to revolutionize the tobacco industry.

The American Tobacco Company

Duke entered the cigarette business around 1880 with his father, Washington Duke, in W. Duke Sons and Company, a smoking-tobacco manufacturer near Durham, North Carolina. When the government reduced the tax on cigarettes by two-thirds, he cut the price of his cigarettes by half. In addition to price cutting, he launched an extensive advertising and promotion campaign for his Duke of Durham and Cameo brands, using huge newspaper ads and billboard displays. By 1889, advertising and promotion outlays amounted to about 20 percent of sales, an unusually high level within the tobacco industry.

In 1884, Duke began to operate a new factory in New York and to control the northern and western parts of the U.S. market. Price cuts and competitive advertising intensified among his and four other major cigarette manufacturers: Allen & Ginter, Kinney Tobacco Company, William S. Kimball & Company, and Goodwin & Company. In 1890, Duke took advantage of the New Jersey incorporation law of 1889 to organize a merger with those four manufacturers to form the American Tobacco Company. With $25 million in capital, the new company immediately became one of the biggest "trusts" or holding companies in the United States. It controlled nearly 90 percent of all domestic cigarette sales.

American Tobacco continued to expand its spending on cigarette advertising, with expenditures exceeding $4 million in 1910. Its competitive prices were the result of Duke's efficient management, which kept operating costs substantially below those of most competitors. Duke's cost-cutting practices included hiring nonunion labor at a wage rate lower than its union counterpart; an exclusive contract with the Bonsack Company for its cigarette-making machines, which cut production costs by fifteen to twenty-five cents per thousand cigarettes; vertical integration through forming extensive networks to perform all functions from purchasing leaf tobacco to warehouse storage to marketing cigarettes through its tobacco product retail chain, the United Cigar Store (which replaced the old industry method of using traveling salespersons); and discontinuing less profitable brands and closing less efficient factories.

By 1900, American Tobacco's profits had risen to be more than half of sales. As public tastes switched to Turkish tobacco, however, American Tobacco's cigarettes declined in popularity. Duke fought back with his own Turkish brands, regaining a market share of 85 percent of cigarette sales by 1910. Market shares for the company's smoking and chewing tobacco also increased, to more than 75 percent of the U.S. market.

American Tobacco bought out about 250 of its competitors before its dissolution in 1911. In 1898, Duke had organized a combination of tobacco plug manufacturers, the Continental Tobacco Company. In 1901, the American and Continental companies were consolidated into the Consolidated Tobacco Company, a holding company that was soon dissolved and reorganized under the original name of the American Tobacco Company. In 1901, it stretched its market power overseas to England by buying Ogden's Limited of Liverpool, a leading British cigarette manufacturer. One year later, Duke negotiated with the Imperial Tobacco Company to form the British-American Tobacco Company to operate in overseas markets.

The success of American Tobacco in the cigarette market did not prevent Duke from diversifying into other tobacco-related products. He waged the so-called Plug Wars by acquiring plug and smoking tobacco manufacturers including Liggett & Myers Tobacco Company and R. J. Reynolds Tobacco Company. In conjunction with its massive advertising campaign, it deliberately sold various "fighting brands" at prices below cost in order to bankrupt competitors. As American Tobacco became the monopoly in the market, advertising intensity subsided to less than 10 percent of sales.

Before American Tobacco was dissolved by order of the Supreme Court, the company had acquired approximately 95 percent of sales of snuff, 85 percent of chewing tobacco and cigarettes, and 75 percent of smoking tobacco. By the end of the nineteenth century, the growth and practices of large trusts, especially those in the oil, sugar, and tobacco industries, had brought the attention of the U.S. Department of Justice, which sought to restore competition in the marketplace.

Sherman Antitrust Act

In 1890, the first major U.S. antitrust legislation, the Sherman Antitrust Act, written by Senator John Sherman, was passed. It outlawed any restraints of trade (section 1) and attempts or conspiracy among competitors to monopolize a market (section 2). The antitrust campaign was intensified by President Theodore Roosevelt. On July 19, 1907, after one of American Tobacco's subsidiaries was indicted for price fixing in the District Court for the Southern District of New York, the Justice Department filed a petition against the entire tobacco trust for violating sections 1 and 2 of the Sherman Act.

In November, 1908, American Tobacco was ruled guilty in a 3-1 vote. That decision was not finalized until May 29, 1911, when the Supreme Court sustained the lower court's verdict. In the Court's opinion, Chief Justice Edward D. White, following logic developed in the Court's ruling against Standard Oil two weeks earlier, used the "rule of reason" principle in regard to American Tobacco's monopolization of the cigarette industry. The rule of reason stated that monopolies were not necessarily unlawful; they violated the law only by acting "unreasonably." White noted that the "undisputed" evidence of "unreasonable" business practices was overwhelming. This evidence included the original formation of the tobacco trust through the buying out of competitors, the use of the trust's power to monopolize the trade in tobacco and the plug and snuff business further by using below-cost pricing, attempts to conceal the trust's practices through secret agreements and creation of brands falsely promoted as independent, the practice of vertical integration with wholesalers and leaf tobacco suppliers to blockade the entry of others into the tobacco trade, and price fixing with some formerly independent tobacco companies.

The case resulted in a dissolution decree, which was issued in November, 1911. The circuit court was directed to form a plan to dissolve the trust and form a new decentralized market structure. As a result, American Tobacco was split into sixteen successor companies, including a new American Tobacco Company, Liggett & Myers Tobacco Company, P. Lorillard Company, R. J. Reynolds Company, and the American Snuff Company. It was dissolved from iGts purchasing subsidiaries and separated from Imperial Tobacco, its overseas subsidiary.

Significance

Along with the Standard Oil case in the same year, the American Tobacco case significantly altered the course of both the U.S. history of big business and the development of antitrust law. The victory of the U.S. government in these two cases highlighted federal efforts to promote competition in U.S. markets.

As for the tobacco industry, however, American Tobacco's successor companies continued to have considerable market power. The dissolution decree gave the new American Tobacco, Liggett & Myers, Lorillard, and Reynolds a combined 80 percent of the smoking and chewing tobacco facilities of that time. Despite declining profits, the successor companies continued to in-

Contemporary editorial cartoon suggesting that the Supreme Court would be going after the tobacco trusts after taking care of the Standard Oil trust. (Library of Congress)

crease advertising spending, which exceeded $10 million in 1912. Their total sales increased from the old American Tobacco's $6.9 billion in 1910 to $11.8 billion in 1912.

In October, 1912, in response to declining market shares, four of the independent companies formed Tobacco Products Corporation. The new trust soon was joined by six more independents. Because the government concentrated its attention on American Tobacco's successor companies after the dissolution decree, the case actually gave birth to other industrial combinations. The next few decades witnessed the rise of Brown & Williamson Tobacco Company and Philip Morris Company, the latter of which grew to become the biggest U.S. tobacco manufacturer by 1990.

In the 1911 Supreme Court decision against American Tobacco, Chief Justice White explained the Court's interpretation and application of the Sherman Act, arguing that not all restraints of trade were violations of the antitrust law, only the "unreasonable" ones. White emphasized that it was not the mere size of American Tobacco in relation to its market that the Court condemned but the evidence of its "unreasonable" restraints of trade. The new doctrine, known as the rule of reason, set a precedent for a new era of Supreme Court antitrust decisions. The rule of reason stayed in force until the Alcoa case in 1945.

The Supreme Court ruling illustrated the need for additional legislation that would define specific business practices that were "unreasonable" and thus illegal. That need led to passage of the Clayton Antitrust Act and the Federal Trade Commission Act in 1914, which respectively declared specific business practices, including attempts to monopolize through mergers and acquisitions, to be "unfair" and gave birth to the Federal Trade Commission as an agency to enforce compliance with the modified antitrust law. In 1938, the Wheeler-Lea Amendment to the Federal Trade Commission Act was passed to give the Federal Trade Commission authority over consumer-protection matters.

Impact on the Tobacco Industry

The dissolution of American Tobacco transformed the structure of the U.S. tobacco industry from a near monopoly to an oligopolistic structure with a few large companies. That character prevailed until the end of the century. The dissolution of American Tobacco immediately resulted in increased competition among its successor companies. Product variety and advertising and promotional efforts increased in attempts to increase brand loyalty. The average advertising expenses in the tobacco industry doubled in the two years following the dissolution. In 1913, R. J. Reynolds Tobacco Company introduced a new brand of cigarettes, Camel. Lorillard responded with its Tiger brand in 1915 and Old Gold in 1926, American Tobacco with Lucky Strike in 1916, and Liggett & Myers with Chesterfield in 1920.

The American Tobacco case, along with the Standard Oil case, signified the government's negative attitude toward merger and acquisition activities. Mergers appeared to level off until the government's failure in prosecuting the merger practices of U.S. Steel in 1920. As for the tobacco industry, even though competition increased with the rise of Brown & Williamson Tobacco Company and Philip Morris Tobacco Company, the biggest three successor companies to American Tobacco—the new American Tobacco, Reynolds, and Liggett & Myers—still maintained considerable market power, as a group controlling between 65 percent and 90 percent of the U.S. tobacco-product sales during the next two decades. Such a market without another major entry became the main evidence used by the Supreme Court to convict the largest three successor companies of conspiracy in monopolization and restraint of trade in 1946.

The practices of the American Tobacco Company contributed important lessons not only in the development of antitrust law but also in the role of marketing and advertising in business practices. Tactics innovated by James Duke and later by American Tobacco's successor companies, including heavy use of advertising, became common in other markets for nearly identical products, such as the market for gasoline. Consequently, in 1938, the government stepped in with passage of the Wheeler-Lea Act, which gave the Federal Trade Commission jurisdiction to regulate advertising and promotional activities.

Jim Lee

Further Reading

Adams, Walter, and James Brock, eds. *The Structure of American Industry.* 10th ed. Upper Saddle River, N.J.: Prentice Hall, 2000. Provides good coverage of the development of the tobacco industry as well as discussions of the industry's structure, price behavior, and performance. Valuable for undergraduate and graduate students in industrial organization.

Areeda, Phillip, Louis Kaplow, and Aaron Edlin. *Antitrust Analysis: Problems, Text, Cases.* 6th ed. New York: Aspen, 2004. Textbook containing case studies of the major antitrust cases in American history. Bibliographic references and index.

Armentano, Dominick T. *Antitrust and Monopoly: Anatomy of a Policy Failure.* 2d ed. Oakland, Calif.: Independent Institute, 1990. Covers major antitrust lawsuits since the Sherman Act and the development of antitrust legislation. Includes discussion of the American Tobacco case. Features an appendix of relevant sections of antitrust laws.

Cox, Reavis. *Competition in the American Tobacco Industry, 1911-1932.* New York: Columbia University Press, 1933. A good study of the performance and competition among the major tobacco companies.

Hovenkamp, Herbert. *Federal Antitrust Policy: The Law of Competition and Its Practice.* 3d ed. St. Paul, Minn.: Thomson/West, 2005. Covers nearly all aspects of U.S. antitrust policy in a manner understandable to readers with no background in economics. Chapter 2 discusses history and ideology in antitrust policy.

Hylton, Keith N. *Antitrust Law: Economic Theory and Common Law Evolution.* New York: Cambridge University Press, 2003. Comprehensive text on economic principles behind antitrust and the development of American antitrust law over more than one hundred years of litigation. Includes a chapter on the Alcoa case. Bibliographic references and index.

Porter, Patrick G. "Origins of the American Tobacco Company." *Business History Review* 43 (Spring, 1969): 59-76. Concise historical study of the tobacco company until its dissolution in 1911 draws comparisons between big tobacco and the oil industry.

Tennant, Richard B. *The American Cigarette Industry.* New Haven, Conn.: Yale University Press, 1950. Detailed history of the cigarette industry through the 1940's. Includes analysis of market behavior using economic models and statistical regression analysis. Excellent business or economics case study for undergraduate-level readers.

U.S. Bureau of Corporations. *Report of the Commissioner of Corporations on the Tobacco Industry.* Washington, D.C.: Government Printing Office, 1908-1909. Presents the findings of a government investigation of the tobacco industry, particularly the American Tobacco Company.

Whitney, Simon N. *Antitrust Policies: American Experience in Twenty Industries.* 2 vols. New York: Twentieth Century Fund, 1958. Chapter 11 of volume 2 provides detailed discussions of the tobacco industry from different perspectives, including its price and product competition and its performance that resulted in the second antitrust lawsuit. Other chapters offer case studies of other major industries. Appendix contains critiques of the studies by economists and government officials.

See also *Alcoa v. Federal Trade Commission; Northern Securities Co. v. United States; Standard Oil v. United States; United States v. United States Steel Corp.*

================

UNITED STATES V. BUTLER

Court: U.S. Supreme Court
Citation: 297 U.S. 1
Date: January 6, 1936
Issues: Congressional powers; Taxation

• The U.S. Supreme Court struck down the regulatory features of the Agricultural Adjustment Act (AAA) of 1933 as inconsistent with the Tenth Amendment, while at the same time interpreting the general welfare clause as providing an independent source of congressional power to spend public money for public purposes.

The first Agricultural Adjustment Act, in order to counter the devastating effects of the Great Depression on agricultural prices, authorized the payment of subsidies to farmers in exchange for a reduction in the production of agricultural commodities. The funding for the payments came from a processing tax levied on the processors of the commodities. William Butler and other receivers of a cotton-processing company refused to pay the tax.

By a 6-3 vote, the Supreme Court ruled that the tax was unconstitutional. Speaking for the majority, Justice Owen J. Roberts argued that the processing tax was not a true tax for raising revenue but part of a system for regulating agricultural production, which was a power reserved to the states under the Tenth Amendment. In this part of his opinion, Roberts simply affirmed *Bailey v. Drexel Furniture Co.* (1922). Roberts then considered whether the subsidies could be justified by the general welfare clause. Although he found that Congress had broad authority to appropriate funds for the general welfare, he denied that Congress could impose regulations as a condition for receiving the funds.

In a famous dissent, Justice Harlan Fiske Stone argued that the act was a valid application of the taxing and spending power of Congress and referred to Roberts's opinion as "a tortured construction of the Constitution." Declaring that the Court should exercise self-restraint, Stone wrote: "Courts are not the only agencies of government that must be assumed to have the power to govern."

Although *Butler* expressed a preference for limited government, its interpretation of the general welfare clause provided later justification for the Social Security Act and other federal programs. In *Mulford v. Smith* (1939), Justice Roberts wrote the majority opinion that upheld the Agricultural Adjustment Act of 1938, despite its great similarity to the act of 1933.

Thomas Tandy Lewis

See also *Bailey v. Drexel Furniture Co.*; *Mulford v. Smith*; *South Dakota v. Dole*; *Steward Machine Co. v. Davis*.

UNITED STATES V. CALIFORNIA

Court: U.S. Supreme Court
Citation: 332 U.S. 19
Date: June 23, 1947
Issues: Federal supremacy

• The U.S. Supreme Court held that the federal government, not the states, had full dominion and mineral rights over the three-mile strip of submerged coastal lands.

The United States sued California in order to establish federal sovereignty over the offshore area three miles seaward from the low-water mark. Until then, the states had exercised de facto control over the area. The question was important because of huge oil and gas reserves that were being discovered. Speaking for a 6-2 majority, Justice Hugo L. Black found that the federal government had always possessed dominion over the entire coastal waters, even if it had allowed the states to control a three-mile strip. Black noted that the U.S. Constitution authorized Congress to decide the issue. Following an angry debate, Congress enacted the Submerged Lands Act of 1953, which gave title of the offshore lands to the coastal states.

Thomas Tandy Lewis

See also *Lucas v. South Carolina Coastal Council; Nollan v. California Coastal Commission; Pennsylvania Coal Co. v. Mahon; Powell v. Alabama.*

United States v. Carolene Products Co.

Court: U.S. Supreme Court
Citation: 304 U.S. 144
Date: April 25, 1938
Issues: Judicial powers; Judicial review

• The fourth footnote to this case, which described the standards of judicial scrutiny and the appropriateness of their use, became the basis of judicial activism on the part of the U.S. Supreme Court.

Although this case is unimportant otherwise, its fourth footnote is regarded as the most important in Supreme Court history because it became the basis for judicial activism in the defense of powerless minorities who were likely to have their Fourteenth Amendment rights denied by state or local governments. The majority opinion in the 5-2 decision was written by Justice Harlan

THE COURT'S THREE LEVELS OF JUDICIAL SCRUTINY

Level	Application	Standard of review	Classifications/restraints
Strict	Suspect classifications and fundamental rights	Is there a compelling state interest in the classification or restraint? Is the classification or restraint narrowly tailored?	Race; aliens (those not performing essential government functions); fundamental rights (right to vote, right to interstate travel, reproductive rights)
Intermediate	Quasi-suspect classifications	Is there an important governmental objective and a substantial relationship between that objective and the classification or restraint?	Gender; illegitimacy
Minimal	Economic regulations and nonsuspect classifications	Is there a good reason to justify the classification or restraint?	Poverty; age discrimination; homosexuality; aliens (performing essential government functions); rights (education, housing, welfare)

Fiske Stone, who was joined by Chief Justice Charles Evans Hughes and Justices Louis D. Brandeis and Owen J. Roberts. Justice Hugo L. Black concurred but dissented in the portion containing the footnote; Justices James C. McReynolds and Pierce Butler dissented; Justices Benjamin N. Cardozo and Stanley F. Reed did not participate.

In essence, the footnote set out the appropriateness of using different standards of judicial scrutiny for different kinds of legislation. The Court's basic presumption is that all laws are constitutional. If unconstitutional laws are passed under ordinary circumstances, the majority of citizens have the option of electing new legislators and repealing the legislation; but this is not true if there are groups of people who are unable to avail themselves of the political process. The Court must use greater scrutiny when dealing with cases involving these groups because the democratic process can be frustrated by laws limiting the right to vote or preventing free expression. Such laws are suspect when they involve groups that are likely to be unable to use the political process to correct bad legislation. Still more important from the Court's point of view are laws that affect discrete and insular minorities despised and feared by the overwhelming majority in society. Prejudice against these groups may prevent normal processes and result in the loss of constitutional protection.

Richard L. Wilson

See also *Craig v. Boren*; *Plyler v. Doe*; *Reapportionment Cases*.

UNITED STATES V. CLASSIC

Court: U.S. Supreme Court
Citation: 313 U.S. 299
Date: May 26, 1941
Issues: Racial discrimination; Voting rights

• Overturning its 1921 decision, the U.S. Supreme Court held that Congress has the power to regulate primaries whenever state law makes them an integral part of the process for electing candidates to federal office.

The precedent set in *Newberry v. United States* (1921), which prevented Congress from regulating party primaries, was one of the foundation blocks for the whites-only primaries of the South. The Supreme Court partially over-ruled *Newberry* in the *Classic* case, which involved charges against a Louisiana election commissioner for deliberately changing the ballots in a congressional primary. Speaking for a 5-3 majority, Justice Harlan Fiske Stone ruled that the federal government, based on Article I of the U.S. Constitution, had the right to ensure the integrity of primary elections if they had a clear relationship to the determination of who would be elected to Congress. *Classic* prepared the way for the landmark case *Smith v. Allwright* (1944).

Thomas Tandy Lewis

See also *Grovey v. Townsend; Newberry v. United States; Smith v. Allwright.*

UNITED STATES V. CRUIKSHANK

Court: U.S. Supreme Court
Citation: 92 U.S. 542
Date: March 27, 1876
Issues: Civil rights and liberties; States' rights

• Based on narrow interpretations of the Fourteenth and Fifteenth Amendments, the U.S. Supreme Court severely limited the authority of the federal government to protect the civil rights of African Americans.

Because state courts rarely prosecuted acts of violence against the freed slaves of the South, the Enforcement Act of 1870 made it a federal crime to engage in a conspiracy to deprive a citizen of constitutional rights. In Colfax, Louisiana, an armed group of white rioters killed about one hundred blacks gathered for a political meeting. Federal prosecutors used the Enforcement Act to prosecute and convict William Cruikshank and two others for participating in the Colfax massacre.

The Supreme Court unanimously held that the indictments were invalid. In a complicated ruling, Chief Justice Morrison R. Waite concentrated on the difference between the rights of state and national citizenship. Any assaults on the rights of state citizenship, which included participation in state politics, were not enforceable in federal courts. In addition, the due process and equal protection clauses of the Fourteenth Amendment authorized federal legislation relating only to actions by state officials, not to acts of private persons. Finally, in charging interference with a Fifteenth Amendment right to vote, the indictments failed to specify that the defendants had been motivated by the race of the victims.

The decision in *United States v. Cruikshank* left protection for most African American rights with the southern states, where few people sympathized with their cause. The decision reflected the national mood, which had become tired of federal intervention in southern politics.

Thomas Tandy Lewis

See also *Civil Rights Cases; Cox v. Louisiana; Griffin v. Breckenridge; Slaughterhouse Cases; United States v. Guest.*

UNITED STATES V. CURTISS-WRIGHT EXPORT CORP.

Court: U.S. Supreme Court
Citation: 299 U.S. 304
Date: December 21, 1936
Issues: Foreign policy; Presidential powers

• The U.S. Supreme Court declared that the federal government possesses broad and inherent powers to deal with other countries and that the president exercises primacy in formulating and conducting foreign policy.

In 1934, Congress passed a joint resolution authorizing the president to prohibit the sale of arms to the warring nations of Bolivia and Paraguay. Congress also provided criminal penalties for violators. President Franklin D. Roosevelt quickly proclaimed an embargo. After the Curtiss-Wright Export Corporation was indicted for disobeying the embargo, it asserted that the congressional resolution was an unconstitutional delegation of legislative power to the president.

By a 7-1 margin, the Supreme Court found nothing unconstitutional about the government's arrangement. Justice George Sutherland distinguished between two kinds of legislation, domestic and foreign, and held that the rule against delegation of duties applied only to the former. He theorized that the powers in foreign affairs derived less from the Constitution than from the inherent attributes of a sovereign country. In the international field, moreover, the president has primacy, and Congress "must often accord to the President a degree of discretion and freedom from statutory restriction which would not be admissible were domestic affairs alone involved."

There has been much controversy concerning *Curtiss-Wright*'s expansive views of inherent presidential powers in foreign affairs. The decision was cited by opponents of the War Powers Act of 1973 and by supporters of executive discretion in the Iran-Contra affair. Probably a majority of legal scholars believe that Sutherland's statements about presidential powers are inconsistent with constitutional principles of separation of powers. In *Regan v. Wald* (1984), the Court recognized that the conduct of foreign affairs is under the domain of both the legislative and executive branches.

Thomas Tandy Lewis

See also *Dames and Moore v. Regan; Humphrey's Executor v. United States; Mc-Culloch v. Maryland; Martin v. Mott; Myers v. United States; Nixon v. Administrator of General Services; United States v. Nixon; Wiener v. United States; Youngstown Sheet and Tube Co. v. Sawyer.*

UNITED STATES V. DARBY LUMBER CO.

Court: U.S. Supreme Court
Citation: 312 U.S. 100
Date: February 3, 1941
Issues: Labor law; Regulation of business

• Using a broad interpretation of the commerce clause, the U.S. Supreme Court upheld a federal law mandating minimum wages and maximum hours for employees producing goods for interstate commerce.

The Fair Labor Standards Act of 1938, the last major piece of New Deal legislation, applied to employees engaged "in commerce" and "in the production of goods for commerce." Fred Darby, owner of a Georgia company making goods to be shipped out of state, was indicted for paying his employees less than the minimum wage. In his appeal, Darby referred to the precedent of *Hammer v. Dagenhart* (1918), which had held that the U.S. Congress, under the commerce clause and the Tenth Amendment, had no authority to regulate activities that were only indirectly connected to interstate commerce. By an 8-0 vote, the Court overturned *Hammer* and upheld the 1938 statute. Justice Harlan Fiske Stone wrote that Congress possessed the comprehensive authority to regulate any intrastate activities that had either a direct or indirect effect on interstate commerce. Only the employees of companies engaging in purely local activities remained outside the protection of the federal minimum-wage law. Stone's landmark opinion specifically repudiated the doctrine of dual federalism, so that the Tenth Amendment would no longer serve as a significant restraint on federal supervision of anything relating to interstate commerce.

Thomas Tandy Lewis

See also *Carter v. Carter Coal Co.*; *Hammer v. Dagenhart*; *National Labor Relations Board v. Jones and Laughlin Steel Corp.*; *United States v. Lopez*; *Wickard v. Filburn.*

UNITED STATES V. E. C. KNIGHT CO.

Court: U.S. Supreme Court
Citation: 156 U.S. 1
Date: January 21, 1895
Issues: Antitrust law

• In its first decision under the Sherman Antitrust Act (1890), the U.S. Supreme Court found that the framers of the act had not intended it to apply to the manufacturing process.

During the 1890's, the American Sugar Company was a large monopoly controlling 98 percent of the refining industry. Responding to a public outcry, President Grover Cleveland's administration filed suit against the monopoly under the Sherman Antitrust Act (1890). By an 8-1 vote, the Supreme Court

Chief Justice Melville W. Fuller. (Albert Rosenthal Collection of the Supreme Court of the United States)

ruled that the law was not applicable because it had not been designed to prevent a monopoly in manufacturing. In the opinion for the majority, Justice Melville W. Fuller wrote that the power to regulate manufacturing belonged exclusively to the states under their police powers and that the regulatory authority of the federal government was limited to interstate commerce. An article manufactured for sale in another state did not become an article of interstate commerce until it was actually transported as commerce. Fuller did not rule on the constitutionality of the Sherman Act because he assumed that the act had been framed according to the "well-settled principles" of dual federalism.

In a strong dissent, Justice John Marshall Harlan broadly defined commerce so that it included the buying and selling of goods. He argued that the U.S. Congress could constitutionally regulate some manufacturers and that it had intended to do so in the Sherman Antitrust Act. He insisted, moreover, that only the federal government had the capacity to deal with large business combinations. Although the Court would accept the "stream-of-commerce" theory in *Swift and Co. v. United States* (1905), it did not fully accept Harlan's view of congressional authority over sugar refineries until *Mandeville Island Farms v. American Crystal Sugar Co.* (1948).

Thomas Tandy Lewis

See also *Hammer v. Dagenhart; Northern Securities Co. v. United States; Swift and Co. v. United States.*

United States v. E. I. du Pont de Nemours and Co.

Court: U.S. Supreme Court
Citation: 366 U.S. 316
Date: May 22, 1961
Issues: Antitrust law; Regulation of commerce

- The U.S. Supreme Court ordered that du Pont disburse its shares of GM stock to du Pont shareholders, marking the largest forced divestiture of an American company under antitrust laws since 1911.

The landmark case *United States v. E. I. du Pont de Nemours and Co.* (353 U.S. 586, 1956) grew out of a study by the Antitrust Division of the Department of Justice of the market power and actions of the General Motors Corporation (GM). That study was begun in September, 1946, by the assistant attorney general in charge of the Antitrust Division, Wendell Berge. At the time, E. I. du Pont de Nemours and Company (commonly known as du Pont) owned more than 20 percent of the equity in GM, so the investigation quickly was expanded to cover the relationship between the two companies and whether, by virtue of its partial ownership, du Pont exercised control over GM.

Shortly thereafter, the inquiry was split into two parts. Antitrust advocates feared that without the differentiation, the courts would be reluctant to require both the dissolution of GM and its divorce from du Pont. To compel production of documents expected to be important in framing the case, a criminal action was filed and a grand jury empaneled in August, 1948, to study the interrelationships among du Pont, GM, United States Rubber Company (USR), and several other companies. When the government was unable to obtain an indictment from the grand jury, it immediately filed a civil action charging that Du Pont's ownership of large blocks of stock in GM and USR gave it de facto control of the companies. The government charged that dealings among the companies were in restraint of trade, thus violating sections 1 and 2 of the Sherman Antitrust Act and section 7 of the Clayton Antitrust Act, as amended by the Celler-Kefauver Act of 1950.

Background to the Case

The root of the case stretched back to a number of du Pont actions, some occurring before World War I. In an effort to diversify, brought on by the decision of the U.S. government to produce its own smokeless powder, du Pont sought alternative uses for its smokeless-powder plants. Additionally, on the advice of company treasurer John Jakob Raskob to its president, Pierre du Pont, the company embarked on an acquisition spree, purchasing entities that manufactured artificial leather, celluloid, rubber-coated fabrics, paints, and varnish. In 1917, du Pont made its first investment in GM, and by 1920 it owned almost 24 percent of the stock in GM.

Many members of the du Pont clan personally invested in the automaker. Including their interests and those of several du Pont trusts along with those of the corporation, the percentage of GM stock owned by du Pont interests rose as high as 38 percent. Despite the fact that beginning in 1923 several family members and the du Pont company began to sell off small portions of the automaker's stock, industry pundits expected that, in the future, GM would be absorbed into du Pont. During the 1920's, members of the du Pont family or its corporation made many other investments, including the purchase of large blocks of stock in United States Steel Corporation (U.S. Steel) and USR.

When the du Pont holdings in U.S. Steel attracted the attention of the Department of Justice's Antitrust Division, they were quickly liquidated. The investments in USR were made only after careful study and with the understanding that the company, while financially weak, was probably the most advanced in the development of a highly productive and disease-resistant rubber tree. There is no question that the family expected that at some time in the future the company would be merged into du Pont. In the meantime, according to papers filed by the government in the case, the resultant interrelationships among du Pont, GM, and USR allegedly obtained favored treatment for GM in tire purchasing and guaranteed USR a market for a large percentage of its output.

In December, 1954, Judge Walter J. LaBuy of the District Court for the Northern District of Illinois found that the defendants were not guilty. In line with its already-well-enunciated, strict antitrust enforcement policy, the Justice Department appealed the decision to the Supreme Court. In June, 1957, the Court reversed the determination, finding that the government had proved a violation of section 7 of the Clayton Act, noting that "[t]he test of a violation is whether, at the time of suit, there is any reasonable possibility that the stock acquisition may lead to a restraint of commerce or tend to create a monopoly."

The 1956 Case

In 1956, the Court had used a wide definition of a market in the du Pont cellophane case. It had accepted the du Pont argument that various packaging products were substitutes and that the market included all of them, thus lowering du Pont's overall percentage share of the market from what it would have been if cellophane wrap had been considered to be a separate market. The Court now narrowed the definition of a market, finding that automotive finishes and fabrics had sufficient peculiar characteristics and uses to differentiate them from other finishes and fabrics, thus creating a distinct line of commerce within the meaning of the Clayton Act. This increased du Pont and GM's shares of the market and made them more vulnerable to adverse antitrust rulings.

The case was remanded to the lower court to determine an appropriate remedy, with the government proposing that du Pont's GM shares be distributed directly to du Pont stockholders. The defendants proposed transferring only the voting rights associated with the GM stock while keeping the rest of the rights accorded to shareholders, such as the right to dispose of the shares at any time deemed propitious. This was referred to as the "pass-through option."

The Internal Revenue Service ruled that shares disbursed according to the government's plan would be treated as income and thus taxable at a rate, depending on the filer's overall income, ranging from 20 to 91 percent. The income would also be taxable by states. Judge LaBuy opted for the "pass-through option," ruling that the government plan would be "harsh and punitive" because many du Pont shareholders would have to sell their GM shares to pay a tax bill on profits generated from making an undesired sale of securities. This would affect not only the sellers but also thousands of other General Motors investors.

The government had the right to appeal the arrangement, but few believed that it would, especially since the specter of the presidential election loomed large and any other solution would negatively affect hundreds of thousands of shareholders. Nevertheless, early in 1960 the government announced that it would file an appeal. In May, the Supreme Court granted the government's petition for *certiorari*, indicating that it would hear the appeal. The market values of all the equities involved reacted negatively to the decision, illustrating that the government action was unexpected.

On May 22, 1961, the Court, by a 4-3 vote, issued its opinion accepting the government's argument and directing divestiture. About sixty-three million GM shares were in question, valued at the time at about $3.5 billion. It was generally agreed that a single massive sale would disrupt the market in GM stock; thus, it was expected that the shares would have to be issued to du Pont shareholders on a pro rata basis. Even according to this scenario, the receipts would be taxable immediately. Responding to the cries of his constituents, Republican senator J. Allen Frear of Delaware convinced Congress to pass a statute providing that, for tax purposes, the market value of GM shares received would be treated as "return of capital." Income tax exposure thus would be postponed for du Pont shareholders as long as they continued to own the shares, provided that the value of the shares received did not exceed the original cost of their du Pont equity.

The new statute directly affected the divestiture timetable as directed by the Court. Originally, in an attempt to lessen the tax impact, the government had asked that the divestiture take place over a span of ten years. With the legislation, the shares were to be distributed within a space of three years, with the du Pont personal and trust holdings being divested over a slightly longer time span. As finally arranged, each du Pont shareholder received three disbursements in three different years. For each du Pont share owned, .50 of a GM share was paid on July 9, 1962; .36 of a share was paid on January 6, 1964; and .50 of a share was paid on January 4, 1965.

Significance

Even though the breakup of GM—the original intent of the antitrust action—was not accomplished, the du Pont-General Motors case is significant because, at the time, it produced the largest divestiture since the breakup of the Standard Oil Company in 1911. The suit against du Pont was filed on the eve of the 1948 presidential election, and its political intent was readily visible to all but the most naïve. First, it improved the antitrust record of the incumbent administration. Second, the Republicans were heavily favored to win and were expected to drop the action, thus providing Democrats with fuel for their claim that their opponents were "soft on big business."

The action is a vivid illustration of the dedication of the Dwight D. Eisenhower administration to a vigorous antitrust enforcement policy. That administration's first secretary of defense was Charles E. Wilson, a former president of General Motors. He is often misquoted as stating, "what is good for General Motors is good for the country"; he actually said in his confirmation hearings before the Senate that "I had always thought that what was good for the country was good for General Motors and vice versa."

There was much partisan rhetoric to the effect that the Republican administration was business oriented and soft on antitrust, but the record in this case alone refutes the latter charge. Attorney General Herbert Brownell, Jr., and his successor, William P. Rogers, chose persons to run the Antitrust Division who were dedicated to vigorous enforcement. The case could have been dropped after the defeat on the district court level, but it was not; the determined stance concerning the divestiture and disbursement of the GM stock, ignoring the political calendar and the interests of the Republican Party's natural constituency, was not required to blunt partisan criticism. Eisenhower administration activism kept the case in the courts.

In terms of the development of legal precedent, the case is little more than an unimportant footnote in the history of Clayton Act enforcement. Less than two years after the filing, the Celler-Kefauver Amendment altered section 7 of the Clayton Act to strengthen its prohibitions. Although the old statute was given a new and much broader interpretation as a result of the case, the precedent has never since been used. Over the next few years, only one other acquisition was investigated in which the precedent could have been cited: the du Pont acquisition of the Remington Arms Company. Although the Antitrust Division prepared a complaint, it was never filed, probably in reaction to the possible cry of the unfairness of applying the precedent again to du Pont before having used it in connection with actions against other companies.

The Supreme Court decisions in the case fit into a pattern of vigorous antitrust enforcement begun in the 1950's and continued through the late 1960's. It was during this period that the government won an unprecedented string of victories in the highest court, extending the interpretation of section 7 of the Clayton Act as amended in 1950. Key actions, many begun during the Eisenhower era and others initiated during the John F. Kennedy and Lyndon B. Johnson years, all were decided in favor of the government. These included opposition to takeovers by Brown Shoe Company, Philadelphia National Bank, and Vons Grocery and to a joint venture of Pennsalt Chemicals Corporation and Olin Mathieson Chemicals Corporation.

Theodore P. Kovaleff

Further Reading

Areeda, Phillip, Louis Kaplow, and Aaron Edlin. *Antitrust Analysis: Problems, Text, Cases.* 6th ed. New York: Aspen, 2004. Textbook containing case studies of the major antitrust cases in American history. Bibliographic references and index.

Chandler, Alfred D., Jr., and Stephen Salsbury. *Pierre S. Du Pont and the Making of the Modern Corporation.* New York: Harper & Row, 1971. A corporate history, particularly informative on the company's diversification and the suit.

Dirlam, Joel B., and I. M. Stelzer. "Du Pont-General Motors Decision: In the Antitrust Grain." *Columbia Law Review* 58 (September, 1958): 24-43. Views the decision as being within the confines of traditional antitrust policy.

Hylton, Keith N. *Antitrust Law: Economic Theory and Common Law Evolution.* New York: Cambridge University Press, 2003. Comprehensive text on economic principles behind antitrust and the development of American antitrust law over more than one hundred years of litigation. Includes a chapter on the Alcoa case. Bibliographic references and index.

Kinnane, Adrian. *DuPont: From the Banks of the Brandywine to Miracles of Science.* Wilmington, Del.: E. I. du Pont de Nemours, 2002. Official corporate history of du Pont, touting the corporation's accomplishments in the fields both of science and of business. Bibliographic references and index.

Kovaleff, Theodore Philip. *Business and Government During the Eisenhower Administration.* Athens: Ohio University Press, 1980. Includes a chapter that details the various antitrust actions filed against the chemical giant in the post-World War II era.

_____. "Divorce American Style: The Du Pont-General Motors Case." *Delaware History* 18 (Spring/Summer, 1978): 28-42. Uses the papers of both the du Ponts and the Antitrust Division to detail the intricacies of the case.

Stocking, George W. "The Du Pont-GM Case and the Sherman Act." *Virginia Law Review* 44 (January, 1959): 1-40. Stocking agrees with the outcome but believes that it was incorrectly based. Rather than violating section 7 of the Clayton Act, he suggests that du Pont's acquisition of GM shares was a restraint of trade, thus violating sections 1 and 2 of the Sherman Act.

"Symposium—The Du Pont-General Motors Decision: The Merger Problem in a New Perspective." *Georgetown Law Journal* 46 (Summer, 1958): 561-700. Participants included Irston R. Barnes, John Blair, Bruce Bromley, Walton Hamilton, William L. McGovern, and Blackwell Smith. Various issues involved in the decision are discussed from a legal perspective.

See also *Federal Trade Commission v. Procter & Gamble Co.*; *United States v. Paramount Pictures, Inc.*; *United States v. United States Steel Corp.*

UNITED STATES V. EICHMAN

Court: U.S. Supreme Court
Citation: 496 U.S. 310
Date: June 11, 1990
Issues: First Amendment guarantees; Symbolic speech

• The U.S. Supreme Court reaffirmed its 1989 decision that flag burning was a constitutionally protected form of free speech.

The Supreme Court, by a 5-4 majority, struck down the 1989 Flag Protection Act, passed by Congress to void the Court's ruling in *Texas v. Johnson* (1989), which overturned a Texas flag-burning statute. Justice William J. Brennan, Jr., in the opinion for the Court, suggested that the justices would probably regard virtually any law directed at forms of flag desecration as unconstitutional because such laws would inevitably imply governmental disapproval of the message inherent in flag burning.

In *Johnson*, the Court declared a Texas statute unconstitutional because it explicitly stated that the desecration must be done to "offend" someone. This provision flew in the face of the cardinal tenet of allowable time, place, and manner regulations—namely, that they may not be used by officials who do not like the ideas expressed. Congress sought to circumvent the *Johnson* holding by carefully avoiding the expression-of-ideas question, but the Court found that the government's purpose was clearly the suppression of ideas and, therefore, that the strict scrutiny test needed to be applied to the congressional enactment. The Court found the 1989 federal law could not pass such a strict test. Justices William H. Rehnquist, Byron R. White, John Paul Stevens, and Sandra Day O'Connor dissented, arguing that there were so many ways that demonstrators could exercise their First Amendment rights that laws preventing flag desecration were not a real infringement on their rights.

Richard L. Wilson

Further Reading

Fridell, Ron. *U.S. v. Eichman: Flag-Burning and Free Speech.* Tarrytown, N.Y.: Marshall Cavendish Benchmark, 2009. Part of its publisher's Supreme Court Milestones series designed for young-adult readers, this volume offers an accessible history and analysis of the *Eichman* case that examines opposing sides in the case, the people involved, and the case's lasting impact. Includes bibliography and index.

See also *Brandenburg v. Ohio; Gitlow v. New York; Schenck v. United States; Texas v. Johnson; Tinker v. Des Moines Independent Community School District; United States v. O'Brien; Whitney v. California.*

===

UNITED STATES V. GUEST

Court: U.S. Supreme Court
Citation: 383 U.S. 745
Date: March 28, 1966
Issues: Civil rights and liberties; Right to travel; States' rights

• The U.S. Supreme Court restricted the state-action doctrine when it gave a broad reading to a Reconstruction-era statute that criminalized conspiracies to interfere with rights "secured" by the U.S. Constitution.

In the southern states during the 1960's, it was almost impossible to convict white citizens who used violence against civil rights activists. After defendants in a Georgia trial were found not guilty of murdering black army officer Lemuel Penn, a federal grand jury indicted them on several charges, including conspiracy to deprive people of the right to interstate travel and conspiracy in making false reports to the police in order to intimidate African Americans from seeking equal utilization of public facilities. A federal district judge dismissed the charges, ruling that the relevant statute did not encompass any Fourteenth Amendment rights that Congress had the authority to enforce.

By a 9-0 vote, the Supreme Court reversed the ruling, but the justices presented a confusing array of opinions about the reasons for the judgment. Eight of the justices voted to uphold the portion of the indictment charging interference with interstate travel. Six of the justices, moreover, endorsed the view that Congress had the authority to punish all conspiracies—with or without state action—to interfere with Fourteenth Amendment rights. Therefore, the justices came close to rejecting the state-action doctrine as articulated in the *Civil Rights Cases* (1883).

The *Guest* decision was soon overshadowed by *Jones v. Alfred H. Mayer Co.* (1968), which recognized Congress's power to legislate against private racial discrimination under the Thirteenth Amendment.

Thomas Tandy Lewis

See also *Jones v. Alfred H. Mayer Co.*; *Moose Lodge v. Irvis*; *United States v. Cruikshank.*

UNITED STATES V. HUDSON AND GOODWIN

Court: U.S. Supreme Court
Citation: 11 U.S. 32
Date: February 13, 1812
Issues: Common law

- The U.S. Supreme Court ended a long-standing dispute by disavowing the existence of a federal common law for crimes.

For ten years, the Democratic Republicans and the Federalists had disagreed over whether there was a federal common law for criminal offenses. Barzillai Hudson and George Goodwin, who published a report linking Thomas Jefferson and Napoleon Bonaparte, were indicted for common-law seditious libel in federal court. The Democratic Republicans believed that the branches of the federal government held only the powers specifically granted by the Constitution and, therefore, federal courts did not have the power to enforce common-law crimes. The Court, on which Democratic Republican appointees were in the majority, dismissed the indictments, resolving the dispute. The case remains a valid holding.

Richard L. Wilson

See also *Erie Railroad Co. v. Tompkins; Johnson v. Louisiana; Tennessee v. Garner.*

UNITED STATES V. KAGAMA

Court: U.S. Supreme Court
Citation: 118 U.S. 375
Date: May 10, 1886
Issues: Native American sovereignty

- The U.S. Supreme Court ruled that Congress had the power to apply federal criminal statutes to Native Americans within tribal lands.

In *Ex parte Crow Dog* (1883), the Supreme Court decided that tribal law applied to crimes committed by Native Americans in Indian country. Congress reacted by passing the Major Crimes Act in 1885, giving federal courts authority over seven major crimes, including murder, committed by Native Americans against Native Americans. The Court unanimously upheld the statute, applying the principles laid down by Chief Justice John Marshall in *Worcester v. Georgia* (1832) to the federal criminal statutes. The Court found that the *Worcester* principles meant that protection of Native Americans was a national obligation and sustained Congress's power to legislate. Although the Court found the common-law guardian-ward notion from *Worcester* appropriate, Congress's authority derived from the Constitution. *Worcester* continues to be cited as appropriate law governing Native American affairs.

Richard L. Wilson

See also *California v. Cabazon Band of Mission Indians; Cherokee Cases; Ex parte Crow Dog; Johnson and Graham's Lessee v. McIntosh; Lone Wolf v. Hitchcock; Santa Clara Pueblo v. Martinez; Talton v. Mayes; Worcester v. Georgia.*

UNITED STATES V. LANZA

Court: U.S. Supreme Court
Citation: 260 U.S. 377
Date: December 11, 1922
Issues: Double jeopardy

- The U.S. Supreme Court, in allowing a bootlegger to be tried in both state and federal court, restricted the protection against double jeopardy.

The Supreme Court unanimously upheld the second indictment of a bootlegger who was tried first in state court for violating the Washington State prohibition law and then charged in federal court for violating the 1919 Volstead Act, using the same evidence. A federal district court blocked trial on the federal charges, but the Supreme Court overturned its decision, arguing that the two levels acted independently of each other. Although *Lanza* remains valid law, this practice has been criticized as the kind of double jeopardy presumably prohibited by the Fifth Amendment.

Richard L. Wilson

See also *Benton v. Maryland*; *Kansas v. Hendricks*; *Palko v. Connecticut*; *United States v. Ursery*.

United States v. Leon

Court: U.S. Supreme Court
Citation: 468 U.S. 897
Date: July 5, 1984
Issues: Evidence

• The U.S. Supreme Court ruled that the Fourth Amendment did not prohibit the admission of criminal evidence obtained from a search conducted pursuant to a warrant issued by a neutral and detached magistrate even if the warrant was ultimately found invalid through no fault of the police officers conducting the search.

Based on an affidavit referring to a confidential informant and various police observations, a state judge issued a search warrant authorizing police officers to search the residences of Alberto Leon and two other suspects. In the ensuing search, the police found large quantities of illegal drugs. At the trial, however, the court determined that the affidavit was insufficient to establish probable cause, and the evidence was thrown out.

By a 6-3 vote, the Supreme Court adopted the good-faith exception, which stipulated that the exclusionary rule would not apply when the police were acting from an "objectively reasonable" belief that a search warrant is valid, even if the warrant later proves to be defective. Justice Byron R. White's majority opinion warned of the social costs of excessive interference with the criminal justice system's "truth-finding function," and he insisted that the exclusionary rule was designed only as a deterrent to police misconduct, not to prevent judicial errors. In dissent, Justice William J. Brennan, Jr., argued that the Fourth Amendment requires the suppression of unconstitutionally seized evidence without any regard to its deterrent effect.

Although the *Leon* ruling was rather narrow, the Court subsequently extended the conditions for applying the good-faith exception to the exclusionary rule. In *Illinois v. Krull* (1987), a 5-4 majority of the justices upheld the admission of evidence obtained in a warrantless search authorized by a statute that was later found unconstitutional. In *Arizona v. Evans* (1995), a 7-2 majority allowed the use of evidence found in a search resulting from police reliance on mistaken court records of outstanding arrest warrants.

Thomas Tandy Lewis

See also *Illinois v. Krull; Mapp v. Ohio; Massachusetts v. Sheppard.*

UNITED STATES V. LOPEZ

Court: U.S. Supreme Court
Citation: 514 U.S. 549
Date: April 26, 1995
Issues: Interstate commerce; Regulation of commerce; Right to bear arms

• The U.S. Supreme Court held that a federal statute was unconstitutional because Congress had overstepped its authority to regulate interstate commerce.

In 1990 Congress passed the Gun-Free School Zones Act, making it a federal crime to possess a gun within one thousand feet of a school. After Alfonso Lopez, Jr., a high school student in Texas, was arrested for taking a handgun to school, he was tried under federal law because the federal penalties were greater than those under state law. A federal court of appeals found that the federal statute violated the Tenth Amendment. Most observers expected the Supreme Court to reverse the judgment because the Court in *Garcia v. San Antonio Metropolitan Transit Authority* (1985) had held that the scope of federal authority to regulate commerce was a political question to be decided by the political process rather than by the Courts.

By a 5-4 vote, however, the Court upheld the ruling. Chief Justice William H. Rehnquist's majority opinion reasoned that possession of guns near a school had nothing to do with interstate commerce and that such an issue is traditionally a concern of local police power. As a principle, he wrote that Congress could regulate only "those activities that have a substantial relationship to interstate commerce."

The *Lopez* decision appeared to mark a renaissance for the principle of dual sovereignty, which had largely been abandoned following *Carter v. Carter Coal Co.* (1936). It was not clear how far the trend would go, but the Court in *Printz v. United States* (1997) held that Congress had no power to force states to enforce federal regulations absent a particular constitutional authorization.

Thomas Tandy Lewis

See also *Carter v. Carter Coal Co.*; *Garcia v. San Antonio Metropolitan Transit Authority*; *Gibbons v. Ogden*; *Gonzales v. Raich*; *Hammer v. Dagenhart*; *McCulloch v. Maryland*; *National League of Cities v. Usery*; *Printz v. United States*; *United States v. Darby Lumber Co.*

UNITED STATES V. LOVETT

Court: U.S. Supreme Court
Citation: 238 U.S. 303
Date: June 3, 1946
Issues: Antigovernment subversion; Labor law

• The U.S. Supreme Court held that the portion of a federal statute prohibiting three named federal employees from receiving governmental compensation was an unconstitutional bill of attainder.

During the early period of the Cold War, a rider to an appropriations statute denied compensation for three persons branded as "subversives" by the House Un-American Activities Committee. Speaking for an 8-0 majority, Justice Hugo L. Black wrote that a legislative act that inflicts punishment on either particular individuals or "easily ascertainable members of a group" without a judicial trial is a bill of attainder.

Expanding on the *Lovett* decision, the Supreme Court in *United States v. Brown* (1950) struck down a statute that prohibited Communist Party members from serving as officers of trade unions because the measure punished "easily ascertainable members of a group." In *Nixon v. Administrator of General Services* (1977), however, the Court rejected former president Richard M. Nixon's contention that a statute giving the general services administration control over his presidential papers and recordings was a bill of attainder.

Thomas Tandy Lewis

See also *Cummings v. Missouri; Hurtado v. California; Nixon v. Administrator of General Services.*

UNITED STATES V. NIXON

Court: U.S. Supreme Court
Citation: 418 U.S. 683
Date: July 24, 1974
Issues: Presidential powers

• The U.S. Supreme Court's ruling in this case played a key role in causing President Richard M. Nixon to resign from office.

Chief Justice Warren E. Burger wrote the unanimous opinion ordering the release of tapes possibly damaging to President Richard M. Nixon. Justice William H. Rehnquist declined to participate, saying he had been a former Justice Department official under Nixon, but the other Nixon appointees, Justices Harry A. Blackmun and Lewis F. Powell, Jr., as well as Burger, participated. As important as this decision was to Nixon, three of his own appointees ruled against him.

In response to questions regarding the burglary of the Democratic Party National Headquarters in the Watergate building, Nixon had contradicted his aides as to his level of involvement in the scandal. When it was revealed that Nixon routinely taped conversations in his office, the Watergate investigators used presidential appointment logs to isolate tapes that they wished to hear. Nixon refused to release the tapes, and the presumably independent special prosecutor Archibald Cox sued to force Nixon to produce them. Nixon fired Cox, but his own two top Justice Department officials resigned before he could force them to remove Cox from office. Newly appointed special prosecutor Leon Jaworski renewed the pursuit for the tapes, and the Supreme Court ruled that they must be released.

Included among the tapes was a conversation so damning that it has been called the "smoking gun" that led to Nixon's resignation just three weeks later. In his opinion, Burger emphasized that the Court must be deferential to the presidency; but this ruling, by concluding that executive privilege was conditional, nonetheless limited the previous presumption that executive privilege was absolute.

Richard L. Wilson

Further Reading

Stefoff, Rebecca. *U.S. v. Nixon: The Limits of Presidential Privilege.* Tarrytown, N.Y.: Marshall Cavendish Benchmark, 2009. Part of its publisher's Supreme Court Milestones series designed for young-adult readers, this volume offers an accessible history and analysis of *United States v. Nixon* that examines opposing sides in the case, the people involved, and the case's lasting impact. Includes bibliography and index.

See also *Butz v. Economou; Dames and Moore v. Regan; Humphrey's Executor v. United States; McCulloch v. Maryland; Martin v. Mott; Mississippi v. Johnson; Nixon v. Administrator of General Services; United States v. Curtiss-Wright Export Corp.; Youngstown Sheet and Tube Co. v. Sawyer.*

===

UNITED STATES V. O'BRIEN

Court: U.S. Supreme Court
Citation: 391 U.S. 367
Date: May 27, 1968
Issues: Symbolic speech

• The U.S. Supreme Court's ruling limited the concept of symbolic speech and affirmed the distinction between thought and action in expression cases.

During the Vietnam War, some students, including David O'Brien, protested the war by burning their draft cards (selective service registration certificates). O'Brien, convicted for destroying a document he was required to keep, challenged the conviction, claiming his action was symbolic speech. By a 7-1 vote, the Supreme Court upheld O'Brien's conviction. In the opinion for the Court, Chief Justice Earl Warren wrote that the government has a substantial interest in continuing the selective service system. The Court stated that there were limits to how far it would extend symbolic speech protections. One unprotected area involved violations of otherwise valid laws. Although the Court believed that the government's right to maintain a selective service system outweighed the incidental limitation on free speech, Justice William O. Douglas dissented on free speech grounds.

Richard L. Wilson

See also *Barnes v. Glen Theatre, Inc.*; *Brandenburg v. Ohio*; *Cohen v. California*; *Schenck v. United States*; *Texas v. Johnson*; *Tinker v. Des Moines Independent Community School District*; *Whitney v. California.*

UNITED STATES V. PARAMOUNT PICTURES, INC.

Court: U.S. Supreme Court
Citation: 334 U.S. 131
Date: May 3, 1948
Issues: Antitrust law; Regulation of commerce

• The U.S. Supreme Court determined that it was a violation of antitrust laws for a film studio to own a chain of movie theaters. The major studios were therefore ordered to divest themselves of the theaters they owned.

During the 1930's, the motion-picture industry was dominated by five major studios—Radio-Keith-Orpheum (RKO), Warner Bros., Paramount, Loews, and Twentieth Century-Fox—that produced, distributed, and exhibited motion pictures. Three other minor firms—Columbia, United Artists, and Universal—produced and distributed significant numbers of motion pictures but did not own any theaters. The five major studios owned theaters accounting for about 45 percent of U.S. film rentals; they owned 70 percent of first-run theaters in cities with populations larger than 100,000 and 60 percent in cities with populations between 25,000 and 100,000. The major studios' theaters were operated by franchise agreements in which film-rental charges were assessed as a percentage of overall receipts. The contracts were detailed and provided circuits (groups of theaters) with options that were not granted to independent theaters.

Distribution of films to independent exhibitors was, nevertheless, an important activity if the profit from a film was to be maximized. Since distributors leased rather than sold films, a film distributor had to be concerned not only with existing leases but also with scheduling future leases. Typically, a film was publicized; distributed to large, high-gross theaters for a "run"; and then distributed to smaller, low-gross theaters (known as "second-run theaters") for additional runs. Because some days of the week generated larger attendance than others and because transportation of films was a time-consuming, costly process, efficient scheduling of all the runs of a given film at different theaters was a critical activity.

Monopolistic Practices

The five major and three minor studios developed numerous business practices to maximize the profits they realized through film distribution. These included specifying admission prices to be charged by the theater; leasing packages of films on an all-or-nothing basis, a practice known as "block-booking"; providing the exhibitor of a film with a promise not to show the film at another theater in the same market for a stipulated period of time, a practice known as "clearance"; and joint operation of theaters in a given market area or a pooling of their revenues. Theater owners complained regularly to the Justice Department and the Federal Trade Commission (FTC) that these business practices excluded entrants into the production and distribution of films and provided the studios with monopoly power in film exhibition.

During the early 1930's, the Justice Department filed numerous antitrust suits against firms in the motion-picture industry, alleging the use of monopolistic contracting practices in particular markets. After a five-year investigation of monopolistic practices in the motion-picture industry, the department decided to use a more systematic approach. In July, 1938, the Justice Department filed an antitrust suit against the eight largest integrated motion-picture firms. The suit alleged a conspiracy to fix prices in first-run theaters in major cities and to restrict the access of independent distributors to first-run films produced by the eight producers charged in the suit. The complaint asked that production and distribution be divorced from exhibition of films.

The government and the five major studios reached a voluntary agreement, in which the Justice Department issued a consent decree, on November 20, 1940. The consent decree—a judicially sanctioned agreement between two parties—prohibited block-booking of more than five feature films, licensing films without first showing them to exhibitors (a practice known as "blind-booking"), or tying the lease of a short film to the lease of a feature film. It also forbade the studios from acquiring substantial numbers of new theaters. It was stipulated that conflicts over clearances were to be resolved by independent arbitrators.

Lower Court Rulings

Complaints from independent exhibitors continued after the consent decree, and in August, 1944, the government asked the studios if they would agree to amend the consent decree to mandate that they sell their theaters. The studios rejected the proposed breakup of their vertically integrated firms, and the government responded by reviving the 1938 antitrust case. The eight different cases resulting from this decision were consolidated as *United States v. Paramount Pictures, Inc.* They were tried before a three-judge panel of the U.S. District Court for the Southern District of New York beginning on October 8, 1945. Augustus N. Hand—a judge on the U.S. Court of Appeals for the Second Circuit who had previously sat on the district court—was temporarily reassigned to the district court to head the panel. On June 11, 1946, Hand issued the opinion of the court. The panel had decided that the studios had not monopolized the production of motion pictures. The court also found, however, that the distribution practices of the five major studios did violate the Sherman Antitrust Act.

Once this opinion was issued, the trial continued to a judgment phase, in which the court heard arguments and solicited proposals from all parties as to the appropriate remedy for the studios' distribution monopoly. The district court's final ruling was issued on January 22, 1947. It ordered both the major and the minor studios to cease practices such as block-booking, dictating minimum ticket prices, requiring "arbitrary" runs and clearances, making "formula deals" that tied a film's rental fee to a percentage of its national gross revenues, and pooling the management of allegedly competing theaters. The court also ordered the major studios to institute competitive bidding in film distribution.

The Supreme Court Ruling

Both sides appealed the case to the U.S. Supreme Court, and on May 3, 1948, the Court, by a 7-1 vote, affirmed portions of the district court's decision and reversed other portions of the decision. Writing for the Court, Justice William O. Douglas condemned many of the trade practices employed by the studios and observed that small independent operators "have been the victim of the massed purchasing power of the larger units in the industry." Douglas rejected, however, the district court's proposed remedy for the violations, that film distribution be conducted by competitive bidding. He argued that firms with the deepest pockets would possess too large an advantage and noted practical difficulties with such auctions. The Court then remanded the case back to the district court for reconsideration of the appropriate remedy for the violations. Justice Felix Frankfurter dissented in part, claiming that, because the lower court had read thousands of pages of evidence that the high court had not seen, the Court should not presume to second guess the district court's judgment.

In 1949, Judge Hand ruled for the district court that divestiture by the studios of their exhibition businesses was necessary to restore competition in the industry. Between 1948 and 1953, four of the five major studios divested their exhibitor subsidiaries. Divestiture of theaters by Loew's was delayed by arguments over the allocation of its debt between the two new production and exhibition companies, but its spin-off of theaters was completed in 1959.

Significance

It is particularly difficult to judge the impact of the *Paramount* case because of the other massive changes in the film industry that occurred in the post-World War II period. The most obvious factor affecting the motion picture industry was the rise of a new and powerful competitor in the entertainment business: television. Between 1946 and 1953, average weekly attendance at film theaters fell from eighty-two million to forty-six million people. Exhibitor net income fell from $325 million to $46 million over the same period. Between 1946 and 1955, consumers reduced the share of their income devoted to theater tickets and concessions by one-half, to 0.5 percent. The number of theaters remained roughly constant, at about nineteen thousand, between 1946 and 1955, but about four thousand indoor theaters were forced to close as a result of competition from a similar number of new drive-in theaters. The drive-ins were often operated by new entrepreneurs, and owners of indoor theaters complained that these theaters were receiving the business they had expected to receive after the *Paramount* decisions.

Television was not the only reason for the film industry's decline. The postwar baby boom left young parents with less leisure time. Hiring babysitters to care for young children raised the cost of seeing movies substantially. Innovations in other entertainment industries, such as nighttime baseball games, created new diversions during a time when people traditionally viewed movies. Movement to the suburbs also meant that individuals spent more time commuting and working on their homes, leaving less time for motion pictures.

The rise of television also changed the product that consumers demanded from Hollywood. Much of the type of entertainment provided by B-films was now provided on a daily basis by network television. To encourage parents to take time away from their busy lives to see a film, the experience had to represent a distinct improvement over two hours of television. Hollywood responded by producing more quality motion pictures, with larger budgets.

The move away from B-films may help explain why admission prices increased at the same time that overall attendance was falling. Individuals were willing to pay more to see a film if the average quality was expected to be higher. The average price of a film at an indoor theater rose from 36 cents in 1948 to $1.24 in 1967, an increase substantially greater than the increase in the consumer price index. The higher prices of films may also have resulted from the closure of competing theaters in some market areas, increased distribution costs brought about by changes in distribution practices mandated by the *Paramount* case, or increased markups imposed by newly independent exhibitors who could set their own ticket prices.

The *Paramount* case also subjected the defendants to a large number of private antitrust suits. Federal courts allowed independent exhibitors to use the *Paramount* decision as evidence that the studios had conspired to violate antitrust laws prior to 1948. An exhibitor needed only to prove that it had been harmed by the conspiracy and show the extent of its damages. Damages in private antitrust suits were trebled, representing substantial potential liabilities for the studios. Film historian Simon Whitney reported that total claims in these private antitrust suits amounted to $600 million but that most claims were ultimately settled at a deep discount.

Another major postwar trend in the motion-picture industry was the decline in the number of foreign and domestic feature films released. From an average of 476 annual releases between 1937 and 1942, the number of releases declined to 295 in 1954 and 283 in 1955. Most of the decline in output was concentrated among the eight largest producers, and much of it was related to the decline in demand for motion-picture entertainment.

Some exhibitors attributed the "product shortage" to the forced sale by the five major studios of their exhibitor subsidiaries. It was alleged that the studios had less of an interest in filling theater screens, since they no longer owned those screens. Ironically, during the early 1950's a trade association of exhibitors (Theater Owners of America) attempted to contract with independent producers to ensure a steady flow of films. In 1955, a second trade association of exhibitors (Allied States Association of Motion Picture Exhibitors) called upon the Justice Department to allow the newly independent exhibitor firms to begin producing their own films.

The Justice Department had argued in the *Paramount* case that the business practices of the five major studios had acted to prevent independent producers from gaining access to theaters. If the decision in fact restored competition to the industry, one would likely observe more independent firms entering the production business. Entrance may well have been stymied by the decline in the film industry after the war. Nevertheless, it is interesting to observe that after the major-studio divestitures, independent firms produced a smaller proportion of domestic feature films. Between 1942 and 1945, independents produced 31 percent of domestic motion picture releases; between 1952 and 1955, independents produced only 21 percent of the total. In addition, over the same period, independents distributed a smaller proportion of foreign feature films.

After the 1950's, it became much more difficult to make meaningful comparisons. By 1960, the studio system that had been in place for more than forty years was coming to an end. Studios ceased to be self-contained entities in which actors, writers, directors, and all other key occupations were under contract. As the nature of film production changed, its relation to distribution changed as well.

Sumner J. La Croix

Further Reading

Adams, Walter, and James W. Brock, eds. *The Structure of American Industry.* 11th ed. Upper Saddle River, N.J.: Pearson/Prentice Hall, 2005. Presents the history, structure, and economics of twelve major American industries. Contains a thoughtful chapter by Barry Litman analyzing the structure, conduct, and performance of the motion picture industry.

Balio, Tino, ed. *The American Film Industry.* Rev. ed. Madison: University of Wisconsin Press, 1985. An excellent review of the film industry's development, including discussions of the industry's early days, its development into an oligopoly during the 1930's, and its reorganization after World War II. Contains a chapter by Michael Conant analyzing the impact of the *Paramount* case on the motion-picture industry.

Blair, Roger, and David Kaserman. *Antitrust Economics.* 2d ed. New York: Oxford University Press, 2008. Uses fundamental principles of economics to analyze major issues in antitrust law. Provides an assessment of numerous controversial business practices and presents original analysis of important antitrust cases. Chapters 11-16 provide a careful analysis of the business practices that were attacked by the Justice Department in the *Paramount* case.

Calvani, Terry, and John Siegfried. *Economic Analysis and Antitrust Law.* 2d ed. Boston: Little, Brown, 1988. Presents short excerpts from many important articles by economists analyzing the impact and efficiency of antitrust law. Chapter 4 provides a general analysis of the business practices that the Justice Department attacked in the *Paramount* case.

Hylton, Keith N. *Antitrust Law: Economic Theory and Common Law Evolution.* New York: Cambridge University Press, 2003. Comprehensive text on economic principles behind antitrust and the development of American antitrust law over more than one hundred years of litigation. Includes a chapter on the Alcoa case. Bibliographic references and index.

Kindem, Gorham, ed. *The American Movie Industry: The Business of Motion Pictures.* Carbondale: Southern Illinois University Press, 1982. Presents the views of established scholars from several fields on the history, marketing strategies, product innovations, industry structure, and contracting practices of the American film industry. Simon Whitney's chapter on antitrust policies and the motion-picture industry provides an excellent analysis of the *Paramount* case's impact.

Lev, Peter. *Transforming the Screen, 1950-1959.* History of the American Cinema 7. New York: Charles Scribner's Sons, 2003. Discusses the state of the motion-picture industry throughout the 1950's in painstaking detail. Contextualizes the results of the *Paramount* decision by explaining the general changes in cinema in the 1950's.

Schatz, Thomas. *Boom and Bust: American Cinema in the 1940's.* History of the American Cinema 6. Berkeley: University of California Press, 1999. Part of a definitive series on the history of the American motion-picture industry; provides a comprehensive overview of the state of the industry in the 1940's. Essential context for the *Paramount* case.

Waldman, Don E. *The Economics of Antitrust: Cases and Analysis.* Boston: Little, Brown, 1986. Waldman presents excerpts from major twentieth century antitrust cases and uses economic theory to analyze the principles used by judges to decide these cases.

See also *City of Renton v. Playtime Theaters; Erznoznik v. Jacksonville; Federal Trade Commission v. Procter & Gamble Co.; Young v. American Mini Theatres.*

UNITED STATES V. REESE

Court: U.S. Supreme Court
Citation: 92 U.S. 214
Date: March 27, 1876
Issues: Voting rights

• The U.S. Supreme Court voided part of the 1870 Enforcement Act, claiming that voting was a privilege, not a right.

Commemorative print celebrating ratification of the Fifteenth Amendment. (Library of Congress)

After refusing to accept an African American's vote, a Kentucky election official was indicted under the 1870 Enforcement Act, which enforced the voting rights provided by the Fifteenth Amendment. Chief Justice Morrison R. Waite wrote the opinion for the 8-1 majority, striking down a section of the 1870 act regarding refusal to accept a vote, on the grounds that the statute did not repeat the precise language of the Fifteenth Amendment. The Supreme Court affirmed that voting was a privilege, not a right, but held that if a state offered the privilege, it must not exclude voters on racial grounds. The Court upheld the Enforcement Act for federal elections, but by omitting state and local elections with its very narrow rulings, the Court allowed southern states to disenfranchise African Americans through poll taxes and literacy, character, and other tests.

Richard L. Wilson

See also *Davis v. Beason; Dunn v. Blumstein; Ex parte Yarbrough; South Carolina v. Katzenbach.*

UNITED STATES V. RICHARDSON

Court: U.S. Supreme Court
Citation: 418 U.S. 166
Date: June 25, 1974
Issues: Standing

• The U.S. Supreme Court made it more difficult for taxpayers to sue the government.

Plaintiff Richardson sued the United States, alleging that the law prohibiting the disclosure of Central Intelligence Agency (CIA) spending violated Article I, section 9, of the U.S. Constitution requiring publication of all public expenditures. The trial court and appellate courts reversed various parts of Richardson's suit but essentially upheld his right to sue in some form. By a 5-4 vote, the Supreme Court overturned this latter conclusion, making taxpayers' suits practically impossible. In his opinion for the Court, Chief Justice Warren E. Burger restored the basic rule that taxpayers may not sue the government unless they show direct personal harm from the government's action. Burger distinguished *Flast v. Cohen* (1968) by giving it such a narrow interpretation that it restored the basic rule of *Frothingham v. Mellon* (1923) for taxpayers' suits. Justice Potter Stewart and Thurgood Marshall wrote dissents in which they were joined by others. The thrust of the dissents was that taxpayers should be able to sue the government for failing an affirmative duty under the Constitution without having to show a personal loss.

Richard L. Wilson

See also *Bivens v. Six Unknown Named Agents; Flast v. Cohen; Frothingham v. Mellon.*

UNITED STATES V. ROBEL

Court: U.S. Supreme Court
Citation: 389 U.S. 258
Date: December 11, 1967
Issues: Antigovernment subversion; Freedom of assembly and association; Freedom of speech

• The U.S. Supreme Court, in a rare move, struck down a congressional enactment for violating the First Amendment.

The McCarran Act of 1950 required members of allegedly subversive organizations, such as the Communist Party, to register with the Subversive Activities Control Board. Communist Party member Eugene F. Robel was indicted for working at a shipyard involved in the defense industry. By a 6-2 vote, the Supreme Court overturned Robel's conviction and a section of the act. The Court argued that because the act made no distinction between active and passive members of allegedly subversive organizations, people could be found guilty by association. Chief Justice Earl Warren, in the opinion for the Court, found that the statute was overbroad in the activities it prohibited. This decision did not directly overturn *Communist Party v. Subversive Activities Control Board* (1961), but its practical effect was to render the board a nullity. Justices Byron R. White and John Marshall Harlan dissented. Justice Thurgood Marshall did not participate.

Richard L. Wilson

See also *Albertson v. Subversive Activities Control Board*; *Aptheker v. Secretary of State*; *Communist Party v. Subversive Activities Control Board*; *Dennis v. United States*; *Scales v. United States*; *Yates v. United States*.

UNITED STATES V. ROSS

Court: U.S. Supreme Court
Citation: 456 U.S. 798
Date: June 1, 1982
Issues: Police powers; Search and seizure

• Through this decision, the U.S. Supreme Court broadly increased the right of police officers to search automobiles without search warrants, so long as the searchers have probable cause.

In *Robbins v. California* (1981), the Supreme Court ruled that police officers could conduct a warrantless search of a package in an automobile only if the contents of the package were in plain view. However, in *Ross*, police conducting a search of a car trunk had opened a closed paper bag to discover that it contained heroin. Later, they also found a zippered pouch that contained cash in the trunk. A lower court denied the defendant's motion to suppress the evidence, and he was convicted of possessing heroin with intent to sell.

By a 6-3 vote, the Supreme Court largely abandoned *Robbins* and ruled that packages in automobiles could be searched without a warrant if the police had probable cause—the same standard a magistrate should use in issuing a warrant. Justice Thurgood Marshall dissented, arguing that a police officer was not trained as a magistrate and should not be given the same power as a magistrate to determine probable cause. Justice William J. Brennan, Jr., joined in the dissent, and Justice Byron R. White agreed with it.

Richard L. Wilson

See also *California v. Acevedo; Mapp v. Ohio; Maryland v. Buie; Michigan Department of State Police v. Sitz.*

UNITED STATES V. SHIPP

Court: U.S. Supreme Court
Citation: 214 U.S. 386
Date: May 24, 1909
Issues: Federalism; Incorporation doctrine

• As the only criminal trial ever conducted by the U.S. Supreme Court, this trial of a local sheriff for contempt demonstrated the Court's authority and raised the question of whether the Sixth Amendment applied to the states. The trial, however, did not appear to establish any precedents.

On January 23, 1906, a violent rape occurred in the city of Chattanooga, Tennessee. Although the evidence was weak, an African American man named Ed Johnson was convicted and sentenced to death by an all-white jury on February 11. Arguing that the trial violated the principles of due process and equal protection, Johnson's lawyer failed to obtain habeas corpus relief in the lower federal courts. He then appealed directly to the U.S. Supreme Court, where he had a personal conversation with Justice John Marshall Harlan, who persuaded his colleagues on the Court to issue a stay of execution and to schedule oral arguments for the case.

The same evening that the stay was announced, an angry mob stormed the county jail and lynched Johnson on a city bridge. There was considerable evidence that the local sheriff, Joseph Shipp, and his deputies had known that the lynching would occur but did nothing to stop it. The attorney general filed charges of criminal contempt with the clerk of the Supreme Court. Following a hearing, Justice Oliver Wendell Holmes announced that the justices unanimously agreed that the Court had jurisdiction to try Shipp and his deputies.

On February 12, 1907, the Shipp trial began in Chattanooga with the taking of evidence, and in March, 1909, the final arguments of the contending attorneys were presented before the Court in Washington, D.C. On May 24, 1909, Chief Justice Melville Fuller announced that the justices had voted six to three that the defendants were guilty. Shipp and two deputies were sentenced to three months imprisonment. Three other defendants were sentenced to terms of two months. After Shipp's prison term was completed in January,

1910, he returned to Chattanooga to an enthusiastic crowd of 10,000 supporters. In 2000, however, a county judge in Chattanooga overturned Ed Johnson's conviction and death sentence.

Thomas Tandy Lewis

See also *Betts v. Brady; Duncan v. Louisiana; Richmond Newspapers v. Virginia; Taylor v. Louisiana.*

UNITED STATES V. SOUTH-EASTERN UNDERWRITERS ASSOCIATION

Court: U.S. Supreme Court
Citation: 322 U.S. 533
Date: June 5, 1944
Issues: Judicial powers

- In this case, the U.S. Supreme Court ruled that the business of insurance companies was not interstate commerce and thus was subject to regulation solely by individual states. However, the ruling was soon superseded by a law enacted by Congress.

Beginning in the mid-nineteenth century, the Supreme Court had consistently held that insurance policies were not interstate commerce and that states were free to regulate the industry, including out-of-state companies that wrote policies in their states. However, the U.S. Justice Department sued the South-Eastern Underwriters Association for price fixing under the Sherman Antitrust Act (1890).

By a 4-3 vote, the Supreme Court found against the underwriters association. In his opinion for the Court, Justice Hugo L. Black explained away several precedential holdings, saying they were all state laws and that this case turned on a federal statute. He found that insurance companies conducting a substantial portion of their business across state lines were engaged in interstate commerce and subject to the Sherman Antitrust Act. Congress disagreed and passed the 1945 McCarren Act specifying that no congressional enactment should be interpreted as preempting state authority over insurance unless the act specifically asserted federal authority, thereby overturning the Court.

Richard L. Wilson

See also *Allgeyer v. Louisiana; O'Gorman and Young v. Hartford Fire Insurance Co.; Paul v. Virginia; Prudential Insurance Co. v. Benjamin.*

United States v. United Mine Workers

Court: U.S. Supreme Court
Citation: 330 U.S. 258
Date: March 6, 1947
Issues: Labor law

• The U.S. Supreme Court upheld congressional enactments allowing the federal courts to issue injunctions when the government was the employer.

A coal shortage resulting from failed contract negotiations between mine operators and the United Mine Workers (UMW) led President Harry S. Truman to declare an emergency, seize the mines, and order the miners back to work. When the union miners refused to work, the government got an injunction against further strikes. When the union members still did not work, the federal court fined the UMW $3.5 million and its president, John Lewis, $10,000. The union claimed the 1932 Norris-La Guardia Act prohibited the federal courts from issuing injunctions, and the government claimed the 1942 War Labor Disputes Act took precedence when the president declared an emergency. By a 7-2 vote, the Supreme Court found that the Norris-LaGuardia Act did not apply when the government was in effect the employer. Chief Justice Frederick M. Vinson wrote the majority opinion, with Justices Felix Frankfurter and Robert H. Jackson concurring only in the judgment. Justices Hugo L. Black and William O. Douglas concurred in part but dissented in part from the majority decision. Justices Frank Murphy and

Wiley B. Rutledge, Jr., dissented. The controversy led Congress to pass the 1947 Taft-Hartley Act curbing labor union powers.

Richard L. Wilson

See also *Keystone Bituminous Coal Association v. DeBenedictis; In re Neagle; Youngstown Sheet and Tube Co. v. Sawyer.*

UNITED STATES V. UNITED STATES DISTRICT COURT

Court: U.S. Supreme Court
Citation: 407 U.S. 297
Date: June 19, 1972
Issues: Search and seizure

• The U.S. Supreme Court prohibited the government from using electronic surveillance without a search warrant.

The administration of President Richard M. Nixon wanted to engage in electronic surveillance of dissident anti-Vietnam War and Civil Rights groups without having to obtain a search warrant. The government claimed that requiring warrants violated the separation-of-powers concept because it enabled the judicial branch to interfere with the executive branch, but by an 8-0 vote, the Supreme Court found the proposed activity would violate both the First and Fourth Amendments to the Constitution. Justice Lewis F. Powell, Jr., wrote the opinion for the Court, with Chief Justice Warren E. Burger and Justices William O. Douglas and Byron R. White concurring. This decision was rendered just a few days after the infamous burglary of the Democratic Party national headquarters in the Watergate complex, which clearly involved electronic surveillance equipment.

Richard L. Wilson

See also *Katz v. United States; Mapp v. Ohio; Olmstead v. United States.*

UNITED STATES V. UNITED STATES STEEL CORP.

Court: U.S. Supreme Court
Citation: 251 U.S. 417
Date: March 1, 1920
Issues: Antitrust law; Regulation of commerce

• The U.S. Supreme Court dismissed the *United States v. United States Steel Corporation* case, ruling that the defendant had not committed conduct in violation of antitrust laws despite its large share of the steel industry.

The United States Steel Corporation (U.S. Steel) was founded in 1901 as the world's first billion-dollar company. It immediately became the dominant firm in the steel industry. A decade after U.S. Steel's formation, the U.S. government challenged the firm's relative size and its leadership in industry pricing as violating the Sherman Antitrust Act. After ten years of litigation, the U.S. Supreme Court dismissed the case of *United States v. United States Steel Corporation* on March 1, 1920. The Court's decision reduced the market power of U.S. Steel by encouraging other mergers within the steel industry.

Until the mid-nineteenth century, the iron and steel industry was competitive and decentralized. In the 1870's, adoption of the Bessemer process of steelmaking, discovered in England, led to large-scale production that gradually changed the development of the structure of the steel industry. In contrast to a rapid increase in steel output, the depression of 1893-1896 resulted in a reduction of demand for steel. Consequently, the price of steel rails dropped from more than one hundred dollars per ton in 1870 to seventeen dollars per ton in 1898. A wave of merger movement took place in the industry as firms attempted to reduce competition.

One of the biggest mergers was organized by financier J. P. Morgan, who bought three major steel producers: Federal Steel, National Steel, and Carnegie Steel. In 1901, the United States Steel Corporation was formed as a trust, or holding company, of these operating firms in addition to ore mines, railroads, and ore-carrying ships. Charles M. Schwab of Carnegie Steel was made president of the company. The new trust immediately accounted for 44 percent of the nation's ingot capacity and 66 percent of steel-casting production.

An economic recession in 1907 reduced the demand for steel. Rather than cutting prices in response to the declining market, U.S. Steel's chairman of the board, Elbert Henry Gary, attempted to stabilize prices through cooperation with competitors. Through a series of well-publicized meetings, known as the Gary dinners, with many steel producers between 1907 and 1911, Gary promoted a policy of cooperation rather than competition among companies.

Gary developed a new pattern of pricing that was generally followed by other producers, a basing-point system known as the Pittsburgh-plus system. U.S. Steel began to quote steel product prices in all market areas on the basis of the Pittsburgh price plus the railroad freight rate from Pittsburgh to the market, regardless of where the products were made. U.S. Steel's policy was disseminated during the Gary dinners, and other steel producers gradually adopted the Pittsburgh-plus system. Other firms also followed U.S. Steel's list of "extras" and price charges quoted to customers.

Despite its cooperative practices with other steel producers, U.S. Steel continued to expand, acquiring seven more companies between 1902 and 1908 and constructing the world's largest steel mill at a city in Indiana named for Gary. The company's expansionary and cooperative actions soon brought public attention, notably from newspaper journalists and labor unions.

Government Antitrust Campaign

During the early twentieth century, following formation of U.S. Steel, the federal government began to prosecute trusts in sugar, oil, and tobacco for illegal monopolization. The relationship between Gary and President Theodore Roosevelt prevented an antitrust suit in 1907, when the president granted advance approval of U.S. Steel's acquisition of the Tennessee Coal, Iron, and Railroad Company. In 1911, as a result of extensive investigations of the steel industry conducted by the U.S. Bureau of Corporations and the Stanley Committee of the House of Representatives, the long-expected antitrust suit could not be avoided. Attorney General George Woodward Wickersham filed suit against U.S. Steel in October, 1911, and asked for divestiture of the corporation. In the *United States v. United States Steel Corporation* case, the Department of Justice filed suit against U.S. Steel, charging monopolization through acquisition of competing firms and price fixing with competitors, both of which constituted unreasonable restraints of trade in the steel industry and violations of the Sherman Act.

Meanwhile, in the early 1910's, successful prosecutions of other major trusts, including Standard Oil and American Tobacco, for violating antitrust law encouraged the U.S. government to wage a war against more trusts and big corporations. The passage of the Clayton Antitrust Act and the formation of the Federal Trade Commission (FTC) in 1914 further strengthened the enforcement of antitrust laws. The Clayton Act forbade specific "unfair" business practices, including price discrimination and acquisition of competing companies in order to reduce market competition.

On June 3, 1915, the U.S. Steel case was dismissed in the District Court of New Jersey. District Judge Joseph Buffington explained the decision, ruling that there was no acceptable evidence of a monopoly, unfair pricing, or monopolization by U.S. Steel in the steel market. In fact, U.S. Steel's share in the iron and steel markets had declined to about 50 percent between 1901 and 1910, while many competitors, such as Bethlehem Steel, Inland Steel, and LaBelle Steel, had grown rapidly during the period. More than eighty competitive steel manufacturers were active in the industry—hardly evidence of a monopoly.

Furthermore, the court did not find any evidence that the defendant attempted to control the supply of iron ore, as its major competitors all had sufficient iron ore supplies. Judge Buffington found the evidence contrary to claims of monopolization and trade restraints. Furthermore, the Gary dinners, which might have constituted evidence of illegal practices as conspiracy to monopolize among firms, were discontinued before the suit was brought. No competitors of U.S. Steel testified against the defendant's allegedly unreasonable business practices. Nevertheless, the federal government appealed the district court's decision to the U.S. Supreme Court.

The Supreme Court Ruling

On March 1, 1920, the Supreme Court reaffirmed the district court's decision in a 4-3 vote. Associate Justice Joseph McKenna delivered the majority opinion, which was similar to that of Buffington. McKenna explained that U.S. Steel was not formed with the intent to monopolize or restrain trade or to restrict competition and that the formation of the steel trust was a natural result of the existing industrial technology, which made mass production efficient. Despite its gigantic size, the corporation did not abuse its market power to increase profits by reducing the wages of its employees or by lowering product quality or output. Furthermore, the Court did not find any evidence of unfair practices or trade restraints. The corporation had no power of its own, and its power to fix prices and maintain price stability arose from the cooperation of its competitors.

Unlike in the American Tobacco (1911) and Standard Oil (1911) cases, both the district court and the Supreme Court found that the size of U.S. Steel itself was not an offense against the Sherman Antitrust Act, since it was not accompanied by "unreasonable" business practices. The failure of the government in prosecuting U.S. Steel signified the Court's tolerance of "good trusts."

Significance

The U.S. Steel case contributed much to the early development of antitrust laws and the course of American industries. It represents the government's early efforts to maintain market competition in the face of mergers. Following victories in the Standard Oil and American Tobacco suits, the case accounted for the federal government's first major failure in prosecuting a big corporation.

Both the district court and the Supreme Court decisions in favor of U.S. Steel were based on the "rule of reason" principle established in the Standard Oil and American Tobacco cases. McKenna reinforced the rule of reason that corporate size alone was no offense against the antitrust laws if not accompanied by anticompetitive conduct. The Supreme Court's confirmation of the rule of reason signified its tolerance of big corporations. Its ruling immediately initiated a new merger movement in the steel industry as well as in other American industries over the next two decades. In addition, the U.S. Steel case set the tone for the government's defeat in the Alcoa antitrust suit in 1924.

Later Events

After the 1920 case, U.S. Steel ceased its expansion, hoping to avoid another antitrust lawsuit. Its share in steel production continued to decline, while competitors, particularly Bethlehem Steel and Republic Steel, began to grow through mergers. Only two years after U.S. Steel's victory over the government, several major steel companies (Midvale, Ordnance, Republic, Inland, Bethlehem, and Lackawanna) proposed the formation of the North American Steel Company, which would have been only slightly smaller in size than U.S. Steel. The proposed merger eventually was broken into two parts and approved by the Justice Department, which hoped to add to the competitive forces acting on U.S. Steel. The Federal Trade Commission filed complaints against both mergers as constituting unfair competition under section 5 of the Federal Trade Commission Act. Although the Midvale-Republic-Inland proposed merger was dropped voluntarily, Bethlehem successfully merged with Lackawanna and Midvale when the U.S. Supreme Court dismissed the FTC's charges in 1927.

Steel mergers continued successfully without challenge from the government until 1935, when Republic acquired Corrigan, McKinney Steel. A suit filed by the Justice Department against the merger was decided by the Northern Ohio District Court in favor of the industry.

In the U.S. Steel antitrust case, the Supreme Court did not find the defendant's cooperative Pittsburgh-plus pricing system to be an illegal type of price fixing. The Clayton Antitrust and Federal Trade Commission Acts, however, explicitly ruled price discrimination illegal. In April, 1921, the FTC filed a complaint that U.S. Steel's Pittsburgh-plus pricing practice constituted price discrimination against western consumers and was an unfair business practice. U.S. Steel obeyed the commission's cease-and-desist order in 1924 and abandoned the pricing policy. Meanwhile, the basing-point policy had spread to other industries, such as cement; the FTC unsuccessfully challenged that industry's use of the policy in 1925. The basing-point system continued to be used until it was explicitly banned by the government in 1948.

The U.S. Steel victory over the government encouraged mergers and the use of basing-point pricing practices, which in turn led to increased efforts on the part of the government to regulate these practices. As for the steel industry, the case marked the end of U.S. Steel's dominance and the rise of its competitors, setting the tone for the oligopolistic market structure that developed. The case also ended cooperative pricing practices among firms and led to the elimination of the practice of price discrimination.

In 1986, U.S. Steel Corporation changed its name to USX Corporation, and its major operating units focused on energy, steel, and other diversified enterprises. In October, 2001, USX Corporation reorganized into United States Steel Corporation, its original name, and Marathon Oil Corporation, which operated the nonsteel parts of USX Corporation.

Jim Lee

Further Reading

Armentano, Dominick T. *Antitrust and Monopoly: Anatomy of a Policy Failure.* 2d ed. Oakland, Calif.: Independent Institute, 1990. Covers major antitrust lawsuits since the Sherman Act, discussing their relationship to economic theory and the development of antitrust legislation. Chapter 4 discusses the U.S. Steel case. Includes an appendix of relevant sections of antitrust laws.

Hovenkamp, Herbert. *Federal Antitrust Policy: The Law of Competition and Its Practice.* 3d ed. St. Paul, Minn.: Thomson/West, 2005. Covers nearly all aspects of U.S. antitrust policy in a manner understandable to people with no background in economics. Chapter 2 discusses "history and ideology in antitrust policy."

Hylton, Keith N. *Antitrust Law: Economic Theory and Common Law Evolution.* New York: Cambridge University Press, 2003. Comprehensive text on economic principles behind antitrust and the development of American antitrust law over more than one hundred years of litigation. Includes a chapter on the Alcoa case. Bibliographic references and index.

Peritz, Rudolph J. R. *Competition Policy in America: History, Rhetoric, Law.* Rev. ed. New York: Oxford University Press, 2001. Explores the influences on U.S.

public policy of the concept of free competition. Discusses congressional debates, court opinions, and the work of economic, legal, and political scholars in this area.

Schroeder, Gertrude. *The Growth of Major Steel Companies, 1900-1950.* Baltimore: Johns Hopkins University Press, 1952. Detailed historical study of the leading steel companies during the first half of the twentieth century. Written for a general audience.

Tarbell, Ida. *The Life of Elbert H. Gary: The Story of Steel.* 1926. Reprint. Whitefish, Mont.: Kessinger, 2003. Penetrating look at the corporate life of the president of U.S. Steel as well as the early development of the company. Includes discussion of Gary's relationships with President Theodore Roosevelt and with organized labor.

U.S. Steel Corporation. *United States Steel Corporation: T.N.E.C.* 3 vols. New York: Author, 1940. Contains economic and statistical studies, charts, and illustrations submitted by U.S. Steel to the Temporary National Economic Committee during court hearings on the steel industry in 1939 and 1940.

Weiss, Leonard. *Economics and American Industry.* New York: John Wiley & Sons, 1961. Chapter 7 provides good coverage of the integration in steel production and market concentration in the early years of the industry. Explores pricing policy, including oligopoly and basing-point systems, with economic models. Valuable for undergraduate economics students.

Whitney, Simon N. *Antitrust Policies: American Experience in Twenty Industries.* 2 vols. New York: Twentieth Century Fund, 1958. Chapter 5 of volume 1 provides historical and legal case studies of the steel industry and U.S. Steel in the first half of the twentieth century. Economic analysis includes changes in market concentration, forms of interindustry competition, and industry performance. Also discusses antitrust laws from an economic perspective and provides a good end-of-chapter summary of historical events.

See also *Alcoa v. Federal Trade Commission; Northern Securities Co. v. United States; Standard Oil v. United States; United States v. American Tobacco Co.; United States v. E. I. du Pont de Nemours and Co.*

UNITED STATES V. URSERY

Court: U.S. Supreme Court
Citation: 518 U.S. 267
Date: June 24, 1996
Issues: Double jeopardy

- The U.S. Supreme Court determined that civil forfeitures in drug-manufacturing and money laundering cases do not cause double jeopardy.

Congress passed laws requiring the forfeiture of property in drug-manufacturing and money-laundering cases. The defendant, Guy Ursery, was required to forfeit his property, including his house, in a drug-manufacturing case. After he was convicted, he sought to have his conviction overturned on grounds that he had already been punished criminally by the forfeiture. He prevailed in a lower court that used *United States v. Halper* (1989) to rule that civil penalties could be as punitive as criminal penalties. The Supreme Court, by a vote of eight to one, upheld the federal government's imposition of civil forfeiture of property in drug-manufacturing and money-laundering cases. Without overturning *Halper* or holding that civil penalties could not be as punitive as criminal penalties, the Court held they were not punishment in this case and therefore could not constitute double jeopardy.

Richard L. Wilson

See also *Kansas v. Hendricks; Palko v. Connecticut; United States v. Lanza.*

UNITED STATES V. VIRGINIA

Court: U.S. Supreme Court
Citation: 516 U.S. 515
Date: June 26, 1996
Issues: Education; Sex discrimination; Women's issues

• The U.S. Supreme Court held that an all-male, state-supported military academy must admit women.

Justice Ruth Bader Ginsburg wrote the opinion for the 7-1 majority in the case requiring Virginia Military Institute, an all-male, state-supported military academy, to admit women. Ginsburg found that Virginia failed to show a persuasive reason for excluding women. She rejected Virginia's proposed alternative, creating a women-only military academy, because the academy was unlikely to ever equal the quality of the existing institute. According to the Court, Virginia's remedy could not offer comparable benefits sufficient to meet the equal-protection clause requirements. Ginsburg rejected as plain error the notion that a substantive comparability inquiry should be used. Chief Justice William H. Rehnquist concurred. Justice Clarence Thomas did not participate and Justice Antonin Scalia dissented.

Richard L. Wilson

See also *Dronenburg v. Zech; Frontiero v. Richardson; Personnel Administrator of Massachusetts v. Feeney; Rostker v. Goldberg.*

UNITED STATES V. WADE

Court: U.S. Supreme Court
Citation: 388 U.S. 218
Date: June 12, 1967
Issues: Miranda rights; Right to counsel

• The U.S. Supreme Court's decision further expanded the defendant's right to counsel beyond its 1966 ruling.

A defendant in a bank robbery case named Wade was placed in a police lineup without having an attorney present. In the lineup, he and the others were required to wear a mask and say, "Put the money in the bag." By a 5-4 vote, the Supreme Court held that this setting and the required statement were self-incriminating and in violation of the Fifth Amendment. In his opinion for the Court, Justice William J. Brennan, Jr., overturned Wade's conviction and stated that the lineup was a critical stage in the proceedings, mandating the appointment of counsel for indigents. The Court's decision greatly expanded the right to counsel that had already been increased by *Miranda v. Arizona* (1966). Chief Justice Earl Warren and Justice William O. Douglas joined in an opinion written by Justice Abe Fortas overturning the conviction but rejecting the Court's finding that the lineup procedures were self-incriminating. Justices John M. Harlan II and Potter Stewart joined in a dissent by Justice Byron R. White upholding the conviction but rejecting the Court's view that the lineup is a critical stage in the proceedings. Justice Hugo L. Black upheld the conviction but rejected the Court's holding that the lineup did not constitute self-incrimination.

Richard L. Wilson

See also *Arizona v. Fulminante*; *Brown v. Mississippi*; *Chambers v. Florida*; *Faretta v. California*; *Harris v. New York*; *Mallory v. United States*; *Malloy v. Hogan*; *Minnick v. Mississippi*.

UNITED STATES V. WONG KIM ARK

Court: U.S. Supreme Court
Citation: 169 U.S. 649
Date: March 28, 1898
Issues: Citizenship; Habeas corpus; Immigration; International law

• The U.S. Supreme Court's *Wong Kim Ark* decision held that children born in the United States, even to temporary sojourners, were subject to U.S. jurisdiction regardless of race or nationality. It effectively extended citizenship to any person born on U.S. soil, regardless of parentage.

After the U.S. Civil War (1861-1865), the Constitution of the United States was amended to deal with the end of slavery and the legal status of the freed slaves. Under then-existing law, notably the 1857 decision in *Dred Scott v. Sandford*, even free African Americans could not become citizens. The Thirteenth Amendment ended slavery. The Fourteenth Amendment, which was drafted to confer citizenship on the newly freed slaves and to protect their rights from infringement by state governments, begins: "All persons born or naturalized in the United States and subject to the jurisdiction thereof, are citizens of the United States and of the State wherein they reside."

The Fourteenth Amendment ended neither racial prejudice nor various racially based legal discriminations. In 1882, 1884, and 1894, Congress passed a series of laws known as the Chinese Exclusion Acts. These statutes were designed to keep persons of Chinese ancestry out of the United States. They were particularly aimed at the importation of Chinese laborers and at the "coolie" system—a form of indentured labor. The acceptance of low wages by imported Chinese immigrants angered many Americans.

Wong Kim Ark was born in San Francisco in 1873. His parents were Chinese subjects permanently domiciled in the United States—in modern terminology, they would have been called resident aliens. They had been in business in San Francisco and were neither employees nor diplomatic agents of the government of China. In 1890, they returned to China after many years in the United States. Wong Kim Ark also went to China in 1890, but he returned to the United States the same year and was readmitted to the country on the grounds that he was a U.S. citizen. In 1894, he again went to China for a temporary visit but was denied readmission to the United States on his return in August, 1895.

The federal government's position was that under the Chinese Exclusion Acts, a Chinese person born to alien parents and who had not renounced his previous nationality was not "born or naturalized in the United States" within the meaning of the citizenship clause of the Fourteenth Amendment. If the government's position was correct, Wong Kim Ark was not a citizen of the United States and was not entitled to readmission to the country. Wong brought a habeas corpus action against the government in the United States District Court for the Northern District of California. That court's judgment in favor of Wong was appealed to the U.S. Supreme Court by the government.

The Supreme Court Ruling

The case was decided on March 28, 1898. Justice Horace Gray wrote the Supreme Court's opinion for a 6-2 majority. Gray's argument begins with the assumption that the citizenship clause of the Fourteenth Amendment has to be read in the context of preexisting law. The Court's opinion begins with a long review of citizenship practices and legal customs. The U.S. tradition had been to distinguish between "natural-born" and naturalized citizens. This distinction came from English common law.

In England, for hundreds of years prior to the American Revolution (1775-1783), all persons born within the king's realms except the children of diplomats and alien enemies were said to have been born under the king's protection and were natural-born subjects. This rule was applied or extended equally to the children of alien parents. Moreover, the same rule was in force in all the English colonies in North America prior to the revolution, and was continued (except with regard to slaves) under the jurisdiction of the United States when it became independent. The first American law concerning naturalization was passed in the First Congress. It and its successor acts, passed in 1802, assumed the citizenship of all free persons born within the borders of the United States. It was not until the passage of the Chinese Exclusion Acts that any U.S. law had sought to alter the rule regarding natural-born citizens.

On the European continent, however, the law of citizenship was different. Most European countries had adopted the citizenship rules of ancient Roman law. Under the Roman civil law, a child takes the nationality of his or her parents. Indeed, when *United States v. Wong Kim Ark* reached the Supreme Court, the government argued that the European practice had become the true rule of international law as it was recognized by the great majority of the countries of the world.

This was the historical and legal context for the Fourteenth Amendment's language "All persons *born* or naturalized in the United States. . ." (emphasis added). According to Justice Gray, the purpose of the Fourteenth Amendment was to extend the rule providing citizenship for natural-born persons to the freed slaves and their children. The amendment did not establish a congressional power to alter the constitutional grant of citizenship. Gray's opinion reviews many of the Court's prior opinions upholding the principle. The Chinese Exclusion Acts, passed after the passage of the Fourteenth

Justice Horace Gray.
(Library of Congress)

Amendment, could not affect the amendment's meaning, according to the majority, and therefore did not affect the established rule of natural-born citizenship.

The grant of constitutional power to Congress to "establish a uniform rule of naturalization" did not validate the Chinese Exclusion Acts. Wong, as a natural-born citizen, had no need of being naturalized. The Court held that "Every person born in the United States and subject to the jurisdiction thereof, becomes at once a citizen of the United States, and needs no naturalization." Moreover, the majority held that Congress's power of naturalization is "a power to confer citizenship, not to take it away." In other words, Congress had the power to establish uniform rules for naturalization but could not alter the plain-language and common-law meaning of the Fourteenth Amendment's citizenship clause.

Dissenting Opinions

The dissenting justices saw the case differently. Chief Justice Melville Fuller wrote an extensive dissent in which Justice John Marshall Harlan joined. In their view, the common-law rule sprang from the feudal relationship between the British crown and children born within the realm. American law was not bound to follow the common-law rule, because there were differences be-tween "citizens" and "subjects." In a republic such as the United States, citi-zenship was a status created by and conferred by the civil law. Because nothing in U.S. law had explicitly endorsed the common-law principle of citizenship, the Fourteenth Amendment did not have to be read so as to include it. Fuller argued that Congress is free to pass statutes that define and interpret the citi-zenship clause of the Fourteenth Amendment. In the dissenters' view, then, the Chinese Exclusion Acts could constitutionally limit the reach of the phrase "born or naturalized in the United States and subject to the jurisdic-tion thereof." Under this interpretation, Wong Kim Ark would not have been a citizen and his exclusion would have been constitutional.

Significance

The Court's decision in this case was important because it stripped the gov-ernment of the power to deny the citizenship of persons born in the United States of alien parents. It essentially meant that any person born on U.S. soil, under virtually any circumstances to any parents, would be a citizen of the United States. Beyond establishing a specific limit upon the ability of Con-gress to pass statutes interpreting or limiting the Fourteenth Amendment, moreover, the decision had a broader implication. It strengthened the princi-ple that Congress lacked the power to pass statutes that modified the meaning of a segment of the Constitution. Congress was bound by the language of the

Constitution itself, and changes to the meaning of that language could be achieved only by amending the document.

Robert Jacobs

Further Reading

Bankston, Carl L., III, ed. *Encyclopedia of American Immigration.* 3 vols. Pasadena, Calif.: Salem Press, 2010. Comprehensive reference source on all aspects of American immigration history, with articles on individual laws, court cases, events, immigrant groups, and other subjects. Profusely illustrated with photographs, maps, charts, and graphs. Extensive appendix materials and bibliographical notes in every article.

Chan, Sucheng, ed. *Entry Denied: Exclusion and the Chinese Community in America, 1882-1943.* Philadelphia: Temple University Press, 1991. Good discussion of the effects and technical aspects of the Chinese Exclusion Acts.

Corwin, Edward S. *The Constitution of the United States of America: Analysis and Interpretation.* Washington, D.C.: Government Printing Office, 1953. Corwin's monumental compilation of constitutional lore is especially strong on issues such as citizenship, whose fundamental rules date back to the nineteenth century.

Federman, Cary. *The Body and the State: Habeas Corpus and American Jurisprudence.* Albany: State University of New York Press, 2006. Historical account of the application of the writ since 1789.

Franklin, Frank George. *The Legislative History of Naturalization in the United States: From the Revolutionary War to 1861.* Chicago: University of Chicago Press, 1906. Discussion of naturalization and citizenship precedents of early U.S. history.

Lee, Erika. "Wong Kim Ark: Chinese American Citizens and U.S. Exclusion Laws, 1882-1943." In *The Human Tradition in California,* edited by Clark Davis and David Igler. Wilmington, Del.: Scholarly Resources, 2002. Examines the history of Chinese Americans in California and the effect of the exclusion laws upon them.

McKenzie, Roderick Duncan. *Oriental Exclusion: The Effect of American Immigration Laws, Regulations, and Judicial Decisions upon the Chinese and Japanese on the American Pacific Coast, 1885-1940.* New York: J. S. Ozer, 1971. Discusses the human aspect of the Chinese exclusion laws.

See also *Frank v. Mangum; McCleskey v. Zant; Scott v. Sandford; Stone v. Powell.*

United States District Court, United States v. *See* United States v. United States District Court

United States Steel Corp., United States v. *See* United States v. United States Steel Corp.

United Steelworkers of America v. Weber

Court: U.S. Supreme Court
Citation: 443 U.S. 193
Date: June 27, 1979
Issues: Affirmative action; Civil rights and liberties; Employment discrimination; Labor law; Racial discrimination

• In *United Steelworkers of America v. Weber,* the U.S. Supreme Court upheld the legality of preferential treatment, making it possible for affirmative action programs to continue.

The passage of Title VII of the Civil Rights Act of 1964 made it illegal for employers in the United States to discriminate against anyone on the basis of race, sex, color, religion, or national origin. Title VII was supposed to create an atmosphere of equal opportunity, in which all candidates theoretically had the same chance to secure a job and other employment benefits. It was soon recognized, however, that prohibiting present and future discrimination would not fully remedy the consequences of past discrimination. Members of groups disadvantaged by prior discrimination did not have the experience, credentials, status, or contacts to compete on an equal footing with those who had never been the target of discrimination.

The government therefore imposed on federal contractors the duty to undertake "affirmative action," that is, to engage in special efforts to hire and promote members of groups that were underrepresented in their workforces. The overall goal was to bring groups that had been discriminated against into statistical parity in the workforce at a faster-than-natural rate. Affirmative action required employers to compare the relevant labor market to their present labor forces and to identify discrepancies and situations in which minorities and women were underrepresented. They then had to file written affirmative action plans that included goals, timetables, and strategies to correct the deficiencies.

Challenges to Affirmative Action

Opponents soon chose to test the validity of affirmative action by questioning the legality of the results the legislation created. Affirmative action has been interpreted in several ways. It was commonly understood that an employer undertaking affirmative action would actively recruit underrepresented groups, eliminate managerial prejudices toward them, and remove employment practices that put victims of previous discrimination at a disadvantage. There has never been a question about the legality of these types of practices. To most employers, however, it seemed that the safest way to comply with affirmative action involved extending preferential treatment to qualified members of underrepresented groups through the use of hiring quotas. This meant, for example, that if women were underrepresented in a particular company, and a woman and a white man applied for a job and had the same qualifications, the woman would be given preference. At the extreme, quotas might also result in the hiring of less-qualified women and people of color over white men. Such practices resulted in what was called reverse discrimination against members of groups that were adequately represented—in particular, white men.

Such a result appeared to be in conflict with Title VII (section 703), which specifically prohibits discrimination in employment based on race, gender, color, religion, or national origin. The basic issue was therefore whether an affirmative action plan that classifies people according to their race, gender, and national origin and then makes employment decisions at least partially based on those classifications violates Title VII. Opponents of affirmative action argued that its practical effect mandated preferential treatment for certain groups of people, while Title VII specifically stated that it did not require the granting of preferential treatment. A series of court cases, most of which reached the U.S. Supreme Court and culminated in the ruling in *United Steelworkers of America v. Weber,* eventually decided the fate of affirmative action.

The Supreme Court initially seemed to take a position against preferential treatment, in *Griggs v. Duke Power Co.* (1971). This case concerned a company that had unintentionally produced a discriminatory effect against African Americans by requiring tests and educational credentials that were not job-related. The decision made it clear that the court considered these practices to be violations of Title VII and that artificial and unnecessary barriers to employment had to be removed. The court also specifically stated, however, that no person or group had a right to preferential treatment simply because of membership in a particular group or because of being the target of prior discrimination.

The arguments against preferential treatment seemed to grow stronger in 1976 with *McDonald v. Santa Fe Trail Transportation Company.* Three men, two white and one black, were charged with the same indiscretion at their workplace. The company fired the two white men but gave the black man a warning. The two white men charged the company with discrimination, but the company responded that Title VII was meant to protect the disadvantaged and that the two white men therefore had no protection. The Supreme Court disagreed, eventually ruling that the term "race" was all-inclusive and Title VII therefore also prohibited discrimination against whites.

Another 1976 ruling, this time by a lower court, ordered American Telephone and Telegraph (AT&T) to pay damages to a white man who had lost a promotion to a woman with less experience and seniority. The promotion decision had been made in the context of a federal consent decree, in which AT&T had agreed to hire and promote women and people of color into jobs previously dominated by white men. The male employee believed that he was nevertheless the victim of sex discrimination, and the court agreed, contending that "innocent employees" should not be made to pay for a company's past discriminatory practices.

The Bakke Case

A more direct blow was dealt to affirmative action in *Regents of the University of California v. Bakke* (1978). The University of California at Davis reserved a percentage of its medical school openings for minority students, and a white applicant, Allan Paul Bakke, was denied admission to the medical school because the white allotment had been filled. In a narrow and indecisive ruling, the Supreme Court affirmed a lower-court order to admit Bakke to the medical school, claiming that the university's admission system violated both the U.S. Constitution's equal protection amendment and Title VII. The Court made it clear that quotas based exclusively on race were illegal in a situation in which no previous discrimination had been shown. The justices did not, however, outlaw the use of quotas in situations where previous discrimination had occurred. The Supreme Court further muddied the waters when it also ruled that although race could not be the sole deciding factor, the university could continue to take race into consideration in its selection system.

The net effect of these decisions placed employers in a difficult position and affirmative action in potential jeopardy. In the light of the various rulings, employers believed that they had to find ways to increase the presence and position of underrepresented groups without causing any discrimination against the white majority. Such a balancing act was extremely difficult, if not impossible. The controversy was at least temporarily settled in 1979 with *United Steelworkers of America v. Weber.*

In 1974, the United Steelworkers of America and Kaiser Aluminum voluntarily entered into a fifteen-plant collective bargaining agreement that included an affirmative action plan designed to remedy racial imbalances in Kaiser's skilled-craft workforce. The plan reserved half of the openings to in-house craft-training programs for African Americans until the percentage of black craft workers at Kaiser mirrored the percentage of blacks in the local labor force. The litigation arose from a charge at the Gramercy plant in Louisiana, where 1.83 percent of the skilled-craft workers were black and 39 percent of the local workforce was black. After the plan was put into operation, seven black and six white workers were selected from the production workforce to enter the training program. Brian Weber, a white production worker, bid for admission into the program and was rejected; he had more seniority than all the black workers who were selected. Weber subsequently filed a class-action suit, alleging that the plan discriminated against whites and was therefore in violation of Title VII.

The basic issue was whether a private-sector employer could voluntarily implement an affirmative action plan that involved preferential treatment when there was no proof of prior discrimination but the workforce did demonstrate racial or sexual imbalance. The Court's majority opinion, authored by Justice William J. Brennan, stated that any employer or union that was trying to eliminate imbalances in its workforce could voluntarily use a plan that involved preferential treatment, even if that plan benefited individuals who had not themselves been the victims of discrimination. In reaching this decision, the justices emphasized that Kaiser's affirmative action plan was the result of negotiation and agreement between the company and the union. The Supreme Court further stipulated that although Title VII does not require preferential treatment, neither does it prohibit it.

The *Weber* decision did not legitimate all quota systems. It stated that in order for a quota system to be lawful, it must be part of a "permissible" affirmative action plan. The Court offered the following guidelines as to what constitutes a permissible plan: It is designed to break down old patterns of discrimination, it does not needlessly trammel the interests of white employees, it does not create an absolute bar to whites, it is a temporary corrective measure, and it has the goal of eliminating racial imbalance.

Writing for the minority, Justice William H. Rehnquist authored a strong dissent in the *Weber* case. He quoted convincing evidence from the *Congressional Record* that indicated that some members of Congress, including strong proponents of the civil rights bill, did indeed intend that Title VII prohibit all preferential treatment.

Significance

Review of the findings of *Weber* and the previous cases results in a multifaceted scenario. If an employer has been found guilty of employment discrimination, affirmative action involving preferential treatment appears to be sanctioned by Title VII, which allows the courts to impose any relief or affirmative action deemed appropriate. In these cases, the affirmative action is viewed as a remedy for illegal behavior—that is, a way to redress an imbalance created by deliberate discrimination. If an employer has an imbalanced workforce but has not been found guilty of discrimination, the courts have no power to order any plan involving preferential treatment. A firm is free, however, to adopt measures voluntarily that result in preferential treatment, provided they are part of a permissible affirmative action plan. Although "permissible" has never been specifically defined, the five criteria laid out in *Weber* are regarded as useful guidelines. Finally, a firm cannot voluntarily adopt preferential treatment tactics that are not part of a permissible affirmative action plan.

The *Weber* ruling is especially noteworthy because it is one of the few in American judicial history in which a court has rejected the actual wording of a statute in favor of what the court interprets as the legislative intent. The Supreme Court acknowledged that Title VII does indeed prohibit all racial discrimination but contended that the law had to be interpreted in the context of the history and purpose of Title VII. The Court held that the primary concern of Title VII was the plight and position of African Americans, and it was therefore illogical to assume that the act would therefore ban all voluntary and race-conscious efforts to correct the effects of past discrimination. In effect, the Court said that despite the inevitable result of reverse discrimination, preferential treatment is permissible when its goal is the correction of long-standing social problems. Based on this reasoning, and despite subsequent challenges, most major firms in the United States implemented affirmative action, and most plans involved some degree of preferential treatment.

The battle was far from over. From its inception, affirmative action has had its detractors and its defenders. Both proponents and opponents of affirmative action continued to make valid and legitimate points about the evils and the benefits of preferential treatment. Some voiced moral and societal objections; opponents protested that it is unfair to require present generations to pay for the sins of predecessors, that affirmative action causes discrimination against white men, and that all employment decisions should be based solely on merit. Detractors further argued that any legislation that allows preferential treatment is bound to increase hostility toward the groups it is meant to help. Others pointed out, however, that relying on the natural progression of time to correct the effects of past discrimination would take far too long and would perpetuate an untenable situation.

Although the *Weber* ruling may have settled prominent legal questions about preferential treatment and affirmative action, it by no means ended the controversy. The continuing debate again took center stage in the late 1980's, when a more conservative Supreme Court handed down a series of decisions unfavorable to affirmative action and equal employment opportunity legislation. Congress quickly responded with the Civil Rights Act of 1991, which basically undid all the conservative Court decisions.

Legislative and judicial activity concerning affirmative action continued to generate uncertainty for businesses, as they did their best to hire and promote women and people of color while still trying to treat individual white men fairly. This balancing act appeared to produce mixed results; for example, affirmative action helped women and people of color gain entry into organizations, but they were not necessarily promoted into higher and more influential positions.

Marie McKendall

Further Reading

Buchholz, Rogene A. "Equal Employment Opportunity." In *Business Environment and Public Policy.* 5th ed. Englewood Cliffs, N.J.: Prentice Hall, 1995. Provides a concise and understandable synopsis of affirmative action. Gives insights into both sides of the issue. Includes an excellent summary of major cases dealing with affirmative action.

Dudley, William, ed. *Racism in America: Opposing Viewpoints.* San Diego, Calif.: Greenhaven Press, 1991. Among other topics, presents a series of essays arguing both for and against affirmative action. Provides moral and societal context to the debate in a lively style.

Eisenberg, Theodore. *Civil Rights Legislation: Cases and Materials.* 5th ed. Newark, N.J.: LexisNexis, 2004. Provides the text of the Supreme Court's *Weber* ruling and those of other significant affirmative action cases. Intended for readers with some background in the law.

Ledvinka, James, and Vida Scarpello. *Federal Regulation of Personnel and Human Resource Management.* 2d ed. Boston: PWS-Kent, 1991. Provides an excellent, easy-to-read history of the controversy surrounding preferential treatment in hiring.

Player, Mack. *Federal Law of Employment Discrimination in a Nutshell.* 6th ed. St. Paul, Minn.: West, 2009. Reference guide to employment discrimination law lays out the highlights in a brief, orderly fashion. Includes table of cases and index.

Weiss, Robert J. *"We Want Jobs": A History of Affirmative Action.* New York: Routledge, 1997. Presents the history of African Americans' struggles to achieve workplace equality.

See also *Griggs v. Duke Power Co.*; *Johnson v. Santa Clara County*; *Regents of the University of California v. Bakke.*

Ursery, United States v. *See* United States v. Ursery

Veazie Bank v. Fenno

Court: U.S. Supreme Court
Citation: 75 U.S. 533
Date: December 13, 1869
Issues: Taxation

- The U.S. Supreme Court upheld Congress's right to tax bank notes issued by a state-chartered bank.

In 1866, in an effort to build revenue to finance the Civil War, Congress passed an act that raised the tax on state bank notes from 1 percent to 10 percent. The Veazie Bank of Maine declined to pay the higher tax, arguing that it was an unconstitutional use of Congress's power to tax because it was a direct tax and levied on a state agency. The Supreme Court, by a 7-2 vote, followed *Hylton v. United States* (1796) and found that a tax on bank notes was not a direct tax in contravention of the Constitution and that the bank—though chartered by Maine—was not a state "instrumentality." It upheld Congress's power to levy such a tax, and Veazie Bank was required to pay. Chief Justice Salmon P. Chase wrote the opinion for the Court, and Justices Samuel Nelson and David Davis dissented.

Richard L. Wilson

See also *Hayburn's Case*; *Hylton v. United States*; *Marbury v. Madison.*

VERNONIA SCHOOL DISTRICT 47J
V. ACTON

Court: U.S. Supreme Court
Citation: 515 U.S. 646
Date: June 26, 1995
Issues: Education; Parental rights; Right to privacy

• The U.S. Supreme Court ruled that public schools may require student athletes to submit to random drug tests as a condition of their participation in interscholastic sports.

In the mid-1980's, teachers and administrators in the public schools in Vernonia, Oregon, began noticing a sharp and progressive increase in drug and alcohol abuse among students, as well as disciplinary problems. Of particular concern were the deleterious effects of alcohol and drug abuse on student athletes, who were not only more susceptible to physical injury than students generally but also believed to be the leaders of the schools' drug culture.

In 1989, after making unsuccessful efforts to deter students' drug and alcohol use through education, the local school board, with parental approval, instituted a compulsory drug-testing policy for all student athletes. Every student wishing to participate in interscholastic athletics was required to sign a form consenting to the drug testing and to obtain a parent's written consent as well. At the beginning of each season of competition, every student athlete was tested; then, throughout the season, 10 percent of the student athletes were tested at random. James Acton, a seventh-grade student, signed up to play district-supported football, but his parents refused to consent to the drug testing. The parents of James Acton then sued the school district.

After the trial court dismissed the lawsuit, the Actons appealed. The U.S. Court of Appeals for the Ninth Circuit struck down the school district's policy, saying that it violated the Fourth Amendment to the U.S. Constitution. The Fourth Amendment guarantees citizens freedom from unreasonable searches and seizures; it reads, "The right of the people to be secure in their persons, houses, papers, and effects, against unreasonable searches and seizures, shall not be violated, and no Warrants shall issue, but upon probable cause, supported by Oath of affirmation, and particularly describing the place to be searched, and the persons or things to be seized." The school district then requested review of the decision from the U.S. Supreme Court.

The Supreme Court Ruling

In *Vernonia School District 47J v. Acton* (1995), the U.S. Supreme Court, by a vote of six to three, reversed the decision of the Ninth Circuit, declaring that the school district's policy did not amount to unreasonable search and seizure under the Fourth Amendment. The Court's opinion was written by Associate Justice Antonin Scalia; he was joined by Chief Justice William H. Rehnquist and Associate Justices Anthony Kennedy, Clarence Thomas, Ruth Bader Ginsburg, and Stephen G. Breyer. Although the justices acknowledged that state-compelled drug testing constitutes a search subject to the demands of the Fourth Amendment, they determined that the school district's testing scheme fit squarely within the "special needs" exception to the Fourth Amendment. This exception holds that an administrative search—a search that is not executed as a pretext for obtaining evidence of criminal activity—does not re-

Under Chief Justice William H. Rehnquist, the Supreme Court became more conservative. Clockwise from upper left, its members were Ruth Bader Ginsburg, David Souter, Clarence Thomas, Stephen Breyer, Anthony Kennedy, Sandra Day O'Connor, Rehnquist, John Paul Stevens, and Antonin Scalia. (Richard Strauss/Smithsonian Institution, Courtesy the Supreme Court of the United States)

quire either a warrant or individualized suspicion so long as the search is a reasonable one.

To determine reasonableness, the Court balanced the strength of the student's privacy interest guaranteed by the Fourth Amendment against any legitimate governmental interest in conducting the search. First considering the individual privacy interest of the student, the opinion noted that unemancipated minors and public school students, because they are in the temporary custody of the state as "schoolmaster," have a lesser expectation of privacy than do adults. Moreover, those expectations are even less for student athletes, who voluntarily subject themselves to a degree of regulation higher than that imposed on students generally. "Public school locker rooms . . . are not notable for the privacy they afford," Justice Scalia wrote.

Finally, because the drug-testing procedures presented conditions of collection that were "nearly identical" to the conditions typically encountered in public restrooms, the Court noted, the nature of the intrusion was negligible. (For the testing, each student athlete entered an empty locker room accompanied by an adult monitor of the same sex. Each male produced a urine sample while remaining fully clothed and with his back to the monitor. Each female produced a sample in an enclosed bathroom stall. The monitor listened for normal sounds of urination, checked the sample for temperature and tampering, and then transferred the sample to a vial.)

The Court then assessed the strength of the government's interest in the drug testing by considering the nature and the immediacy of the government's concern. The nature of the concern, the opinion held, was "important—indeed perhaps compelling." The majority, as had the district court, agreed that drug use in schools has negative effects not only on the actual users but also on the entire student body and the faculty because of disruptions to the educative process. Additionally, the justices agreed that drug use presents substantial physical risks—reduction in the oxygen-carrying capacity of the blood and increased body temperature, for example—to student athletes in particular. Finally, the immediacy of the concern was heightened by the school district's findings that drug use was increasing among the student body in large part because other students looked up to student athletes who were drug abusers themselves.

Given the decreased expectation of privacy among student athletes, the unobtrusive nature of the search, and the severity of the need met by the search, the Court held the policy to be reasonable and, therefore, constitutional.

Three justices—John Paul Stevens, David Souter, and Sandra Day O'Connor—disagreed. In an opinion written by Justice O'Connor, the dissenters found the policy unreasonable, and thus unconstitutional, for four primary reasons: First, the school board policy dispensed with the standard requirement of individualized suspicion; second, there was a strong basis for concluding that vigorous suspicion-based testing would have "gone a long way" toward solving the drug problem; third, there was no evidence at all of a drug problem at the actual grade school attended by James Acton; and fourth, the choice of student athletes as the class to subject to suspicionless testing was unreasonable. If the school district was really concerned about the rise in drug-related disorders and disruptions of the educative process, the dissenters noted, a far more reasonable course of action would have been to test those students who had violated published school rules against severe disruptions in class and around campus. In sum, the dissenters asserted, no justifiable reason existed to drug test every student athlete in the entire school district.

Significance

Vernonia School District 47J v. Acton marked the first time the U.S. Supreme Court had sustained the use of random, suspicionless drug testing outside the public-employment context. It did so with some apprehension, however, cautioning against the assumption that suspicionless drug testing would readily pass "constitutional muster." Even so, the Court extended the holding in *Vernonia* seven years later in the case of *Board of Education of Independent School District No. 92 of Pottawatomie County v. Earls* (2002), in which it upheld a public school policy that required suspicionless drug testing of all students who participated in any extracurricular activity. Central to the Court's position in both cases was the fact that the policies at hand dealt with minors temporarily entrusted to the care of the state. It is, therefore, highly questionable whether a similar policy would be upheld outside of the public school context. For example, government would probably not be allowed to drug test all persons entering or leaving a known drug-ridden neighborhood, even though the need to fight the scourge of drugs may provide a compelling governmental interest.

Richard A. Glenn

Further Reading

Alexander, Kern, and M. David Alexander. *American Public School Law.* 7th ed. Belmont, Calif.: Wadsworth Cengage Learning, 2009. Textbook aimed at graduate students provides a comprehensive analysis of legal cases involving a multitude of issues that affect public schools, including student privacy rights against unreasonable searches and seizures.

Gold, Susan Dudley. *Vernonia School District v. Acton: Drug Testing in the Schools.* Tarrytown, N.Y.: Marshall Cavendish Benchmark Books, 2006. Volume intended for young readers presents discussion of the *Vernonia* case and of subsequent Supreme Court decisions involving the Fourth Amendment and mandatory drug testing of public school students.

Hudson, David L., Jr. *Rights of Students.* 2d ed. Philadelphia: Chelsea House, 2010. Uses a point-counterpoint format to examine various topics related to civil liberties in U.S. public schools.

Persico, Deborah A. *Vernonia School District v. Acton: Drug Testing in Schools.* Springfield, N.J.: Enslow, 1999. Volume intended for young-adult readers discusses the facts, issue, holding, rationale, and significance of the 1995 Supreme Court decision.

Raskin, Jamin B. *We the Students: Supreme Court Cases for and About Students.* 3d ed. Washington, D.C.: CQ Press, 2008. Designed to help students achieve literacy on their constitutional rights as students. Includes learning exercises, case excerpts, and discussion prompts.

Stephens, Otis H., and Richard A. Glenn. *Unreasonable Searches and Seizures: Rights and Liberties Under the Law.* Santa Barbara, Calif.: ABC-CLIO, 2006. Examines the Fourth Amendment from its historical origins through controversies of the early twentieth century. Analyzes the Supreme Court's efforts to reconcile the constitutional rights of public school students with the government's interest in promoting a safe learning environment. Includes chronology of relevant Fourth Amendment decisions and annotated bibliography.

See also *Ferguson v. City of Charleston*; *National Treasury Employees Union v. Von Raab*; *Seminole Tribe v. Florida.*

VILLAGE OF SKOKIE V. NATIONAL SOCIALIST PARTY OF AMERICA

Court: U.S. Supreme Court
Citation: 432 U.S. 43
Date: June 14, 1977
Issues: Freedom of speech

• The *Skokie* decision upheld a broad interpretation of free speech, declaring that the promotion of even as odious an ideology as Nazism is protected by the First Amendment.

Frank Collin, a neo-Nazi leader of the National Socialist Party of America (NSPA), sought permission to hold an NSPA demonstration in Marquette Park, a white neighborhood of Chicago. The city, fearing a repeat of riots and racial assaults which had occurred during the previous three summers, used various legal devices to deny the Nazi Party a parade permit. Collin met or circumvented those requirements, until ultimately the city required a $250,000 bond to pay for any damages which might arise from the parade. The American Civil Liberties Union (ACLU) helped Collin challenge the city's requirement in federal court.

While the Marquette case was being litigated, Collin decided to move his demonstration to the village of Skokie, a largely Jewish suburb whose citizens included several thousand survivors of the Holocaust. Like Marquette Park, Skokie tried to stop Collin's group from demonstrating, securing from the Cook County Circuit Court an injunction against the NSPA. Skokie also quickly passed several ordinances which restricted the granting of parade permits through strict insurance-bond requirements, a prohibition on the display of certain military uniforms, and a prohibition on the dissemination of material promoting or inciting racial or religious hatred. Thus, there were two issues to be contested: the ordinances and the injunction.

In *Village of Skokie v. National Socialist Party of America*, the Illinois Supreme Court invalidated the injunction on First Amendment grounds, finding that there were not adequate grounds for the prior restraint of the NSPA's symbolic speech. Invoking *Cohen v. California* (1971), the Court rejected Skokie's claim that the symbols of the NSPA, including the swastika, amounted to "fighting words" which were not protected speech. The issue of the ordinances was decided by the U.S. district court in *Collin v. Smith*, which also held in favor of the NSPA. That ruling was upheld upon appeal to the U.S. appeals court.

Despite Collin's legal successes, various Jewish and other groups from around the country threatened to block the planned Nazi march on Skokie. As Collin considered his options, the federal district court in Chicago, obviously heeding the *Skokie* decision, ruled in *Collin v. O'Malley* (1978) that Collin be granted the original parade permit for Marquette Park without the bond requirement. Collin moved the demonstration back to Marquette Park.

The *Skokie* decision (along with *Collin v. Smith* and *Collin v. O'Malley*) reflected a firm commitment to a broad interpretation of free speech. Although the U.S. Supreme Court in earlier years had noted that free speech is not a limitless right (as in the case of "fighting words" against specific individuals), in these cases the federal and state courts refused to find hateful speech directed against a general group (in this case, Jews) to be unprotected.

Steve D. Boilard

See also *Allegheny County v. American Civil Liberties Union Greater Pittsburgh Chapter; Cohen v. California; Cox v. New Hampshire; Edwards v. South Carolina; Reno v. American Civil Liberties Union.*

VIRGINIA, UNITED STATES V. *See* UNITED STATES V. VIRGINIA

VIRGINIA V. BLACK

Court: U.S. Supreme Court
Citation: 538 U.S 343
Date: April 7, 2003
Issues: Civil rights and liberties; Freedom of expression

• This U.S. Supreme Court decision on cross burning ruled that state laws criminalizing cross burning that is done with the intent to intimidate do not violate the First Amendment.

After the Civil War, cross burning was used as a form of intimidation by southern white supremacists. A Virginia statute prohibited cross burning in public places or on private property when it was done for the purpose of intimidation. In 1998, Barry Black, a Ku Klux Klan (KKK) member who supervised a cross burning in an open field, was convicted by a Virginia jury whose members were instructed that burning a cross was sufficient evidence of an intent to intimidate. In another incident, Richard Elliott and Jonathan O'Mara attempted to burn a cross on a neighbor's lawn. O'Mara pleaded guilty, and Elliott was convicted by a jury that was instructed to find that the defendant intended to intimidate his neighbors when he burned the cross. The Virginia Court of Appeals upheld the convictions in both cases, but the Virginia Supreme Court found the state's anti-cross-burning law unconstitutional. Virginia appealed to the U.S. Supreme Court, which granted *certiorari*.

Justice Sandra Day O'Connor delivered the opinion for the Court on the question of the constitutionality of a state statute prohibiting cross burning. Writing for a six-member majority, she held that a state could single out cross burning done with the intent to intimidate, even if the state did not criminalize all other intimidating messages. As the Court had held in *R.A.V. v. City of St. Paul* (1992), its leading hate speech case, a state could prohibit the worst illustrations of the very reason that an entire category of speech is unprotected. Cross burning, she concluded, was a particularly virulent form of intimidation practiced by the KKK—the kind of true threat that the First Amendment permits states to ban.

When the court turned to the question of the constitutionality of the Virginia statute, seven justices agreed that the Virginia statute was unconstitutional, but there was no majority opinion. Justice O'Connor in a plurality opinion, joined by Chief Justice William Rehnquist and Justices John Paul Stevens and Stephen Breyer, found that the Virginia statute violated the First Amendment, because it permitted the jury to ignore the fact that a cross may be constitutionally burned at Klan rallies as a symbol of solidarity and to infer from the cross burning itself that the defendant had the intent to intimidate.

In a separate opinion, Justices David Souter, joined by Justices Anthony Kennedy and Ruth Bader Ginsberg, found that the Virginia statute was an unconstitutional content-based distinction, because it had selected a symbol with a particular content from the field of all proscribable intimidating or threatening expressions and made its use criminal.

As the Supreme Court's first opportunity in a decade to revisit *R.A.V. v. City of St. Paul*, *Virginia v. Black*, confirmed that cross burning with the intent to intimidate is not protected by the First Amendment. As a result, states may punish cross burning done with the intent to intimidate as long as their criminal laws clearly require prosecutors to prove that the cross burning is intended as a threat.

William Crawford Green

Further Reading

Gerstenfeld, Phyllis B. *Hate Crimes: Causes, Controls, and Controversies.* Thousand Oaks, Calif.: Sage Publications, 2004.

Levin, Jack. *The Violence of Hate: Confronting Racism, Anti-Semitism, and Other Forms of Bigotry.* Boston: Allyn & Bacon, 2002.

Perry, Barbara. *In the Name of Hate: Understanding Hate Crimes.* New York: Routledge, 2001.

Streissguth, Thomas. *Hate Crimes.* New York: Facts On File, 2003.

See also *R.A.V. v. City of St. Paul; Texas v. Johnson; Wisconsin v. Mitchell.*

VIRGINIA V. TENNESSEE

Court: U.S. Supreme Court
Citation: 148 U.S. 503
Date: April 3, 1893
Issues: States' rights

- The U.S. Supreme Court established the rules governing state compacts.

Although Virginia and Tennessee had agreed to a joint boundary based on an 1803 survey, this agreement had never been ratified by Congress, and as a result Virginia tried to have the survey results nullified. By an 8-0 vote, the Supreme Court held that Congress did not have to explicitly recognize every compact and had to ratify only those that ceded federal power to states. Justice Stephen J. Field, in his opinion for the Court, found that Congress had implicitly recognized the boundary in various indirect ways. Justice John Marshall Harlan did not participate.

Richard L. Wilson

See also *Virginia v. West Virginia.*

VIRGINIA V. WEST VIRGINIA

Court: U.S. Supreme Court
Citation: 206 U.S. 290
Date: May 27, 1907
Issues: States' rights

- The U.S. Supreme Court decided the terms of the financial settlement between Virginia and West Virginia after their separation as a result of the Civil War.

Virginia wanted West Virginia to pay about one-third of the pre-Civil War debt based on the total square miles of territory it lost when West Virginia separated from the state in 1863. West Virginia wanted to pay only for the proportion of the debt actually spent in its portion of the preexisting state—a much smaller sum. The special master appointed to resolve the issue determined that West Virginia should pay a sum based on excluding nonslave property value at the time of separation—a sum that fell between the two figures. When West Virginia still refused to pay, Virginia sought judicial enforcement. Chief Justice Melville W. Fuller wrote the unanimous decision for the Court, ratifying the findings of the special master. Eventually West Virginia agreed to pay, taking until 1939 to finish paying this debt.

Richard L. Wilson

See also *Virginia v. Tennessee.*

WABASH, ST. LOUIS, AND PACIFIC RAILWAY CO. V. ILLINOIS

Court: U.S. Supreme Court
Citation: 118 U.S. 557
Date: October 25, 1886
Issues: Regulation of commerce

• In striking down a state law regulating railroad pricing policies, the U.S. Supreme Court encouraged Congress to enact national standards.

During the second half of the nineteenth century, state legislatures used their police powers to regulate the intrastate commerce of railroads, and the railroads faced great confusion and inconsistencies as they crossed state lines. In 1852 the Supreme Court had ruled that states could enact indirect but not direct burdens on interstate commerce. In the *Wabash* case, the issue was an Illinois law that prohibited a difference between long-haul and short-haul rates, and the Court ruled that such rate regulations placed a direct burden on the federal commerce power. In response to the decision, Congress passed the Interstate Commerce Act of 1887, which established the first independent federal agency for regulating businesses. In the 1930's, the Court gave up the direct versus indirect test in favor of a functional balancing approach.

Thomas Tandy Lewis

See also *Cooley v. Board of Wardens of the Port of Philadelphia*; *Shreveport Rate Cases*; *Smyth v. Ames.*

WADE, UNITED STATES V. *See* UNITED STATES V. WADE

WALLACE V. JAFFREE

Court: U.S. Supreme Court
Citation: 472 U.S. 38
Date: June 4, 1985
Issues: Education; Establishment of religion

- The Court ruled against a state law permitting a moment of silence for "meditation or voluntary prayer" in the public schools, based on the law's sectarian intent.

In 1978, the Alabama legislature authorized a one-minute period of silence to begin each school day in the public schools, and about half of the states in the 1970's passed similar laws. Many citizens, especially in the South, wanted public schools also to conduct oral prayer activities. In 1981, the Alabama legislature specified that the period of silence could be used "for meditation or voluntary prayer," and the next year the legislature ignored U.S. Supreme Court precedents and authorized teachers to lead willing students in a vocal prayer.

Ishmael Jaffree, an outspoken humanist of Mobile County, became angry when teachers of his minor children conducted prayer activities, with peer ridicule for those not participating. After local officials refused to stop the practice, Jaffree filed a complaint in federal court against various officials, including Governor George Wallace. The complaint challenged the constitutionality of the 1981 and 1982 laws. Although the district court ruled against Jaffree, based on the argument that the Supreme Court had been mistaken in 1947 when it made the establishment clause applicable to the states, the court of appeals reversed the judgment and found that the two laws were unconstitutional because they advanced and encouraged religious activities.

The U.S. Supreme Court unanimously affirmed the unconstitutionality of the 1982 law allowing vocal prayers, and the Court voted six to three to strike down the 1981 law allowing a moment of silence for meditation or prayer. Writing the majority opinion, Justice John Paul Stevens focused all of his attention on the 1981 law. Failing to find any secular motive behind the law, Stevens argued that the expression "meditation or voluntary prayer" indicated the legislature's desire to "endorse prayer as a favored practice," and he quoted the sponsor as introducing the bill as "an effort to return voluntary prayer to our public schools." Stevens found no problem with the simple moment of silence as enacted in the law of 1978.

In a long and vigorous dissent, Justice William H. Rehnquist reviewed the history of the establishment clause and rejected the idea that the clause required a "wall of separation between church and state." He concluded that the Framers intended only to prevent a national establishment of religion and to prohibit federal preference for one religion over another. Chief Justice Warren Burger's dissent emphasized that only two years earlier, in *Marsh v. Chambers* (1983), the Court had relied on history to allow oral prayers in legislative sessions. He wrote that to treat prayer as a step toward an established religion "borders on, if it does not trespass, the ridiculous." The dissenters did not reject the idea that the establishment clause applied to the states through the Fourteenth Amendment.

In the *Jaffree* decision, the Court went rather far in insisting on neutrality between religion and secularism in the public schools. The majority of the Court made it clear that a moment of silence was acceptable so long as schools did not encourage students to use the time for religious activity. In 1992 the Court would again deal with the issue of state-encouraged prayer in *Lee v. Weisman*, ruling that invocations and benedictions at public school graduation ceremonies violated the First Amendment.

Thomas Tandy Lewis

See also *Abington School District v. Schempp; Engel v. Vitale; Lee v. Weisman; Swann v. Charlotte-Mecklenburg Board of Education.*

WALZ V. TAX COMMISSION

Court: U.S. Supreme Court
Citation: 397 U.S. 664
Date: May 4, 1970
Issues: Establishment of religion

• The U.S. Supreme Court upheld property tax relief for religious institutions.

Chief Justice Warren E. Burger wrote the opinion for the 8-1 majority, holding that New York state's exemption of religious institutions from paying property taxes did not violate the establishment of religion clause. The Supreme Court found that this law, which implemented a provision of the New York state constitution, was sufficiently remote from entanglement of the government in religion that it did not attempt to establish religion. The law exempted all real estate owned by an association organized exclusively for religious purposes. Justice William O. Douglas dissented.

Richard L. Wilson

See also *Engel v. Vitale; Illinois ex rel. McCollum v. Board of Education; Lee v. Weisman; United States v. Richardson; Wallace v. Jaffree.*

WARDS COVE PACKING CO. V. ATONIO

Court: U.S. Supreme Court
Citation: 490 U.S. 642
Date: June 5, 1989
Issues: Civil rights and liberties; Employment discrimination; Labor law; Racial discrimination

• This decision threatened to narrow the scope of the law against employment discrimination sharply.

Five salmon canneries, owned by Wards Cove Packing Company and Castle & Cooke, recruited seasonal labor for the peak of the fishing season at remote areas in Alaska. Unskilled cannery workers were recruited from Alaska Natives in the region and through the Seattle local of the International Longshoreman's and Warehouseman's Union; two-thirds of these employees were either Alaska Natives or Filipino Americans, including Frank Atonio and twenty-one other plaintiffs.

Higher-paid on-site noncannery support staff, including accountants, boat captains, chefs, electricians, engineers, managers, and physicians, were recruited from company offices in Oregon and Washington, largely by word of mouth; some 85 percent of these employees were white. For all employees, the companies provided race-segregated eating and sleeping facilities.

Plaintiff cannery workers, who believed that they were qualified to hold support staff positions but were never selected for these higher-paying jobs, filed suit in 1974 against the companies under Title VII of the Civil Rights Act of 1964. Their argument was based on statistics that showed ethnic differences in the two classes of workers, cannery versus noncannery. In addition to evidence of segregated company housing, they asserted disparate treatment and adverse impact arguments regarding criteria and procedures used to screen them out. Among these criteria, they claimed that there were preferences for relatives of existing employees (nepotism), rehire preferences, English language requirements, failure to promote from within, and a general lack of objective screening and selection criteria. The procedures to which they objected were separate hiring channels and word-of-mouth recruitment rather than open postings of job opportunities.

Justice Byron White delivered the opinion of a divided Court (the vote was 5-4). According to the majority, the comparison between ethnic groups in the two types of jobs was irrelevant because they were drawn from different labor market pools. The Court then went beyond the case to assert that a statistical difference between ethnic groups does not give *prima facie* evidence of discrimination under Title VII unless intent to discriminate is proved. To provide that proof, plaintiffs must show that specific criteria, even vague and subjective criteria, statistically account for the difference. Moreover, an employer may defend criteria that have been proved to account for the difference if they are "reasoned."

The decision had a deleterious impact on efforts to redress employment discrimination, as it reversed the broad language of *Griggs v. Duke Power Co.* (1971) by requiring proof of intent, by allowing the use of separate hiring channels, and by no longer insisting that employers must prove that biased hiring criteria are absolutely essential for job performance. Congress responded by passing the Civil Rights Act of 1991, which codified the original *Griggs* ruling into law.

Michael Haas

See also *Firefighters Local Union No. 1784 v. Stotts et al.; Griggs v. Duke Power Co.; Local 28 of Sheet Metal Workers International Association v. Equal Employment Opportunity Commission; Martin v. Wilks; Meritor Savings Bank v. Vinson; Runyon v. McCrary; Washington v. Davis; Weeks v. Southern Bell.*

WARE V. HYLTON

Court: U.S. Supreme Court
Citation: 3 U.S. 199
Date: March 7, 1796
Issues: Federal supremacy; Foreign policy; Treaties

- The Supreme Court established that U.S. treaties prevail over conflicting state laws.

The 1783 Treaty of Paris ending the Revolutionary War specified that the newly independent states would not interfere with the collection of prewar debts, but Virginia passed a law allowing its citizens to pay the Virginia treasury in depreciated currency and receive a certificate satisfying the debt. John Marshall, who later became chief justice, unsuccessfully represented a Virginia debtor, losing the only case he argued before the Supreme Court. The Court clearly ruled the treaty valid and binding on Virginia because of the supremacy clause, Article VI of the Constitution, which established the supremacy of federal treaties over conflicting state laws. Justices Samuel Chase, William Paterson, James Wilson, and William Cushing each wrote a serial opinion as was the custom at the time. Justices Oliver Ellsworth and James Iredell did not participate, but Iredell later submitted a written opinion for the record.

Richard L. Wilson

See also *Goldwater v. Carter; Marbury v. Madison; Martin v. Hunter's Lessee; Missouri v. Holland; United States v. Alvarez-Machain.*

WASHINGTON V. DAVIS

Court: U.S. Supreme Court
Citation: 426 U.S. 229
Date: June 7, 1976
Issues: Employment discrimination; Equal protection of the law

- The U.S. Supreme Court ruled that plaintiffs must show a discriminatory intent, not merely a disparate impact, to prevail under the equal protection requirements of the Fifth and Fourteenth Amendments.

In 1970 African American plaintiffs challenged the constitutionality of a hiring and promotion policy of the District of Columbia police department. They objected to the use of Test 21, which attempted to measure verbal skills and reading ability, because African American applicants failed the test at a rate four times that of white applicants. They were encouraged by *Griggs v. Duke Power Co.* (1971), when the Supreme Court interpreted Title VII so that employers had to demonstrate the business necessity of any employment policies having a disparate impact on racial minorities. The plaintiffs in the *Washington* case had to rely on the Fifth Amendment because at the time they filed suit Title VII did not apply to governmental agencies.

By a 7-2 vote, the Court upheld the use of the examination. Justice Byron R. White's opinion for the majority emphasized that an employment practice is not unconstitutional "solely because it has a racially disproportionate impact." Citing numerous precedents, White concluded that the Court had employed the "purposeful discrimination" test when examining claims of a constitutional violation. Addressing the questions of when and how one might infer discriminatory intent, White wrote that disproportionate impact was "not irrelevant," but that it had to be considered within the context of the totality of relevant facts. The Constitution did not require scientific proof that requirements were related to job performance, but employers had to show that there was a reasonable relationship between the two. White found that Test 21 was neutral on its face and rationally related to the legitimate governmental purpose of improving the communication skills of police officers.

The *Washington* decision did not disturb the Court's earlier rulings in regard to Title VII of the Civil Rights Act of 1964, prohibiting many employment requirements that had a disproportionate effect on minorities. It also actually had little influence in regard to the racial effects of employment requirements because Title VII was expanded to include governmental employees in 1972. The decision was important, however, for nonemployment cases such as *McCleskey v. Kemp* (1987), in which the Court disregarded statistical studies when examining the constitutionality of capital punishment.

Thomas Tandy Lewis

See also *Arlington Heights v. Metropolitan Housing Development Corp.*; *Griggs v. Duke Power Co.*; *McCleskey v. Kemp*.

WASHINGTON V. GLUCKSBERG

Court: U.S. Supreme Court
Citation: 521 U.S. 702
Date: June 26, 1997
Issues: Medical ethics

• The U.S. Supreme Court held that the U.S. Constitution does not guarantee any right to have assistance in committing suicide.

In *Cruzan v. Director, Missouri Department of Health* (1990), the Supreme Court "assumed and strongly suggested" that the due process clause of the Fourteenth Amendment protects the traditional right of competent adults to refuse medical treatment, including life-support systems. Building on this substantive reading of the due process clause, the Ninth Circuit struck down Washington state's ban on assisted suicide, and it recognized that terminally ill competent adults have the right to hasten their deaths with medication prescribed by physicians.

The Supreme Court unanimously reversed the lower court's ruling. Speaking for a majority, Chief Justice William H. Rehnquist found that the decision to terminate medical treatment was fundamentally different from providing active assistance in a suicide. The use of substantive due process, he emphasized, should be limited to protecting those rights and liberties that are "deeply rooted in this Nation's history and traditions," and he noted that this tradition had almost universally rejected any notion of a right to commit suicide. Washington's law, moreover, furthered the state's legitimate interest in protecting human life.

Four justices, while concurring in Rehnquist's ruling, expressed more ex-

ARGUMENTS FOR AND AGAINST PHYSICIAN-ASSISTED SUICIDE

Arguments for	Arguments against
Decisions about time and circumstances of death are personal; competent persons should have the autonomous right to choose death.	Assisted suicide is morally wrong because it contradicts strong religious and secular traditions supporting the sanctity of life.
Like cases should be treated alike. If competent, terminally ill patients may hasten death by refusing treatment, those for whom treatment refusal will not hasten death should be allowed the option of assisted death.	There is an important difference between passively letting someone die and actively killing a person. The two options are not equivalent.
Suffering may go beyond physical pain; there are other physical and psychological burdens for which physician-assisted suicide may be a compassionate response to suffering.	There is a potential for abuse; persons lacking access to care and support may be pushed into assisted death; moreover, assisted death may become a cost-containment strategy.
Although society has a strong interest in preserving life, that interest lessens when a person becomes terminally ill and has a strong desire to end life. A complete prohibition on assisted death excessively limits personal liberty.	Physicians have a long ethical tradition against taking life. Their Hippocratic oath pledges them not to "administer poison to anyone where asked" and to "be of benefit, or at least do no harm."
Assisted deaths already occur secretly, as when the administration of morphine may be a covert form of euthanasia. Legalization of physician-assisted suicide would promote open discussion of the subject.	Physicians occasionally make mistakes, and there may be uncertainties in diagnoses, and the state has an obligation to protect lives from such mistakes.

Source: Ethics in Medicine, University of Washington School of Medicine (http://eduserv.hscer.washington.edu/bioethics/topics/pas.html).

pansive views of individual rights to personal autonomy protected by substantive due process, recognizing some right to avoid pain and suffering.

Thomas Tandy Lewis

See also *Cruzan v. Director, Missouri Department of Health*; *Griswold v. Connecticut*; *Moore v. City of East Cleveland*.

Watkins v. United States

Court: U.S. Supreme Court
Citation: 354 U.S. 178
Date: June 17, 1957
Issues: Congressional powers

- In this decision, the U.S. Supreme Court ruled that when a congressional committee conducts an investigation, the due process clause requires that it must clearly articulate the subject matter of the investigation and that all questions must be pertinent to the investigation.

During the early years of the Cold War, the House Un-American Activities Committee asked broad-ranging questions of people suspected of having supported communist causes. John Watkins, a former labor leader, agreed to answer questions about his own relationship to the Communist Party but refused to answer questions about whether his personal acquaintances had been affiliated with the party in the past. He angered the committee when he declared that the information was not relevant to the investigation. For his refusal to cooperate, he was convicted of contempt of Congress.

By a 6-1 vote, the Supreme Court reversed the conviction. Speaking for the Court, Chief Justice Earl Warren emphasized that a congressional committee must clearly articulate the purposes of its investigation and that it cannot compel witnesses to answer questions without giving them a fair opportunity to learn whether an answer is required. A committee has no right to expose the private life of an individual unless justified by a legitimate function of Congress. Warren expressed concern, moreover, that the committee was threatening First Amendment values. Although recognizing that the power to conduct investigations was inherent in the legislative process, he insisted that Congress must respect the constitutional rights of witnesses when gathering information.

Thomas Tandy Lewis

See also *Barenblatt v. United States; Kilbourn v. Thompson.*

WEBSTER V. REPRODUCTIVE HEALTH SERVICES

Court: U.S. Supreme Court
Citation: 492 U.S. 490
Date: July 3, 1989
Issues: Reproductive rights; Right to privacy

- Sixteen years after *Roe v. Wade*, the U.S. Supreme Court's decision in *Webster v. Reproductive Health Services* allowed states to set some restrictions on abortion.

Seldom has a U.S. Supreme Court ruling been as controversial as that in the case of *Roe v. Wade*. Prior to this decision, abortion regulation was left to the states. In 1973, however, the Court examined state abortion laws with respect to the right to privacy, a right that is not explicitly protected by the U.S. Constitution but that the Court had previously decided was implied by it. Although the Court's decision in *Roe v. Wade* recognized that states properly have interests in safeguarding health, in maintaining medical standards, and in protecting potential life, there was no case in which these rights were upheld by the Supreme Court. After *Roe* and prior to 1989, state laws restricting abortion were consistently struck down.

Pro-choice groups were satisfied with the Court rulings. Pro-life groups, however, were left with a situation in which they could find few legal avenues through which to express their dissent. Perhaps partly for that reason, a small minority turned to civil disobedience. Randall Terry, founder of Operation Rescue, an organization that sought to shut down abortion clinics by blocking access to the facilities, reasoned that it was time for those who believed that abortion is murder to begin to take action as though they were preventing murder.

Only a very few pro-lifers, however, were involved in tactics such as those used by Operation Rescue. Most attempted to work within the few legal avenues available in the aftermath of *Roe v. Wade*. The first of these avenues was constitutional amendment. Since 1973, the right-to-life movement had held an annual march to Washington, D.C., on the January 22 anniversary of *Roe v. Wade*, protesting the decision and calling for a constitutional amendment prohibiting abortion. They consistently failed to gather sufficient support for such an amendment. A second legal avenue was to lobby against congressional funding for abortion. This tactic often worked. It could not, however, be used to contest the legality of abortion, a very important goal for pro-lifers. A third possibility was to work for a change in the composition of the Supreme Court. This avenue eventually led to a window of opportunity for pro-life groups in 1989.

The Court majority in *Roe v. Wade* had been steadily eroding as a result of retirements and appointments to the Court by President Ronald Reagan. Only three of the justices who made up the 7-2 majority in 1973 remained on the Court in 1989. On January 9, 1989, this Court, which was clearly more conservative than the one that had adjudicated *Roe v. Wade*, decided to hear the case of *Webster v. Reproductive Health Services*.

Issues in the Webster Case

The *Webster* case involved a Missouri statute that stated that life begins at conception and that unborn children have interests in life, health, and well-being that can be protected. It forbade the use of public funds to counsel or encourage a woman to have an abortion, made abortions more difficult to obtain after twenty weeks of pregnancy, and forbade public hospitals and employees to perform or assist in abortions not necessary to save the life of the mother. The Missouri law also required a physician to perform and record tests on fetal gestational age, weight, and lung maturity if there was reason to believe that the mother was twenty or more weeks pregnant. The state claimed that a fetus of that age may be viable given modern technology. The state of Missouri was in effect arguing that the U.S. Constitution does not protect a fundamental right to abortion.

Webster v. Reproductive Health Services drew seventy-six *amicus curiae* (friend of the court) briefs, more than any other case in recent history. Among the groups that filed briefs urging pro-life action were the Christian Action Council, Americans United for Life, the National Right to Life Committee, the U.S. Catholic Conference, the National Association of Evangelicals, and JustLife. Groups urging pro-choice action included Planned Parenthood, the American Civil Liberties Union, the Religious Coalition for Abortion Rights, the National Organization for Women, and the National Abortion Rights Action League. The presidential administration of George H. W. Bush also submitted a brief. The administration position was that *Roe v. Wade* should be overruled and that Missouri should not be required either to fund abortion counseling or to use public employees or facilities to perform abortions. Bush had campaigned on an antiabortion platform and was on the record as favoring a constitutional amendment barring abortions except in cases of rape and incest and to save the life of the mother.

Pro-life and pro-choice groups swung into action. Legal representatives for Reproductive Health Services contended that the right to choose an abortion is properly among the fundamental freedoms protected by the Constitution. Acting Solicitor General William C. Bryson directly contradicted that contention in the brief submitted for the Bush administration. He stated that a supposed fundamental right to abortion can draw no support from either the text of the Constitution or U.S. history. Pro-choice historians argued that abortion should not be restricted in 1989 because abortion was neither uncommon nor illegal in the early nineteenth century. Pro-life groups countered that slavery, child labor, and the disenfranchisement of women were also common and legal at that time.

Religious leaders tended to focus on their belief in a fundamental right to life, and thus sided with the pro-lifers. Not all religious persons were on the pro-life side of the argument, however. Faith Evans, president of the Religious Coalition for Abortion Rights, pledged at a press conference that the religious community would not allow restrictions and erosion of the rights guaranteed by *Roe v. Wade*. Mark Ellingsen, a Lutheran pastor in Salisbury, North Carolina, argued that human life should be defined not by biological viability but by the more specifically human characteristic of relationality. If this definition were to be accepted, no human rights would be denied in the case of an abortion because it is impossible for a fetus to be involved in a relationship. Finally, some religious groups, such as the United Methodists, argued that women could be exploited by boyfriends, spouses, and even governments if the choice of whether to bear children is not firmly in women's own hands.

The Supreme Court Ruling

On July 3, 1989, the Supreme Court ruling in the case of *Webster v. Reproductive Health Services* upheld Missouri's abortion restrictions. The Supreme Court would no longer be the primary locus of the abortion controversy. Power would now reside as well in state and national legislative bodies, and with the governors of the states.

With that expanded battlefront in mind, pro-life activists in every state began developing strategies to limit abortion. They planned for the introduction of legislation that could include requiring doctors to give women detailed information about fetal development and possible complications from abortion, granting some veto power to the father of the unborn child, and prohibiting abortion for reasons such as the sex of the child, inconvenience, or financial hardship.

One year after the *Webster* decision, in 1990, approximately three hundred bills had been introduced across most of the forty-four state legislatures that held sessions in that year. Pennsylvania was the first state to take legislative action, passing a bill that set limits on late abortion; mandated notification of husband, informed consent, and a twenty-four-hour waiting period before an abortion; and banned sex-selection abortion and the use of aborted fetuses for medical research. South Carolina and Michigan passed laws requiring parental consent before a minor's abortion. West Virginia passed a law setting limits on state-funded abortions. Indiana established subsidies for the adoption of special-needs children as an alternative to abortion.

Attempts to pass pro-life legislation were not always successful, however. In Idaho, Louisiana, and Mississippi, restrictive laws were passed by the legislature but vetoed by the governor. Florida governor Robert Martinez miscalculated badly in calling a special legislative session to bar public funding for abortion and to require fetal viability tests: 65 percent of the electorate opposed the special session, and 71 percent favored leaving Florida's permissive abortion laws alone or even expanding them. Martinez's popularity rating subsequently plunged to 24 percent.

Significance

Although the 1989 *Webster v. Reproductive Health Services* decision did not result in any drastic curtailment in the number of abortions performed in the United States, at least not in the short run, pro-life groups rightly hailed it as a significant change of policy on the part of the Supreme Court, one that allowed them to have a greater share in the decision-making processes regarding abortion.

With more legislative possibilities open to them than at any time since 1973, pro-life groups began to suffer from internal divisions. Although the official policy of all major pro-life groups was to oppose abortion even in cases of rape and incest, some groups were willing to compromise on that issue in order to get laws passed that would severely restrict the number of abortions performed each year. Doug Scott, director of public policy for the Christian Action Council, said that he would feel responsible for the other 99 percent of the abortions performed if he were not willing to work with the system on the 1 to 3 percent of all abortions that are done following rape or incest. Others sided with Nellie Gray, president of March for Life, who was opposed to any exceptions or compromises. Such thinking, she said, bargains some human lives away. How is it right, she asked, to say that we will defend babies, but not those babies who are conceived through rape or incest?

Still other pro-lifers believed that to applaud the *Webster* decision, and to scramble to pass more legislation along the lines of the Missouri statute that it upheld, was to skew the pro-life position in an unfortunate direction. Kathleen Hayes, director of publications for Evangelicals for Social Action and

JustLife, pointed out that although the *Webster* decision served to protect more of the unborn, it did little for their often-desperate mothers. It thus fell short, in her opinion, of being fully pro-life.

In 1989, survey results showed that 69 percent of Americans believed that the lives of unborn babies should be protected, and 67 percent believed that a woman should have the right to choose to have an abortion. The American public seemed to oppose both "abortion on demand" and government control of a woman's reproductive capacity. Such survey results explain why either side in this debate has been capable of winning a majority, as findings depend on how the issue is phrased.

The abortion issue had become extremely polarized as a result of the Supreme Court decision in *Roe v. Wade*, which effectively removed abortion from the give-and-take of the legislative process. In other developed nations, in which the abortion issue was settled legislatively rather than judicially, political compromises had long since been worked out. Those compromises were remarkably similar to one another and also remarkably similar to what most Americans seem to want, if results of public opinion polls are a reliable indication. The compromises attempted to balance compassion for pregnant women and concern for fetal life.

The abortion issue is morally complex. It involves concerns about life, choice, gender, responsibility, and dependence. *Roe v. Wade* did not do justice to the complexity of the moral issues involved, nor did it do justice to the complexity of American moral sentiment surrounding abortion. In the *Roe* decision, the Supreme Court allowed one important value, that of privacy, to take priority over all others. In so doing, it closed the door for sixteen years on the business of weighing and deciding among competing interests and values. *Webster v. Reproductive Health Services* reopened that door.

Ann Marie B. Bahr

Further Reading
Balkin, Jack M., ed. *What Roe v. Wade Should Have Said: The Nation's Top Legal Experts Rewrite America's Most Controversial Decision.* New York: New York University Press, 2005. Eleven constitutional scholars rewrite the opinions in the landmark case using sources available at the time of its decision. Authors take positions for and against the right to abortion.

Biskupic, Joan. "Abortion Protagonists Gird for Crucial Court Test: No Matter What the Outcome, a New Flurry of Activity Seems Certain in Congress, State Legislatures." *Congressional Quarterly Weekly Report* 47 (April 8, 1989): 753-758. One of the best single articles available on *Webster v. Reproductive Health Services*, and among the most comprehensive. Describes the case and its history and tells where individual members of Congress, the Supreme Court, the administration, and the states stood on the eve of the decision. Also includes abortion statistics from the Alan Guttmacher Institute.

Dellinger, Walter. "Day in Court: No One Wins if *Roe* Is Restricted." *The New Republic*, May 8, 1989, 11-12. Expresses the pro-choice side of the debate. Written from a secular point of view.

Glendon, Mary Ann. "A World Without *Roe*: How Different Would It Be?" *The New Republic*, February 20, 1989, 19-20. Insightful article, written by a professor of law at Harvard University, discusses the problems with *Roe*. Analyzes how *Roe v. Wade* blocked the normal legislative avenues for debate and discussion on difficult issues.

Hayes, Kathleen. "Fully Pro-Life." *Sojourners* 18 (November 22, 1989). Discussion of the topic of abortion takes a pro-life position that is both nuanced and morally sensitive.

Hull, N. E. H., and Peter Charles Hoffer. *Roe v. Wade: The Abortion Rights Controversy in American History*. Lawrence: University Press of Kansas, 2001. Provides a complete legal history of abortion in the United States from colonial times to the early twenty-first century.

Lawton, Kim A. "Confrontation's Stage Is Set: A Supreme Court Decision Marks the Beginning of a New Era in the Abortion Debate, an Era Long Awaited by Abortion Foes." *Christianity Today* 33 (August 18, 1989): 36-38.

_____. "Could This Be the Year? Supreme Court Observers Say the 1973 *Roe v. Wade* Decision Could Be Restricted—and Perhaps Overturned—This Term." *Christianity Today* 33 (April 7, 1989): 36-38.

_____. "Taking It to the States: In Light of the Supreme Court's *Webster* Decision, Pro-life Activists Focus on States as the New Abortion Battlefields." *Christianity Today* 33 (November 3, 1989): 36-38. *Christianity Today* provided the most sustained pro-life coverage of the 1989 challenge to *Roe v. Wade* and its aftermath. These three articles provide a sample of the periodical's coverage.

McGurn, William. "What the People Really Say." *National Review*, December 22, 1989, 26-29. Analyzes the abortion debate from a neutral point of view, neither pro-life nor pro-choice in orientation.

Meeks, Catherine. "To Respect Life." *Sojourners* 18 (November 22, 1989). States the pro-life position with a greater degree of moral sensitivity than is often found.

O'Connor, Karen. *No Neutral Ground? Abortion Politics in an Age of Absolutes*. Boulder, Colo.: Westview Press, 1996. Focuses on the dilemma of abortion as a political issue. Examines key court cases and events in the history of the abortion debate in the United States.

Ranck, Lee. "A Special Issue on Abortion." *Christian Social Action* 3 (April,

1990): 1-16. Expresses the pro-choice side of the debate. Written from a religious point of view.

Reagan, Leslie J. *When Abortion Was a Crime: Women, Medicine, and Law in the United States, 1867-1973.* Berkeley: University of California Press, 1997. Examines the history of abortion during the period when it was illegal in the United States and portrays the experiences of women who sought illegal abortions. Draws on court records, police reports, and coroners' reports, among other sources.

See also *Akron v. Akron Center for Reproductive Health; Bigelow v. Virginia; Doe v. Bolton; Harris v. McRae; Maher v. Roe; Planned Parenthood of Central Missouri v. Danforth; Roe v. Wade; Rust v. Sullivan; Thornburgh v. American College of Obstetricians and Gynecologists.*

WEEKS V. SOUTHERN BELL

Court: U.S. Court of Appeals for the Fifth Circuit
Citation: 408 F.2d 228
Date: March 4, 1969
Issues: Civil rights and liberties; Employment discrimination; Labor law; Sex discrimination; Women's issues

• This opinion by a federal appeals court strictly interpreted the Civil Rights Act of 1964 with regard to the prohibition of discrimination in employment based on sex, thus opening many jobs to women.

In 1966, Lorena W. Weeks, an employee of Southern Bell for nineteen years, applied for the job of switchman. Her employer refused to consider her application, stating that the decision had been made that women would not be employed as switchmen. Weeks responded by filing a complaint with the Equal Employment Opportunity Commission (EEOC) stating that the refusal to hire women as switchmen violated the Civil Rights Act of 1964. An investigation by the EEOC indicated that Weeks might have a valid claim of discrimination based on sex.

Southern Bell argued that the job of switchman was an exception to the law because it required the lifting of heavy objects and emergency work. The Court responded that Southern Bell had not proven the position to be an exception to the law. While "men are stronger on average than women," the court stated, "it is not clear that any conclusions about relative lifting ability would follow." The Court ruled that many women are capable of performing the duties of a switchman.

Donald C. Simmons, Jr.

See also *County of Washington v. Gunther; Frontiero v. Richardson; Geduldig v. Aiello; Hoyt v. Florida; Phillips v. Martin Marietta Corp.; Rosenfeld v. Southern Pacific; Stanton v. Stanton.*

WEEKS V. UNITED STATES

Court: U.S. Supreme Court
Citation: 232 U.S. 383
Date: February 24, 1914
Issues: Evidence; Right to privacy; Search and seizure

- In order to enforce the privacy values of the Fourth Amendment, the Court ordered that illegally obtained evidence must be excluded from criminal trials in federal courts; this order is commonly called the "exclusionary rule."

After Fremont Weeks was arrested for illegally sending lottery tickets through the U.S. mail service, a federal marshal accompanied by a police officer, without a search warrant, broke into Weeks's private home and seized incriminating evidence. Although the defendant argued that the search and seizure contradicted the requirements of the Fourth Amendment, the resulting evidence was used to convict him in a federal district court. Weeks appealed his case to the U.S. Supreme Court.

Until the *Weeks* decision, American courts had followed the common-law practice of allowing federal prosecutors to use evidence unlawfully seized by law-enforcement officers. Many constitutional scholars had argued that the traditional practice encouraged governmental violations of liberties guaranteed in the Constitution, and they insisted that it was inconsistent with the Fourth Amendment's purpose of treating people's houses as their castles.

Based on this point of view, the Supreme Court in *Boyd v. United States* (1886) criticized and implicitly rejected the common-law practice, but the

Court stopped short of explicitly ruling the inadmissibility of evidence obtained illegally. The *Boyd* pronouncements on privacy values, without any means of enforcement, appeared to have no impact on the behavior of those who enforced the laws.

In *Weeks* an impatient Court unanimously required federal courts thereafter to apply the exclusionary rule in all criminal prosecutions. In the official opinion, Justice William Day declared that without the exclusionary rule, the Fourth Amendment was of "no value" and "might as well be stricken from the Constitution." The noble goal of punishing the guilty must not be used as an excuse to sacrifice the "fundamental rights" established by the Constitution. Day's opinion did not clearly articulate whether the application of the exclusionary rule was an individual right guaranteed by the Constitution or whether it was simply a judicial device developed to prevent unreasonable searches and seizures. Although these two views would continue to be debated by the Court, most justices have accepted Day's conclusion that the exclusionary rule is the only practical means of requiring government to conform to constitutional rules.

The immediate impact of the *Weeks* decision was limited, because it did not apply to state courts where most criminal prosecutions took place. When the Court ruled that the Fourth Amendment was binding on the states in *Wolf v. Colorado* (1949), the Court did not require states to follow the exclusionary rule, and until *Elkins v. United States* (1960), the so-called silver platter doctrine permitted federal prosecutors to make use of evidence illegally seized by agents of the states. Finally, in *Mapp v. Ohio* (1961), the Supreme Court required the application of the exclusionary rule in state courts. The exclusionary rule has always been controversial, for it sometimes makes it more difficult to prosecute criminals. Critics argue that there are alternative means of protecting the rights of the Fourth Amendment, but defenders reply that the alternatives do not provide effective protection.

Thomas Tandy Lewis

See also *Boyd v. United States; Brown v. Mississippi; Chimel v. California; Mapp v. Ohio; Rummel v. Estelle; Wolf v. Colorado.*

WEEMS V. UNITED STATES

Court: U.S. Supreme Court
Citation: 217 U.S. 349
Date: May 2, 1910
Issues: Cruel and unusual punishment

• The U.S. Supreme Court overturned a sentence as cruel and unusual for the first time, interpreting the term as referring to punishments that were unnecessarily cruel and grossly excessive for the crime.

Paul Weems, a coast guard officer in the Philippines, was found guilty of falsifying the public record and sentenced to fifteen years at *cadena*, a punishment of Spanish origin that required the prisoner to serve the entire term at hard labor bound by heavy chains around his wrists and ankles. Although the sentence was given under Philippine law, the Philippine Bill of Rights contained a provision almost identical to the Eighth Amendment. By a 4-2 margin, the Supreme Court ordered Weems released. Writing for the majority, Justice Joseph McKenna recognized that the concept of cruelty changed over time and that a punishment for a particular crime was cruel when disproportionately harsh in comparison with those levied for more serious crimes.

Thomas Tandy Lewis

See also *Furman v. Georgia; Harmelin v. Michigan; Hutto v. Davis; Louisiana ex rel. Francis v. Resweber; Robinson v. California; Rummel v. Estelle; Stanford v. Kentucky; Trop v. Dulles.*

WEINBERGER V. WIESENFELD

Court: U.S. Supreme Court
Citation: 420 U.S. 636
Date: March 19, 1975
Issues: Sex discrimination

• The U.S. Supreme Court overturned a provision of the Social Security Act that awarded benefits to widows but not widowers.

In the aftermath of *Reed v. Reed* (1971), in which the Supreme Court ruled that classifying by gender is an equal protection violation, the Court faced the problem that many "benign" classifications favored women over men. In *Kahn v. Shevin* (1974), the Court was badly divided when it upheld a Florida law giving tax relief to widows but not to widowers. In *Weinberger*, however, the Court unanimously struck down a provision of the Social Security Act that awarded benefits to widows but not widowers. Justice William J. Brennan, Jr., wrote the opinion for the Court. Chief Justice Warren E. Burger, and Justices Lewis F. Powell, Jr., and William H. Rehnquist concurred.

Richard L. Wilson

See also *County of Washington v. Gunther; Frontiero v. Richardson; Geduldig v. Aiello; Hoyt v. Florida; Meritor Savings Bank v. Vinson; Reed v. Reed; Rosenfeld v. Southern Pacific; Stanton v. Stanton.*

WESBERRY V. SANDERS

Court: U.S. Supreme Court
Citation: 376 U.S. 1
Date: February 17, 1964
Issues: Reapportionment and redistricting

• This decision required that congressional districts within a state be approximately equal in size.

The topic of representation in Congress and state legislatures—with the related issues of apportionment and districting—was long avoided by the federal courts. When in the 1946 case of *Colegrove v. Green* the U.S. Supreme Court was asked to consider the imbalance in size of congressional districts in Illinois (which had not been redistricted since 1901), it declined to enter "the political thicket" and said that such matters were the proper concern of legislative bodies. In 1929, Congress had stopped mandating that states redraw district lines after each census. The result was that by the 1960's there were substantial inequalities in the sizes of congressional (and state legislative) districts in many states, a situation that usually meant the decided over-representation of rural populations.

An important indication that change might be on the way came in the case of *Baker v. Carr* (1962). In this case the U.S. Supreme Court ruled that questions of apportionment and districting were within the jurisdiction of federal courts, effectively reversing the doctrine it had followed in the *Colegrove* case. The court took up the question directly when it agreed to hear *Wesberry v. Sanders*. This case had its origins in a class-action suit by voters in Fulton County, Georgia, who claimed that they were cheated of fair representation. They pointed out that their urban and suburban fifth district was approximately three times larger than the rural ninth district, though each was represented by one congressman. The Court upheld their challenge by a 7-2 majority. It based its decision on Article I, section 2 of the Constitution, which says that representatives should be chosen "by the People of the several States." The court interpreted this to mean that one person's vote should be equal to another's.

Wesberry was followed by other "reapportionment decisions." In *Reynolds v. Sims* (also 1964) the Court reached a similar conclusion with regard to state legislative districts (though grounding its decision here in the Fourteenth Amendment's equal protection clause).

By mandating equality in population among congressional districts, the Court brought a considerable shift in congressional representation and political power from rural areas to urban and—especially—suburban ones that would continue for the rest of the century. Other decisions had a similar effect at the state level, though the Court did tolerate greater differences in size among state legislative districts than among congressional districts. Once established, the doctrine of "one person, one vote" raised other questions, such as the extent to which racial and ethnic considerations should be factored into apportionment and districting.

William C. Lowe

See also *Baker v. Carr; Colegrove v. Green; Reynolds v. Sims.*

WEST COAST HOTEL CO. v. PARRISH

Court: U.S. Supreme Court
Citation: 300 U.S. 379
Date: March 29, 1937
Issues: Employment discrimination; Labor law; Sex discrimination; Women's issues

- In this case, the U.S. Supreme Court upheld a state minimum wage law and signaled the end of an era declaring many similar state laws unconstitutional on the basis of substantive due process.

The state of Washington enacted a minimum wage law for women in 1913. Elsie Parrish, a hotel chambermaid, sued her employer, the West Coast Hotel Company, for her minimum wage under the terms of the Washington law. She was seeking $14.50 for forty-eight hours of work. The Washington Supreme Court upheld the law, and the employer appealed to the U.S. Supreme Court. Chief Justice Charles Evans Hughes, writing for the narrow five-member majority, upheld the law under the U.S. Constitution's Fourteenth Amendment. The majority held that the protection of women workers was a legitimate end for the states to regulate. Further, a minimum wage for women provides for their subsistence and is a permissible means for the state to achieve the desired end.

This decision reversed several earlier cases which had declared similar state statutes unconstitutional under the Lochner doctrine. This doctrine was generally based on the Court's 1905 decision in *Lochner v. New York*, which struck down a New York maximum hours law as unconstitutional. The Lochner doctrine applied the Fourteenth Amendment due process clause to invalidate state legislation under the grounds of substantive due process. The Court had held state regulation of business activities to be an invasion of the fundamental freedom of individuals to enter into contracts of their own free choice. Such an argument was used many times to strike down state laws as unconstitutional that protected workers such as maximum hours laws.

The West Coast Hotel Company case is significant in that it was decided during the era of the "Court-packing plan" of President Franklin D. Roosevelt, during which the Court majority changed and reversed some of its earlier decisions. The *West Coast Hotel* decision vote by Justice Owen J. Roberts is cited as the "switch in time that saved nine" when he apparently changed his vote from his position in an earlier case. The Court then started to uphold many pieces of the Roosevelt administration's New Deal legislation and signaled the beginning of the modern era of judicial scrutiny of state and federal legislation.

Subsequently, the rationale of the Court has been criticized for relying too much on an argument that it is necessary to provide special protection to women in the workplace. In many early cases, during the period 1906-1937, courts had been willing to uphold legislation that characterized women as weaker and in need of more state protection. These laws have since generally given way to less sexually stereotypical laws that apply to all employees, not simply women.

Scott A. White

See also *Allgeyer v. Louisiana; Lochner v. New York; Morehead v. New York ex rel. Tipaldo.*

WEST RIVER BRIDGE CO. V. DIX

Court: U.S. Supreme Court
Citation: 47 U.S. 507
Date: January 31, 1848
Issues: Freedom of contract

• The U.S. Supreme Court expanded eminent domain to prevail over contracts the state made with private parties and further established that police power cannot be contracted away.

The state of Vermont had signed a one-hundred-year contract with the West River Bridge Company but later decided to build a free road over the toll bridge. Although the state paid the bridge company for its property and franchise, the bridge company hired the famed Daniel Webster to represent it, maintaining that the state's action violated the contracts clause. By a 7-1 vote, the Supreme Court ruled against the bridge company. In the opinion for the Court, Peter V. Daniel wrote that the state could not contract away its basic police power and that eminent domain prevailed over Vermont's earlier contract. Justice James M. Wayne dissented, and Justice John McKinley did not participate.

Richard L. Wilson

See also *Barron v. Baltimore; Berman v. Parker; Hawaii Housing Authority v. Midkiff; Kelo v. City of New London; Nollan v. California Coastal Commission; Stone v. Mississippi.*

WEST VIRGINIA STATE BOARD OF EDUCATION V. BARNETTE

Court: U.S. Supreme Court
Citation: 319 U.S. 624
Date: June 14, 1943
Issues: Education; Freedom of expression

- In 1940, the U.S. Supreme Court ruled that it was constitutional for public schools to expel children who refused to salute the American flag. Three years later, in *West Virginia State Board of Education v. Barnette,* the Court overturned its decision, ruling that under the First Amendment the state had no authority to compel political speech.

In 1872, in the state of Pennsylvania, a new American religious sect was born that, in time, spread around the globe. Its founder was Charles Taze Russell, who became the first president of the Watch Tower Bible and Tract Society. The members of the new sect were called by a variety of names, including Russellites and Bible Students. In time, however, they came most commonly to be known as Jehovah's Witnesses.

Members of the sect became unpopular with many Americans because of both their religious beliefs and their aggressive door-to-door proselytizing. Jehovah's Witnesses believed that they alone were God's chosen people, and they believed that the clergy of other faiths were working for Satan. While they did not spare Protestant and Jewish clergy, they reserved the worst of their epithets for the Roman Catholic hierarchy. Many people who opened their doors to Jehovah's Witnesses' knocks became quite irate when they heard their religions and their clergy maligned. Even when the Witnesses were clearly unwelcome, they would return repeatedly.

Besides being offended by their proselytizing tactics, many people questioned whether Jehovah's Witnesses were loyal Americans. Witnesses were willing to obey the laws of the United States or any other government under which they lived, as long as the laws were not contrary to what they believed to be God's law. Because they believed that God had no interest in World War I, Jehovah's Witnesses refused to serve in the American military and, consequently, went to prison. Witnesses in Germany experienced a similar fate. Both sides in the war perceived Jehovah's Witnesses as unpatriotic and disloyal.

As events in Europe unfolded in the 1930's, increasing the possibility that the United States might once again be involved in a world war, local American communities sought to inculcate patriotism and penalize nonconformity. Such was the case in Minersville, Pennsylvania. Pursuant to state law, the school board in that town sought to encourage patriotism in public school children by making a flag salute ceremony, including the Pledge of Allegiance, a required part of the school day. Believing the flag salute to be the equivalent of worshiping a graven image, which is prohibited in the Old Testament, children of Jehovah's Witnesses refused to participate in the ceremony. The penalty for their refusal was expulsion.

The Witnesses' Case

The Jehovah's Witnesses sought a decision from the federal courts exempting them on religious grounds from participation in the flag salute ceremony. They were successful in the lower federal courts, but the school board appealed to the U.S. Supreme Court. In 1940, in the case of *Minersville v. Gobitis*, the Supreme Court, with only one justice dissenting, reversed the lower courts and upheld the right of a school board to require patriotic exercises, such as the flag salute ceremony, of all students regardless of their religious beliefs. Justice Felix Frankfurter, writing for the majority, noted that the purpose of the flag salute was the promotion of national unity. He considered such promotion to be a matter of educational policy with which courts should not interfere. Persons were free to hold whatever religious beliefs they chose, but their beliefs did not entitle them to exemption from public policies of general application.

Following the *Gobitis* decision, such patriotic ceremonies became increasingly common in the public schools of the nation, forcing hard choices on Jehovah's Witnesses with children in the public schools. Many chose to follow their religion rather than the law, and their children were expelled from school. In some instances, after expulsion the children were treated as delinquents, taken from their families, and placed in institutions. Also in the after-

Justice Felix Frankfurter.
(Library of Congress)

math of the *Gobitis* decision, Jehovah's Witnesses increasingly became victims of violence. Violence against them had existed before the Supreme Court decision, but it increased afterward. At various times, as they sought to promulgate their religion, they were attacked by mobs, had dogs turned loose on them, and had rocks and boiling water thrown at them.

In the midst of this wave of violence, one event occurred that offered the Witnesses some hope in the legal arena. In another Supreme Court case involving Jehovah's Witnesses, three justices who had been with the majority in *Minersville v. Gobitis* took the highly unusual step of saying that they had reconsidered the matter and now believed the earlier case to have been incorrectly decided. The statement was almost an invitation to the Witnesses to try again. They had their opportunity in *West Virginia State Board of Education v. Barnette*.

Relying on the *Gobitis* opinion for its authority, the West Virginia State Board of Education had adopted a resolution ordering that the flag salute become a regular school activity. The Witnesses again sought judicial vindication of their rights when some of their children were expelled for refusing to salute the flag. The case again progressed to the Supreme Court, and this time, the Court ruled in favor of the Jehovah's Witnesses.

Positions of the Justices

Harlan Fiske Stone, who had been the lone dissenter in the *Gobitis* case, had become chief justice of the United States in 1941. In addition to the chief justice, the Witnesses knew they had the support of the three justices who had indicated that they had changed their minds: Hugo L. Black, William O. Douglas, and Frank Murphy. Only one more vote was needed for a majority. Justice Robert H. Jackson, who had been appointed to the Court by President Franklin D. Roosevelt in 1941, provided that vote. Chief Justice Stone assigned Justice Jackson the task of writing the opinion of the Court, which was handed down on Flag Day, June 14, 1943.

Justice Jackson viewed the controversy from a different perspective than had the justices in the *Gobitis* majority. To them, the question was whether the religious beliefs of the Jehovah's Witnesses exempted them from the compulsory flag salute. To Justice Jackson, the question was whether the state had the authority to compel children to salute the flag in the first place. He did not consider the controversy to revolve around the free exercise of religion but rather around the freedom of speech. He saw no need to determine whether the religious convictions of the Witnesses exempted them from the requirement to salute the flag if the state lacked the authority to make the flag salute a legal duty.

In Justice Jackson's opinion, the First Amendment's guarantee of freedom of speech deprived the state of authority to compel the flag salute, because the freedom of the individual to speak implies the freedom of the individual not to speak what he does not believe. Jackson denied that patriotism needed to be propped up by compulsory ceremonies. He further denied that the Court was invading the sphere of competence of school boards. Through the due process clause of the Fourteenth Amendment, the First Amendment's guarantee of freedom of speech placed limitations on what states and their instrumentalities, such as school boards, could do. He asserted that it was the responsibility of the Court to see that limitations imposed by the Bill of Rights were not exceeded. In this case, the West Virginia State Board of Education had exceeded one of these limitations. The compulsory flag salute was unconstitutional.

Justice Frankfurter, an Austrian Jew and naturalized citizen who had written the majority opinion in *Minersville v. Gobitis*, was now in the position of having to write a dissent. Clearly uncomfortable with the possibility of being perceived as one who sanctioned the persecution of unpopular minorities, he reminded the majority that he himself was a member of "the most vilified and persecuted minority in history." Frankfurter asserted that he would have voted with the majority if his personal opinion were all that mattered. As a judge, however, he could not permit his personal opinion to control his vote.

He continued to consider the flag salute an educational exercise, one which did not interfere with anyone's freedom of speech.

Frankfurter noted that Jehovah's Witnesses, children and parents, were free to use their right of free speech to denounce the flag salute and everything it stood for. If any law attempted to prevent that, Frankfurter said that he would be the first to rule that it was unconstitutional. He continued to believe, however, that a compulsory flag salute ceremony was a legitimate educational measure within the scope of school officials' authority.

Significance

West Virginia State Board of Education v. Barnette, by overruling *Minersville v. Gobitis*, removed the legitimacy which the Court had conferred on compulsory flag salute exercises in 1940. Moreover, because the decision was rendered on the basis of the right to freedom of speech rather than the right to free exercise of religion, persons could choose not to participate in the flag salute even if they held no specifically religious beliefs prohibiting their participation. It was, however, the Jehovah's Witnesses and others who refused to salute the flag for religious reasons who were the primary beneficiaries of the decision.

The Supreme Court's *Barnette* decision, in combination with other factors, resulted in decreased persecution of Jehovah's Witnesses. Mindful of the need for enforcement to give weight to the Court's ruling, the Department of Justice conscientiously sought to enforce that ruling without engaging in widespread prosecutions. United States attorneys spoke with school officials who attempted to require flag salutes and tried to persuade them to end the practice. The threat of federal prosecution usually brought compliance.

Also contributing to the decreased persecution of the Jehovah's Witnesses was that the nation was at war. The flag salute controversy had been going on for a long time, but by 1943 most Americans had more on their minds than a few children who would not salute the flag. Adolf Hitler was clearly a greater threat than the school behavior of children of the Jehovah's Witness sect.

Beyond its effect upon the Jehovah's Witnesses, the Court's decision in *West Virginia State Board of Education v. Barnette* contributed to a growing body of law asserting that the First Amendment protected both the right to speak and the right to refuse to speak, as well as the rights to act and to refuse to act when the actions in question were primarily expressive or interpretable as a form of speech. It was the precedent of the *Barnette* case, for example, that led the Court to decide in 1989 that flag burning was a constitutionally protected form of speech, since the earlier decision suggested that neither speech nor expressive actions could be curtailed for the purpose of preserving the American flag's symbolic value.

Patricia A. Behlar

Further Reading

Conant, Michael. *Constitutional Structure and Purposes: Critical Commentary.* Westport, Conn.: Greenwood Press, 2001. Commentary on a range of constitutional issues. Includes sections on both the Supreme Court's flag salute cases and its flag desecration cases. Bibliographic references and index.

Dilliard, Irving. "The Flag-Salute Cases." In *Quarrels That Have Shaped the Constitution,* edited by John A. Garraty. Rev. ed. New York: Harper & Row, 1987. Brief account of the flag salute cases written for the general reader. Although its primary focus is on the reasoning of the justices of the Supreme Court, it does not neglect the plight of the Jehovah's Witnesses.

Jackson, Robert H. *Dispassionate Justice: A Synthesis of the Judicial Opinions of Robert H. Jackson.* Edited by Glendon Schubert. Indianapolis: Bobbs-Merrill, 1969. Includes Justice Jackson's majority opinion in *West Virginia State Board of Education v. Barnette,* as well as discussion of Jackson's position in other Jehovah's Witnesses cases.

Lee, Francis Graham. *Church-State Relations.* Westport, Conn.: Greenwood Press, 2002. Discusses the flag salute cases in the context of the general history of separation of church and state in the United States. Bibliographic references and index.

Manwaring, David Roger. *Render unto Caesar: The Flag Salute Controversy.* Chicago: University of Chicago Press, 1962. Thorough case study of the flag salute controversy. Discusses the parties to the cases, the opinions of Supreme Court Justices, public reactions to the decisions, and the impact of the decisions.

Penton, M. James. *Apocalypse Delayed: The Story of Jehovah's Witnesses.* Toronto, Ont.: University of Toronto Press, 1985. A useful history of the Jehovah's Witnesses by a Canadian historian who was himself a fourth generation Jehovah's Witness until being expelled for heresy. Includes some discussion of the flag salute controversy. Contains bibliography and index.

Simon, James F. *The Antagonists: Hugo Black, Felix Frankfurter, and Civil Liberties in Modern America.* New York: Simon & Schuster, 1989. Using an engaging writing style to reach a general audience, the author focuses on the above-named justices, emphasizing their human qualities and their competition for leadership on the Supreme Court. He devotes several pages to their conflict in the flag salute controversy. Indexed, well researched and documented, but no bibliography.

See also *Cantwell v. Connecticut; Cox v. New Hampshire; Lovell v. City of Griffin; Minersville School District v. Gobitis; Murdock v. Pennsylvania.*

WESTON V. CHARLESTON

Court: U.S. Supreme Court
Citation: 27 U.S. 624
Date: March 18, 1829
Issues: Taxation

• The U.S. Supreme Court reaffirmed an earlier ruling in holding that states could not tax instruments of the federal government.

The city of Charleston, South Carolina, sought to place a tax on the earnings from bonds issued by the U.S. government. The Supreme Court, by a 4-2 vote, ruled that this tax was unconstitutional. It reaffirmed its holding in *McCulloch v. Maryland* (1819) that states and their subunits could not tax an instrument of the United States. Chief Justice John Marshall wrote the opinion for the Court at a time when there were only six members because of the death of Robert Trimble. Justices William Johnson and Smith Thompson dissented.

Richard L. Wilson

See also *Collector v. Day; Dobbins v. Erie County; Graves v. New York ex rel. O'Keefe; Helvering v. Davis; McCray v. United States; McCulloch v. Maryland.*

WHITNEY V. CALIFORNIA

Court: U.S. Supreme Court
Citation: 274 U.S. 357
Date: May 26, 1927
Issues: Freedom of assembly and association

• The U.S. Supreme Court refined the clear and present danger concept to clearly require an imminence test.

Charlotte Whitney was a member of the International Workers of the World (IWW) and briefly a member of the Communist Labor Party, which advocated the overthrow of the U.S. government. There was no indication that Whitney did more than attend meetings, but the jury convicted her on criminal syndicalism charges. The Supreme Court unanimously sustained her conviction and the California state criminal syndicalism statute under which she was convicted. Justice Edward T. Sanford, in his opinion for the Court, cited the state's power to protect the public from violence resulting from political action.

Justices Oliver Wendell Holmes and Louis D. Brandeis concurred, with some very significant differences from the majority. They argued that Whitney's lawyers failed her and therefore the conviction needed to stand, but they believed her lawyers might have succeeded had they used the argument that clear and present danger needed to be imminently present for her to be convicted. The justices insisted that imminence was a crucial requirement before the government could restrain speech. Only with the concept of imminence did the clear and present danger doctrine offer much hope of protecting free speech. Eventually Whitney was overturned by the Court in *Brandenburg v. Ohio* (1968).

Richard L. Wilson

See also *Abrams v. United States; Brandenburg v. Ohio; Dennis v. United States; Elfbrandt v. Russell; Gitlow v. New York; Lovell v. City of Griffin; Schenck v. United States; Stromberg v. California.*

WHREN V. UNITED STATES

Court: U.S. Supreme Court
Citation: 517 U.S. 806
Date: June 10, 1996
Issues: Police powers; Search and seizure

• This U.S. Supreme Court ruling on Fourth Amendment protections upheld the authority of police officers to stop automobiles whenever there is probable cause of minor traffic violations, even if circumstances suggest that the officers are motivated by considerations of race or physical appearance of the motorists.

Because the U.S. Supreme Court has ruled that stopping a motorist to issue a ticket for a traffic violation does not constitute an arrest, officers do not need to issue Miranda warnings to cited motorists. Nevertheless, anything that such motorists say to officers while receiving their citations may be used against them in court, should their cases go to trial. (Brand-X Pictures)

In what is considered a "high-drug area" of Washington, D.C., plainclothes officers in an unmarked vehicle noticed a truck occupied by two young African Americans who were waiting at a stop sign for about twenty seconds. The truck then turned without signaling and left the intersection at an excessive speed. When the officers stopped the truck—presumably to warn the driver about a possible traffic violation—they observed plastic bags that appeared to contain cocaine. The officers arrested the two men, who were later convicted of violating federal drug laws.

At trial, defense attorneys argued unsuccessfully that the evidence should be suppressed. Because plainclothes officers almost never enforce minor traffic violations, the attorneys asserted that the officers' justification for stopping the truck was pretextual. Indeed, the circumstances of the case strongly suggested that the officers were motivated by vague suspicions that were influenced by the location and race of the defendants. To prevent abuses such as racial profiling, the defense attorneys proposed an alternative test for automobile stops.

After reviewing the case, the Supreme Court unanimously upheld the original convictions and rejected the alternative test proposed by the defense. In the opinion for the Court, Justice Antonin Scalia wrote, "the decision to stop an automobile is reasonable where the police have probable cause to believe that a traffic violation has occurred." He argued that the Court's precedents had never held that the existence of probable cause depends on the subjective motivation of police officers. Although acknowledging that the Fourth Amendment prohibits selective law enforcement based on considerations such as race, Scalia could see "no reasonable alternative to the traditional common-law rule that probable cause justified a search and seizure."

Many civil libertarians criticized the *Whren* decision as inconsistent with the spirit of the Fourth and Fourteenth Amendments. The broad scope of the ruling allows the police almost unfettered discretion for deciding to stop select vehicles for minor traffic violations that would usually be ignored. After making stops, the police may then seize suspicious objects in plain view, check drivers for the smell of alcohol, frisk occupants for weapons based on reasonable suspicion, and request permission to search the entire vehicle.

Critics argue that the *Whren* holding provides a rationale for selectively investigating individuals based on an intuitive hunch rather than probable cause. Such discretion is especially controversial because of evidence that officers sometimes engage in racial profiling, because of either unconscious bias or supervisors' instructions. Some African Americans complain that the decision has increased the practice of stopping drivers for "the crime of driving while black."

Thomas Tandy Lewis

Further Reading
O'Brien, David M. *Constitutional Law and Politics.* 6th ed. New York: W. W. Norton, 2005.
Whitebread, Charles, and Christopher Slobogin. *Criminal Procedures: An Analysis of Cases and Concepts.* 4th ed. New York: Foundation Press, 2000.

See also *California v. Acevedo; Carroll v. United States; Harris v. United States; Illinois v. Caballes; Illinois v. Krull; Knowles v. Iowa; New York v. Belton; United States v. Ross.*

WICKARD V. FILBURN

Court: U.S. Supreme Court
Citation: 317 U.S. 111
Date: November 9, 1942
Issues: Interstate commerce; Regulation of commerce

- This case effectively eliminated the use of the interstate commerce clause of the Constitution as a restraint on federal authority.

Beginning in 1933, the federal government attempted to raise farm prices by measures intended to restrict output. After the Agricultural Adjustment Act of 1933 had been declared unconstitutional in 1936, Congress adopted the Agricultural Adjustment Act of 1938. The law authorized the secretary of agriculture to establish a national acreage allotment for wheat that would be translated into a permissible quota for each farmer. Farmers were given an opportunity to reject the national quota level in an annual referendum vote. Production in excess of the quota would incur a financial penalty.

Roscoe Filburn, an Ohio farmer, produced 239 bushels of wheat in excess of his allotment and was assessed a penalty of $117. He obtained an injunction from a federal district court against Secretary of Agriculture Claude Wickard. Filburn used much of his wheat output on his own farm, chiefly for feed and seed. He claimed that the government policy went beyond the boundaries of interstate commerce. He further argued that a speech by Wickard had misled farmers into supporting the quota in the referendum, and that the increase in penalties by a statutory amendment in May, 1941, was improper when applied to production already undertaken.

The U.S. Supreme Court rejected Filburn's claim and upheld federal authority. The contentions concerning Wickard's speech and the penalty increase, both of which had been accepted by the district court, were dismissed. As for the commerce clause, the Court noted its previous broad construction in *United States v. Darby Lumber Co.* (1941), upholding the federal minimum-wage law. They acknowledged that the 1938 law extended regulatory authority to production not entering commerce but being consumed on the farm. Such an extension was not improper: "[E]ven if appellee's activity be local and though it may not be regarded as commerce, it may still . . . be reached by Congress if it exerts a substantial economic effect on interstate commerce." Home-consumed production of wheat in the aggregate was a potentially important influence on the price of wheat. The propriety of such regulation was a political question, said the Court, rather than an issue of constitutionality.

Taking this decision and the *Darby* case in combination, the Supreme Court clearly served notice that it was not inclined to limit the scope of federal authority by reference to the commerce clause. Thus the doctrine of *United States v. E. C. Knight Co.* (1895), that "commerce succeeds to [that is, follows] manufacture, and is not a part of it," was put aside. It is probably not mere coincidence that the *Filburn* case came during World War II, which involved such extreme extensions of federal authority as the military draft and direct controls over wages and prices. The decisions in *Filburn* and *Darby* also removed obstacles to later extensions of federal authority into employment discrimination, health and safety, and environmental protection.

Paul B. Trescott

See also *Carter v. Carter Coal Co.*; *Mulford v. Smith*; *Swift and Co. v. United States*; *United States v. Darby Lumber Co.*; *United States v. E. C. Knight Co.*

WIENER V. UNITED STATES

Court: U.S. Supreme Court
Citation: 357 U.S. 349
Date: June 30, 1958
Issues: Presidential powers

• In this decision, the U.S. Supreme Court upheld a broad presidential power over removal of executive officials but limited removal of quasi-judicial officials.

In *Myers v. United States* (1926), the Supreme Court upheld a virtually unchecked presidential power to remove officials, but this power had been limited by *Humphrey's Executor v. United States* (1935), in which the Court permitted Congress to set some limits for quasi-judicial or quasi-legislative officials. Harry S. Truman had appointed Wiener to the War Claims Commission. The length of his appointment had no limits, but President Dwight D. Eisenhower asked him to step down in 1953. After being removed by Eisenhower, Wiener filed suit, asking for back pay. The court of claims dismissed his suit. The Supreme Court followed *Humphrey's Executor* and upheld a broad presidential authority to remove executive branch officials but limited the removal of quasi-judicial officials. Because Wiener's post was quasi-judicial, the Court found in his favor and granted back pay.

Richard L. Wilson

See also *Dames and Moore v. Regan*; *Goldwater v. Carter*; *McCulloch v. Maryland*; *Martin v. Mott*; *Mississippi v. Johnson*; *Nixon v. Administrator of General Services*; *United States v. Curtiss-Wright Export Corp.*; *United States v. Nixon*; *Youngstown Sheet and Tube Co. v. Sawyer.*

WILLIAMS V. FLORIDA

Court: U.S. Supreme Court
Citation: 399 U.S. 78
Date: June 22, 1970
Issues: Juries

• The U.S. Supreme Court authorized a reduction in the size of juries from twelve to six.

Defendant Williams was convicted of a felony by a six-member jury because Florida allowed six-person juries for all criminal cases except capital murder. Williams argued that the smaller jury denied him of his Sixth Amendment right to trial by jury. The Supreme Court held, seven to one, that six people were enough to have on either a civil or a criminal jury (absent a state constitution or law mandating twelve jurors) on the state or federal level. The Court's decision has been widely criticized for offering no evidence for its conclusion that six-member juries are adequate, but the Court later reaffirmed its decision and six-member juries are now commonplace.

Richard L. Wilson

See also *Ballew v. Georgia*; *Johnson v. Louisiana*.

WILLIAMS V. MISSISSIPPI

Court: U.S. Supreme Court
Citation: 170 U.S. 213
Date: April 25, 1898
Issues: Juries

• The U.S. Supreme Court ignored its 1886 ruling and upheld the murder conviction of an African American in a trial in which no African Americans served on the jury.

Williams, an African American from Mississippi, had been convicted of murder by an all-white jury. Williams argued, in line with *Yick Wo v. Hopkins* (1886), that his indictment and conviction by all-white grand and petit juries violated the Fourteenth Amendment's equal protection clause. At the time in Mississippi, African Americans were effectively excluded from jury service because only qualified voters could serve, and poll taxes and literacy tests rendered most African Americans unable to vote. The Court distinguished *Yick Wo* and its principle that a racially fair law could be voided if it was administered in a discriminatory manner from the facts of this case, saying that Williams did not prove that the actual practice of Mississippi's suffrage laws was unfair. As a result of this ruling, other southern states quickly followed Mississippi and passed laws designed to prevent African Americans from voting. White primaries, poll taxes, and literacy tests became common in the South until white primaries were banned in the 1940's and discriminatory voting practices were stopped by the 1964 and 1965 Voting Rights Acts.

Richard L. Wilson

See also *Batson v. Kentucky; Chinese Exclusion Cases; Edmonson v. Leesville Concrete Co.; Yick Wo v. Hopkins.*

WILLSON V. BLACKBIRD CREEK MARSH CO.

Court: U.S. Supreme Court
Citation: 27 U.S. 245
Date: March 20, 1829
Issues: Regulation of commerce

• The U.S. Supreme Court's decision signaled a retreat from the strong nationalistic position the Court took in an 1824 case.

A Delaware statute allowed the Blackbird Creek Marsh Company to dam a minor navigable stream to drain a swamp. In *Gibbons v. Ogden* (1824), the Supreme Court took a strong nationalistic stand defending the federal power to regulate commerce. *Gibbons* would have allowed the Court to invalidate the Delaware statute, but the Court chose to uphold the statute on the grounds that the federal government had not exercised its power. This brief observation was developed into a theory that the federal government could lose its dominance in interstate commerce if it allowed its power to lie dormant under what came to be called the doctrine of the dormant commerce power. This weakened the already somewhat elusive commerce power of Congress. Chief Justice John Marshall wrote the unanimous decision at a time when there were only six members because of the death of Robert Trimble.

Richard L. Wilson

See also *Gibbons v. Ogden; McCray v. United States; McCulloch v. Maryland.*

WILSON V. ARKANSAS

Court: U.S. Supreme Court
Citation: 514 U.S. 927
Date: May 22, 1995
Issues: Police powers; Right to privacy; Search and seizure

- This U.S. Supreme Court ruling on Fourth Amendment protections held that police officers, when conducting searches, are normally expected to knock and announce their presence before entering private homes, except when special circumstances justify exceptions to this common-law requirement.

In 1992, Sharlene Wilson sold illegal drugs to undercover agents working for the Arkansas state police. Based on this information, police officers obtained warrants to arrest Wilson and search her home. When they arrived, the main door to the house was open and the screen door was unlocked. After entering the house without knocking, the officers notified her of the warrants. They placed her under arrest, and their search uncovered substantial amounts of illicit narcotics.

At Wilson's trial, her defense attorneys entered a motion to have the evidence collected in her home suppressed. They asserted that the search had been unconstitutional because the police had ignored the common-law obligation of knocking and announcing their presence and authority before entering a private home. The motion was denied, and Wilson was found guilty.

After Arkansas's highest court upheld the conviction, the U.S. Supreme Court agreed to review the case.

A unanimous Supreme Court held that the knock-and-announce principle is a significant part of an inquiry into whether a search-and-seizure passes the reasonableness standards of the Fourth Amendment. In writing the official opinion in the case, Justice Clarence Thomas referred to a long-standing endorsement of the knock-and-announce principle in the common law, combined with a wealth of founding-era commentaries, statutes, and cases supporting the principle. Based on this history, Thomas concluded that an unannounced entry into a home is unreasonable in most circumstances.

However, the Court's opinion also acknowledged that the common-law principle has never been applied as an inflexible rule that requires announcement before entry in all situations. Law enforcement may be faced with exigent circumstances, including a credible threat of physical harm to the police or reasons to believe that physical evidence would probably be destroyed if advance notice were given. The Court therefore remanded the case back to the state courts and directed the judges to consider whether the police had a reasonable justification for neglecting to knock and announce their presence before entering Wilson's home. If the police were unable to articulate a strong rationale, the conviction of Wilson would be rendered invalid, and in the event of another trial, prosecutors would not be able to introduce the seized narcotics as evidence. The *Wilson* ruling sent a firm message to law-enforcement officers not to ignore the principle of knock-and-announce.

Thomas Tandy Lewis

Further Reading

Franklin, Paula. *The Fourth Amendment.* New York: Silver Burdett Press, 2001.

LaFave, Wayne R. *Search and Seizure: A Treatise on the Fourth Amendment.* 3d ed. St. Paul, Minn.: West Publishing, 1996.

O'Brien, David M. *Constitutional Law and Politics.* 6th ed. New York: W. W. Norton, 2005.

Wetterer, Charles M. *The Fourth Amendment: Search and Seizure.* Springfield, N.J.: Enslow, 1998.

See also *California v. Greenwood; Hudson v. Michigan; Massachusetts v. Sheppard.*

Winship, In re. *See* In re Winship

WISCONSIN V. MITCHELL

Court: U.S. Supreme Court
Citation: 509 U.S. 476
Date: June 11, 1993
Issues: First Amendment guarantees

• This hate crime case was the first of its type to be heard by the U.S. Supreme Court; this landmark decision has opened the way for more extensive hate crime legislation, and it signalled that such legislation would be upheld as constitutional by the court in most cases.

Following a showing of the 1988 film *Mississippi Burning*, several African American men and boys congregated at an apartment complex to talk about the film. After a discussion of a scene in the film in which a young African American boy is beaten by a white man, the accused, Todd Mitchell, asked those who joined him outside if they were ready to go after a white man.

Walking on the opposite side of the street and saying nothing, fourteen-year-old Gregory Riddick approached the complex. Mitchell selected three individuals from the group to go after Riddick. The victim was beaten, and his tennis shoes were stolen.

In a Kenosha, Wisconsin, trial court, Mitchell was convicted as a party to the crime of aggravated battery. By Wisconsin law, this crime carries a maximum prison sentence of two years. Mitchell's sentence was extended to four years, however, under a state statute commonly known as the "hate crimes" statute. This statute provides for sentence extensions if it can be determined that the victim was selected because of his or her race, religion, color, disability, sexual orientation, national origin, or ancestry.

Mitchell appealed his conviction and the extended sentence. His conviction was upheld by the court of appeals, but the Supreme Court of Wisconsin reversed the decision of the appellate court. Wisconsin's Supreme Court held that the "hate crimes" statute violated the defendant's First Amendment protection for freedom of speech because it was unconstitutionally overbroad and punished only what the state legislature found to be offensive. Moreover, the state Supreme Court believed that this statute would have a "chilling effect" on a citizen's freedom of speech; that is, a citizen would fear reprisal for actions which might follow the utterance of prejudiced or biased speech.

The U.S. Supreme Court reversed the state court's decision. Chief Justice

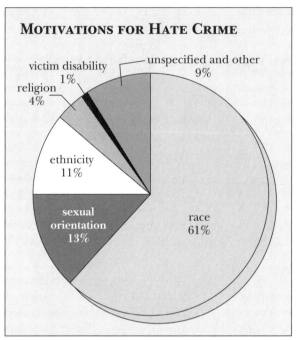

MOTIVATIONS FOR HATE CRIME

victim disability 1%
religion 4%
unspecified and other 9%
ethnicity 11%
sexual orientation 13%
race 61%

Source: U.S. Bureau of Justice Statistics, 2005. Data are based on nearly 3,000 incidents of hate crime reported to the National Incident-Based Reporting System (NIBRS) in 1997-1999. Because of rounding, percentages do not add up to 100.

William Rehnquist wrote the opinion in this unanimous decision. The Court held that Mitchell's First Amendment rights to free speech had not been violated. The Court pointed out that the statute was not aimed at speech but at conduct, which is not protected by the First Amendment. The Court also addressed the "chilling effect" of the statute, finding that such would not be the case and that the state Supreme Court's hypothesis was far too speculative to be entertained. This decision indicates that the Supreme Court appears ready to uphold legislation designed to enhance punishment for criminal acts based on bigotry and bias without making bigoted or biased speech itself a crime.

Donna Addkison Simmons

See also *R.A.V. v. City of St. Paul; Virginia v. Black.*

WISCONSIN V. YODER

Court: U.S. Supreme Court
Citation: 406 U.S. 205
Date: May 15, 1972
Issues: Education; Freedom of religion

• In the 1960's, Amish farmers in New Glarus, Wisconsin, refused to send their children to the public schools on the basis of the group's religious convictions, an action that violated Wisconsin's Compulsory Education Law. In 1972, the case was heard by the U.S. Supreme Court, which affirmed the right of the Amish to educate their children in Amish homes and schools.

The Amish are an Anabaptist Christian group with deeply held religious views and a conservative lifestyle; they follow a strict code of behavior known as the Ordnung (German for "order"), which is modified periodically as decided by the Amish bishops. Their teachings stress humility and simplicity, cooperation and community, ties to the land, service to society, and limits on modernization.

Beyond a basic education, the Amish view the public schools as inconsistent with, even hostile to, their system of values and beliefs and thus a barrier to integrating their children into the Amish way of life. They see high school as a purveyor of temptation that also interferes with the use of adolescents as farm labor. The consolidation of many rural schools in the 1960's meant the bussing of children to the city schools, a change of paramount concern to the Amish because they saw it as a threat to their rural lifestyle as well as to the cohesion of the group. The public schools exposed Amish children to notions of individuality, competition, status, and circumstances such as holiday celebrations that were in conflict with Amish religious views.

The Yoder Case

Jonas Yoder, a father in the Amish community at New Glarus, Wisconsin, did not want his daughter to take physical education in the public schools because participation would require non-Amish attire. The issue was taken to the state legislature, which made no exception, and subsequently the Amish decided to build and staff their own schools modeled after Amish schools elsewhere in the country. In the summer of 1968, three Amish fathers informed Superintendent Kenneth Glewen of the New Glarus District that they would not comply with Wisconsin's Compulsory Education Law that mandates children ages seven to sixteen to attend school. Glewen asked the Amish to enroll their children in the district until the third Friday in September, so that the district would not lose state funding. The Amish community refused to participate in the deception and kept their children out of the public school, so that the district ultimately lost about twenty thousand dollars in state funds.

Hearing of the Amish dilemma, the Reverend William C. Lindholm, a Lutheran pastor from Michigan, engaged the support of the National Committee for Amish Religious Freedom (NCARF) and contacted a Pennsylvania attorney, William B. Ball, about representing the Amish in court. Critical of compulsory education, Ball accepted the case and based his arguments on the First Amendment to the U.S. Constitution and religious freedoms. In April, 1969, the three Amish fathers, Jonas Yoder, Wallace Miller, and Adin Yutzy, were found in contempt of the law and each fined five dollars in Green County Court. Yoder and Miller were members of the Old Order Amish Church, and Yutzy was a member of the Conservative Amish Mennonite Church, groups bound by the same conservative doctrine. A former Amish and professor at Temple University, John A. Hostetler, provided the key testimony in the case as it proceeded through the courts: first in the Wisconsin District Court, where the decision was upheld against the Amish; then the Wisconsin Supreme Court, where the decision was reversed; and finally in the U.S. Supreme Court, which handed down a decision in favor of the Amish on May 15, 1972.

The Supreme Court Ruling

With a vote of six to one (William O. Douglas dissenting), the justices ruled that the First and Fourteenth Amendments to the U.S. Constitution protected the rights of the Amish to maintain and staff their own schools and to limit their formal education to the eighth grade. Chief Justice Warren E. Burger wrote, "The Amish objection to formal education beyond eighth grade is firmly grounded in central religious beliefs." Attendance at non-Amish schools could result in censure by the church community because non-Amish values were a threat to the community and a danger to eternal salvation. In arguing the case, Ball repeatedly invoked two earlier Supreme Court cases: *Pierce v. Society of Sisters* (1925), a decision that supported parental rights, and *Sherbert v. Verner* (1963), a decision that upheld religious liberty.

Although the Amish shunned the limelight, they were satisfied with the ruling; tensions over the issue eased, and the American public generally supported the Amish position. Even after the decision, some Amish parents around the country continued to send their children to public elementary schools, although Amish schools had become the norm by the late 1970's.

Significance

Wisconsin v. Yoder was a historic decision that sparked discussion and debate and left a legacy of ambiguity and criticism. Scholarly observers criticized the justices for conferring special judicial protection to a single religious group. Some argue that the justices did not give proper consideration to the children and the importance of the state in providing and regulating education. For the Amish of New Glarus, the case brought unwanted notoriety, a serious circumstance in a culture that shuns attention, deplores vanity, and avoids confrontation of any kind. The Amish prefer to resolve their differences within the Amish world, avoiding the courts and litigation. They generally do not challenge higher authorities, nor do they serve in public office, preferring subjection over active forms of citizenship. Ironically, the Amish relinquished control of the case to non-Amish players who did not live the Amish lifestyle, such as Ball, Lindholm, and the coalition of lawyers, clergy, and scholars on the NCARF. Many believed that William Ball manipulated the Amish to serve his own moral and political interests, specifically his fight against secular humanism in the public schools.

Wisconsin v. Yoder illustrates how a small, local event can be easily catapulted to national significance—in this case, led by advocates outside of the litigant community. At the same time, it provides a poignant example of how the lives of litigants can be transformed by an experience in the national spotlight. The litigation sparked controversy within the Amish group at New Glarus and ultimately led to the disintegration of the community as people moved to other Amish settlements. Between 1973 and 1976, about two-thirds of the community relocated. Some farmers cited the lack of good, flat land for farming in the area; others pointed to a dispute with state authorities over barn sanitation regulations. Dissension arose between conservatives and progressives over the matter of farm machinery. The death of Dan Miller, caught in a tractor-propelled forklift, led some to believe that the Amish were being punished for inappropriate modernization. Tired of the criticism and notoriety that came to him, Jonas Yoder and his family left their New Glarus farm for a new life in Missouri. For Yoder and his community, it was not acceptable to live in the camera's eye of interviews and photographs.

The Yoder case arrived before the Supreme Court at a time of significant turnover and adjustment among the justices, and legal scholars have analyzed the decision in this light. They point to lingering questions about the interpretation of religious liberty, the rights of parents versus children, home schooling, and the legal implications of this decision for other sectarian groups.

Ann M. Legreid

Further Reading

De Walt, Mark W. *Amish Education in the U.S. and Canada.* Lanham, Md.: Rowman & Littlefield, 2006. Detailed description of the history, philosophy, and classroom practices of the Amish, including cases by state and province.

Harrison, Maureen, and Steve Gilbert, eds. *Freedom of Religion Decisions of the United States Supreme Court.* San Diego, Calif.: Excellent Books, 1996. Details on the Yoder court, a summary of the case, and the decision presented by Chief Justice Warren Burger.

Peters, Shawn Francis. *The Yoder Case: Religious Freedom, Education, and Parental Rights.* Lawrence: University Press of Kansas, 2003. Complete history of the case, criticism of the decision, and an analysis of its legacy.

See also *Pierce v. Society of Sisters; Sherbert v. Verner.*

WITHERSPOON V. ILLINOIS

Court: U.S. Supreme Court
Citation: 391 U.S. 510
Date: June 3, 1968
Issues: Capital punishment; Juries

• In this groundbreaking decision, the U.S. Supreme Court decided that prospective jurors with reservations about the death penalty could not be excluded from service in a criminal proceeding.

The Sixth Amendment to the U.S. Constitution guarantees accused citizens the right to trial by an impartial jury of peers. This deceptively simple guarantee has come under fire in cases too numerous to mention. During the 1960's, many noteworthy cases advanced to the Supreme Court regarding the composition and unanimity of the jury in criminal cases. In 1968, the *Witherspoon* case compounded the jury-selection question with the issue of capital punishment.

Using an Illinois statute, the prosecution at William Witherspoon's murder trial in Cook County, Illinois, eliminated almost half of the potential jurors by challenging those who had reservations about their ability to impose a death sentence. This exclusion occurred without any determination of the level of reservation; that is, the potential jurors were excluded for any degree of uncertainty about imposition of a death sentence. The defendant, Witherspoon, appealed his case on the grounds that such a broad exclusion of jurors prevented him from being tried by an impartial jury as guaranteed in the Sixth Amendment. Witherspoon claimed that a jury absent of those opposed or at least uncertain about capital punishment would under no circumstances be impartial or representative of the community.

The Supreme Court agreed in a majority opinion written by Justice Potter Stewart. Witherspoon's death sentence was voided by the Court; however, his conviction was not overturned. The Court agreed with the defendant that a jury devoid of objectors to capital punishment was sure to be "woefully short" of the impartiality guaranteed by the Sixth Amendment and extended to the states under the Fourteenth Amendment. In the majority opinion, the Court stated that those prospective jurors who expressed a total disinclination toward ever imposing the death penalty could be excluded; however, persons who merely had reservations in the matter could not be excluded for their reservations alone.

The Court went on to state that juries must attempt to mirror the feelings of the community. In any given community there will be a certain number of people who are unsure of their feelings about capital punishment. This point of view should not be avoided in jury selection, the Court ruled, as inclusion of such undecided jurors will ensure neutrality on the sentencing issue and will allow the jury more adequately to reflect the conscience of the community.

While ruling that a jury totally committed to the imposition of the death penalty cannot be selected deliberately, as this would deprive a defendant of life without due process, the Court did not issue a constitutional rule that would have required the reversal of every jury selected under the Illinois statute. The Court did not state that a jury composed of persons in favor of capital punishment would be predisposed to convict, only that such a jury would be predisposed in the sentencing element of a trial.

The *Witherspoon* decision was an early test of the Supreme Court's position on capital punishment as well as on jury composition and selection. The Court indicated its willingness to uphold criminal convictions while examining the sentencing procedures being used in the states. At no point in its opinion did the Court express disfavor for the death penalty; rather, the opinion targeted only the constitutional implications of the jury-selection process. In other words, the *Witherspoon* decision indicated that within constitutional bounds, communities would be left to choose whether to impose the death penalty.

Donna Addkison Simmons

See also *Coker v. Georgia; Furman v. Georgia; Gregg v. Georgia; Harmelin v. Michigan.*

WOLF V. COLORADO

Court: U.S. Supreme Court
Citation: 338 U.S. 25
Date: June 27, 1949
Issues: Evidence; Search and seizure

• The decision of the U.S. Supreme Court in this search and seizure case emphasized the importance of the individual protections guaranteed by the Fourth Amendment against illegal searches and seizures but failed to mandate use of the exclusionary rule in state courts.

The U.S. Supreme Court has heard a number of cases related to the protection against unlawful searches and seizures guaranteed by the Fourth Amendment of the U.S. Constitution. Until early in the twentieth century, rules of common law allowed the admission of illegally obtained evidence in criminal trials throughout the country. A case decided by the U.S. Supreme Court in 1914, *Weeks v. United States*, changed the rules of evidence in federal criminal proceedings by instituting an "exclusionary rule" that required the barring of illegally obtained evidence in those trials.

The exclusionary rule in criminal trials prohibits the use of evidence which has been gained from an unconstitutional search and seizure. This rule was designed to give teeth to the Fourth Amendment in order to protect the integrity of trial courts from tainted evidence and to decrease police misconduct in the collection of evidence.

Wolf v. Colorado was the first case to argue that this exclusionary rule should also be mandatory for state criminal proceedings. Wolf was accused and convicted of performing illegal abortions. The evidence introduced at trial included his appointment book, which had been taken by a deputy sheriff without a warrant. After acquiring the appointment book, the deputy sheriff questioned patients whose names he saw in the book. By doing so, he obtained enough evidence to charge the doctor with performing illegal abortions. Wolf appealed his conviction on the basis that the evidence used to convict him was a product of an illegal search and seizure in violation of his Fourth Amendment liberties.

Writing for the majority, Justice Felix Frankfurter stated with undeniable enthusiasm that the Fourth Amendment protections are a vital and basic part of the concept of "ordered liberty." That is to say, the protections against illegal searches and seizures are fundamental to the American notion of freedom. The Court sustained Wolf's conviction, however, and stopped short of requiring use of the exclusionary rule in state courts. Rather, state courts were given the option of using or not using evidence which was obtained illegally.

Justice Hugo Black wrote a concurring opinion, and Justice William Douglas wrote the dissenting opinion, which was joined by Justices Frank Murphy and Wiley Rutledge. It is important to note that the dissenting justices only disagreed with the Court's finding inasmuch as the Court failed to exclude the evidence.

This decision stood throughout the 1950's; however, by the turn of the decade, the Court was beginning to fine tune this position. Several loopholes in the earlier *Weeks* decision were closed, and by 1961, the Court was ready to hold the states accountable for Fourth Amendment protections through the application of the Fourteenth Amendment. *Mapp v. Ohio* (1961) extended the application of the exclusionary rule to state criminal proceedings, effectively overturning the decision rendered in *Wolf.*

This controversial rule of evidence has been revisited on numerous occasions in both judicial and political arenas. Indeed, throughout the 1970's and 1980's, the Court itself continued to redefine the criteria for determining that evidence had been obtained illegally. Critics of the exclusionary rule tout the numbers of criminals released and unpunished, the apathy among police forces across the nation, and so on. Advocates of the exclusionary rule seek to remind policy makers and the public of dangers of unrestrained governmental interference and police powers. Both sides continue to argue their cases in the light of the ever-changing political landscape.

Donna Addkison Simmons

See also *Escobedo v. Illinois*; *Mapp v. Ohio*; *Weeks v. United States.*

WOLFF PACKING CO. V. INDUSTRIAL RELATIONS

Court: U.S. Supreme Court
Citation: 262 U.S. 522
Date: June 11, 1923
Issues: Freedom of contract; Regulation of business

- Taking a broad view of economic freedom, the U.S. Supreme Court placed the majority of businesses outside the reach of state regulations.

The 1920 Court Industrial Relations Act of Kansas provided for compulsory arbitration of labor disputes in several key industries and authorized a regulatory commission to decide wages and working conditions in many circumstances. The Supreme Court ruled unanimously that the law violated the freedom of contract as protected by the Fourteenth Amendment. Chief Justice William H. Taft's opinion for the Court was influential because of its narrow definition of the "affected with a public interest" justification for regulating private businesses. Taft mentioned three categories of affected businesses: those operating under a public grant of privilege, such as public utilities; occupations historically recognized as performing a special service, such as inns or cabs; and powerful businesses, such as monopolies, which without regulation might subject the public to exorbitant charges and arbitrary control.

For the next decade, Taft's definition of "affected with a public interest" served as a theoretical basis for striking down numerous state regulations. In *Nebbia v. New York* (1934), however, the Court rejected the public interest theory of *Wolff Packing Co.*, and it accepted the idea that states had the authority to regulate all kinds of businesses, large or small.

Thomas Tandy Lewis

See also *Munn v. Illinois*; *Nebbia v. New York*; *Tyson v. Banton.*

WONG KIM ARK, UNITED STATES V. *See* UNITED
STATES V. WONG KIM ARK

WOODRUFF V. PARHAM

Court: U.S. Supreme Court
Citation: 8 Wall. (75 U.S.) 123
Date: November 8, 1869
Issues: Taxation

• The U.S. Supreme Court ruled that the states could levy nondis-
criminatory sales taxes on goods from other states.

The U.S. Constitution prohibits states from taxing imports, and it authorizes
Congress to regulate interstate commerce. In *Brown v. Maryland* (1827), the
Supreme Court interpreted these two provisions to mean that the states
could not tax an imported commodity while it was in its original packaging.
In *Woodruff v. Parham*, by an 8-1 vote, the Court held that this limitation did
not apply to goods coming from other states. Recognizing that a state might
use its taxing power to interfere with interstate commerce, the Court emphasized that states could not enact discriminatory taxes to insulate their own citizens from competition. In *Welton v. Missouri* (1876), therefore, the Court
struck down a license tax imposed only on sellers of products manufactured
outside the state.

Thomas Tandy Lewis

See also *Bailey v. Drexel Furniture Co.*; *Brown v. Maryland*; *License Cases.*

WOODSON V. NORTH CAROLINA

Court: U.S. Supreme Court
Citation: 428 U.S. 280
Date: July 2, 1976
Issues: Capital punishment

• The U.S. Supreme Court held that laws requiring a mandatory death penalty were inconsistent with the Eighth Amendment.

Following *Furman v. Georgia* (1972), North Carolina enacted a statute requiring the death penalty for persons convicted of first-degree murder. Woodson, an accomplice in a robbery/murder, asserted that the law was unconstitutional. In a 5-4 vote, the Supreme Court agreed. Justice Byron R. White argued that the law violated "evolving standards of decency" for three reasons: First, it provided no opportunity for "particularized consideration" of the circumstances and motivation of the crime; second, capital punishment is a unique form of punishment that requires individualized sentencing; and third, the law might encourage juries to find a defendant innocent in order to escape the death sentence. *Woodson* was consistent with the more well-known case of *Gregg v. Georgia* (1976), which was announced on the same day.

Thomas Tandy Lewis

See also *Furman v. Georgia; Gregg v. Georgia; Harmelin v. Michigan.*

WORCESTER V. GEORGIA

Court: U.S. Supreme Court
Citation: 6 Pet. (31 U.S.) 515
Date: February 20, 1832
Issues: Native American sovereignty; Treaties

- The U.S. Supreme Court held that the federal government had exclusive jurisdiction over territories owned by Native Americans. It also recognized that the tribes retained significant claims to sovereignty.

The Reverend Samuel Worcester was a Christian missionary who was convicted and imprisoned for disobeying a Georgia law that required white men to have a state license to live in Indian territory. When Worcester appealed his conviction, the Supreme Court had clear jurisdiction to consider the case under a writ of error. By a 5-1 margin, the Court held that the Georgia law violated three legal principles: the commerce clause of the U.S. Constitution, the Cherokee treaties with the federal government, and the residual sovereignty rights of the Cherokee Nation. In a far-reaching opinion, Chief Justice John Marshall wrote that the Indian tribes remained "distinct, independent political communities," possessing their own territory and substantial elements of sovereignty within their boundaries.

Although the Court's order to free Worcester was ignored by Georgia's courts, he was eventually pardoned by the governor. The *Worcester* decision did not immediately help the Cherokee because it did not place any restrictions on the actions of the federal government. President Andrew Jackson, who disliked the decision, was in the process of using his authority to force the

President Andrew Jackson.
(Library of Congress)

Cherokee to leave Georgia and go to Oklahoma—a mass migration known as the Trail of Tears. *Worcester's* concept of limited Indian sovereignty proved to be very influential during the twentieth century.

Thomas Tandy Lewis

Further Reading

Gold, Susan Dudley. *Worcester v. Georgia: American Indian Rights.* Tarrytown, N.Y.: Marshall Cavendish Benchmark, 2009. Part of its publisher's Supreme Court Milestones series designed for young-adult readers, this volume offers an accessible history and analysis of *Worcester v. Georgia* case that examines opposing sides in the case, the people involved, and the case's lasting impact. Includes bibliography and index.

Vinzant, John Harlan. *The Supreme Court's Role in American Indian Policy.* El Paso, Tex.: LFB Scholarly Publications, 2009. Study of the U.S. Supreme Court's role in reducing the sovereignty of Native American tribes.

See also *California v. Cabazon Band of Mission Indians; Cherokee Cases; Ex parte Crow Dog; Johnson and Graham's Lessee v. McIntosh; Lone Wolf v. Hitchcock; Santa Clara Pueblo v. Martinez; Talton v. Mayes; United States v. Kagama.*

=====

WYATT V. STICKNEY

Court: U.S. District Court for the Middle District of Alabama
Citation: 325 F. Supp 781 (M.D. Ala.1971), 334
Date: March 12, 1971
Issues: Medical ethics

• A federal judge declared that mental patients incarcerated against their will without criminal proceedings had a right to adequate therapy. The case created minimum standards for the care of people with mental retardation and mental illness.

Progress in psychology and psychiatry in the twentieth century made many mental institutions appear backward. Many American states used their asylums as pens into which the aged, the retarded, and the ill were herded to keep them away from the rest of society. Institutions often lacked finances to provide inmates with adequate treatment. For therapists, the issue was ethical and medical: Improved techniques could not help patients who were not treated, while confinement without treatment could make patients worse. For lawyers, the issue was constitutional and procedural: Patients were committed against their wishes by civil proceedings that lacked the protections constitutionally guaranteed to defendants in criminal trials. For mental patients, the issue was sanity and survival: Forced hospitalization without much hope of recovery or rehabilitation sentenced many of them to a living death.

For many therapists and lawyers, the resolution of ethical, medical, and constitutional issues was a "right to treatment." Existing law mandated states merely to avoid harming inmates and to provide reasonable custodial conditions. A right to treatment required that a state provide adequate treatment when it committed persons to mental hospitals. The right of every individual to life and liberty made it insufficient for the state merely to care; it demanded that the state make at least a minimal attempt to cure.

Morton Birnbaum, a lawyer and medical doctor, wrote the seminal defense of a constitutional, legal, and moral right to treatment in 1960. Birnbaum noted that many mental patients could be helped if mental facilities and staffs were professionalized and funded. Many states, however, ignored mental hospitals, in part because patients did not vote or otherwise threaten or concern officials. Birnbaum argued that the due process clause of the Fourteenth Amendment ("nor shall any State deprive any person of life, liberty, or property, without due process of law") prohibited states from confining persons to institutions without treatment because treatment was the only excuse for depriving them of liberty. Reports from the American Medical Association, the American Bar Association, the American Psychiatric Association, and the Subcommittee on Constitutional Rights of the Senate Judiciary Committee reinforced Birnbaum's description of the inadequacies of psychiatric confinement across the United States.

Legal Precedents

Increased attention to such conditions inspired laws in many U.S. states and in the District of Columbia. The statute for the nation's capital was held to mandate a right to treatment by the Court of Appeals for the District of Columbia in *Rouse v. Cameron* (1966). Judge David L. Bazelon's opinion in that case suggested that the Constitution might authorize a right to treatment even if the statute had not. The conditions that drove legislatures and courts to formulate a right to treatment were characterized by the Bryce State Mental Hospital in Tuscaloosa, Alabama. Alabama spent less than any other state on mental patients, so Bryce was poorly funded. Lack of funds and overcrowding contributed to the inadequacy of facilities. Most patients had no privacy in lavatories or dormitories. Patients were offered poor clothing, inadequate and unsanitary nutrition (Bryce budgeted fifty cents per patient per day for food), and few productive outlets or activities. Some patients had no beds. Many patients were constantly drugged. Many went days without bathing, in some cases because dozens had to share a single shower. On one surprise visit, reporters found walls and toilets covered with excrement and floors soaked with urine.

Budget cuts at Bryce in 1970 rendered an inadequate staff skeletal. Those who dealt directly with patients included only one clinical psychologist with a doctoral degree, three medical doctors with some psychiatric training, two social workers, and no board-certified psychiatrist. Other staff were overworked and underqualified. Nurse's aides, for example, were not required to have graduated from high school. Most nonprofessionals were minimally supervised. Many of the staff exhibited indifference or brutality toward their charges, some of whom suffered deaths that were arguably preventable. These conditions made it unclear whether Bryce was meeting even the traditional legal standard of reasonable care. Inadequate funds, facilities, and staffing made individualized treatment of patients impossible. Of the hospital's more than five thousand residents, almost half were aged or retarded patients who neither required nor received any psychiatric care. Most patients, convicted of no crimes but committed to Bryce and not free to leave, received little treatment. At best, Bryce Hospital maintained its residents without helping them. At worst, it maimed them through neglect and indifference.

Bryce employees laid off because of budget cuts and citizens concerned about the rights of mental patients protested the budget cuts and demanded a higher standard of care. Largely on their own, they formulated a constitutional right to treatment similar to the views propounded by Birnbaum and Bazelon. On October 23, 1970, they filed suit in federal court in the name of several patients at Bryce and their legal guardians. Heading the list of plaintiffs was Ricky Wyatt, a patient at the hospital. The leading defendant was Dr. Stonewall B. Stickney, the mental health officer for Alabama. Chief Judge Frank M. Johnson, Jr., of the U.S. District Court for the Middle District of Alabama heard *Wyatt v. Stickney* on January 4, 1971, and issued his first decision (there was no jury) on March 12.

The District Court Ruling

Judge Johnson found that, even before budget cuts, Bryce failed to meet minimal medical or custodial standards for treatment. Since most patients were not getting treatment, he reasoned, they were in effect imprisoned at Bryce. He found this especially true for the geriatric, mentally retarded, and other nonpsychotic inmates who should not have been forced into the asylum. For the truly mentally ill, Judge Johnson followed the logic that Birnbaum had articulated a decade earlier. "Due process" required trial and conviction before imprisonment, but most patients at Bryce had been involuntarily committed without criminal proceedings. Judge Johnson concluded in a brief, candid, and remarkably dispassionate opinion that because the only constitutionally acceptable reason for depriving noncriminal patients of their liberties was therapy or cure, patients had a constitutional right to treatment.

Alabama insisted that it lacked the money necessary to make treatment available to the inmates, but Judge Johnson replied that constitutional rights could not be sacrificed to economics. Alabama would have to find the money to treat people whom it sent to its hospitals because, Judge Johnson argued, "There can be no legal (or moral) justification for the State of Alabama's failing to afford . . . adequate treatment . . . to the several thousand patients who have been civilly committed."

Ten years of ethical, medical, and legal arguments had found their way into constitutional law. In a second decision announced on December 10, 1971, Judge Johnson defined the right to treatment more extensively. The Constitution demanded that each state provide a humane environment, a sufficient complement of qualified staff, and treatment planned around the needs of individual inmates. Judge Johnson detailed how Bryce and other mental hospitals in Alabama had defaulted on each criterion. In subsequent decisions for more than a decade, Judge Johnson would wrestle with the difficulties of achieving state compliance with his decrees, but a constitutional right to treatment had been declared. If the state deprives individuals of freedom "for their own good," it must make at least a minimal effort to secure the individuals that good.

Significance

Wyatt v. Stickney led to a decade of litigation, appeals, and maneuvers within federal courts and resulted in Alabama's mental health system being run by a federal appointee. The most direct impact of the right to treatment was to make critical scrutiny of Alabama's institutions routine. During the extended litigation, all three Alabama mental institutions were included in the cases. Having defined the right to treatment as a constitutional requirement for individualized treatment by qualified staff in a humane environment, Judge Johnson required institutions to justify their practices by each criterion in that definition. Judge Johnson also set up "human rights committees" to monitor implementation of reforms and expose any shortcomings in compliance with court orders.

Immediately, then, the Wyatt case inspired Judge Johnson to lead a revolution in treatment of the mentally ill. The demand for individualized treatment compelled institutional staff to diagnose and respond to the problems of patients or to release them. At the very least, the state could "warehouse" the mentally ill only if it prepared an inventory of inmates and their problems. Each patient would receive more attention, and the retarded and the aged who did not belong in a mental institution would be reassigned to more appropriate residences.

Confinement without treatment often makes healthy people sick and sick people sicker, so individualized treatment forced the state to suit treatment regimens to the reasons for confinement. Defendants found not guilty of crimes because of insanity could no longer be imprisoned without hope of release. The court and its agents evaluated the qualifications of staff and ordered the hiring of more and better trained attendants. To augment the amount of attention each patient could anticipate, the maximum population at each institution was reduced, in part through removal of inmates who were not mentally ill. Patients who read and understood the court's decrees became more conscious of their rights and less docile, forcing staff to be more professional and humane. Recalcitrant staff unwilling to upgrade their care left or were reassigned.

A broader impact of *Wyatt* was to expose existing conditions and to institute routine means of improving the environment at mental institutions. The human rights committees, the U.S. Department of Justice, and even the Federal Bureau of Investigation were drawn into the Alabama case to contest often extravagant claims of improvement and to force the state to meet its newly defined constitutional responsibilities. The committee for Partlow Mental Hospital, for example, recruited a former patient from Partlow to inform outsiders about true conditions in the hospital. Judge Johnson and his agents and advisers would eventually define, in great detail, minimal standards for treatment. The constant threat of judicial, federal, or citizen intervention gave patients a phalanx of champions and the state a host of critics to please.

The secrecy of mental institutions had been breached. Judge Johnson's declaration was implemented elsewhere more quickly and to a greater extent than in Alabama. More than a dozen states legislated expanded rights for inmates of mental institutions. Many courts readily accepted *Wyatt v. Stickney* as precedent. Lawyers and doctors began to work out its implications in professional and political discussions. A less immediate but perhaps more profound impact of this landmark case was to encourage citizens and professionals concerned about mental health to push governments to do more for institutionalized mental patients. Procedural safeguards before and after commitment were expanded and strengthened in many jurisdictions to differentiate asylums from prisons in a substantial manner.

The U.S. Supreme Court implicitly reaffirmed the right to treatment in *Jackson v. Indiana* (1972) when it stated that involuntary commitment must advance some justifiable purpose. This means both that states must articulate and defend their purpose when they deprive individuals of freedom and that the incarceration must advance that purpose. In *Youngberg v. Romeo* (1982), the court also found that the Eighth Amendment ban on cruel and unusual punishment and the due process clause of the Fourteenth Amendment demanded adequate care and training for the institutionalized retarded. Both decisions clearly imply a right to treatment.

Perhaps the most far-reaching impact of *Wyatt v. Stickney* was to induce communities to care for many patients outside institutions. The duty to provide individualized treatment inclined many states to remove all but the most seriously ill patients from state institutions. Many aged and retarded citizens began living in communities rather than asylums, which represented a boon to individual liberty. The right to treatment did not in itself force states to upgrade their treatment of the mentally ill. It was, however, an important prod to doctors, lawyers, and other citizens to remember that the infirm are entitled to care and protection.

William Haltom

Further Reading

Birnbaum, Morton. "The Right to Treatment." *American Bar Association Journal* 46 (May, 1960): 499-505. Presents the seminal argument that set out in legal terms the right of involuntarily institutionalized mental patients to minimal therapy and moved some reformers to try to secure a "right to treatment."

Cooper, Phillip J. *Hard Judicial Choices: Federal District Court Judges and State and Local Officials.* New York: Oxford University Press, 1988. Chapter 6 provides an overview of conditions in mental institutions and raises the major psychological, mental, penal, and legal issues. Chapter 7 chronicles the lengthy litigation in *Wyatt v. Stickney.* Readers unfamiliar with legal jargon and judicial process will have some difficulty understanding parts of these chapters, but the coverage makes it worth the trouble.

Neier, Aryeh. *Only Judgment.* Middletown, Conn.: Wesleyan University Press, 1982. Engaging book by a leading activist for human rights features an informative chapter on legal attempts to reform mental institutions. Readers unfamiliar with legal writing will be able to understand and appreciate this analysis of what the legal process can and cannot do about the rights of the involuntarily institutionalized.

_____. *Taking Liberties: Four Decades in the Struggle for Rights.* New York: Public-Affairs, 2003. Memoir focuses on the author's work as a human rights activist. Chapter 3, "Opening Asylums," offers discussion relevant to the topic of the right to treatment.

Saks, Elyn R. *Refusing Care: Forced Treatment and the Rights of the Mentally Ill.* Chicago: University of Chicago Press, 2002. Examines when, if ever, a mentally ill person should be treated against his or her will. Includes case studies.

"The Wyatt Case: Implementation of a Judicial Decree Ordering Institutional Change." *Yale Law Journal* 84 (May, 1975): 1338-1379. Excellent account of how fiscal and political resistance undermined enforcement of the right to treatment. Shows that rights as enunciated by courts are often severely compromised by government agencies that "lost" in court. Somewhat technical.

Yarbrough, Tinsley E. *Judge Frank Johnson and Human Rights in Alabama.* 2d ed. Tuscaloosa: University of Alabama Press, 2002. Accessible and interesting chronicle of the first decades of Judge Johnson's career provides details about conditions at mental institutions in Alabama and about the political and legal forces arrayed in the battle over the right to treatment.

See also *Atkins v. Virginia; Ford v. Wainwright; Furman v. Georgia; Gregg v. Georgia; Penry v. Lynaugh.*

Yakus v. United States

Court: U.S. Supreme Court
Citation: 321 U.S. 414
Date: March 27, 1944
Issues: Congressional powers; Judicial review; Separation of powers; Warfare and terrorism

• In approving the Emergency Price Control Act of 1942, the Supreme Court upheld congressional power to limit judicial review in lower federal courts and to authorize an administrative agency to use wide latitude in fixing maximum prices and rents.

Soon after the United States entered World War II in 1941, Congress established the Office of Price Administration to set "fair and equitable" price controls for limiting inflation. Although violators of the regulations were tried in federal district courts, the statute specified that these courts could not rule on the constitutionality of the controls. Decisions of the courts were then reviewed by a special tribunal before going to the Supreme Court. Essentially the statute was designed to defer judicial review until late in the war effort. When Albert Yakus, a wholesaler of meats, was criminally punished under the Emergency Price Control Act of 1942, he challenged its constitutionality.

Speaking for a 6-3 majority, Chief Justice Harlan Fiske Stone upheld Yakus's conviction. Although the Court in 1935 had imposed substantial limitations on the delegation of legislative powers, Stone found that the 1942 delegation was acceptable because Congress had provided standards to guide the agency's work. Likewise, Stone wrote that the limitations on the courts were acceptable because there was sufficient opportunity for judicial review. In dissent, Justice Wiley B. Rutledge, Jr., wrote that although Congress might ex-

President Harry S. Truman visiting the Supreme Court in 1945. He faces Chief Justice Harlan Fiske Stone (bottom left). To Truman's right, Justices Hugo L. Black and Felix Frankfurter; second row, left to right; Justices Stanley F. Reed, Harold H. Burton, Wiley B. Rutledge, Jr., Frank Murphy; third row, left: Justice William O. Douglas. (Library of Congress)

clude the courts from the administrative process, if the courts were involved, they must be able to consider the constitutionality of their decisions. Rutledge's dissent is widely respected. The Court appeared to affirm the delegation portion of *Yakus* in *Mistretta v. United States* (1989).

Thomas Tandy Lewis

See also *Budd v. New York; Calder v. Bull; Chicago, Milwaukee, and St. Paul Railway Co. v. Minnesota; Fletcher v. Peck; Hayburn's Case; Hylton v. United States; Marbury v. Madison; Mistretta v. United States; Stuart v. Laird.*

YARBROUGH, EX PARTE. *See* EX PARTE YARBROUGH

YATES V. UNITED STATES

Court: U.S. Supreme Court
Citation: 354 U.S. 298
Date: June 17, 1957
Issues: Freedom of assembly and association; Freedom of speech

• The U.S. Supreme Court's decision in this case advanced protections for both freedom of speech and freedom of assembly or political association; this case rendered ineffective the government's attempt to prosecute members of the Communist Party of America under the Smith Act.

Following the rise of communism around the globe, leaders in the United States moved to stamp out any signs of communist activity in the country. Fourteen middle-level Communist Party leaders were accused under the Smith Act (1940) of organizing and participating in a conspiracy to advocate the forceful overthrow of the United States government. In a stunning 6-1 decision, with two justices not participating, the Supreme Court reversed their convictions, acquitting five and remanding the remaining nine for new trials.

The Court maintained that the government had waited much too long to charge the defendants with organizing the Communist Party in the United States. Indeed, the Court stated that the three-year statute of limitations had expired. The Court also found that the trial judge had been mistaken in his directions to the jury in regard to what they must find in order to convince the defendants on the advocacy charges. Finally, the Court declared the evidence in several cases to be entirely insufficient. After this decision was rendered, the government dropped all nine of the remanded cases.

The question before the court was simple enough. When placed in balance, which is of greater consequence: the value of preserving free speech or the value of preserving a government's interest which might be adversely affected by such speech? This basic question continues to raise controversy and foster strong emotions even though the issue of communism itself has been removed.

In an earlier case, *Dennis v. United States* (1951), the Court upheld the Smith Act as constitutional, allowing for numerous conspiracy convictions from 1951 through 1957. The Yates decision did not directly overrule Dennis, but it clarified the distinction between advocating illegal acts and holding abstract doctrinal beliefs which, the Court said, had been ignored by trial courts. After *Yates*, the government was required to show very specific illegal acts by the accused in order to gain a conviction. Membership in a political organization was insignificant in and of itself. Strict standards of proof had to be met.

This decision marked a dramatic and important change in the Court's attitude toward the Smith Act and a move away from the *Dennis* decision. Only four years later, however, the Court upheld a section of the Smith Act which made it a crime to be a member of a group advocating the overthrow by force of the government. This case, *Scales v. United States* (1961), was neither a retreat from *Yates* nor a return to *Dennis*, because the Court insisted that evidentiary requirements similar to those found in *Yates* be met. That is, a person's "membership" has to meet certain criteria. It must be both knowing and active. Additionally, the person must show "specific intent" to bring about the forceful overthrow of the government. This case, in combination with *Yates*, made conviction under the Smith Act virtually impossible.

Donna Addkison Simmons

See also *Brandenburg v. Ohio; Dennis v. United States; Elfbrandt v. Russell; Lovell v. City of Griffin; Noto v. United States; Scales v. United States; Whitney v. California.*

YICK WO V. HOPKINS

Court: U.S. Supreme Court
Citation: 118 U.S. 356
Date: May 10, 1886
Issues: Regulation of business

• The U.S. Supreme Court clearly expanded the reach of the Fourteenth Amendment but its decision in this case was ignored until the mid-twentieth century.

In a move that clearly targeted Chinese laundries, San Francisco required all laundries to have an operating license approved by the board of supervisors. These licenses were granted only to laundries in brick buildings, while most Chinese laundries were wooden. Yick Wo had operated a family laundry business for twenty-two years, and the laundry had been found safe in its last city inspection, which took place about a year before. When denied a license, Yick Wo challenged this regulation by continuing to operate his laundry. He was jailed for refusing to pay a fine.

Although the California supreme court denied his petition for habeas corpus, the Supreme Court directed his release. The Court unanimously found the ordinance was a vastly greater exercise of a local government's police power than was justified by circumstances. As such, the ordinance represented class legislation in violation of the Fourteenth Amendment. Although Yick Wo's attorneys had alleged the ordinance was a violation of the 1880 Sino-American treaty, the Court rested the decision on the Fourteenth Amendment, clearly implying the incorporation doctrine used in the twentieth century. Changes in the political climate and in Court membership led this important ruling to be ignored except when it could benefit corporations.

Richard L. Wilson

See also *Chinese Exclusion Cases; Williams v. Mississippi.*

YOUNG, EX PARTE. *See* EX PARTE YOUNG

Young v. American Mini Theatres

Court: U.S. Supreme Court
Citation: 427 U.S. 50
Date: June 24, 1976
Issues: Zoning

• The U.S. Supreme Court upheld zoning ordinances that significantly restricted the location of theaters and bookstores dealing in sexually explicit materials.

Detroit's anti-Skid Row ordinance required that adult stores (those dealing in sexually explicit materials) be dispersed and that they be located at least five hundred feet from residential areas. The ordinance applied to all erotic materials, whether or not they were legally obscene. By a 5-4 vote, the Supreme Court upheld the ordinance. In a plurality opinion, Justice John Paul Stevens made the following points: First, sexually explicit materials were entitled to less First Amendment protection than other forms of expression; second, the zoning regulations did not totally eliminate the availability of the materials; and third, the city had a valid interest in preserving the character of its neighborhoods. In a concurring opinion, Justice Lewis F. Powell, Jr., emphasized that the ordinances placed only "incidental and minimal" limits on the expression of producers and the choice of consumers. The Court has often reaffirmed the basic approach of the *Young* decision.

Thomas Tandy Lewis

See also *Erznoznik v. Jacksonville; Freedman v. Maryland; Miller v. California; Mutual Film Corp. v. Industrial Commission of Ohio; Times Film Corp. v. City of Chicago.*

Younger v. Harris

Court: U.S. Supreme Court
Citation: 401 U.S. 37
Date: February 23, 1971
Issues: Federal supremacy

• The U.S. Supreme Court reinforced the doctrine of abstention, prohibiting federal judges from intervening in most state court proceedings before they have been finalized.

During the controversial Vietnam War, John Harris, Jr., was indicted in a California court for violating a criminal syndicalism statute that was virtually identical to the law that had been ruled unconstitutional in *Brandenburg v. Ohio* (1969). Finding that the law violated the First and Fourteenth Amendments, a three-judge federal court issued an injunction restraining district attorney Evelle Younger from prosecuting Harris.

By an 8-1 vote, the Supreme Court lifted the injunction. Justice Hugo L. Black's opinion for the majority emphasized the concept of comity, which requires mutual respect between federal and state governments. A long-established policy prohibited federal courts from interfering with state proceedings except under very limited conditions, as when expressly authorized by an act of Congress or when a person could show a likely danger of irreparable damages. In contrast to the exception allowed in *Dombrowski v. Pfister* (1965), Black concluded that Harris had not shown that state officials were guilty of bad faith or harassment. The possibility that a prosecution might create a chilling effect on free speech was not an adequate reason to justify a federal injunction. Black also argued that the federal courts should not pass judgments on state statutes without the benefit of interpretations of the state courts.

Dissenting, Justice William O. Douglas argued that the logic of *Dombrowski* required the federal courts to use special vigilance in periods of repression when enormous sanctions were imposed on those "who assert their First Amendment Rights in unpopular causes."

Thomas Tandy Lewis

See also *Brandenburg v. Ohio; Dombrowski v. Pfister; Ex parte Young; Martin v. Hunter's Lessee.*

Youngstown Sheet and Tube Co. v. Sawyer

Court: U.S. Supreme Court
Citation: 343 U.S. 579
Date: June 2, 1952
Issues: Presidential powers; Regulation of business; Warfare and terrorism

- During the Korean War, the U.S. Supreme Court disallowed the president's right to invoke emergency powers in order to seize and operate private businesses without prior congressional approval.

Fearful that a long strike would damage the war effort, President Harry S. Truman issued an executive order instructing the secretary of commerce to take over the steel plants and maintain full production. Although there was no statutory authority for the seizure, the president argued that the policy was valid under his inherent powers as president and commander in chief. The steel companies argued that the seizure was unconstitutional unless authorized by an act of Congress. They emphasized that Congress, in passing the Taft-Hartley Act (1947), had considered but rejected an amendment permitting the president to seize industrial facilities in order to resolve labor disputes.

By a 6-3 vote, the Supreme Court ruled in favor of the companies. Writing for the majority, Justice Hugo L. Black rejected Truman's defense based on the existence of an inherent executive power. Reflecting his desire to adhere closely to the text of the Constitution, Black wrote that "the Constitution is neither silent nor equivocal about who shall make laws which the President is to execute." In concurring opinions, several justices recognized an inherent executive power transcending the enumerated powers in Article II of the Constitution but joined the decision because Congress had specifically refused to give the president the kind of power that Truman had exercised. All members of the majority apparently agreed that Congress could have legitimately ordered or authorized the seizure of the steel mills. The three dissenters argued that presidents had been allowed to exercise similar emergency powers in the past.

The steel seizure case did not represent a complete repudiation of the theory of inherent presidential powers. The decision did make it clear, however, that the president is not invested with unbridled discretion in the name of na-

President Harry S. Truman. (Library of Congress)

tional security. When examining the limits of executive actions, moreover, the Court indicated that it would consider both the explicit and the implicit will of Congress.

Thomas Tandy Lewis

See also *Dames and Moore v. Regan; Goldwater v. Carter; Humphrey's Executor v. United States; Martin v. Mott; Mississippi v. Johnson; Myers v. United States; United States v. Nixon; Wiener v. United States.*

ZABLOCKI V. REDHAIL

Court: U.S. Supreme Court
Citation: 434 U.S. 374
Date: January 18, 1978
Issues: Children's rights; Equal protection of the law; Parental rights

- The Court ruled that a Wisconsin law prohibiting the marriage of residents failing to comply with court-ordered child-support payments and obligations unconstitutionally interfered with the right of personal choice in marriage and family life.

On September 27, 1974, Roger Redhail was denied an application for a marriage license by Thomas Zablocki, the clerk of Milwaukee County, on the grounds that Redhail had not complied with state family law. The Wisconsin Family Code made Redhail's ability to marry dependent on his payment of child support from a previous relationship and on assurances that minor children were not and would not become wards of the state.

Redhail, unmarried, unemployed, and poor, had not paid court-ordered child support, and his illegitimate daughter had received benefits under the Aid to Families with Dependent Children program since her birth. He challenged the law. On August 31, 1976, a federal district court said that the Wisconsin law violated the equal protection clause of the Fourteenth Amendment to the U.S. Constitution. The U.S. Supreme Court agreed and ruled that the state significantly interfered with the fundamental right to marry, the most important relation in family life and a liberty protected by the Fourteenth Amendment. Individuals, including "deadbeat dads," may make personal decisions relating to marriage without unjustified governmental interference.

Steve J. Mazurana and Dyan E. Mazurana

See also *Gomez v. Perez; Goodridge v. Department of Public Health; Louisville, Cincinnati, and Charleston Railroad Co. v. Letson; Stanton v. Stanton.*

ZADVYDAS V. DAVIS

Court: U.S. Supreme Court
Citation: 533 U.S. 678
Date: June 28, 2001
Issues: Immigration

- In cases in which no country is willing to accept a noncitizen who is under order of deportation, the controversial Zadvydas decision restricted the length of time of detentions, except when the government can demonstrate aggravating circumstances that require additional detention.

A resident alien in the United States, Kestutis Zadvydas had been born to Lithuanian parents in a German camp for displaced persons. However, after he acquired a long criminal record, the Immigration and Naturalization Service (INS) ordered his deportation. Both Germany and Lithuania refused to admit him because he was not a citizen of either country, and no other country could be found to accept him. According to applicable U.S. law, following a final deportation order, an alien was to be held in custody for a period of up to ninety days. If the alien was still in the country after the removal period had expired, INS personnel would conduct an administrative review to decide between further detention or supervised release.

After Zadvydas's custody had lasted longer than ninety days, he petitioned a U.S. district court for a writ of habeas corpus. The court ruled in Zadvydas's favor, based on the theory that the government would never deport him, thereby resulting in permanent confinement without a criminal trial, which violated constitutional requirements of due process. The court of appeals, however, reversed the decision, based on the theory that an eventual deportation was not impossible, thereby providing a rationale for continuing the administrative detention.

In a 5-4 opinion, the U.S. Supreme Court held that the "the statute, read in light of the U.S. Constitution's demands, limits an alien's post-removal-period detention to a period reasonably necessary to bring about that alien's removal from the United States." Writing the opinion for the Court, Justice Stephen G. Breyer explained that since indefinite detention of aliens without trials would raise serious constitutional objections, the federal courts were obligated to construe the statute as containing an "implicit reasonable time limitation."

Although deportation proceedings were "civil and assumed to be nonpunitive," the government's two justifications did not appear adequate to an indefinite civil detention. First, the possibility of flight appeared weak, since no country wanted to accept Zadvydas; second, the use of preventive detention to protect the community was only allowed for individuals judged to be especially dangerous. Balancing Zadvydas's "liberty interests" with the risk of his committing crimes, Breyer wrote that the INS could detain him for an additional six months, after which it would have to demonstrate strong proof to justify further detention.

Justices Antonin Scalia and Anthony Kennedy both expressed strong dissenting opinions. They argued that Justice Breyer had misread the relevant statute, and also that he had failed to give adequate consideration to several precedents, especially *Shaughnessy v. United States ex rel. Mezei* (1953), which appeared to put no time limit for detaining an alien under an order of detention. Describing the majority opinion as a claim for the "right of release into this country by an individual who concededly has no legal right to be here," Scalia declared, "There is no such constitutional right."

Thomas Tandy Lewis

See also *Abrams v. United States; Chinese Exclusion Cases; Immigration and Naturalization Service v. Chadha.*

ZELMAN V. SIMMONS-HARRIS

Court: U.S. Supreme Court
Citation: 536 U.S. 639
Date: June 27, 2002
Issues: Education; Establishment of religion

• Continuing a permissive trend in the use of tax money for parochial schools, the U.S. Supreme Court approved an Ohio program of providing low-income families with tax-subsidized vouchers to pay for tuition at private schools.

As part of plan to increase educational opportunity, the legislature of Ohio enacted a statute with a Pilot Scholarship Program that provided vouchers for low-income students to attend private schools of their choice from kindergarten through the eighth grade, with the announced goal of improving academic achievement. During the 1990-2000 school year, 96 percent of the students participating in the program attended religiously affiliated schools, and 82 percent of the participating schools had religious affiliations. Susan Tave Zelman, Ohio's superintendent of public instruction, joined with other Ohio taxpayers to initiate a lawsuit alleging that the program violated the establishment clause of the First Amendment. The challengers prevailed in both the District Court and the Court of Appeals.

The lower courts based their decision on the three-pronged test in *Lemon v. Kurtzman* (1971), which required a secular purpose, a secular primary impact, and no "excessive entanglement" between government and religion. For some time, however, the Supreme Court had been applying the *Lemon* test permissively, with less and less insistence on a "high wall" of separation between church and state. In *Mueller v. Allen* (1983), the Court had upheld a Minnesota law permitting a tax deduction for tuition costs at private schools, even though 95 percent of the deductions were for attendance at parochial schools. More recently, in *Mitchell v. Helms* (2000), the justices by a 5-4 margin had upheld a federal program of providing religious schools with computers and other equipment, despite the likelihood that some equipment might be occasionally used for religious instruction.

In the *Zelman* case, the Supreme Court reversed the lower courts' rulings and upheld the constitutionality of the Ohio voucher program. Speaking for a 5-4 majority, Chief Justice William H. Rehnquist reasoned the program was "entirely neutral with respect to religion." Developing a "private choice test," he argued that the Court's precedents had consistently recognized a distinction between government aid going directly to the schools and assistance going to private individuals who are given adequate secular options. He emphasized that the government had done nothing to encourage the students to attend parochial rather than nonreligious schools. In a strong dissent, Justice David H. Souter countered that the program involved the use of tax funds to subsidize religious indoctrination.

Although the *Zelman* decision created great controversy, it was unlikely that vouchers would be offered in many other places. Between 1970 and 2000, eight states held elections to decide the issue, and each time the voters rejected the proposal, usually by a vote of more than 65 percent.

Thomas Tandy Lewis

See also *Agostini v. Felton; Everson v. Board of Education of Ewing Township; Flast v. Cohen; Lemon v. Kurtzman; Mueller v. Allen; Pierce v. Society of Sisters.*

ZORACH V. CLAUSON

Court: U.S. Supreme Court
Citation: 343 U.S. 306
Date: April 28, 1952
Issues: Establishment of religion

• The U.S. Supreme Court upheld a released-time program on the grounds that the religious instruction did not take place on school property or require the expenditure of public funds, and there was no evidence that students were being pressured into attending the religious classes.

In *Illinois ex rel. McCollum v. Board of Education* (1948), the Court ruled that an on-campus released-time program violated the establishment clause of the First Amendment. In *Zorach*, the justices voted six to three to approve a New York program in which students with parental permission left campus to participate in religious activities while other students attended study hall. Speaking for the Court, Justice William O. Douglas emphasized the need for religious accommodation and asserted that Americans "are a religious people whose institutions presuppose a Supreme Being." The three dissenters argued that the location of the program was not the central issue, and they found that New York was using the coercive apparatus of the public school system in order to encourage religious activities. Douglas later repudiated his accommodationist statements in *Zorach*.

Although *Zorach* remains good law, released-time programs have largely been replaced by policies allowing religion-oriented students to have equal access to school facilities. In *Board of Education v. Mergens* (1990), the Court approved of the Equal Access Act of 1984, which requires public secondary schools to permit students to voluntarily meet for religious activities if they are permitted to meet for other purposes.

Thomas Tandy Lewis

See also *Abington School District v. Schempp; Good News Club v. Milford Central School; Illinois ex rel. McCollum v. Board of Education.*

ZURCHER V. THE STANFORD DAILY

Court: U.S. Supreme Court
Citation: 436 U.S. 547
Date: May 31, 1978
Issues: Freedom of the press; Search and seizure

• The U.S. Supreme Court held that newspaper offices do not have any special protection from searches and seizures.

Local police clashed with demonstrators at Stanford University Hospital, and the school paper, *The Stanford Daily*, printed a photograph of the ruckus. Police hoped to find more photographs and obtained a warrant to search the paper's office where, finding no pictures, they instead read confidential files. The paper sued under the First and Fourth Amendments, and the lower federal courts agreed. However, the Supreme Court ruled five to three against the Stanford paper. In his opinion for the Court, Justice Byron R. White wrote that there was no special Fourth Amendment protection governing searches of press offices. Justices Potter Stewart and Thurgood Marshall dissented, arguing that under the circumstances, the warrant did threaten press operations and have a negative effect on potential news sources. Justice John Paul Stevens found the warrant unconstitutional because the newspaper was not under suspicion. Media outrage at the Court's decision led to passage of the 1980 Privacy Protection Act.

Richard L. Wilson

See also *Branzburg v. Hayes*; *Cohen v. Cowles Media Co.*; *Grosjean v. American Press Co.*; *Mapp v. Ohio*; *Miami Herald Publishing Co. v. Tornillo*; *Near v. Minnesota*; *New York Times Co. v. United States*; *Richmond Newspapers v. Virginia*.

Appendixes

Supreme Court Justices

Alphabetical listing of Supreme Court justices. Birth and death dates follow names. Names of justices who served as chief justice of the United States through at least part of their time on the Supreme Court are underlined. A dagger symbol (†) after a tenure date indicates that the justice died while in office.

Samuel Alito (1950-)
Associate justice: 2006-
Appointed by: George W. Bush
Career highlights: Conservative jurist. Significant opinions: *Gonzales v. Carhart* (2007); *Parents Involved in Community Schools v. Seattle* (2007); *District of Columbia v. Heller* (2008); *Citizens United v. Federal Election Commission* (2010).

Henry Baldwin (1780-1844)
Associate justice: 1830-1844†
Appointed by: Andrew Jackson
Career highlights: First justice consistently to write separate opinions expressing his views. Significant opinion: *Holmes v. Jennison* (1840). Other publication: *A General View of the Origin and Nature of the Constitution and Government of the United States* (1937).

Philip Pendleton Barbour (1783-1841)
Associate justice: 1836-1841†
Appointed by: Andrew Jackson
Career highlights: Significant opinion: *New York v. Miln* (1837).

Hugo L. Black (1886-1971)
Associate justice: 1937-1971
Appointed by: Franklin D. Roosevelt
Career highlights: Author of incorporation doctrine, which held that the major provisions of the Bill of Rights were imposed on the states through the due process clause of the Fourteenth Amendment. Significant opinions: *Adamson v. California* (1947) (dissenting opinion); *Barenblatt v. United States* (1959) (dissenting opinion); *Gideon v. Wainwright* (1963); *Pointer v. Texas* (1965); *Illinois v. Allen* (1970); *New York Times Co. v. United States* (1971) (concurring opinion).

Harry A. Blackmun (1908-1999)
ASSOCIATE JUSTICE: 1970-1994
APPOINTED BY: Richard M. Nixon
CAREER HIGHLIGHTS: Defender of a general constitutional right of privacy. Significant opinions: *Roe v. Wade* (1973); *Andresen v. Maryland* (1976); *New York v. Burger* (1987); *California v. Acevedo* (1991).

John Blair, Jr. (1732-1800)
ASSOCIATE JUSTICE: 1790-1796
APPOINTED BY: George Washington
CAREER HIGHLIGHTS: Significant opinion: *Chisholm v. Georgia* (1793).

Samuel Blatchford (1820-1893)
ASSOCIATE JUSTICE: 1882-1893†
APPOINTED BY: Chester Arthur
CAREER HIGHLIGHTS: Wrote one of the earliest opinions interpreting the scope of the privilege against self-incrimination. Energetic supporter of substantive due process doctrine. Significant opinions: *Chicago, Milwaukee, and St. Paul Railway. Co. v. Minnesota* (1890); *O'Neil v. Vermont* (1892); *Councilman v. Hitchcock* (1892).

Joseph P. Bradley (1813-1892)
ASSOCIATE JUSTICE: 1870-1892†
APPOINTED BY: Ulysses S. Grant
CAREER HIGHLIGHTS: Author of *Boyd v. United States* (1886), the first case offering a significant interpretation of the Fourth and Fifth Amendments. Significant opinions: *Legal Tender Cases* (1871) (concurring opinion); *Civil Rights Cases* (1885); *Munn v. Illinois* (1886).

Louis D. Brandeis (1856-1941)
ASSOCIATE JUSTICE: 1916-1939
APPOINTED BY: Woodrow Wilson
CAREER HIGHLIGHTS: As a lawyer was a social reformer known as the "people's attorney." As a justice, argued states should be free to experiment with social and economic regulation and was a consistent defender of individual rights. Significant opinions: *Whitney v. California* (1927) (concurring opinion); *Olmstead v. United States* (1928) (dissenting opinion); *New State Ice Co. v. Liebmann* (1932) (dissenting opinion).

William J. Brennan, Jr. (1906-1997)
Associate Justice: 1956-1990
Appointed by: Dwight D. Eisenhower
Career highlights: Author of many important Warren Court-era opinions on individual rights; opposed death penalty. Significant opinions: *Baker v. Carr* (1962); *Wong Sun v. United States* (1963); *New York Times Co. v. Sullivan* (1964); *United States v. Wade* (1967); *Warden v. Hayden* (1967); *Coleman v. Alabama* (1970); *Gregg v. Georgia* (1976) (dissenting opinion); *Craig v. Boren* (1976); *Dunaway v. New York* (1979); *Pennsylvania v. Muniz* (1990).

David J. Brewer (1837-1910)
Associate Justice: 1890-1910†
Appointed by: Benjamin Harrison
Career highlights: Believed many forms of governmental economic and social regulation were unconstitutional under substantive due process doctrine. Significant opinions: *Reagan v. Farmers' Loan & Trust Co.* (1894); *In re Debs* (1895); *Muller v. Oregon* (1908).

Stephen G. Breyer (1938-   )
Associate Justice: 1994-
Appointed by: Bill Clinton
Career highlights: Specialist in administrative law; liberal jurist on most issues; author of textbooks and *Active Liberty: Interpreting Our Democratic Constitution* (2005). Significant opinions: *Turner Broadcasting System v. FCC* (1997); *Bush v. Gore* (2000) (dissent); *Zadvydas v. Davis* (2001); *Clinton v. Jones* (2007).

Henry B. Brown (1836-1913)
Associate Justice: 1891-1906
Appointed by: Benjamin Harrison
Career Highlights: Author of "separate but equal" doctrine concerning racial classifications. Significant opinions: *Pollock v. Farmers' Loan & Trust Co.* (1895) (dissenting opinion); *Plessy v. Ferguson* (1896); *Holden v. Hardy* (1898).

Warren E. Burger (1907-1995)
Chief Justice: 1969-1986
Appointed by: Richard M. Nixon
Career highlights: Critical of Warren-era expansion of constitutional rights available to criminal defendants, but unsuccessful in reversing those decisions. Revived separation of powers as an important constitutional

doctrine. Significant opinions: *Harris v. New York* (1971); *South Dakota v. Opperman* (1976); *United States v. Chadwick* (1977); *Richmond Newspapers, Inc. v. Virginia* (1980) (plurality opinion); *INS v. Chadha* (1983); *Nix v. Williams* (1984); *United States v. Sharpe* (1985).

Harold Hitz Burton (1888-1964)
ASSOCIATE JUSTICE: 1945-1958
APPOINTED BY: Harry S. Truman
CAREER HIGHLIGHTS: Generally, opposed expansion of rights for criminal defendants in state courts. Significant opinions: *Louisiana v. Resweber* (1947) (dissenting opinion); *Haley v. Ohio* (1948) (dissenting opinion); *Henderson v. United States* (1950).

Pierce Butler (1866-1939)
ASSOCIATE JUSTICE: 1923-1939†
APPOINTED BY: Warren Harding
CAREER HIGHLIGHTS: Opposed most New Deal regulatory measures. Significant opinions: *Olmstead v. United States* (1928) (dissenting opinion); *United States v. Schwimmer* (1929).

James F. Byrnes (1879-1972)
ASSOCIATE JUSTICE: 1941-1942
APPOINTED BY: Franklin D. Roosevelt
CAREER HIGHLIGHTS: Last justice who became a lawyer without attending law school. Resigned from the Court to assist the president in the war effort. Served as secretary of state in the Truman administration.

John Archibald Campbell (1811-1889)
ASSOCIATE JUSTICE: 1853-1861
APPOINTED BY: Franklin Pierce
CAREER HIGHLIGHTS: Resigned soon after Alabama's secession from the Union and became assistant secretary of war for the Confederacy. Significant opinion: *Scott v. Sandford* (1857) (concurring opinion).

John Catron (1786-1865)
ASSOCIATE JUSTICE: 1837-1865†
APPOINTED BY: Andrew Jackson
CAREER HIGHLIGHTS: Significant opinions: *License Cases* (1847); *Scott v. Sandford* (1857) (concurring opinion).

Benjamin N. Cardozo (1870-1938)
ASSOCIATE JUSTICE: 1932-1938†
APPOINTED BY: Herbert Hoover
CAREER HIGHLIGHTS: Distinguished career on the New York Court of Appeals and the United States Supreme Court. One of the great jurists in American history. Significant opinions: *Baldwin v. Seelig* (1935); *Palko v. Connecticut* (1937); *Stewart Machine Co. v. Davis* (1937). Other writings: *The Nature of the Judicial Process* (1921); *The Growth of the Law* (1924); *The Paradoxes of Legal Science* (1928).

Salmon P. Chase (1808-1873)
CHIEF JUSTICE: 1864-1873†
APPOINTED BY: Abraham Lincoln
CAREER HIGHLIGHTS: Ardent abolitionist. Presided over impeachment trial of President Andrew Johnson. Significant opinions: *Ex parte Milligan* (1866) (concurring opinion); *Ex parte McCardle* (1869); *United States v. Klein* (1871).

Samuel Chase (1741-1811)
ASSOCIATE JUSTICE: 1796-1811†
APPOINTED BY: George Washington
CAREER HIGHLIGHTS: Signer of the Declaration of Independence, ardent Federalist, and only justice ever impeached, although not convicted by the Senate. Significant opinions: *Ware v. Hylton* (1796); *Calder v. Bull* (1798).

Tom C. Clark (1890-1977)
ASSOCIATE JUSTICE: 1949-1967
APPOINTED BY: Harry S. Truman
CAREER HIGHLIGHTS: Author of *Mapp v. Ohio* opinion, which imposed the exclusionary rule on states. Retired from the Court when his son, Ramsey Clark, became attorney general. Significant opinions: *Jenks v. United States* (1957) (dissenting opinion); *Mapp v. Ohio* (1961); *School District of Abington v. Schempp* (1963); *Sheppard v. Maxwell* (1966).

John Hessin Clarke (1857-1945)
ASSOCIATE JUSTICE: 1916-1922
APPOINTED BY: Woodrow Wilson
CAREER HIGHLIGHTS: Resigned from the Court to advocate United States entry into the League of Nations. Significant opinions: *Hammer v. Dagenhart* (1918) (dissenting opinion); *Abrams v. United States* (1919).

Nathan Clifford (1803-1881)
ASSOCIATE JUSTICE: 1858-1881†
APPOINTED BY: James Buchanan
CAREER HIGHLIGHTS: Author of opinion that Court could declare congressional statute unconstitutional on grounds other than constitutional text, in *Loan Association v. Topeka* (1874).

Benjamin R. Curtis (1809-1874)
ASSOCIATE JUSTICE: 1851-1857
APPOINTED BY: Millard Fillmore
CAREER HIGHLIGHTS: Defense counsel for President Johnson during his impeachment trial. Significant opinions: *Cooley v. Board of Wardens of the Port of Philadelphia* (1851); *Scott v. Sandford* (1857) (dissenting opinion).

William Cushing (1732-1810)
ASSOCIATE JUSTICE: 1790-1810†
APPOINTED BY: George Washington
CHIEF JUSTICE: 1796
APPOINTED BY: George Washington
CAREER HIGHLIGHTS: In more than twenty years of service, wrote only nineteen opinions. Significant opinion: *Ware v. Hylton* (1796). Chief justice for only one week before he decided to decline the office and remain as an associate justice.

Peter V. Daniel (1784-1860)
ASSOCIATE JUSTICE: 1842-1860†
APPOINTED BY: Martin Van Buren
CAREER HIGHLIGHTS: Consistent advocate of states' rights. Significant opinions: *Cooley v. Board of Wardens of the Port of Philadelphia* (1851) (concurring opinion); *Scott v. Sandford* (1857) (concurring opinion).

David Davis (1815-1886)
ASSOCIATE JUSTICE: 1862-1877
APPOINTED BY: Abraham Lincoln
CAREER HIGHLIGHTS: Resigned from the Court to take a seat in the United States Senate. Significant opinion: *Ex parte Milligan* (1866).

William R. Day (1849-1923)
ASSOCIATE JUSTICE: 1903-1922
APPOINTED BY: Theodore Roosevelt
CAREER HIGHLIGHTS: Author of the exclusionary rule remedy for Fourth

Amendment violations in federal courts. Significant opinions: *Weeks v. United States* (1914); *Hammer v. Dagenhart* (1918).

William O. Douglas (1898-1980)
Associate Justice: 1939-1975
Appointed by: Franklin D. Roosevelt
Career highlights: An iconoclast and one of the most outspoken justices. Defender of a broad scope for First Amendment and other individual rights. Significant opinions: *Terminiello v. Chicago* (1949); *Griswold v. Connecticut* (1965); *Argersinger v. Hamlin* (1972). Other writings: *Go East, Young Man* (1974); *The Court Years, 1939-1975* (1980); and more than thirty other books.

Gabriel Duvall (1752-1844)
Associate Justice: 1811-1835
Appointed by: James Madison
Career highlights: One of the first members of the Court to hold strong antislavery views.

Oliver Ellsworth (1745-1807)
Chief Justice: 1796-1800
Appointed by: George Washington
Career highlights: As a senator, the main author of the Judiciary Act of 1789, which established the federal court system.

Stephen J. Field (1816-1899)
Associate Justice: 1863-1897
Appointed by: Abraham Lincoln
Career highlights: A zealous advocate of substantive due process doctrine as a means of protecting business from governmental regulation. Survived an assassination attempt by a political rival. Significant opinions: *Slaughterhouse Cases* (1873) (dissenting opinion); *Munn v. Illinois* (1877) (dissenting opinion). Other writing: *Personal Reminiscences of Early Days in California* (1893).

Abe Fortas (1910-1982)
Associate Justice: 1965-1969
Appointed by: Lyndon B. Johnson
Career highlights: As a lawyer, successfully argued in *Gideon v. Wainwright* (1963), that the right to counsel be applied to the states. Longtime adviser and confidant of President Johnson. Nominated for chief justice in 1968,

but withdrew. Resigned after disclosure of alleged financial impropriety involving a former client. Significant opinions: *In re Gault* (1967); *Tinker v. Des Moines Independent Community School District* (1969).

Felix Frankfurter (1882-1965)
ASSOCIATE JUSTICE: 1939-1962
APPOINTED BY: Franklin D. Roosevelt
CAREER HIGHLIGHTS: Opposed imposition of many provisions of the Bill of Rights on the states through the due process clause of the Fourteenth Amendment. Fought with Justice Black over this issue for more than twenty years. Significant opinions: *Adamson v. California* (1947) (concurring opinion); *Wolf v. Colorado* (1949); *Rochin v. California* (1952).

Melville W. Fuller (1833-1910)
CHIEF JUSTICE: 1888-1910†
APPOINTED BY: Grover Cleveland
CAREER HIGHLIGHTS: Opposed an expansive reading of the Congress' power under the commerce clause. Significant opinions: *United States v. E. C. Knight Co.* (1895); *Pollock v. Farmers' Loan & Trust Co.* (1895); *Champion v. Ames* (1903) (dissenting opinion).

Ruth Bader Ginsburg (1933-   )
ASSOCIATE JUSTICE: 1993-
APPOINTED BY: Bill Clinton
CAREER HIGHLIGHTS: Argued cases before the Court that established intermediate scrutiny under the equal protection clause of the Fourteenth Amendment for gender-based regulations. Emphasized rights of women and minorities. Significant opinions: *United States v. Virginia Military Academy* (1996); *Olmstead v. L.C.* (1999); *Bush v. Gore* (2000) (dissenting opinion); *Ricci v. DeStefano* (2009) (dissenting opinion).

Arthur J. Goldberg (1908-1990)
ASSOCIATE JUSTICE: 1962-1965
APPOINTED BY: John F. Kennedy
CAREER HIGHLIGHTS: Resigned to become ambassador to the United Nations with expectation that he would be permitted to settle the Vietnam War. Significant opinions: *Escobedo v. Illinois* (1964); *Aguilar v. Texas* (1964); *Griswold v. Connecticut* (1965) (concurring opinion).

Horace Gray (1828-1902)
Associate Justice: 1882-1902†
Appointed by: Chester Arthur
Career highlights: Significant opinions: *Sparf v. Hansen* (1895); *United States v. Wong Kim Ark* (1898).

Robert C. Grier (1794-1870)
Associate Justice: 1846-1870
Appointed by: James Polk
Career highlights: Significant opinions: *Moore v. Illinois* (1852); The *Prize Cases* (1863).

John Marshall Harlan (1833-1911)
Associate Justice: 1877-1911†
Appointed by: Rutherford B. Hayes
Career highlights: No other justice has written as many dissenting opinions which later became the law of the land. Significant opinions: *Pollock v. Farmers' Loan & Trust Co.* (1895) (dissenting opinion); *Plessy v. Ferguson* (1896) (dissenting opinion); *Lochner v. New York* (1905) (dissenting opinion); *Berea College v. Kentucky* (1908) (dissenting opinion).

John Marshall Harlan II (1899-1971)
Associate Justice: 1955-1971
Appointed by: Dwight D. Eisenhower
Career highlights: Author of the modern approach to the scope of the Fourth Amendment. Significant opinions: *Katz v. United States* (1967) (concurring opinion); *Simmons v. United States* (1968); *Spinelli v. United States* (1969).

Oliver Wendell Holmes, Jr. (1841-1935)
Associate Justice: 1902-1932
Appointed by: Theodore Roosevelt
Career highlights: Most influential justice in the twentieth century; wrote with an elegant style unmatched in the history of the Court. Significant opinions: *Lochner v. New York* (1905) (dissenting opinion); *Schneck v. United States* (1919); *Abrams v. United States* (1919) (dissenting opinion); *Pennsylvania Coal Co. v. Mohan* (1922). Other writings: *Kent's Commentaries on American Law* (editor of 12th edition, 1873); *The Common Law* (1881).

Charles Evans Hughes (1862-1948)
ASSOCIATE JUSTICE: 1910-1916
APPOINTED BY: William Howard Taft
CHIEF JUSTICE: 1930-1941
APPOINTED BY: Herbert Hoover
CAREER HIGHLIGHTS: Resigned from the Court to run (unsuccessfully) as the
Republican nominee for president in 1916; later served as secretary of state in
the Harding Administration. After returning to the Court as chief justice,
successfully defended the Court against President Roosevelt's Court-packing
plan. Significant opinions: *Home Building & Loan Association v. Blaisdell* (1934);
Brown v. Mississippi (1936); *NLRB v. Jones and Laughlin Steel Corp.* (1937).

Ward Hunt (1810-1886)
ASSOCIATE JUSTICE: 1873-1882
APPOINTED BY: Ulysses S. Grant
CAREER HIGHLIGHTS: Usually a supporter of legislation protecting rights of
African Americans; in circuit trial, rejected Susan Anthony's claim that the
Fourteenth Amendment applied to voting rights for women.

James Iredell (1751-1799)
ASSOCIATE JUSTICE: 1790-1799†
APPOINTED BY: George Washington
CAREER HIGHLIGHTS: Significant opinion: *Chisholm v. Georgia* (1793) (dissent-
ing opinion).

Howell E. Jackson (1832-1895)
ASSOCIATE JUSTICE: 1893-1895†
APPOINTED BY: Benjamin Harrison
CAREER HIGHLIGHTS: Moderate southerner who supported an expansive role
for national government; strongly dissented on income tax in *Pollock v. Farm-
ers' Loan & Trust* (1895).

Robert H. Jackson (1892-1954)
ASSOCIATE JUSTICE: 1941-1954†
APPOINTED BY: Franklin D. Roosevelt
CAREER HIGHLIGHTS: Took a leave from the Court to serve as chief prosecu-
tor in the Nuremberg war crimes trial of Nazi leaders. Publicly feuded with
Justice Black over this and other matters. Significant opinion: *West Virginia
State Board of Education v. Barnette* (1943). Other writings: *The Struggle for Ju-
dicial Supremacy* (1941); *The Supreme Court in the American System of Govern-
ment* (1955).

John Jay (1745-1829)
Chief Justice: 1789-1795
Appointed by: George Washington
Career highlights: In 1795, resigned to become governor of New York, and in 1800 declined nomination as chief justice. Only author of *The Federalist Papers* to serve on the Supreme Court. Significant opinion: *Chisholm v. Georgia* (1793).

Thomas Johnson (1732-1819)
Associate Justice: 1791-1793
Appointed by: George Washington
Career highlights: Wrote only one opinion.

William Johnson (1771-1834)
Associate Justice: 1804-1834†
Appointed by: Thomas Jefferson
Career highlights: Only member of the Court during this period who directly challenged Chief Justice Marshall's views on the Constitution. Significant opinions: *Gibbons v. Ogden* (1824) (concurring opinion); *United States v. Hudson and Goodwin* (1832).

Anthony M. Kennedy (1936-   )
Associate Justice: 1988-
Appointed by: Ronald Reagan
Career highlights: Expanded administrative search exception to warrant requirement to individuals. Significant opinions: *Skinner v. Railway Labor Executives' Association* (1989); *Illinois v. Perkins* (1990).

Joseph R. Lamar (1857-1916)
Associate Justice: 1911-1916†
Appointed by: William Howard Taft
Career highlights: Significant opinion: *Gompers v. Bucks Stove and Range Company* (1911).

Lucius Quintus Cincinnatus Lamar (1825-1893)
Associate Justice: 1888-1893†
Appointed by: Grover Cleveland
Career highlights: Significant opinions: *In re Neagle* (1890) (dissenting opinion); *Field v. Clark* (1892) (dissenting opinion).

Henry Brockholst Livingston (1757-1823)
ASSOCIATE JUSTICE: 1807-1823†
APPOINTED BY: Thomas Jefferson
CAREER HIGHLIGHTS: Approved state prosecutions of seditious libel while on New York Supreme Court; strong supporter of Chief Justice Marshall; eight opinions on prize ship cases; questions of his judicial ethics in communications about cases.

Horace H. Lurton (1844-1914)
ASSOCIATE JUSTICE: 1910-1914†
APPOINTED BY: William Howard Taft
CAREER HIGHLIGHTS: Oldest justice ever appointed; conservative judicial values; former Confederate officer who supported states' rights under the Tenth Amendment.

Joseph McKenna (1843-1926)
ASSOCIATE JUSTICE: 1898-1925
APPOINTED BY: William McKinley
CAREER HIGHLIGHTS: In 1924, after old age rendered him incompetent but he remained on the Court, the other justices agreed to decide no case where his vote was the deciding one. Significant opinions: *Hoke v. United States* (1913); *Hammer v. Dagenhart* (1918) (dissenting opinion); *Gilbert v. Minnesota* (1920).

John McKinley (1780-1852)
ASSOCIATE JUSTICE: 1838-1852†
APPOINTED BY: Martin Van Buren
CAREER HIGHLIGHTS: Kentuckian who supported state sovereignty in *Bank of Augusta v. Earle* (1839) and other cases; frequently absent from the Court.

John McLean (1785-1861)
ASSOCIATE JUSTICE: 1830-1861†
APPOINTED BY: Andrew Jackson
CAREER HIGHLIGHTS: Adamant antislavery justice. Significant opinions: *Prigg v. Pennsylvania* (1842) (dissenting opinion); *Ex parte Dorr* (1844); *Scott v. Sandford* (1857) (dissenting opinion).

James Clark McReynolds (1862-1946)
ASSOCIATE JUSTICE: 1914-1941
APPOINTED BY: Woodrow Wilson
CAREER HIGHLIGHTS: Arguably, the most reactionary and bigoted, and cer-

tainly the least congenial justice ever to serve on the Supreme Court. Opposed use of individual rights in criminal cases and New Deal regulatory measures. Significant opinions: *Berger v. United States* (1921) (dissenting opinion); *Carroll v. United States* (1925) (dissenting opinion); *Pierce v. Society of Sisters* (1925); *Stromberg v. California* (1931) (dissenting opinion); *Powell v. Alabama* (1932) (dissenting opinion).

John Marshall (1755-1835)
CHIEF JUSTICE: 1801-1835†
APPOINTED BY: John Adams
CAREER HIGHLIGHTS: "Great chief justice" who established preeminent role of the Supreme Court in interpreting the Constitution. No other justice has ever so dominated the Supreme Court. His last constitutional law decision held the Bill of Rights did not apply to the states. Significant opinions: *Marbury v. Madison* (1803); *McCulloch v. Maryland* (1819); *Gibbons v. Ogden* (1824); *Barron v. Baltimore* (1833).

Thurgood Marshall (1908-1993)
ASSOCIATE JUSTICE: 1967-1991
APPOINTED BY: Lyndon B. Johnson
CAREER HIGHLIGHTS: Former lead lawyer for the NAACP, successfully argued *Brown v. Board of Education* (1954) and other cases before the Supreme Court. Viewed the Constitution as providing significant protection for the individual against unjust actions by the government. Adamantly opposed to the death penalty. Significant opinions: *United States v. Wilson* (1975); *Gregg v. Georgia* (1976) (dissenting opinion); *Donovan v. Dewey* (1981); *Oliver v. United States* (1984) (dissenting opinion); *Skinner v. Railway Labor Executives' Association* (1989) (dissenting opinion); *Florida v. Bostick* (1991) (dissenting opinion).

Stanley Matthews (1824-1889)
ASSOCIATE JUSTICE: 1881-1889†
APPOINTED BY: James Garfield
CAREER HIGHLIGHTS: Closest Senate confirmation vote (24-23). Significant opinions: *Hurtado v. California* (1884); *Yick Wo v. Hopkins* (1886).

Samuel F. Miller (1816-1890)
ASSOCIATE JUSTICE: 1862-1890†
APPOINTED BY: Abraham Lincoln
CAREER HIGHLIGHTS: Opposed using the Fourteenth Amendment to block state regulations of business activity and favored the use of individual rights

to check the power of the federal government. Significant opinions: *Slaughterhouse Cases* (1873); *Kilbourn v. Thompson* (1881); *United States v. Lee* (1882).

Sherman Minton (1890-1965)
ASSOCIATE JUSTICE: 1949-1956
APPOINTED BY: Harry S. Truman
CAREER HIGHLIGHTS: Consistently held for the government in criminal cases. Significant opinions: *United States v. Rabinowitz* (1950); *United States ex rel. Knauff v. Shaughnessy* (1950).

William H. Moody (1853-1917)
ASSOCIATE JUSTICE: 1906-1910
APPOINTED BY: Theodore Roosevelt
CAREER HIGHLIGHTS: Believed states were free to confer or withhold individual rights from criminal defendants. Significant opinions: *Twining v. New Jersey* (1908); *Londoner v. Denver* (1908).

Alfred Moore (1755-1810)
ASSOCIATE JUSTICE: 1800-1804
APPOINTED BY: John Adams
CAREER HIGHLIGHTS: Wrote only one opinion.

Frank Murphy (1890-1949)
ASSOCIATE JUSTICE: 1940-1949†
APPOINTED BY: Franklin D. Roosevelt
CAREER HIGHLIGHTS: Argued vigorously for the availability of individual rights as checks on governmental power and opposed the expansion of the scope of warrantless searches and seizures. Significant opinions: *Thornhill v. Alabama* (1940); *In re Yamashita* (1946) (dissenting opinion); *Harris v. United States* (1947) (dissenting opinion); *Wolf v. Colorado* (1949) (dissenting opinion).

Samuel Nelson (1792-1873)
ASSOCIATE JUSTICE: 1845-1872
APPOINTED BY: John Tyler
CAREER HIGHLIGHTS: Significant opinions: *Scott v. Sandford* (1857) (concurring opinion); *Prize Cases* (1863) (dissenting opinion); *Ex parte Milligan* (1866) (dissenting opinion).

Sandra Day O'Connor (1930-   )
ASSOCIATE JUSTICE: 1981-2006
APPOINTED BY: Ronald Reagan
CAREER HIGHLIGHTS: First woman to serve on the Supreme Court. A moderate jurist, she served as the swing vote in 5-4 rulings from the 1990's until her retirement in 2006. Significant opinions: *Strictland v. Washington* (1984); *Oregon v. Elstad* (1985); *Florida v. Bostick* (1991); *Grutter v. Bollinger* (2003).

William Paterson (1745-1806)
ASSOCIATE JUSTICE: 1793-1806†
APPOINTED BY: George Washington
CAREER HIGHLIGHTS: Significant opinions: *Hylton v. United States* (1796); *Stuart v. Laird* (1803).

Rufus W. Peckham (1838-1909)
ASSOCIATE JUSTICE: 1896-1909†
APPOINTED BY: Grover Cleveland
CAREER HIGHLIGHTS: Author of best-known substantive due process case, *Lochner v. New York* (1905). Believed states were not required to offer defendants all of the rights found in the Bill of Rights. Significant opinions: *Crain v. United States* (1896); *White v. United States* (1896); *Allegeyer v. Louisiana* (1897); *Maxwell v. Dow* (1900).

Mahlon Pitney (1858-1924)
ASSOCIATE JUSTICE: 1912-1922
APPOINTED BY: William Howard Taft
CAREER HIGHLIGHTS: Rejected attempts to apply the Bill of Rights to state criminal justice systems and read the scope of those rights narrowly in federal criminal cases. Significant opinions: *Frank v. Mangum* (1915); *Pierce v. United States* (1920); *Berger v. United States* (1921) (dissenting opinion).

Lewis Franklin Powell, Jr. (1907-1998)
ASSOCIATE JUSTICE: 1972-1987
APPOINTED BY: Richard M. Nixon
CAREER HIGHLIGHTS: Author of modern "open fields" exception to the Fourth Amendment and of opinion cutting back access to federal habeas corpus for state prisoners. Significant opinions: *Barker v. Wingo* (1972); *Doyle v. Ohio* (1976); *Stone v. Powell* (1976); *Solem v. Helm* (1983); *Oliver v. United States* (1984); *Batson v. Kentucky* (1986).

Stanley F. Reed (1884-1980)
Associate Justice: 1938-1957
Appointed by: Franklin D. Roosevelt
Career highlights: Significant opinions: *McNabb v. United States* (1943) (dissenting opinion); *Adamson v. California* (1947); *Winters v. New York* (1948); *Gallegos v. Nebraska* (1951); *Carlson v. Landon* (1952); *Brown v. Allen* (1953).

William H. Rehnquist (1924-2005)
Associate Justice: 1972-1986
Appointed by: Richard M. Nixon
Chief Justice: 1986-2005†
Appointed by: Ronald Reagan
Career highlights: As associate justice, opposed the Warren-era expansion of constitutional rights of defendants. Author of many opinions limiting the scope of these decisions and adamant critic of the exclusionary rule. As chief justice, led the Court in the creation of more exceptions to the warrant requirement of the Fourth Amendment and of limitations on the use of the exclusionary rule. Presided over impeachment trial of President Bill Clinton; leader of the conservative wing of the court. Significant opinions: *Rakas v. Illinois* (1978); *Illinois v. Gates* (1983); *Colorado v. Connelly* (1986); *United States v. Salerno* (1987); *Arizona v. Youngblood* (1988); *Michigan Department of State Police v. Sitz* (1990); *Bush v. Gore* (2000); *United States v. Morrison* (2000).

John G. Roberts (1955-   )
Chief Justice: 2005-
Appointed by: George W. Bush
Career highlights: Conservative jurist. Significant opinions: *Gonzales v. Carhart* (2007); *Parents Involved in Community Schools v. Seattle* (2007); *District of Columbia v. Heller* (2008); *Citizens United v. Federal Election Commission* (2010).

Owen J. Roberts (1875-1955)
Associate Justice: 1930-1945
Appointed by: Herbert Hoover
Career highlights: Changed his vote and saved the Supreme Court from President Franklin D. Roosevelt's Court-packing plan, commonly known as a "switch in time that saved the nine." Consistent defender of individual rights in criminal cases. Significant opinions: *Grau v. United States* (1932); *Herndon v. Lowry* (1937); *Hague v. Committee for Industrial Organization* (1939); *Cantwell v. Connecticut* (1940); *Betts v. Brady* (1942).

John Rutledge (1739-1800)
Associate Justice: 1790-1791
Appointed by: George Washington
Chief Justice: 1795
Appointed by: George Washington
Career highlights: As associate justice, wrote no opinions and attended no sessions of the Supreme Court. Resigned to become chief justice of the South Carolina Court of Common Pleas. After returning to the U.S. Supreme Court, took oath and presided over only one session, during which only two cases were heard before the Senate rejected his appointment.

Wiley B. Rutledge, Jr. (1894-1949)
Associate Justice: 1943-1949†
Appointed by: Franklin D. Roosevelt
Career highlights: Significant opinions: *Thomas v. Collins* (1944); *In re Yamashita* (1946) (dissenting opinion).

Edward T. Sanford (1865-1930)
Associate Justice: 1923-1930†
Appointed by: Warren Harding
Career highlights: Held that the First Amendment applied to the states through the due process clause of the Fourteenth Amendment. Significant opinions: *Gitlow v. New York* (1925); *Fiske v. Kansas* (1927).

Antonin Scalia (1936-   )
Associate Justice: 1986-
Appointed by: Ronald Reagan
Career highlights: Intellectual leader of the conservative wing of the Court; proponent of interpreting the Constitution according to its original meaning. Significant opinions: *Illinois v. Rodriguez* (1990); *California v. Hodari D.* (1991); *United States v. Williams* (1992).

George Shiras, Jr. (1832-1924)
Associate Justice: 1892-1903
Appointed by: Benjamin Harrison
Career highlights: Dissenting opinions offered modern view of the protections offered by the Fifth Amendment. Significant opinions: *Mattox v. United States* (1895) (dissenting opinion); *Wong Wing v. United States* (1896); *Brown v. Walker* (1896) (dissenting opinion).

Sonia Sotomayor (1957-   )
ASSOCIATE JUSTICE: 2009-
APPOINTED BY: Barack Obama
CAREER HIGHLIGHTS: First Hispanic justice; during her eleven years on the U.S. Court of Appeals for the Second Circuit, her record was moderate liberal on most issues.

David H. Souter (1939-   )
ASSOCIATE JUSTICE: 1990-2009
APPOINTED BY: George H. W. Bush
CAREER HIGHLIGHTS: Although thought to have conservative views, he almost always voted with the liberal wing of the Court on issues of federalism, separation between religion and government, abortion, and affirmative action. Significant opinions: *Planned Parenthood v. Casey* (1992); *Washington v. Glucksburg* (1997); *Bush v. Gore* (2000).

Edwin M. Stanton (1814-1869)
ASSOCIATE JUSTICE: 1869†
APPOINTED BY: Ulysses S. Grant
CAREER HIGHLIGHTS: Died four days after he was confirmed by the Senate.

John Paul Stevens (1920-   )
ASSOCIATE JUSTICE: 1975-2010
APPOINTED BY: Gerald Ford
CAREER HIGHLIGHTS: Usually joined the liberal wing of the Court; emphasis on judicial protection for individual liberties. Significant opinions: *Payton v. New York* (1980); *United States v. Jacobsen* (1984); *Maryland v. Garrison* (1987). (On May 10, 2010, President Barack Obama nominated U.S. solicitor general Elena Kagan [b. 1960] to fill Justice Stevens's seat on the Court.)

Potter Stewart (1915-1985)
ASSOCIATE JUSTICE: 1958-1981
APPOINTED BY: Dwight D. Eisenhower
CAREER HIGHLIGHTS: Leader in development of Supreme Court's approach to interpreting the scope of the Fourth Amendment in modern times. Famous for his quip concerning attempts to define obscenity: ". . . I know it when I see it; and the motion picture involved in this case is not that." Significant opinions: *Jacobellis v. Ohio* (1964) (concurring opinion); *Massiah v. United States* (1964); *Stoner v. California* (1964); *Katz v. United States* (1967); *Chimel v. California* (1969); *Gregg v. Georgia* (1976) (plurality opinion); *Brewer v. Williams* (1977); *Rhode Island v. Innis* (1980).

Harlan Fiske Stone (1872-1946)
ASSOCIATE JUSTICE: 1925-1941
APPOINTED BY: Calvin Coolidge
CHIEF JUSTICE: 1941-1946†
APPOINTED BY: Franklin D. Roosevelt
CAREER HIGHLIGHTS: As associate justice, was author of footnote four in *United States v. Carolene Products Co.*, a key doctrinal innovation leading to modern equal protection analysis under the Fourteenth Amendment. As chief justice, led the Supreme Court during the difficult years of World War II. Significant opinions: *United States v. Butler* (1936) (dissenting opinion); *United States v. Carolene Products Co.* (1938); *Minersville School District v. Gobitis* (1940); *United States v. Classic* (1941); *United States v. Darby Lumber Co.* (1941); *Ex parte Quirin* (1942); *Yakus v. United States* (1944).

Joseph Story (1779-1845)
ASSOCIATE JUSTICE: 1812-1845†
APPOINTED BY: James Madison
CAREER HIGHLIGHTS: Intellectual leader of the Supreme Court who also wrote many of the most significant early commentaries on American law. Significant opinions: *Martin v. Hunter's Lessee* (1816); *Charles River Bridge v. Warren Bridge Co.* (1837) (dissenting opinion); *United States v. Schooner Amistad* (1841); *Swift v. Tyson* (1842). Other writings: *Commentaries on the Constitution of the United States* (1833) (3 volumes); *Commentaries on Equity Jurisprudence* (1834); and numerous other books and articles.

William Strong (1808-1895)
ASSOCIATE JUSTICE: 1870-1880
APPOINTED BY: Ulysses S. Grant
CAREER HIGHLIGHTS: Author of opinions opening jury service to African Americans. Significant opinions: *Strauder v. West Virginia* (1880); *Ex parte Virginia* (1880); *Virginia v. Rives* (1880).

George Sutherland (1862-1942)
ASSOCIATE JUSTICE: 1922-1938
APPOINTED BY: Warren Harding
CAREER HIGHLIGHTS: Intellectual leader of the Supreme Court's opposition to New Deal regulatory measures; supported selective application of the Bill of Rights to state criminal justice systems. Significant opinions: *Powell v. Alabama* (1932); *Berger v. United States* (1935); *Carter v. Carter Coal Co.* (1936).

Noah H. Swayne (1804-1884)
ASSOCIATE JUSTICE: 1862-1881
APPOINTED BY: Abraham Lincoln
CAREER HIGHLIGHTS: Most consistent supporter of President Lincoln's orders concerning prosecution of the Civil War. Significant opinion: *Slaughterhouse Cases* (1873) (dissenting opinion).

William Howard Taft (1857-1930)
CHIEF JUSTICE: 1921-1930
APPOINTED BY: Warren Harding
CAREER HIGHLIGHTS: Only president ever to serve on the Court. As chief justice he actively sought to influence appointments to the Supreme Court. Author of property-based view of the scope of the Fourth Amendment. Significant opinions: *Myers v. United States* (1926); *Olmstead v. United States* (1928).

Roger Brooke Taney (1777-1864)
CHIEF JUSTICE: 1836-1864†
APPOINTED BY: Andrew Jackson
CAREER HIGHLIGHTS: Pro-slavery and states' rights chief justice; author of the infamous *Scott v. Sandford* opinion. Resisted many of President Lincoln's orders concerning the prosecution of the Civil War. Significant opinions: *Charles River Bridge v. Warren Bridge Co.* (1837); *License Cases* (1847); *Scott v. Sandford* (1857).

Clarence Thomas (1948-   )
ASSOCIATE JUSTICE: 1991-
APPOINTED BY: George H. W. Bush
CAREER HIGHLIGHTS: Most controversial modern Supreme Court appointment; accused of sexual harassment during confirmation process. Consistently conservative on most issues. Significant opinions: *Gonzales v. Carhart* (2007); *Parents Involved in Community Schools v. Seattle* (2007); *District of Columbia v. Heller* (2008); *Citizens United v. Federal Election Commission* (2010).

Smith Thompson (1768-1843)
ASSOCIATE JUSTICE: 1824-1843†
APPOINTED BY: James Monroe
CAREER HIGHLIGHTS: Significant opinion: *Cherokee Nation v. Georgia* (1831) (dissenting opinion).

Thomas Todd (1765-1826)
ASSOCIATE JUSTICE: 1807-1826†
APPOINTED BY: Thomas Jefferson
CAREER HIGHLIGHTS: Never disagreed with Chief Justice Marshall on any constitutional issue.

Robert Trimble (1777-1828)
ASSOCIATE JUSTICE: 1826-1828†
APPOINTED BY: John Q. Adams
CAREER HIGHLIGHTS: Significant opinions: *The Antelope Case* (1827); *Ogden v. Saunders* (1827).

Willis Van Devanter (1859-1941)
ASSOCIATE JUSTICE: 1911-1937
APPOINTED BY: William Howard Taft
CAREER HIGHLIGHTS: Significant opinion: *McGrain v. Daugherty* (1927).

Fred M. Vinson (1890-1953)
CHIEF JUSTICE: 1946-1953†
APPOINTED BY: Harry S. Truman
CAREER HIGHLIGHTS: Significant opinions: *Harris v. United States* (1947); *Shelley v. Kraemer* (1948); *Dennis v. United States* (1951); *Stack v. Boyle* (1951).

Morrison R. Waite (1816-1888)
CHIEF JUSTICE: 1874-1888†
APPOINTED BY: Ulysses S. Grant
CAREER HIGHLIGHTS: Significant opinions: *United States v. Cruikshank* (1876); *Munn v. Illinois* (1877).

Earl Warren (1891-1974)
CHIEF JUSTICE: 1953-1969
APPOINTED BY: Dwight D. Eisenhower
CAREER HIGHLIGHTS: Second only to Chief Justice Marshall in impact on the Supreme Court's role. Led expansion of constitutional rights for defendants in state courts and the transformation of the meaning of the equal protection clause of the Fourteenth Amendment. Significant opinions: *Brown v. Board of Education* (1954); *Watkins v. United States* (1957); *Spano v. New York* (1959); *Reynolds v. Sims* (1964); *Miranda v. Arizona* (1966); *Terry v. Ohio* (1968).

Bushrod Washington (1762-1829)
ASSOCIATE JUSTICE: 1789-1829†
APPOINTED BY: John Adams
CAREER HIGHLIGHTS: Almost always agreed with Chief Justice Marshall's views. Significant opinion: *Ogden v. Saunders* (1827).

James M. Wayne (1790-1867)
ASSOCIATE JUSTICE: 1835-1867†
APPOINTED BY: Andrew Jackson
CAREER HIGHLIGHTS: Significant opinion: *Louisville, Cincinnati and Charleston Railroad Co. v. Letson* (1844).

Byron R. White (1917-   )
ASSOCIATE JUSTICE: 1962-1993
APPOINTED BY: John F. Kennedy
CAREER HIGHLIGHTS: Critical of the exclusionary rule and expansive view of the scope of protection offered by the Fourth Amendment. Significant opinions: *Miranda v. Arizona* (1966) (dissenting opinion); *Camara v. Municipal Court of the City and County of San Francisco* (1967); *Duncan v. Louisiana* (1968); *Chambers v. Maroney* (1970); *United States v. Matlock* (1974); *Stone v. Powell* (1976) (dissenting opinion); *United States v. Leon* (1984); *New Jersey v. T.L.O.* (1985); *California v. Greenwood* (1988).

Edward D. White (1845-1921)
ASSOCIATE JUSTICE: 1894-1910
APPOINTED BY: Grover Cleveland
CHIEF JUSTICE: 1910-1921†
APPOINTED BY: William Howard Taft
CAREER HIGHLIGHTS: Holder of erratic positions on governmental powers to regulate economy. As associate justice, significant opinions: *Talton v. Mayes* (1896); *Rasmussen v. United States* (1905). As chief justice, significant opinions: *Standard Oil Co. v. United States* (1911); *Selective Draft Law Cases* (1918).

Charles Evans Whittaker (1901-1973)
ASSOCIATE JUSTICE: 1957-1962
APPOINTED BY: Dwight D. Eisenhower
CAREER HIGHLIGHTS: Supplied the critical vote in a series of 5-4 decisions in which the Supreme Court rejected individual rights claims in state criminal cases. Significant opinion: *Draper v. United States* (1959).

James Wilson (1742-1798)
ASSOCIATE JUSTICE: 1789-1798†
APPOINTED BY: George Washington
CAREER HIGHLIGHTS: While on the Court, was imprisoned for failure to pay his debts. Significant opinion: *Chisholm v. Georgia* (1793).

Levi Woodbury (1789-1851)
ASSOCIATE JUSTICE: 1845-1851†
APPOINTED BY: James Polk
CAREER HIGHLIGHTS: Rejected abolitionists' arguments for limiting the impact of the fugitive slave clause of the Constitution. Significant opinion: *Jones v. Van Zandt* (1847).

William B. Woods (1824-1887)
ASSOCIATE JUSTICE: 1881-1887†
APPOINTED BY: Rutherford B. Hayes
CAREER HIGHLIGHTS: Narrowly interpreted the Fourteenth Amendment; overturned the Ku Klux Klan Act of 1871 in *United States v. Harris* (1883) based on the Tenth Amendment. Other significant opinions: *United States v. Lee* (1882) (dissenting opinion); *United States v. Harris* (1883); *Presser v. Illinois* (1886).

BIBLIOGRAPHY

General Works on the Supreme Court

Ackerman, Bruce. *We the People 2: Transformations.* Cambridge, Mass.: Harvard University Press, 1998. Controversial book viewing the Supreme Court as essentially a political institution, arguing that in times of crisis the Court has been a participant in social movements that have produced constitutional revolutions.

Agresto, John. *The Supreme Court and Constitutional Democracy.* Ithaca, N.Y.: Cornell University Press, 1994. About one-third of this book is a historical analysis of the work of the Court, and the remainder discusses the Court's role in American political life, stressing its interaction with the other two branches.

Baum, Lawrence. *The Supreme Court.* 10th ed. Washington, D.C.: CQ Press, 2010. Brief but nevertheless comprehensive introduction to the U.S. Supreme Court. This up-to-date new edition pays particular attention to changes in the Court under John Roberts since he became chief justice in 2005.

Bloch, Susan Low, Vicki C. Jackson, and Thomas G. Krattenmaker. *Inside the Supreme Court: The Institution and Its Procedures.* 2d ed. St. Paul, Minn.: Thomson/West, 2008. Legal textbook that analyzes the U.S. Supreme Court from the nomination process to modern proposals for reforms of the Court.

Faigman, David L. *Laboratory of Justice: The Supreme Court's Two-Hundred-Year Struggle to Integrate Science and the Law.* New York: Henry Holt, 2004. Argues that scientific beliefs have always influenced the Court's decisions and that the process has often been unsystematic and haphazard, as in the Court's early justification of racism and eugenics.

Fisher, Louis. *The Supreme Court and Congress: Rival Interpretations.* Washington, D.C.: CQ Press, 2009. Study of the interaction between the judicial and legislative branches of the federal government, with particular attention to the conflicts between Congress and the Supreme Court over the Court's power of judicial review.

Gibson, James L. *Citizens, Courts, and Confirmations: Positivity Theory and the Judgments of the American People.* Princeton, N.J.: Princeton University Press, 2009. Study of interrelationships among the Supreme Court, the media, and the general public, looking at the role of the media in influencing public support of the Court.

Greenburg, Jan Crawford. *Supreme Conflict: The Inside Story of the Struggle for Control of the United States Supreme Court.* New York: Penguin, 2007. Drawing on highly placed sources close to the justices of the U.S. Supreme Court, legal affairs journalist Greenburg examines interrelationships among the justices in an effort to show how they reach their decisions in cases.

Hall, Kermit L., ed. *The Oxford Companion to the Supreme Court of the United States.* 2d ed. New York: Oxford University Press, 2005. This single-volume reference on the Court has more than a thousand articles by specialists that include biographies, studies of individual decisions, and major issues confronting the Court.

Hensley, Thomas, Christopher Smith, and Joyce Baugh. *The Changing Supreme Court: Constitutional Rights and Liberties.* 2d ed. Belmont, Calif.: Thomson/Wadsworth, 2007. Scholarly and interesting text arranged topically, with both qualitative analysis and quantitative scales of liberal/conservative voting patterns of the justices.

Jost, Kenneth. *The Supreme Court A to Z.* 4th ed. Washington, D.C.: CQ Press, 2007. Encyclopedic reference work with more than 350 alphabetically arranged entries on all aspects of the U.S. Supreme Court, including specific legal issues, such as intellectual property, international law, and sentencing guidelines. Well illustrated and exhaustively indexed.

Kahn, Ronald, and Ken I. Kersch, eds. *The Supreme Court and American Political Development.* Lawrence: University Press of Kansas, 2006. Collection of original essays exploring the evolution of constitutional doctrine as seen through U.S. Supreme Court rulings. Chapters include a selection of historical case studies that illuminate how the Court has built its authority as it has defined individual rights and government powers.

Levy, Leonard, and Kenneth Karst, eds. *Encyclopedia of the American Constitution.* 2d ed. 6 vols. New York: Macmillan Reference, 2000. These large volumes provide detailed accounts of doctrines, terms, and cases relating to the American Constitution and constitutional law, written by recognized scholars.

Lewis, Thomas Tandy, ed. *U.S. Supreme Court.* 3 vols. Pasadena, Calif.: Salem Press, 2007. Comprehensive reference work on the Supreme Court that contains substantial discussions of all the Court's justices, many court cases, and the organization and procedures of the Court.

McCloskey, Robert G. *The American Supreme Court.* 4th ed. Chicago: University of Chicago Press, 2005. Presents a complete overview of the structure, functions, history, and direction of the Supreme Court and an appreciation of its role in the U.S. political and governmental system.

Maltzman, Forrest, et al. *Crafting Law on the Supreme Court: The Collegial Game.* New York: Cambridge University Press, 2000. Argues that the justices are constrained by the choices of the other justices, requiring them to make compromises and alliances in order to build majority opinions.

Maroon, Fred J., and Suzy Maroon. *The Supreme Court of the United States*. West Palm Beach, Fla.: Lickle Publishing, 1996. Contains 130 color photographs of the Supreme Court building—both inside and outside—a photo-essay on the progress of an appeal through the Court, and a brief history of the Court.

O'Brien, David. *Storm Center: The Supreme Court in American Politics*. 8th ed. New York: W. W. Norton, 2008. Informed introduction to the Supreme Court's role in debating and often deciding the legal outcomes of controversial issues.

Powers, Stephen, and Stanley Rothman. *The Least Dangerous Branch? Consequences of Judicial Activism*. Westport, Conn.: Greenwood Press, 2002. Two moderately conservative critics express their distrust of judicial power and dislike for the Court's ruling in cases of affirmative action, busing, prison reform, and criminal procedures.

Savage, David G. *Guide to the U.S. Supreme Court*. 4th ed. Washington, D.C.: CQ Press, 2004. Comprehensive reference source on the Supreme Court, covering its origins, history, organization, procedures, justices, and major decisions.

_____. *The Supreme Court and the Powers of the American Government*. 2d ed. Washington, D.C.: CQ Press, 2009. Study of the impact of major Supreme Court decisions on the executive and legislative branches of the federal government.

Schwartz, Bernard. *Decision: How the Supreme Court Decides Cases*. New York: Oxford University Press, 1996. Schwartz examines four major ways that cases are decided: leadership by a strong chief justice, leadership on given issues by forceful individual justices, general cooperation of justices dealing with a weak chief justice, and decision by vote switching.

Spaeth, Harold J., and Jeffrey A. Segal. *Majority Rule or Minority Will: Adherence to Precedent on the U.S. Supreme Court*. New York: Cambridge University Press, 2001. Asserts that quantitative data show that justices are rarely influenced by precedent, even though many justices, such as Sandra Day O'Connor, claim otherwise. Interesting from a methodological perspective.

Stephens, Otis H., Jr., and John M. Scheb. *American Constitutional Law*. 4th ed. Belmont, Calif.: Thomson/Wadsworth, 2008. One of the best of the college textbooks, organized topically with a strong historical perspective, containing many selections from Supreme Court decisions.

Urofsky, Melvin I., and Paul Finkelman. *A March of Liberty: A Constitutional History of the United States*. 2d ed. 2 vols. New York: Oxford University Press, 2004. Written primarily to serve as a textbook for college courses, this is a readable and scholarly account of the Constitution and its interpretation by the Supreme Court.

Wiecek, William M. *Liberty Under Law: The Supreme Court in American Life.* Baltimore, Md.: Johns Hopkins University Press, 1988. This clear and succinct summary of the history of the Court is aimed at those who have no background in law. Its judgments about people and events are carefully considered, with some bias in favor of an activist Court.

Wrightman, Lawrence. *The Psychology of the Supreme Court.* New York: Oxford University Press, 2006. Using modern academic concepts and research, an eminent social psychologist's examination of the factors that influence behavior, including social background, appointment, role of the law clerks, the chief justice, and daily interaction with other justices.

Justices

Biskupic, Joan. *American Original: The Life and Constitution of Supreme Court Justice Antonin Scalia.* New York: Farrar, Straus and Giroux, 2009. Analytical biography of Supreme Court justice Antonin Scalia by a legal affairs reporter of *USA Today.* Biskupic focuses on Scalia's tenure on the Court, closely examining Scalia's positions on important issues through a survey of prominent cases.

———. *Sandra Day O'Connor: How the First Woman on the Supreme Court Became Its Most Influential Justice.* New York: ECCO, 2005. Drawing on papers of justices and hundreds of interviews, this fascinating biography portrays the complexity of the woman who became the axis of many key decisions.

Compston, Christine. *Earl Warren: Justice for All.* New York: Oxford University Press, 2002. Relatively short biography with many illustrations, portraying Chief Justice Warren as a courageous man with strong moral commitments, written primarily for general readers.

Cray, Ed. *Chief Justice: A Biography of Earl Warren.* New York: Simon & Schuster, 1997. Based on personal papers and interviews of his associates, and long considered the most complete biography of Warren, it does not have as much legal analysis, however, as G. Edward White's *Earl Warren: A Public Life* (New York: Oxford University Press, 1982).

Dworkin, Ronald. *The Supreme Court Phalanx: The Court's New Right-wing Bloc.* New York: New York Review Books, 2008. Critical appraisal of the increasing conservatism of the U.S. Supreme Court under George W. Bush's 2005 appointees, John Roberts and Samuel Alito.

Friedman, Leon, and Fred L. Israel, eds. *The Justices of the United States Supreme Court: Their Lives and Major Opinions.* 5 vols. New York: Chelsea House, 1997. Interesting scholarly essays devoting about twenty-five pages to each justice. This latest edition has an essay on Justice Stephen Breyer.

Greenhouse, Linda. *Becoming Justice Blackmun: Harry Blackmun's Supreme Court Journey.* New York: Henry Holt, 2005. Using Justice Harry A. Blackmun's voluminous records, *The New York Times*'s specialist on the Supreme Court has written a fascinating account of the debates within the Court and in the left-leaning direction of Blackmun's thinking.

Gronlund, Mimi Clark. *Supreme Court Justice Tom C. Clark: A Life of Service.* Austin: University of Texas Press, 2010. First full study of the life and career of Supreme Court associate justice Tom C. Clark. Includes a foreword by his son, former U.S. attorney general Ramsey Clark.

Gunther, Gerhard. *Learned Hand: The Man and the Judge.* New York: Alfred A. Knopf, 1994. A former clerk to both judge Learned Hand and Chief Justice Earl Warren, Gunther explains why Hand—though he never sat on the U.S. Supreme Court—had a major impact on the Court's workings with the powerful opinions he wrote during his fifty-two years as a federal judge.

Hirsch, H. N. *The Enigma of Felix Frankfurter.* New York: Basic Books, 1981. Attempting to explain Frankfurter's evolution from a civil libertarian to an advocate of judicial restraint, Hirsch relies upon speculative psychoanalytic theories in this scholarly and valuable contribution.

Hockett, Jeffrey. *New Deal Justice: The Constitutional Jurisprudence of Hugo L. Black, Felix Frankfurter, and Robert H. Jackson.* New York: Rowman & Littlefield, 1996. Engrossing and well-researched analysis of President Franklin D. Roosevelt's most notable Court appointees that emphasizes their regional, cultural, and ideological disagreements.

Holzer, Henry Mark. *The Supreme Court Opinions of Clarence Thomas, 1991-2006: A Conservative's Perspective.* Jefferson, N.C.: McFarland, 2007. Drawing on the most important of the nearly 350 opinions that Justice Clarence Thomas wrote during his first fifteen years on the Supreme Court, Holzer argues that Thomas has had a formidable intellectual influence on the Court. Holzer sees Thomas as a consistent defender of federalism, separation of powers, limited judicial review, and regard for individual rights as contemplated by the Constitution's Framers. Includes an appendix listing all Thomas's written opinions.

Hutchinson, Dennis. *The Man Who Once Was Whizzer White: A Portrait of Justice Byron R. White.* New York: Free Press, 1998. Scholarly study of a competent justice who valued his privacy and attempted to make good decisions in particular cases rather than formulating constitutional doctrines or worrying about consistency.

Irons, Peter. *Brennan vs. Rehnquist: The Battle for the Constitution.* New York: Alfred A. Knopf, 1994. Fascinating comparative analysis of two strong ideological voices that dominated the Court for many years. However, while

Irons consistently agrees with Brennan's views, he finds it difficult to be fair when discussing those of Rehnquist.

Jeffries, John C., Jr. *Justice Lewis F. Powell, Jr.* New York: Charles Scribner's Sons, 1994. Justice Powell's former clerk has written a penetrating analysis of how this moderately conservative justice was often the swing vote in important cases dealing with school desegregation, abortion, capital punishment, and racial preference in school admissions.

Marion, David E. *The Jurisprudence of Justice William J. Brennan, Jr.: The Law and Politics of Libertarian Dignity.* Lanham: Rowman & Littlefield, 1997. Marion contends that Brennan was the most important liberal justice of the twentieth century, emphasizing his great influence on political discourse and public policy.

Maveety, Nancy. *Justice Sandra Day O'Connor: Strategist on the Supreme Court.* Lanham, Md.: Rowman & Littlefield, 1996. Maveety provides a brief biographic introduction before embarking on a scrupulous analysis of how O'Connor reached her decisions and the tactics by which she made herself as influential as possible on the Court.

Murphy, Bruce Allen. *Fortas: The Rise and Ruin of a Supreme Court Justice.* New York: William Morrow, 1988. Fascinating tale of a man tricked into taking a seat on the Supreme Court, bringing ruin on himself by violating the separation of powers in principle and practice as well as by unethical financial dealings, and making possible the right-leaning trend of the Court after his time.

_____. *Wild Bill: The Legend and Life of William O. Douglas.* New York: Random House, 2003. Excellent account of the controversial libertarian and unique individualist who wrote more opinions and dissents than any other justice, while also having more marriages and surviving more impeachment attempts.

Newman, Roger K. *Hugo Black: A Biography.* New York: Pantheon Books, 1994. About half of this thorough biography is devoted to Justice Hugo L. Black's service on the Court as an effective defender of individual rights and liberties. Newman includes much detailed information about Black's life, including his youthful involvement with the Ku Klux Klan.

Newmyer, R. Kent. *John Marshall and the Heroic Age of the Supreme Court.* Baton Rouge: Louisiana State University, 2001. With a good balance between Marshall's private life and his jurisprudence, this work is recognized as the best one-volume biography on the "great chief justice."

_____. *Justice Joseph Story: Statesman of the Old Republic.* Chapel Hill: University of North Carolina Press, 1985. Describes the remarkable evolution of Joseph Story as a person and a legal thinker.

Polenberg, Richard. *World of Benjamin Cardozo: Personal Values and the Judicial*

BIBLIOGRAPHY

Process. Cambridge, Mass.: Harvard University Press, 1999. Well-written and detailed account that emphasizes Justice Cardozo's strong commitment to moral values.

Powe, L. A. Scot, Jr. *The Supreme Court and the American Elite, 1789-2008.* Cambridge, Mass.: Harvard University Press, 2009. Lively, opinionated exploration of U.S. Supreme Court history that sees the Court as overly concerned with solidifying its primacy through a series of pretentious opinions. Powe looks especially closely at how the Rehnquist Court overturned congressional attempts at progressive legislation by drawing on rigid interpretations of the Constitution.

Rosen, Jeffrey. *The Supreme Court: The Personalities and Rivalries That Defined America.* New York: Times Books, 2007. Exploration of how the personal styles of individual justices have shaped their decisions on the U.S. Supreme Court. Rosen focuses on comparisons between President Thomas Jefferson and Chief Justice John Marshall, Justice Oliver Wendell Holmes and Justice John Marshall Harlan, Justice William O. Douglas and Justice Hugo Black, and Justice Antonin Scalia and Chief Justice William Rehnquist.

Ross, Michael. *Justice of Shattered Dreams: Samuel Freeman Miller and the Supreme Court During the Civil War Era.* Baton Rouge: Louisiana State University Press, 2003. Excellent biography revealing that the author of the Court's decision in the *Slaughterhouse Cases* was a former slave owner who defended Abraham Lincoln's war policies and became a champion of African American rights.

Rossum, Ralph. *Antonin Scalia's Jurisprudence: Text and Tradition.* Lawrence: University Press of Kansas, 2006. Comprehensive and sympathetic analysis of the six hundred Supreme Court opinions and other writings of the witty, argumentative, and conservative justice.

St. Clair, James, and Linda Gugin. *Chief Justice Fred M. Vinson of Kentucky: A Political Biography.* Lexington: University Press of Kentucky, 2002. Study of an amiable chief justice who presided over the Court as it became embroiled in the critical issues of racial discrimination and freedom of expression.

Smith, Jean Edward. *John Marshall: Definer of a Nation.* New York: Henry Holt, 1996. One of the best of several biographies of the chief justice who is considered the most influential legal statesman to have served on the Supreme Court.

Stebenne, David L. *Arthur J. Goldberg, New Deal Liberal.* New York: Oxford University Press, 1996. In addition to a scholarly analysis of Goldberg's brief but significant tenure on the Supreme Court, this book provides a useful background account of postwar liberalism and Goldberg's work as general counsel to the United Steelworkers of America.

Strum, Philippa. *Louis D. Brandeis: Justice for the People.* Cambridge, Mass.: Harvard University Press, 1984. Attempts to reconcile some of the polarities of Justice Louis D. Brandeis's thought by portraying him as a person with Jeffersonian sensibilities who had to cope with the complexities of an age of rapid urban and industrial growth.

Thomas, Andrew Peyton. *Clarence Thomas: A Biography.* New York: Encounter Books, 2002. Highly critical biography that includes information about Justice Thomas's benefits from affirmative action, his discussions of *Roe v. Wade* before his confirmation, his two marriages, and his vexed relationship with Anita Hill.

Tushnet, Mark. *Making Constitutional Law: Thurgood Marshall and the Supreme Court, 1961-1991.* New York: Oxford University Press, 1997. Justice Marshall's former clerk, Tushnet argues that Marshall had more impact on civil rights before joining the Court than he did afterward and explores Marshall's growing frustrations on issues of busing and affirmative action.

Urofsky, Melvin I., ed. *Biographical Encyclopedia of the Supreme Court: The Lives and Legal Philosophies of the Justices.* Washington, D.C.: CQ Press, 2006. Useful scholarly essays about the justices and their views on jurisprudence.

White, G. Edward. *Oliver Wendell Holmes: Sage of the Supreme Court.* New York: Oxford University Press, 2000. Scholarly study of Justice Holmes's personality, ideas, and writings, from his early life in Boston and courageous service during the Civil War through his thirty years on the Supreme Court.

Yarbrough, Tinsley. *John Marshall Harlan: Great Dissenter of the Warren Court.* New York: Oxford University Press, 1991. Impressively researched and gracefully written portrait of a moderately conservative justice whose lengthy, careful, and learned opinions were admired even by judicial lawyers who disagreed with his conclusions.

———. *Judicial Enigma: The First Justice Harlan.* New York: Oxford University Press, 1995. Explores the discontinuity between Justice John Marshall Harlan's early life as a slave owner and his later liberal dissents in cases affecting civil rights and due process.

Court History

Belknap, Michal R. *The Supreme Court Under Earl Warren, 1953-1969.* Columbia: University of South Carolina Press, 2005. The best single volume on the justices and cases during one of the most significant periods in the history of the Supreme Court.

Casto, William A. *The Supreme Court in the Early Republic: The Chief Justiceships of John Jay and Oliver Ellsworth.* Columbia: University of South Carolina Press, 1995. Insightful study of a neglected period of Court history, the pre-John Marshall years, when the Court combined English law and colonial practice with the emergence of new legal doctrines and forms appropriate to the U.S. Constitution.

Ely, James M., Jr. *The Chief Justiceship of Melville W. Fuller, 1888-1910*. Columbia: University of South Carolina Press, 1995. An eminent law professor, Ely defends the thesis that Fuller and his fellow justices were not simply defenders of wealth and business interests but were motivated by a desire to preserve individual liberty, albeit conceived primarily in economic terms.

Hoffer, Peter Charles, Williamjames Hull Hoffer, and N. E. H. Hull. *The Supreme Court: An Essential History*. Lawrence: University Press of Kansas, 2007. Wide-ranging survey of Supreme Court history that discusses the changing intellectual, social, cultural, economic, and political climate surrounding the Court's work. Each of the book's fifteen chapters traces the Court's history through a tenure of a single chief justice.

Huebner, Timothy. *The Taney Court: Justices, Rulings, and Legacy*. Santa Barbara: ABC-CLIO, 2003. Useful account of the Court's decisions concerning slavery, federalism, and property rights from 1836 to 1864.

Irons, Peter H. *A People's History of the Supreme Court*. New York: Penguin Books, 2000. Colorfully written and filled with insightful portraits of justices, lawyers, and litigants alike, this book praises the liberal justices for having advanced the principles of liberty and equality.

Keck, Thomas M. *The Most Activist Supreme Court in History: The Road to Modern Judicial Conservatism*. Chicago: University of Chicago Press, 2004. Despite conservatives' long-standing advocacy of judicial restraint, Keck finds that both liberal and conservative justices on the Rehnquist Court actively attempted to overturn legislation and precedents that they disliked.

Lazarus, Edward. *Closed Chambers: The Rise, Fall, and Future of the Modern Supreme Court*. New York: Penguin Books, 1999. Justice Harry A. Blackmun's former law clerk concentrates on capital punishment, race relations, and abortion to describe a sometimes dysfunctional court engaging in jealous and partisan bickering and rubber-stamping opinions written by clerks. Some of his contentions have been criticized as inaccurate.

Leuchtenberg, William E. *The Supreme Court Reborn: The Constitutional Revolution in the Age of Roosevelt*. New York: Oxford University Press, 1995. The work of a noted pro-New Deal historian, presenting a comprehensive description of the Court's turn from laissez-faire to activist government.

Lurie, Jonathan. *The Chase Court: Justices, Rulings, and Legacy*. Santa Barbara: ABC-CLIO, 2004. Useful account of the work of the Court from 1864 to 1873.

McKenna, Marian. *Franklin Roosevelt and the Great Constitutional War: The Court-Packing Crisis of 1937*. New York: Fordham University Press, 2002. Portrays President Franklin D. Roosevelt as initiating a "reorganization of the federal judiciary" on the advice of Attorney General Homer Cummings with the support of a "grad coalition."

Renstrom, Peter. *The Stone Court: Justices, Rulings, and Legacy.* Santa Barbara: ABC-CLIO, 2003. Useful account of the work of the Court during World War II.

Scaturro, Frank J. *The Supreme Court's Retreat from Reconstruction: A Distortion of Constitutional Jurisprudence.* Westport, Conn.: Greenwood Press, 2000. Castigates the Court for not opposing the development of Jim Crow, arguing that the Court departed from the intent of the Framers of the Fourteenth and Fifteenth Amendments.

Schwartz, Bernard. *A History of the Supreme Court.* New York: Oxford University Press, 1993. Excellent one-volume history of the Supreme Court with interesting descriptions of major justices and detailed descriptions of landmark decisions.

Schwartz, Herman, ed. *The Burger Court: Counter-Revolution or Confirmation?* New York: Oxford University Press, 1998. Impressive collection of writings about the Supreme Court and its controversial rulings during the often tumultuous period from 1969 to 1987, with writings by distinguished legal scholars and practitioners.

Semonche, John. *Keeping the Faith: A Cultural History of the U.S. Supreme Court.* Lanham, Md.: Rowman & Littlefield, 1998. Portraying the Supreme Court as a guardian of the progressive values of liberty and equality, Semonche portrays the justices as "the high priests of the American civil religion."

Shesol, Jeff. *Supreme Power: Franklin Roosevelt vs. the Supreme Court.* New York: W. W. Norton, 2010. Detailed study of President Franklin D. Roosevelt's struggle with the Supreme Court during the late 1930's, when he attempted to increase the size of the Court so he could "pack" it with his own appointees.

Silver, David M. *Lincoln's Supreme Court.* Urbana: University of Illinois Press, 1998. Classic study of President Abraham Lincoln's manipulation of the Supreme Court during the Civil War in order to attain maximum discretion.

Sloan, Cliff, and David McKean. *The Great Decision: Jefferson, Adams, Marshall, and the Battle for the Supreme Court.* New York: PublicAffairs, 2009. Lively account of the political and judicial struggle behind the epochal *Marbury v. Madison* case, in which the Supreme Court asserted its power of judicial review.

Tushnet, Mark. *A Court Divided: The Rehnquist Court and the Future of Constitutional Law.* New York: W. W. Norton, 2005. Balanced work arguing that the rumors of a "Rehnquist Revolution" were highly exaggerated, in large part because of the conservative justices' strong disagreements on abortion and other social issues.

Urofsky, Melvin I. *Division and Discord: The Supreme Court Under Stone and Vinson, 1941-1953.* Columbia: University of South Carolina Press, 1997. Readable and often entertaining account of strong and combative justices on the Court wrestling with the issues associated with World War II and the Cold War.

Vinzant, John Harlan. *The Supreme Court's Role in American Indian Policy.* El Paso, Tex.: LFB Scholarly Publications, 2009. Study of the U.S. Supreme Court's role in reducing the sovereignty of Native American tribes.

Wiecek, William. *The History of the Supreme Court of the United States: The Birth of the Modern Constitution, 1941-1953.* New York: Cambridge University Press, 2006. Scholarly and highly detailed study of the important changes in the twelve years before Earl Warren became chief justice.

Woodward, Bob, and Scott Armstrong. *The Brethren: Inside the Supreme Court.* New York: Simon & Schuster, 1979. Based primarily on interviews with former clerks, the book provides informative and interesting insight into the personalities and ideas of the justices during the first decade of the Burger Court.

Yarbrough, Tinsley. *The Burger Court: Justices, Rulings, and Legacy.* Santa Barbara: ABC-CLIO, 2000. Part of the publisher's Supreme Court Handbooks Series, the book provides a balanced analysis of the rulings of the Court and their impact from 1969 until 1986.

Zelden, Charles L. *The Supreme Court and Elections: Into the Political Thicket.* Washington, D.C.: CQ Press, 2010. Collection of historical essays and documents tracing the U.S. Supreme Court's rulings on voting rights issues throughout U.S. history.

The Court and Rights and Liberties

Abraham, Henry, and Barbara Perry. *Freedom and the Court: Civil Rights and Liberties in the United States.* 8th ed. Lawrence: University Press of Kansas, 2003. Readable, lively, and trustworthy text of how the Supreme Court has interpreted the Bill of Rights and the Fourteenth Amendment, providing both technical analysis and discussion of the human impact.

Abrams, Floyd. *Speaking Freely: Trials of the First Amendment.* New York: Penguin Books, 2006. Written by one of the premier First Amendment lawyers, the book has discussions of modern controversies such as campaign finance reform and rights of journalists, as well as comparison with other countries.

Alderman, Ellen, and Caroline Kennedy. *In Our Defense: The Bill of Rights in Action.* New York: Avon Books, 1991. Highly readable and compelling work that includes nineteen vignettes of real-life cases in which ordinary people have relied upon one or more of the liberties and rights guaranteed by the first ten amendments.

Alley, Robert S., ed. *The Constitution and Religion: Leading Supreme Court Cases on Church and State.* Amherst, N.Y.: Prometheus Books, 1999. This collection presents full texts of the most significant cases on the topic in a comprehensive and nonpartisan fashion and includes reference to debates on original intent.

Amar, Akhil Reed. *The Bill of Rights: Creation and Reconstruction.* New Haven, Conn.: Yale University Press, 2000. Historical approach, arguing that the Reconstruction projects and particularly the Fourteenth Amendment transformed the Bill of Rights in applying to the states and in protecting the rights of minorities.

Ball, Howard. *The Supreme Court and the Intimate Lives of Americans: Birth, Sex, Marriage, Childrearing, and Death.* New York: New York University Press, 2004. Analysis of the controversial "liberty interest" issues, including abortion, parental rights, gay rights, the right to die, and physician-assisted suicides.

Barnett, Randy, ed. *The Rights Retained by the People: The History and Meaning of the Ninth Amendment.* Fairfax, Va.: George Mason University Press, 1989. Excellent collection of essays advocating a variety of interpretations about the most elusive of the first ten amendments.

Bartee, Alice F. *Privacy Rights: Cases Lost and Cases Won Before the Supreme Court.* New York: Rowman & Littlefield, 2006. Examines the arguments and processes behind eight historic decisions concerning four privacy issues: birth control, gay rights, abortion, and the right to die.

Bradley, Craig M. *The Failure of the Criminal Procedure Revolution.* Philadelphia: University of Pennsylvania Press, 1993. Compared with other industrial countries, Bradley argues that the U.S.'s piecemeal, case-by-case development of criminal procedures has produced a system that is overly complex and cumbersome. He advocates a comprehensive code that is nationally applicable.

Charles, Patrick J. *The Second Amendment: The Intent and Its Interpretation by the States and the Supreme Court.* Jefferson, N.C.: McFarland, 2009. Interesting analysis of the Second Amendment, agreeing with the *Heller* decision on an individual right but questioning whether the amendment's intent was to allow citizens to protect their homes.

Clancy, Thomas K. *The Fourth Amendment: Its History and Interpretation.* Durham, N.C.: Carolina Academic Press, 2008. Comprehensive guide to the historical jurisprudence relating to search and seizure.

Cornell, Saul. *A Well Regulated Militia: The Founding Fathers and the Origins of Gun Control in America.* New York: Oxford University Press, 2006. Although written before *Heller,* this is probably the most informed and balanced account of the Second Amendment's shifting interpretations.

Cortner, Richard C. *The Supreme Court and the Second Bill of Rights: The Fourteenth Amendment and the Nationalization of the Bill of Rights.* Madison: University of Wisconsin Press, 1981. Brilliant account of the development of the incorporation doctrine and its application to the first eight amendments.

Curtis, Michael Kent. *No State Shall Abridge: The Fourteenth Amendment and the Bill of Rights.* Durham: Duke University Press, 1990. Professor Curtis makes a strong case for the controversial thesis that the Republicans who framed the Fourteenth Amendment intended to make the first eight amendments—or at least most of their provisions—applicable to the states.

Davis, Abraham L., and Barbara Luck Graham. *The Supreme Court, Race, and Civil Rights: From Marshall to Rehnquist.* Thousand Oaks, Calif.: Sage Publications, 1995. Combines a narrative text with cases emphasizing the human dimensions of the politically disadvantaged in each historical era, with about three-quarters of the book devoted to the Court under Earl Warren, Warren E. Burger, and William H. Rehnquist.

Ely, James W., Jr. *The Guardian of Every Other Right: A Constitutional History of Property Rights.* 3d ed. New York: Oxford University Press, 2008. Scholarly and interesting account, with a great deal of information on topics such as the takings clause and the liberty of contract doctrine.

Epstein, Lee, and Thomas G. Walker. *Constitutional Law for a Changing America: A Short Course.* 4th ed. Washington, D.C.: CQ Press, 2009. Designed for undergraduate college students, this work combines an interesting and scholarly narrative with many selections from Supreme Court cases.

Foley, Michael. *Arbitrary and Capricious: The Supreme Court, the Constitution, and the Death Penalty.* New York: Praeger, 2003. Dispassionate history of almost one hundred rulings on capital punishment from 1878 to 2002, concluding that the quest for a fair and discrimination-free process remains as elusive as ever.

Glendon, Mary Ann. *Rights Talk: The Impoverishment of Political Discourse.* New York: Free Press, 1993. Polemical work arguing that a single-minded emphasis on individual legal entitlements has distracted from other values such as care, responsibility, and practical compromises.

Greenhouse, Linda, and Reva Siegel. *Before Roe v. Wade: Voices That Shaped the Abortion Debate Before the Supreme Court's Ruling.* New York: Kaplan, 2010. Most thorough study of the Supreme Court's 1973 *Roe v. Wade* decision on abortion rights. Written by a Pulitzer Prize-winning journalist with thirty years of experience following the Court and a law professor, this book examines the background to the case, the process leading to the Court's decision, and the impact the decision has since had.

Hall, Kermit, ed. *By and for the People: Constitutional Rights in American History.*

Arlington Heights, Ill.: Harlan Davidson, 1991. Commemorating the bicentennial of the Bill of Rights, this volume brings together eleven concisely written articles about significant aspects of the amendments, each written by an authority in the field.

Hemmer, Joseph J., Jr. *Communication Law: The Supreme Court and the First Amendment.* Rev. ed. Lanham, Md.: University Press of America, 2006. Introductory textbook on the First Amendment designed for courses in communication law in journalism, communication, and political science departments.

Hixson, Richard. *Pornography and the Justices: The Supreme Court and the Intractable Obscenity Problem.* Carbondale: Southern Illinois University Press, 1996. Chronological examination of how the Court has dealt with obscene material within the context of decision making in evolving social mores.

Howard, John R. *The Shifting Wind: The Supreme Court and Civil Rights from Reconstruction to Brown.* Albany: State University of New York Press, 1999. Study of how the Court allowed the establishment of Jim Crow segregation in the late nineteenth century and then worked gradually to dismantle it.

Jackson, Donald Wilson. *Even the Children of Strangers: Equality Under the U.S. Constitution.* Lawrence: University Press of Kansas, 1992. Traces the complex meanings that have been attached to the notion of equal protection during its evolving treatment by the Supreme Court and uses the methodology of social sciences to establish an argument that entitlement to equal protection should always be presumed.

Kalven, Harry, Jr. *A Worthy Tradition: Freedom of Speech in America.* New York: Harper & Row, 1988. Scholarly account of cases dealing with free expression from 1919 to 1974.

Klarman, Michael J. *From Jim Crow to Civil Rights: The Supreme Court and the Struggle for Racial Equality.* New York: Oxford University Press, 2006. Detailed account of how the constitutional law on race changed from *Plessy v. Ferguson* (1896) to *Brown v. Board of Education* (1954).

Kopel, David, Stephen Halbrook, and Alan Korwin. *Supreme Court Gun Cases: Two Centuries of Gun Rights Revealed.* Phoenix, Ariz.: Bloomfield Press, 2004. Finding ninety-two relevant cases, this controversial book argues that the Supreme Court has recognized gun possession as a personal right.

Koppelman, Andrew. *The Gay Rights Question in Contemporary American Law.* Chicago: University of Chicago Press, 2003. Critiques arguments on both sides of the gay rights issue, discussing whether or not discrimination against gays is legally or morally defensible. Also provides some history regarding court decisions concerning gay rights.

Latzer, Barry. *Death Penalty Cases: Leading U.S. Supreme Court Cases on Capital Punishment.* Burlington, Mass.: Butterworth Heinemann, 1997. After an introductory chapter, Latzer presents excerpts from twenty-two cases between 1968 and 1991, omitting most footnotes and citations but preserving the essence of the arguments and reasoning.

Levy, Leonard. *The Establishment Clause: Religion and the First Amendment.* Durham: University of North Carolina Press, 1994. Written from a proseparatist perspective, an eminent professor discusses the formation of the establishment clause and includes two thought-provoking chapters about Supreme Court decisions on cases involving aid to parochial schools, religious ceremonies, and nativity scenes.

McInnis, Thomas. *The Evolution of the Fourth Amendment.* Lanham, Md.: Lexington Books, 2009. Describes and analyzes the different approaches of the Supreme Court in interpreting the prohibition on unreasonable searches and seizures.

Mackey, Thomas C. *Pornography on Trial: A Handbook with Cases, Laws, and Documents.* Santa Barbara: ABC-CLIO, 2003. Well-written and organized handbook that can be used by researchers as well as students and general readers.

McKinnon, Catherine. *Only Words.* Cambridge, Mass.: Harvard University Press, 1996. The intellectual leader of feminine legal theory, McKinnon argues that the goal of equality justifies proscribing those forms of pornography that degrade or subordinate women.

Manfredi, Christopher P. *The Supreme Court and Juvenile Justice.* Lawrence: University Press of Kansas, 1997. Manfredi provides a readable and insightful historical treatment of the evolution of the juvenile court movement, with the weight of the treatment on discussions of *Kent v. United States* (1966) and *In re Gault* (1967).

Morgan, Richard E. *Disabling America: The "Rights Industry" in Our Time.* New York: Basic Books, 1984. Conservative attack on the Supreme Court's expansive interpretations of defendants' rights since the due process revolution of the Warren Court.

Noonan, John T., Jr., and Edward Gaffney, Jr. *Religious Freedom: History, Cases, and Other Materials on the Interaction of Religion and Government.* New York: Foundation Press, 2001. Valuable collection of more than nine hundred pages of documents and essays about religious freedom and governmental relationship to religion from the colonial period until the twenty-first century.

Peck, Robert S. *Libraries, the First Amendment, and Cyberspace: What You Need to Know.* Chicago: American Library Association, 1999. Written for librarians by a lawyer who specializes in First Amendment issues, this is a useful guide about topics like confidentiality laws, the exclusion of "indecent" materials, and inappropriate uses of the Internet.

Perry, Michael J. *We the People: The Fourteenth Amendment and the Bill of Rights.* New ed. New York: Oxford University Press, 2002. Denying that the modern Supreme Court has engineered a "judicial usurpation of politics," Perry generally defends the Court's application of the Fourteenth Amendment in the areas of racial segregation, affirmative action, abortion, and discrimination based on sex and sexual orientation.

Peters, Shawn. *Judging Jehovah's Witnesses: Religious Persecution and the Dawn of the Rights Revolution.* Lawrence: University Press of Kansas, 2000. Vivid analysis of the legal suppression of members of the Jehovah's Witnesses from 1938 to 1955 and how their struggle expanded civil liberties.

Pinello, Daniel R. *Gay Rights and American Law.* New York: Cambridge University Press, 2003. Examines the development of gay rights throughout the American legal system, including both the Supreme Court and appellate courts. Covers nearly four hundred court decisions between 1980 and 2000.

Price, Polly J. *Property Rights: Rights and Liberties Under the Law.* Santa Barbara: ABC-CLIO, 2003. Historical account of the constitutional status of private property; written for a general audience.

Rehnquist, William. *All the Laws but One: Civil Liberties in Wartime.* New York: Alfred A. Knopf, 1999. In this interesting analysis that emphasizes the experiences of the Civil War and World War II, Chief Justice Rehnquist argues that wars necessitate a balancing between constitutional liberties and the demands of national security.

Roberson, Cliff. *Constitutional Law and Criminal Justice.* New York: Taylor & Francis, 2009. Includes a wealth of information about principles and practices relating to the Fourth Amendment and the exclusionary rule.

Saunders, Kevin. *Violence as Obscenity: Limiting the Media's First Amendment Protection.* Durham, N.C.: Duke University Press, 1996. Argues that the definition of obscenity should be expanded to include explicit and offensive violence, which should be regulated because of its harm to society.

Savage, David. *The Supreme Court and Individual Rights.* Washington, D.C.: CQ Press, 2009. Written by an outstanding scholar, this is an excellent historical account current through the Court's 2007-2009 term.

Schwartz, Bernard. *The Great Rights of Mankind: A History of the American Bill of Rights.* Madison, Wis.: Madison House, 1992. Perhaps the best short history about the first ten amendments, including summaries of major judicial interpretations through the Rehnquist Court.

Smith, Jeffrey. *War and Press Freedom: The Problem of Prerogative Power.* New York: Oxford University Press, 1999. Richly documented work about the restrictions on the press in the name of "national security" from the adoption of the First Amendment until the Gulf War of 1991. A professor of journalism, Smith argues that unrestricted freedom of the press is less dangerous than governmental suppression.

Smith, Rodney K. *Public Prayer and the Constitution.* Wilmington, Del.: Scholarly Resources, 1987. Cogent analysis of the Constitution's establishment clause, rejecting the idea of a "wall of separation" in favor or Madison's view that the government should neither promote nor proscribe religious observations.

Spitzer, Robert J. *The Right to Bear Arms: Rights and Liberties Under the Law.* Santa Barbara: ABC-CLIO, 2001. History of the Second Amendment and its controversies, including the relevant opinions by the Supreme Court.

Stossen, Nadine. *Defending Pornography: Free Speech, Sex, and the Fight for Women's Rights.* New York: New York University Press, 2000. A former president of the American Civil Liberties Union, Stossen argues that pornography's good effects outweigh the bad—thus any attempt to censor pornography produces more evils than it prevents.

Urofsky, Melvin I., ed. *One Hundred Americans Making Constitutional History: A Biographical History.* Washington, D.C.: CQ Press, 2004. Collection of stories, each in about two thousand words, about the key individuals whose cases resulted in Supreme Court decisions.

Volokh, Eugene. *First Amendment: Law, Cases, Problems, and Policy Arguments.* New York: Foundation Press, 2001. Exhaustive collection of documents and commentary related to the principles of the First Amendment.

Waksman, David, and Debbie Goodman. *The Search and Seizure Handbook.* Englewood Cliffs, N.J.: Prentice Hall, 2009. Clearly written guide explaining Fourth Amendment principles for law-enforcement officers working in the current criminal justice system.

Wallace, Jonathan, and Mark Manga. *Sex, Laws, and Cyberspace.* New York: M & T Books, 1996. Balanced work that examines the complex issues relating to free expression over the Internet, with suggested compromises for monitoring the Internet while preserving the values of the First Amendment.

Whitebread, Charles, and Paul Marcus. *Gilbert Law Summaries: Criminal Procedure.* 16th ed. New York: Harcourt Brace Jovanovich Legal and Professional Publications, 2004. Clearly written and concise reference summarizing the Supreme Court's rulings in all areas of criminal procedures.

Zalman, Marvin. *Criminal Procedure: Constitution and Society.* 5th ed. Upper Saddle River, N.J.: Prentice Hall, 2007. Central tenants of criminal procedure with helpful chapters on search warrants, the exclusionary rule, and related topics.

Constitutional Interpretation

Amar, Akhil Reed. *America's Constitution: A Biography.* New York: Random House, 2005. Examines in turn each article of the Constitution and explains how the Framers drew on English models, existing state constitutions, and other sources in structuring the three branches of the federal government and in defining the relationship of that government to the states.

Barber, Sotirios A. *The Constitution of Judicial Power: Defending the Activist Tradition.* Baltimore, Md.: Johns Hopkins University Press, 1997. Criticizing moral relativism, Barber argues that judicial activism is traceable to *The Federalist Papers* (1788) but must be properly rooted in a philosophy of moral realism to be sound and effective.

Barron, Jerome A., and C. Thomas Dienes. *Constitutional Law in a Nutshell.* 6th ed. St. Paul, Minn.: West, 2005. Compact reference on the law for those with a legal or political science background.

Beard, Charles Austin. *The Supreme Court and the Constitution.* Mineola, N.Y.: Dover, 2006. First published during the early 1920's, this classic study of the U.S. Supreme Court remains an important work. This facsimile reprint edition includes a new introduction and bibliographies by Alan F. Westin.

Bickel, Alexander M. *The Least Dangerous Branch: The Supreme Court at the Bar of Politics.* New Haven, Conn.: Yale University Press, 1990. An eminent law professor who advocated judicial restraint, Bickel writes that *Marbury v. Madison* (1803) provided a somewhat shaky foundation for the practice of judicial review and argues that decisions opposed by the majority of the people will not endure in the long term.

Bobbitt, Philip. *Constitutional Fate: Theory of the Constitution.* New York: Oxford University Press, 1984. Systematic analysis of the nature of interpretation, considering six types of constitutional arguments: historical, textual, structural, prudential, doctrinal, and ethical.

Bork, Robert. *The Tempting of America: The Political Seduction of the Law.* New York: Macmillan, 1990. Scholarly but accessible critique of legal activism and a powerful and eloquent polemic cogently arguing the necessity of returning to the original intent of the authors of the Constitution. The tone of the work is sometimes angry.

Breyer, Stephen G. *Active Liberty: Interpreting Our Democratic Constitution.* New York: Alfred A. Knopf, 2005. Disagreeing with Justice Antonin Scalia's emphasis on original intent and literalism, Justice Breyer argues that abstract conceptions like "due process" should be interpreted according to the broad democratic goals of the Constitution.

Cox, Archibald. *The Court and the Constitution.* Boston: Houghton Mifflin, 1987. This historically organized work reviews the issues and debates of various eras to demonstrate the process by which the Court continually keeps the Constitution a vital and creative instrument of government.

Dworkin, Ronald. *Freedom's Law: The Moral Reading of the Constitution.* Cambridge, Mass.: Harvard University Press, 1996. Series of essays by a liberal theorist advocating the use of abstract moral principles at the most general possible level in interpreting the text of the U.S. Constitution.

Ely, John Hart. *Democracy and Distrust: A Theory of Judicial Review.* New York: Oxford University Press, 1990. Important work of jurisprudence that advocates special judicial protection for democratic processes, including free expression, while favoring judicial restraint toward legislative choices. Ely rejects the substantive due process doctrine and denies that the Constitution protects a right to abortion.

Kahn, Ronald. *The Supreme Court and Constitutional Theory, 1953-1993.* Lawrence: University Press of Kansas, 1994. In an effort to revise and clarify the perceptions of the Court under Warren E. Burger, Kahn begins by refining and clarifying the essence of the Warren Court and then embarks on an illuminating comparison.

Kautz, Steven, ed. *The Supreme Court and the Idea of Constitutionalism.* Philadelphia: University of Pennsylvania Press, 2009. Collection of original articles tied together by the notion that the U.S. Supreme Court has been a principal battlefield in the developing "culture war" since the late twentieth century. Individual essays explore the philosophical and historical origins of the idea of constitutionalism, theories of constitutionalism in American history, constitutionalism in other countries, and tensions between constitutionalism and democracy.

Leyh, Gregory, ed. *Legal Hermeneutics: History, Theory, and Practice.* Berkeley: University of California Press, 1992. Fourteen interesting essays with a diversity of viewpoints about the historical and philosophical assumptions about the nature of language and the art of interpretation.

Nelson, William E. *The Fourteenth Amendment from Political Principle to Judicial Doctrine.* Cambridge, Mass.: Harvard University Press, 1995. Nelson argues that the Framers of the Fourteenth Amendment wanted to affirm the public's long-standing rhetoric of equality, which gives support to the expansive interpretations of the equal protection clause during the twentieth century.

Parrish, Michael E. *The Supreme Court and Capital Punishment: Judging Death.* Washington, D.C.: CQ Press, 2010. Comprehensive history of U.S. Supreme Court rulings on capital punishment issues. Particular attention is given to the role of race in death-penalty cases, the constitutionality of specific methods of execution, public opinion, and the execution of minors and mentally ill defendants.

Pollock, Earl E. *The Supreme Court and American Democracy: Case Studies on Judicial Review and Public Policy.* Westport, Conn.: Greenwood Press, 2009. Written by an attorney, this book explores the U.S. Supreme Court's role in public policy issues by examining specific cases relating to abortion, affirmative action, capital punishment, freedom of expression, gay rights, physician-assisted suicide, presidential powers, property rights, racial discrimination, religion, slavery, and voting rights. Pollock summarizes the constitutional principles underlying the Court's rulings and recounts the background and aftermath of key cases.

Posner, Richard A. *Problematics of Moral and Legal Theory.* Cambridge, Mass.: Harvard University Press, 1999. Posner, a brilliant judge known for his use of economic theory, argues that moral philosophy is too subjective to be useful in constitutional interpretation, and he endorses pragmatic and empirical conclusions based on concrete facts.

Scalia, Antonin. *A Matter of Interpretation: Federal Courts and the Law.* Princeton, N.J.: Princeton University Press, 1999. Justice Scalia condemns the idea of a "living Constitution," advocates constitutional interpretation based on textual analysis and a search for the original meaning—not subjective intent—and advocates the same approach in constitutional and statutory interpretations. The volume includes critiques by Lawrence Tribe and others.

Segal, Jeffrey, and Harold Spaeth. *Supreme Court and the Attitudinal Model Revised.* New York: Cambridge University Press, 2006. Criticizing the "legal model," two political scientists argue that the justices' ideological views on issues such as business regulation provide the best means for explaining and predicting their decisions.

Tribe, Lawrence, and Michael Dorf. *On Reading the Constitution.* Cambridge, Mass.: Harvard University Press, 1991. Brief defense of a broad and liberal interpretation of the Constitution, combining the common-law tradition, textual analysis, and concern for American values. Its discussions of the Ninth Amendment and *Bowers v. Hardwick* (1986) are especially interesting.

Wellington, Harry H. *Interpreting the Constitution: The Supreme Court and the Process of Adjudication.* New Haven, Conn.: Yale University Press, 1991. Covering a range of cases from 1803 to 1973, Wellington treats the Constitution as a living document and rejects the utility and even the possibility of interpreting it solely in terms of the original intent of its Framers.

Whittington, Keith E. *Political Foundations of Judicial Supremacy: The Presidency, the Supreme Court, and Constitutional Leadership in U.S. History.* Princeton, N.J.: Princeton University Press, 2007. Clearly written study of the U.S. Supreme Court's power of judicial review arguing that the Court's status as the ultimate authority on the U.S. Constitution has been thrust upon it by the legislative and executive branches of the federal government.

_____. *Constitutional Interpretation: Textual Meaning, Original Intent, and Judicial Review.* Lawrence: University Press of Kansas, 1999. Cogent defense of moderate "originalism," insisting that it is possible to know some of the principles of the Framers of the Constitution. Whittington criticizes the subjectivism of contemporary postmodernism and deconstructionism.

Court Rulings

Baker, Liva. *Miranda: Crime, Law, and Politics.* New York: Atheneum, 1983. Detailed account that places the pivotal *Miranda v. Arizona* case within the context of sociopolitical conceptions about criminal behavior in the modern era.

Cretacci, Michael A. *Supreme Court Case Briefs in Criminal Procedure.* Lanham, Md.: Rowman & Littlefield, 2008. Designed for use as a text or reference manual for law-enforcement and criminal justice students and personnel in these fields, this substantial volume contains a collection of Supreme Court case briefs outlining various criminal procedures in the United States.

Epps, Garrett. *To an Unknown God: Religious Freedom on Trial.* New York: St. Martin's Press, 2001. Detailed account of *Employment Division v. Smith* (1990), in which Native American Al Smith's religious use of peyote led to decisions providing less protection for religious freedom.

Fehrenbacher, Don E. *The Dred Scott Case: Its Significance in American Law and Politics.* New York: Oxford University Press, 2001. Masterful examination of the Court's most infamous ruling, placing it within the legal aspects of the slavery controversy.

Fisher, Louis. *In the Name of National Security: Unchecked Presidential Power and the Reynolds Case.* Lawrence: University Press of Kansas, 2006. Examination of *United States v. Reynolds* (1953), which established the right of the federal government when sued to withhold evidence in the name of national security.

_____. *Nazi Saboteurs on Trial: A Military Tribunal and American Law.* 2d ed. Lawrence: University Press of Kansas, 2005. Study of the World War II case *Ex parte Quirin,* arguing that the justices yielded to public pressure in failing to protect due process rights.

Friendly, Fred W. *Minnesota Rag: The Dramatic Story of the Landmark Supreme Court Cast That Gave New Meaning to Freedom of the Press.* New York: Random House, 1981. A television executive and professor of journalism, Friendly has written a colorful account of *Near v. Minnesota* (1931), a landmark case in the evolution of freedom of the press.

Friendly, Fred W., and Martha Elliott. *The Constitution: That Delegate Balance.* New York: Random House, 1984. Written to accompany a television series, this volume includes sixteen well-written and interesting chapters, each of which is devoted to one or more Supreme Court cases involving a constitutional right.

Garrow, David. *Liberty and Sexuality: The Right to Privacy and the Making of Roe v. Wade.* Berkeley: University of California Press, 1998. A model of top-notch journalism, this meticulously researched and carefully presented work is a vast treatment of the political and legal debate over abortion spanning more than fifty years.

Irons, Peter. *The Courage of Their Convictions: Sixteen Americans Who Fought Their Way to the Supreme Court.* New York: Penguin Books, 1988. This fascinating work portrays pivotal cases touching on religion, race, protest, or privacy, from *Minersville School District v. Gobitis* (1940) to *Bowers v. Hardwick* (1986). Includes a lengthy statement by a principal in each of the cases.

_____. *Justice at War: The Story of the Japanese-American Internment Cases.* Berkeley: University of California Press, 1993. A lawyer who helped reverse some of the convictions he discusses, Irons provides an exhaustive account of *Hirabayashi v. United States* (1943) and *Korematsu v. United States* (1944).

Kens, Paul. *Judicial Power and Reform Politics: The Anatomy of Lochner v. New York.* Lawrence: University Press of Kansas, 1990. Informed and readable account of the famous case that came to symbolize the early Supreme Court's use of the substantive due process doctrine to overturn labor regulations.

Labbe, Ronald M. *The Slaughterhouse Cases.* Lawrence: University Press of Kansas, 2006. Detailed examination of the Court's narrow interpretation of the privileges or immunities clause of the Fourteenth Amendment that prevented application of the Bill of Rights to the states through a half century.

Lewis, Anthony. *Gideon's Trumpet.* New York: Vintage Books, 1989. Originally published in 1964, this is the fascinating story of Clarence Gideon who established the right of poor persons to counsel in felony cases.

_____. *Make No Law: The Sullivan Case and the First Amendment.* New York: Random House, 1992. As a reporter, Lewis covered the development of the *New York Times Co. v. Sullivan* case, the libel suit that expanded the right to criticize public officials.

Killenbeck, Mark R. *McCulloch v. Maryland.* Lawrence: University Press of Kansas, 2006. The case that established Congress's broad discretion when passing laws "necessary and proper" to its enumerated powers.

Patterson, James T. *Brown v. Board of Education: A Civil Rights Milestone and Its Troubled Legacy.* New York: Oxford University Press, 2002. Following a concise narrative with a fascinating cast of characters, Patterson argues that some of the unintended consequences of the *Brown* decision have not helped African Americans.

Schwartz, Bernard. *Behind Bakke: Affirmative Action and the Supreme Court.* New York: New York University Press, 1988. Superb recounting of the *Bakke* case (1978) with the legal background and issues embedded in it.

Smolla, Rodney. *Jerry Falwell v. Larry Flint: The First Amendment on Trial.* New York: St. Martin's Press, 1988. Scholarly but highly readable analysis of an important freedom of speech case, written by a recognized authority on the First Amendment.

Swanson, Wayne. *The Christ Child Goes to Court.* Philadelphia: Temple University Press, 1989. Interesting case study of the crèche case, *Lynch v. Donnelly* (1984), providing detailed information about the judicial process as well as the local politics of Rhode Island.

Tushnet, Mark, ed. *I Dissent: Great Opposing Opinions in Landmark Supreme Court Cases.* Boston: Beacon Press, 2008. Collection of dissenting opinions in thirteen major Supreme Court cases, including *Marbury v. Madison, Brown v. Board of Education, Griswold v. Connecticut,* and *Lawrence v. Texas.* Tushnet places each case in its historical perspective, with an overview of the principal issues at stake.

Van Geel, T. R. *Understanding Supreme Court Opinions.* 6th ed. New York: Longman, 2008. Designed as a supplement to constitutional law casebooks, this legal textbook pays particular attention to the legal reasoning behind the Supreme Court's written opinions.

Vile, John. *The Essential Supreme Court Decisions: Summaries of Leading Cases in U.S. Constitutional Law.* 15th ed. Lanham, Md.: Rowman & Littlefield, 2010. Standard reference work on Supreme Court cases pertaining to constitutional law, with concise analyses of major cases through 2008.

Joseph M. McCarthy, updated by Thomas Tandy Lewis and the Editors

GLOSSARY

abstention. Doctrine or policy under which the federal courts delay or refrain from ruling in state cases until the issues have been definitely resolved by the state courts.

acquittal. Finding that a criminal defendant is not guilty.

actual malice. Libel in which material was published with knowledge that it was false or with reckless disregard toward its truthfulness.

adjudication. Process of reaching a decision in a court of law.

adversarial system. Judicial system, such as that of the United States, in which two opposing parties confront each other in a court of law.

affidavit. Written statement of facts made voluntarily under oath or affirmation.

affirm. To uphold a decision made by a lower court.

aggravation. Circumstances relating to the commission of a crime that cause it to be treated more seriously than average instances of that crime.

amicus curiae **brief.** Latin for "friend of the court." A document filed by a person or organization not directly involved in the litigation in order to supply arguments and evidence supporting one side of the dispute.

amnesty. Pardon granted to a person guilty of having committed a political crime.

annotated codes. Statutes organized by topic and accompanied by brief descriptions of cases referring to the statutes.

appeal. Process of bringing a decision of a lower court to a higher court for a review of the judgment.

appellant. Party that loses in a lower court and attempts to have the judgment reversed in a higher court.

appellate jurisdiction. Authority of a higher court to hear a case appealed from a lower court.

appellee. Party that prevails in the lower court and then responds when the case is taken to a higher court by an appellant.

arraignment. Early stage of the criminal process in which charges are read to a defendant and he or she enters a plea of guilty, not guilty, or *nolo contendere.*

arrest. Act of taking a person into custody for the purpose of charging that person with having committed a crime.

arrest warrants. Documents issued by judicial officers directing law-enforcement officers to arrest persons accused of committing crimes.

assembly and association, freedom of. Fundamental right to associate with other people and organizations without unwarranted government restrictions.

attorney-client privilege. Right of a person not to disclose any matters discussed with an attorney in the course of professional consultation.

bail. Money or other property given to obtain the release from custody of a criminal defendant and to guarantee that the defendant will thereafter appear in court.

balancing test. Judicial approach in which a court weighs the relative importance of competing legal principles and governmental interests.

bench warrant. Order issued by a court directing that a law-enforcement officer bring the person named in the warrant before the court, usually because that person has failed to obey a previous order of the court to appear.

bifurcated trial. Division of a trial into separate phases for determining guilt and punishment.

bill of attainder. Legislative act inflicting punishment without a trial on named individuals or the members of a group.

Bill of Rights, U.S. First ten amendments to the United States Constitution that safeguard various individual liberties, including rights for persons suspected of or accused of having committed crimes.

brief. Concise statement of the facts and arguments in a case, or a written document presenting an argument to a court about some matter.

broad construction. Interpretation that goes beyond the literal meaning of the words in a legal text.

burden of proof. Obligation of presenting enough evidence to establish the truthfulness of an assertion.

capital offenses. Felonies that may be punished by the death penalty.

capital punishment. Punishment by death.

case law. Rules and principles derived from judicial decisions, including constitutional and statutory interpretations.

censorship. Narrowly defined, a governmental action preventing something from being published or said; broadly defined, any governmental restriction on expression.

certification, writ of. Relatively rare procedure in which a lower court requests a higher court to rule on specific legal questions in order to apply the law correctly.

certiorari. Latin for "to make certain." A writ in which a higher court orders an inferior court to send up the record of a particular case.

chain of custody. Account of the possession of the evidence from its discovery and initial possession until it is offered as evidence in court.

checks and balances. Constitutional arrangement that puts limits on the powers of each of the three branches of government in order to prevent an excessive concentration of power.

circumstantial evidence. Evidence from which a primary issue may be inferred.

citation. Standard form used to indicate where to find a statute or a court case. For example, the citation of *Mapp v. Ohio* is 367 U.S. 643 (1961), indicating that the case is found in volume 367 of *United States Reports* beginning on page 643.

civil infraction. Noncriminal violation of a law, such as a minor traffic violation.

civil law. Laws that relate to relationships among private parties, in contrast to criminal law. Also, the legal tradition derived from Roman law, in contrast to the common-law tradition.

civil liberties. Freedoms from government control or restraint, especially those freedoms guaranteed in the Bill of Rights.

civil rights. Positive rights protected by the government, especially those rights found in the equal protection clause of the Fourteenth Amendment and the Civil Rights laws.

civil rights laws. Federal and state statutes designed to prevent invidious discrimination in areas such as employment, education, public accommodations, and voting rights.

class-action suit. Lawsuit brought in behalf of all persons sharing similar circumstances with those of the plaintiff.

clear and convincing evidence. Intermediate standard of proof that is more demanding than "preponderance of evidence" and less demanding than "beyond a reasonable doubt."

comity. Principle by which the courts of one jurisdiction accept the validity of the judicial proceedings of another jurisdiction.

commerce. Broad term that refers to trade, traffic, transportation, communication, or intercourse by way of trade or traffic.

commerce clause. Statement in Article I of the Constitution that gives Congress the authority to regulate commerce among the states, with foreign countries, and with the Native American tribes.

common law. Ever-changing body of principles and rules that have evolved from prevailing customs and judicial decisions rather than from legislative statutes.

compelling interest. Interest of the highest order; required by government to justify suspect classifications or restrictions on fundamental rights.

Comstock laws. Series of nineteenth century statutes, promoted by Anthony Comstock, which made it a crime to send "indecent" or "obscene" materials, including information about family planning, through the U.S. mail.

concurrent jurisdiction. Judicial authority that is shared by different courts of law, especially between federal and state courts.

concurring opinion. Written statement of a judge or justice who agrees with the decision of the majority but writes separately in order to emphasize a particular matter or to disagree with the reasoning used in the opinion of the court.

confession. Admission of guilt.

confrontation clause. Sixth Amendment right of a criminal defendant to observe the testimony of prosecution witnesses and to cross-examine these witnesses.

consent decree. Court-enforced agreement that is reached by the mutual consent of all parties to a lawsuit.

conspiracy. Crime in which two or more persons make plans to commit a specific criminal act.

constitution. Supreme law of a country defining the structures and prerogatives of governmental institutions and the legal rights of individuals.

constitutional courts. Those federal courts established by Congress under the authority of Article III, section 1, of the U.S. Constitution.

construction. Synonym for interpretation.

contempt of court. Failure to carry out a court order, or an action that obstructs, embarrasses, or shows disrespect for a court of law.

continuance. Delay of a judicial proceeding.

controlled substances. Drugs proscribed by law.

conviction. Final determination that a criminal defendant is guilty made as a result of a trial or a plea bargain.

corporal punishment. Physical punishment.

counsel. Lawyer authorized to represent a party.

courts of appeals. At the federal level, those constitutional courts having appellate jurisdiction over decisions by district courts except in the few cases in which there is a right to a direct appeal to the Supreme Court.

crime. Positive or negative act considered as a wrong against society and classified as either a misdemeanor or a felony.

criminal law. Body of law defining and providing for the punishment of crimes, in contrast to civil law, which applies to relationships between private parties.

cruel and unusual punishment. Punishment that is disproportionately severe in relation to a crime or otherwise excessive.

custodial interrogation. Questioning by the police of a suspect held in custody.

de facto. Latin for "in fact." An existing situation that arises from private decisions rather than governmental action. De facto segregation is considered beyond the jurisdiction of the courts because no state action is involved.

de jure. Latin for "by law." A condition that results from law or official governmental action.

declaratory judgment. Judicial ruling declaring the legal rights of the parties to a dispute but not imposing any remedy or relief.

defendant. Party being sued in a civil case or charged with a crime in a criminal case. At the appellate level, the party moved against is called the respondent or appellee.

deposition. Questioning of a witness under oath outside of court that is transcribed by a court reporter or otherwise recorded.

dicta. Statements in a judicial opinion that are not a part of the actual decision.

discovery, pretrial. Procedures for allowing parties to a court case to exchange and discover relevant information prior to the trial.

dismiss motion. Motion made by defense in a criminal case arguing that grounds exist to discontinue charges against a defendant without a trial, or—in some cases after a trial has begun—without submitting case to a jury for a verdict.

dissenting opinion/dissent. Written statement by a judge or justice who disagrees with a decision reached by the majority.

district courts. In the federal system, the trial courts with original jurisdiction.

diversity cases. Lawsuits involving parties residing in different states.

docket. Schedule of cases awaiting action in a court.

double jeopardy. Trying of a person twice for the same crime in the same jurisdiction.

dual sovereignty (dual federalism). Theory of federalism that holds that the national and state governments are sovereign in their respective spheres, so that the national government must not invade a sphere reserved to the states by the Tenth Amendment.

due process of law. Requirement that government must use fair and established procedures whenever it deprives a person of life, liberty, or property. Also, requirement that laws must be fair and reasonable in substance as well as in procedures.

elastic clause (necessary and proper clause). Authority of Congress under Article I, section 8, to select any means appropriate to achieving the enumerated powers.

eminent domain. Government's power to take property for a public purpose by providing just compensation.

enumerated powers. Prerogatives given to the national government in Article I, section 8, of the Constitution.

equity. Historically, a system of jurisprudence developed in England to supplement the common law by emphasizing principles of fairness rather than the letter of the law.

establishment clause. Statement in the First Amendment prohibiting any direct governmental support or favoritism for religion or religious institutions.

ex parte. Latin for "from one side." A hearing in which only one party to a dispute is present, especially a hearing to consider a petition for a writ of habeas corpus.

ex post facto law. Latin for "from after the fact." A retroactive statute that criminalizes an action that was legal when it occurred or increases punishment for a criminal act after it was committed.

excessive bail. Unreasonable large sum of money imposed as a requirement for a defendant to be released before a trial.

exclusionary rule. Constitutional interpretation holding that evidence obtained by illegal means cannot be introduced by the prosecution in a criminal trial.

exclusive jurisdiction. Situation in which only one particular type of court can hear a certain kind of case.

exigent circumstances. Emergency situation demanding immediate action, such as allowing the police to enter into private property without a search warrant.

extradition. Surrender by one country to another of a person accused or convicted of a crime in the other country.

federal question (national question). Legal issue that involves the U.S. Constitution, congressional legislation, or a treaty.

federal system (federalism). Constitutional arrangement that distributes political powers between the national government and regional governments.

felony. Serious crime that carries a possible penalty of at least a year in prison.

fighting words doctrine. Idea that utterances addressed at a person are not protected by the First Amendment if they are inherently likely to provoke a violent response from an average addressee.

free exercise clause. Guarantee in the First Amendment to believe and practice the religion of one's choice.

frisk. Precautionary pat-down of a suspect for weapons in order to protect an officer and other persons.

full faith and credit clause. Provision in Article IV of the Constitution requiring that states must recognize the records and legal proceedings of other states.

fundamental rights. Those rights, regardless of whether they are explicitly mentioned in the Constitution, that the courts have decided are essential to liberty and human dignity, including First Amendment freedoms, the right to vote, and the right to privacy.

gag order. Judge's instructions requiring certain parties to refrain from speaking publicly or privately about a particular trial.

gerrymandering. Drawing of an election district in a strange shape in order to give an advantage to a political party or special interest.

good faith exception. Exception to the exclusionary rule, so that the prosecution can introduce evidence acquired by the police in an invalid search and seizure when the police had good reason to believe the search was legal at the time.

grand jury. Citizens appointed to hear evidence relating to crimes and to determine whether criminal indictments should be brought against particular individuals.

habeas corpus. From Latin for "you have the body." An order to a custodial officer to bring a person held in custody before a judge in order to explain the legal justification for holding the person.

harmless error. Procedural or substantive mistake that does not affect the final result of a judicial proceeding.

hate crime. Crimes in which a victim is chosen on the basis of race, ethnicity, religion, gender, or sexual orientation.

hate speech. Offensive communication expressing disdain for persons of ethnic, religious, or other social categories.

Hicklin test. Obsolete standard for judging obscenity, taken from *Regina v. Hicklin* (1886), that allowed government to proscribe a literary work if an isolated section might tend to "deprave and corrupt" children.

immunity. Exemption from criminal prosecution in return for testimony in a criminal case.

in re. Latin for "in reference to." A designation used in judicial proceedings when there are no formal adversaries.

inadmissible. Materials that under the established rules of law cannot be admitted as legal evidence.

incitement standard. Doctrine that government cannot punish seditious speech unless it is directed at provoking illegal action that is likely to occur.

incompetent to stand trial. Condition, often the result of a mental illness, under which a criminal defendant is unable to understand the charges and proceeding against him or to assist in the preparation of his own defense.

incorporation (or absorption). Doctrine under which most provisions of the Bill of Rights have been "incorporated" or "absorbed" into the due process clause of the Fourteenth Amendment so that they are applicable to state and local governments.

indictment. Formal charge issued by a grand jury against a person for a particular crime.

indigent. Poor.

inevitable discovery. Doctrine that illegally obtained evidence is admissible in a criminal trial if it appears inevitable that the evidence would have been discovered by legal means.

information. Formal accusation of a crime issued by a prosecutor in order to initiate a criminal trial without a grand jury indictment. Because the grand jury requirement of the Fifth Amendment has never been incorporated, several states allow prosecutions to be initiated by information.

inherent powers. Powers of an official or a government that derive from the concept of sovereignty and do not depend upon explicit provisions of a constitution or statutes.

injunction. Judicial order prohibiting or requiring certain acts by designated persons.

intermediate scrutiny. Judicial standard requiring government to justify a challenged policy by demonstrating its substantial relationship to an important government interest. Courts use the standard to scrutinize allegations of gender discrimination.

interpretivism. Interpretative approach that attempts to determine the meanings conveyed by the text itself, without reference to nontextual considerations such as natural law or sociological theory.

Jim Crow. System of laws in the South that required racial segregation, in effect from the late nineteenth century until passage of the Civil Rights laws of the 1960's.

judgment of the court. Court's official ruling in a particular case or controversy, excluding the reasoning used in the ruling.

judicial restraint. View that judges should be careful not to inject their own ideas about "good" or "wise" public policy in their decisions; as distinguished from "judicial activism."

judicial review. 1) In American constitutional law, authority of a court to invalidate legislative and executive acts if they are inconsistent with constitutional principles. 2) In a general sense, the review of any issue by a court of law.

jurisdiction. Legal authority of a court to hear and to decide a particular case or controversy.

jurisprudence. Philosophy of law.

just compensation clause. Statement in the Fifth Amendment requiring that owners whose property is taken under the eminent domain power must be fairly compensated for their loss.

justiciable question. Legal issue that can be appropriately and effectively decided in a court of law.

Lemon test. Based on an interpretation of the establishment clause in *Lemon v. Kurtzman* (1971), a three-part requirement that public aid to religious schools must have a secular purpose, a primary effect that neither advances nor inhibits religion, and no excessive entanglement between government and religion.

libel. Written defamation of another person's character or reputation.

literacy tests. Requirement of a reading test in order to vote, generally used to prevent African Americans from voting in the South; now illegal.

litigant. Party to a lawsuit.

magistrate. Judge with minor or limited authority.

mandamus, writ of. Latin for "we command." A court order directing a public official or organization to perform a particular duty.

mandatory jurisdiction. Requirement of a court to hear a certain category of cases.

Miranda warning. Notice to a detained suspect by a police officer advising the person of the rights to remain silent and to have the assistance of counsel.

misdemeanor. Crime with a maximum penalty of one year or less in jail; less serious than a felony.

mistrial. Premature termination of a trial because of some misconduct or other unusual occurrence.

moot question. Status of a lawsuit that no longer involves a justiciable controversy either because the issue has been resolved or the conditions have so changed that the court is unable to grant the requested relief.

motion. Request for a court to take some action.

natural law. Legal principles derived from general moral intuitions.

natural rights. Idea that all governments at all times have the obligation of respecting basic human rights, either because of human nature or a divine purpose.

necessary and proper clause. See **elastic clause**.

Obiter dicta. Latin for "said in passing." Incidental statements in a court's opinion that are not necessary to support the decision and are not binding as precedent.

objection. Challenge to testimony or other evidence offered in court, or to other action taken in court.

obscenity. Sexually explicit materials that are not protected by the First Amendment according to the three-prong test of *Miller v. California* (1973).

obstruction of justice. Crime of interfering with the administration of justice such as by improperly influencing a witness or destroying evidence.

open fields doctrine. Principle that privacy rights under the Fourth Amendment do not apply to unoccupied areas outside a home's yard.

opinion of the Court. Opinion endorsed by a majority or a controlling plurality of the participating justices. It both announces the decision and explains the rationale for the decision.

ordinance. Most commonly refers to an enactment by a local government.

original intent. Meaning of a document according to the person or persons who produced it. There is disagreement about whether modern courts should attempt to follow the original understanding of the Constitution.

original jurisdiction. Authority of a court to conduct trials and decide cases in the first instance, as distinguished from appellate jurisdiction. The Supreme Court has original jurisdiction in cases involving foreign diplomats or states as parties.

overbreadth doctrine. Principle that governmental policies that directly or indirectly restrict constitutional rights are unconstitutional unless they are narrowly tailored to advance a sufficiently important governmental interest.

overrule. Action of a court that explicitly reverses or makes void an earlier decision about the same legal issue by the same court.

penal codes. Collections of laws defining criminal conduct.

penumbra. Theory that the Constitution casts partial shadows that expand constitutional protection to include broad values such as privacy; associated especially with Justice William O. Douglas.

per curiam. Latin for "by the court." An unsigned or collectively written opinion by a court.

peremptory challenge. Right of an attorney to exclude a prospective juror without explaining the reasons for doing so.

perjury. Deliberate false statement made under oath.

petit jury. Jury, normally composed of twelve persons, that hears a trial and renders a verdict.

petitioner. Party seeking relief in a court of law.

petty (petit) offenses. Minor crimes that are punished by fines or short jail sentences. The Supreme Court has held that a jury trial is not required if the maximum penalty is less than six months.

plain error rule. Rule allowing an appellate court to reverse a trial court decision on some issue even if the person appealing did not complain about the issue at trial, as is normally required.

plain meaning rule. Principle that the words of constitutional and statutory texts should be interpreted according to the common meanings of ordinary language.

plain view rule. Doctrine that allows a police officer to seize contraband that is readily visible to the officer's naked eye, so long as the officer is legally in the place where the contraband is observed.

plaintiff. Party who initiates a civil action or sues to obtain a remedy for an injury.

plea. Response of a criminal defendant to the charge or charges contained in an indictment.

plea bargain. Agreement between a criminal defendant and a prosecutor whereby the defendant pleads guilty in return for a reduction in the charges or the recommended punishment.

plenary consideration. When the Supreme Court gives full consideration for a case, including the submission of briefs and oral arguments.

plurality opinion. Opinion that receives the highest number of votes in an appellate court but without a majority of the judges.

police power. Recognized authority of the states to protect the public's safety, health, morality, and welfare. The national government has gradually acquired overlapping prerogatives by way of the commerce and welfare clauses.

political question doctrine. Principle that the federal courts allow elected officials to resolve political controversies that do not involve constitutional issues.

political speech. Communication about public affairs that is considered to have the highest level of First Amendment protection.

pornography. Broad term that refers to sexually oriented materials ranging from constitutionally protected forms of "indecency" to unprotected "obscenity."

precedent. Prior decision resolving a legal issue that serves as a model or guide for deciding cases involving the same or a similar issue.

preemption. Doctrine that allows Congress to enact a statute that brings an area of authority under the primary or exclusive jurisdiction of the national government, even though the matter was previously under the jurisdiction of the states.

preferred freedoms doctrine. Idea that First Amendment freedoms should have priority among constitutional rights and liberties. Although influential in the 1940's, the doctrine has generally been replaced by that of "fundamental rights."

preponderance of evidence. Standard of proof in civil cases, requiring evidence that an assertion is more probable than a contrary assertion.

preventive detention. Practice of denying bail to a person awaiting trial on the grounds that the person's release would endanger the public safety.

prima facie. Latin for "at first sight." An argument that is sufficiently persuasive to prevail unless effectively refuted by the opposing side.

prior restraint. Most extreme form of government censorship, restraining expression before its publication or broadcast.

privacy, right of. Constitutionally protected liberty to engage in intimate personal conduct and to exercise personal autonomy without unjustified governmental interference.

probable cause. Sufficient evidence to lead a reasonable person to conclude that it is highly likely that certain evidence will be found in a particular place or that a certain individual has probably committed a crime.

probate. Court procedures for determining whether a will is valid or invalid.

procedural due process. Constitutional requirement that the methods and procedures used in the enforcement of laws must be fair, such as the requirements of the Sixth Amendment.

proportionality. Extent to which a particular punishment is 1) commensurate with the harm done in a criminal act or 2) proportional to the penalties given for other crimes of similar magnitude.

prosecutors. Lawyers, such as district attorneys and U.S. attorneys, who represent the government in cases against persons accused of having committed crimes.

public defenders. Attorneys appointed by government to defend persons accused of crimes who cannot afford to hire their own lawyers.

public safety exception. Immediate threat to the public's safety that allows police officers to ask suspects particular questions before giving the Miranda warnings.

punitive damages. In a civil suit, a monetary award that is added to payment for compensatory damages in order to punish the defendant and serve as a deterrent.

rational basis test. Standard requiring that a challenged law must bear a reasonable relationship to a legitimate governmental interest. This test is used when a case does not involve a suspect classification or a fundamental right.

real evidence. Actual object that is used as evidence, rather than a description by a witness.

reapportionment. Redrawing of the boundaries of a voting district based on population.

reasonable doubt. Degree of uncertainty that would lead a prudent person of sound mind to hesitate to make a decision of personal significance.

reasonable expectation of privacy. Person's right to expect that activities in certain places are private, so that government agents cannot intrude in such places except under the provisions of the Fourth Amendment.

reasonable suspicion. Objective circumstances that lead a prudent person to think that a person is likely involved in criminal activity; more than a hunch but less than probable cause.

reasonableness. Legal standard attempting to determine what decisions and actions would be expected of a prudent and reasonably intelligent person within a particular set of circumstances.

rebuttable presumption. Presumption in law that can be refuted by adequate evidence, as distinguished from an irrebuttable presumption that cannot be refuted by evidence.

recuse. Decision of a judge not to participate in a case because of a conflict of interest or another disqualifying situation.

regulatory taking. Government regulations that eliminate the useful value of private property, requiring compensation under the Fifth Amendment.

remand. Superior court's decision to return a case to a lower court for additional action, usually with specific instructions about how to proceed.

reprieves. Postponement of the execution of a criminal sentence.

republican government. Political system with elected representatives and without hereditary rulers.

reserved powers. Police powers retained by the states in the Tenth Amendment.

respondent. Party against whom a legal action is taken.

restrictive covenant. Contract that prohibits transfer of property to one or more classes of persons, usually minorities.

reverse. Judgment of an appellate court setting aside a decision of a lower court.

reversible errors. Significant errors committed by trial courts sufficient to justify appellate courts to overrule the results obtained at trial.

rule of four. Principle that the Supreme Court will not review a case unless four justices vote to accept it.

saving construction. Doctrine that the courts, given two plausible interpretations of a statute, will choose the one that allows the statute to be found constitutional.

search warrants. Judicial orders allowing law-enforcement personnel to enter and search specified locations.

seditious speech. Communications intended to incite insurrection or overthrow of the government.

selective incorporation. Practice of making applicable to the states those provisions of the Bill of Rights considered fundamental or essential to a regime of ordered liberty.

self-incrimination. Declaration or action by which persons implicate themselves in a crime; prohibited by the Fifth Amendment and provisions of most state constitutions.

sentencing. Pronouncing of punishment on a person convicted of having committed a crime.

separation of church and state. Interpretation of the First Amendment requiring a "wall of separation" between religion and government.

separation of powers. Constitutional division of authority among the legislative, executive, and judicial branches of government.

seriatim. Latin for "serially." The practice of each judge writing a separate opinion without a single "opinion of the court."

sexual harassment. Type of discrimination in employment or education involving sexual advances or requests for sexual favors, interpreted as a violation the Civil Rights Act of 1964.

slander. Speaking of false and malicious words that harm the reputation of another person or group.

solicitor general. High official of the Department of Justice who argues the government's position before the Supreme Court.

sovereign immunity. Principle of precluding lawsuits against a government without its consent.

sovereignty. Supreme political authority that is exercised by an independent country. In addition to the sovereignty of the national government, the states and the Indian tribes retain sovereignty in particular spheres.

standing to sue. Status of a party who has the right to bring legal action because of a direct harm.

stare decisis. Latin for "let the decision stand." The doctrine, emphasized in the common-law tradition, that a legal issue settled in a judicial decision should be followed as precedent in future cases presenting the same issue. The Supreme Court is not required to practice the doctrine, especially in regard to constitutional issues.

state action. Official action by an agent of the state or "under color of state law." Such action is an essential element for "equal protection" and "due process" claims under the Fourteenth Amendment.

statute. Generally applicable law enacted by a legislature, to be distinguished from constitutional law, common law, administrative law, or case law.

strict construction. Literal or narrow reading of the words of a document, especially the Constitution.

strict necessity doctrine. Doctrine that a court should consider a constitutional issue only when necessary to decide a particular case.

strict scrutiny. Judicial approach for considering laws that abridge fundamental rights or utilize a suspect classification scheme involving race or national origin. When considering such laws, the courts require government to show that the law is narrowly tailored to advance a compelling state interest, so that laws usually do not survive strict scrutiny.

subpoena. Latin for "under penalty." A judicial order requiring a person to appear before a grand jury, a court, or a legislative hearing.

summary judgment. Court decision rendered without a full hearing or without the benefit of briefs.

supremacy clause. Provision in Article VI of the Constitution declaring that the Constitution, with federal legislation and treaties consistent with it, is the supreme law of the land.

suspect classification. Government categorization of people based on characteristics such as race or national origin, resulting in a special benefit or disadvantage.

swing vote. Deciding vote in a 5-4 Supreme Court decision.

symbolic speech. Act that expresses a message through means other than spoken or written language. An example is the desecration of the flag.

textual analysis. Approach to interpretation that concentrates on the language in a legal text rather than on extratextual considerations.

tort. Willful or negligent injury to a person or property, which is a common basis for a civil lawsuit.

total incorporation. Judicial doctrine holding that all of the first eight amendments should be incorporated into the Fourteenth Amendment and thus applied to the states.

ultra vires. Latin for "beyond powers." An action that goes beyond the legal authority of a person or agency performing it.

unenumerated rights. Constitutionally protected rights not explicitly mentioned in the Constitution. Such rights are usually defended by the substantive due process doctrine or the Ninth Amendment.

Uniform Code of Military Justice (UCMJ). Code of laws enacted by Congress to govern people serving in the military.

vacate. In criminal justice proceedings, to set aside or rescind a court order or decision.

vagueness doctrine. Doctrine holding that a law violates due process principles if it is not written precisely enough to make it clear which actions are illegal.

venue. Location where a legal proceeding takes place.

vested rights. Long-established rights, especially property rights, which cannot be taken from a person without due process of law.

viewpoint discrimination. Governmental exclusion of a category of expression when the exclusion is not reasonable in the light of the forum.

voir dire. French for "to see, to speak." The process in which prospective jurors are questioned by attorneys or judges in order to select juries for trials.

waiver. Voluntary and intentional relinquishment of a legal right. Citizens have the right to waive their rights, so long as there is no coercion by the police.

warrant. Court order authorizing the police to make an arrest or conduct a search and seizure.

white primary. Primary election in the "one-party South" that prohibited participation by African Americans.

wiretap. Surreptitious monitoring of telephone conversations by law-enforcement officials.

witnesses. Persons who offer formal testimony in legal proceedings.

writ. Written court order.

yellow dog contract. Requirement, illegal since 1932, that an employee must agree not to join a labor union as a condition of employment.

TIME LINE OF CASES

February 12, 1837	*Charles River Bridge v. Warren Bridge*, 247
February 16, 1837	*New York v. Miln*, 773
March 9, 1839	*Bank of Augusta v. Earle*, 153
March 4, 1840	*Holmes v. Jennison*, 537
March 10, 1841	*Groves v. Slaughter*, 499
January 25, 1842	*Swift v. Tyson*, 1007
March, 1842	*Commonwealth v. Hunt*, 289
March 1, 1842	*Prigg v. Pennsylvania*, 851
March 4, 1842	*Dobbins v. Erie County*, 331
February 23, 1843	*Bronson v. Kinzie*, 201
March 7, 1844	*Louisville, Cincinnati, and Charleston Railroad Co. v. Letson*, 640
January 21, 1847	*License Cases*, 625
March 5, 1847	*Jones v. Van Zandt*, 586
January 31, 1848	*West River Bridge Co. v. Dix*, 1144
January 3, 1849	*Luther v. Borden*, 646
February 7, 1849	*Passenger Cases*, 817
February 6, 1852	*Pennsylvania v. Wheeling and Belmont Bridge Co.*, 825
February 20, 1852	*Genesee Chief v. Fitzhugh*, 436
March 2, 1852	*Cooley v. Board of Wardens of the Port of Philadelphia*, 294
February 6, 1856	*Dodge v. Woolsey*, 331
February 19, 1856	*Murray's Lessee v. Hoboken Land and Improvement Co.*, 743
March 6, 1857	*Scott v. Sandford*, 937
March 7, 1859	*Ableman v. Booth*, 89
March 14, 1861	*Kentucky v. Dennison*, 597
May 28, 1861	*Ex parte Merryman*, 379
March 10, 1863	*Prize Cases*, 853
January 11, 1864	*Gelpcke v. Dubuque*, 434
April 3, 1866	*Ex parte Milligan*, 381
March 20, 1867	*Cummings v. Missouri*, 310
April 15, 1867	*Mississippi v. Johnson*, 719
April 12, 1869	*Ex parte McCardle*, 377
	Texas v. White, 1023
November 1, 1869	*Paul v. Virginia*, 818
November 8, 1869	*Woodruff v. Parham*, 1171
December 13, 1869	*Veazie Bank v. Fenno*, 1111
April 3, 1871	*Collector v. Day*, 287
May 1, 1871	*Legal Tender Cases*, 620

May 20, 1895	*Pollock v. Farmers' Loan and Trust Co.*, 845
May 27, 1895	*In re Debs*, 565
May 18, 1896	*Plessy v. Ferguson*, 835
	Talton v. Mayes, 1008
March 1, 1897	*Allgeyer v. Louisiana*, 126
	Chicago, Burlington, and Quincy Railroad Co. v. Chicago, 254
February 28, 1898	*Holden v. Hardy*, 536
March 7, 1898	*Smyth v. Ames*, 968
March 28, 1898	*United States v. Wong Kim Ark*, 1100
April 25, 1898	*Williams v. Mississippi*, 1157
December 18, 1899	*Cumming v. Richmond County Board of Education*, 309
February 26, 1900	*Maxwell v. Dow*, 689
May 27, 1901	*Insular Cases*, 571
January 5, 1903	*Lone Wolf v. Hitchcock*, 634
February 23, 1903	*Champion v. Ames*, 239
March 14, 1904	*Northern Securities Co. v. United States*, 783
May 31, 1904	*McCray v. United States*, 656
January 30, 1905	*Swift and Co. v. United States*, 1000
February 20, 1905	*Jacobson v. Massachusetts*, 579
April 17, 1905	*Lochner v. New York*, 627
May 27, 1907	*Virginia v. West Virginia*, 1120
January 27, 1908	*Adair v. United States*, 92
February 3, 1908	*Loewe v. Lawlor*, 633
February 24, 1908	*Muller v. Oregon*, 735
March 23, 1908	*Ex parte Young*, 386
November 9, 1908	*Twining v. New Jersey*, 1038
May 24, 1909	*United States v. Shipp*, 1088
April 6, 1910	*Redd v. State of Georgia*, 861
May 2, 1910	*Weems v. United States*, 1140
January 23, 1911	*Muskrat v. United States*, 744
May 15, 1911	*Gompers v. Buck's Stove and Range Co.*, 459
	Standard Oil v. United States, 976
May 29, 1911	*Coyle v. Smith*, 302
	United States v. American Tobacco Co., 1045
February 19, 1912	*Pacific States Telephone and Telegraph Co. v. Oregon*, 806
February 24, 1914	*Weeks v. United States*, 1138
June 8, 1914	*Shreveport Rate Cases*, 954

February 23, 1915	*Mutual Film Corp. v. Industrial Commission of Ohio*, 745
April 19, 1915	*Frank v. Mangum*, 420
June 21, 1915	*Guinn v. United States*, 501
January 8, 1917	*Clark Distilling Co. v. Western Maryland Railway Co.*, 275
April 9, 1917	*Bunting v. Oregon*, 220
November 5, 1917	*Buchanan v. Warley*, 215
January 7, 1918	*Selective Draft Law Cases*, 943
June 3, 1918	*Hammer v. Dagenhart*, 509
March 3, 1919	*Schenck v. United States*, 933
November 10, 1919	*Abrams v. United States*, 91
March 1, 1920	*United States v. United States Steel Corp.*, 1092
April 19, 1920	*Missouri v. Holland*, 721
January 3, 1921	*Duplex Printing Co. v. Deering*, 347
May 2, 1921	*Newberry v. United States*, 774
May 16, 1921	*Dillon v. Gloss*, 326
December 19, 1921	*Truax v. Corrigan*, 1037
May 15, 1922	*Bailey v. Drexel Furniture Co.*, 145
November 13, 1922	*Ozawa v. United States*, 801
December 11, 1922	*Pennsylvania Coal Co. v. Mahon*, 824
	United States v. Lanza, 1071
February 19, 1923	*Moore v. Dempsey*, 726
April 9, 1923	*Adkins v. Children's Hospital*, 105
June 4, 1923	*Frothingham v. Mellon*, 423
	Massachusetts v. Mellon, 684
	Meyer v. Nebraska, 693
June 11, 1923	*Wolff Packing Co. v. Court of Industrial Relations*, 1170
1924	*Alcoa v. Federal Trade Commission*, 116
March 2, 1925	*Carroll v. United States*, 235
June 1, 1925	*Pierce v. Society of Sisters*, 830
June 8, 1925	*Gitlow v. New York*, 452
May 24, 1926	*Corrigan v. Buckley*, 296
October 12, 1926	*Euclid v. Ambler Realty Co.*, 373
October 25, 1926	*Myers v. United States*, 746
February 28, 1927	*Tyson v. Banton*, 1039
March 7, 1927	*Nixon v. Herndon*, 778
May 2, 1927	*Buck v. Bell*, 216
May 26, 1927	*Whitney v. California*, 1151
June 4, 1928	*Olmstead v. United States*, 794

April 18, 1966   *Elfbrandt v. Russell*, 361
June 6, 1966   *Sheppard v. Maxwell*, 951
June 13, 1966   *Katzenbach v. Morgan*, 591
    Miranda v. Arizona, 712
November 14, 1966   *Adderley v. Florida*, 104
January 9, 1967   *Time v. Hill*, 1029
January 23, 1967   *Keyishian v. Board of Regents*, 600
March 13, 1967   *Klopfer v. North Carolina*, 604
April 11, 1967   *Federal Trade Commission v. Procter & Gamble Co.*, 392
May 15, 1967   *In re Gault*, 567
May 29, 1967   *Afroyim v. Rusk*, 111
    Reitman v. Mulkey, 870
June 12, 1967   *Loving v. Virginia*, 644
    United States v. Wade, 1099
December 11, 1967   *United States v. Robel*, 1086
December 18, 1967   *Katz v. United States*, 589
March 5, 1968   *Harris v. United States*, 516
May 20, 1968   *Duncan v. Louisiana*, 344
May 27, 1968   *Green v. County School Board of New Kent County*, 474
    United States v. O'Brien, 1076
June 3, 1968   *Witherspoon v. Illinois*, 1166
June 10, 1968   *Flast v. Cohen*, 409
    Terry v. Ohio, 1017
June 17, 1968   *Jones v. Alfred H. Mayer Co.*, 585
November 12, 1968   *Epperson v. Arkansas*, 368
February 24, 1969   *Tinker v. Des Moines Independent Community School District*, 1032
March 4, 1969   *Weeks v. Southern Bell*, 1137
April 7, 1969   *Kirkpatrick v. Preisler*, 604
    Stanley v. Georgia, 983
April 21, 1969   *Shapiro v. Thompson*, 945
June 9, 1969   *Brandenburg v. Ohio*, 196
    Red Lion Broadcasting Co. v. Federal Communications Commission, 860
June 16, 1969   *Powell v. McCormick*, 848
June 23, 1969   *Benton v. Maryland*, 164
    Chimel v. California, 257
September 26, 1969   *Bowe v. Colgate-Palmolive*, 185
October 29, 1969   *Alexander v. Holmes County Board of Education*, 123

July 2, 1976	*Gregg v. Georgia*, 477
	Woodson v. North Carolina, 1172
July 6, 1976	*Stone v. Powell*, 987
December 7, 1976	*General Electric v. Gilbert*, 435
December 8, 1976	*Alsager v. District Court*, 127
December 20, 1976	*Craig v. Boren*, 303
December 27, 1976	*Marvin v. Marvin*, 678
January 11, 1977	*Arlington Heights v. Metropolitan Housing Development Corp.*, 136
March 1, 1977	*United Jewish Organizations of Williamsburgh v. Carey*, 1041
May 31, 1977	*Moore v. City of East Cleveland*, 725
June 14, 1977	*Village of Skokie v. National Socialist Party of America*, 1116
June 20, 1977	*Maher v. Roe*, 665
June 27, 1977	*Bates v. State Bar of Arizona*, 161
June 28, 1977	*Nixon v. Administrator of General Services*, 776
June 29, 1977	*Coker v. Georgia*, 283
January 18, 1978	*Zablocki v. Redhail*, 1188
March 21, 1978	*Ballew v. Georgia*, 153
April 26, 1978	*First National Bank of Boston v. Bellotti*, 409
May 15, 1978	*Santa Clara Pueblo v. Martinez*, 927
May 23, 1978	*Marshall v. Barlow's*, 674
May 31, 1978	*Zurcher v. The Stanford Daily*, 1193
June 6, 1978	*Monell v. Department of Social Services*, 725
June 15, 1978	*Tennessee Valley Authority v. Hill*, 1011
June 26, 1978	*Penn Central Transportation Co. v. City of New York*, 822
June 28, 1978	*Regents of the University of California v. Bakke*, 864
June 29, 1978	*Butz v. Economou*, 225
March 5, 1979	*Orr v. Orr*, 798
June 5, 1979	*Personnel Administrator of Massachusetts v. Feeney*, 828
June 26, 1979	*Hutchinson v. Proxmire*, 548
June 27, 1979	*United Steelworkers of America v. Weber*, 1105
July 2, 1979	*Columbus Board of Education v. Penick*, 288
December 13, 1979	*Goldwater v. Carter*, 456
February 19, 1980	*Snepp v. United States*, 969
March 18, 1980	*Rummel v. Estelle*, 916
April 15, 1980	*Payton v. New York*, 821
April 22, 1980	*Mobile v. Bolden*, 724

CATEGORIZED LIST OF ENTRIES

INDEXES

PHOTO INDEX

Subject Index

Note that index references to pages 1243-1258 are glossary entries.

Fighting words doctrine, 245-246, 280, 610, 758, 857, 1015, 1117, 1248

Filburn, Roscoe, 1154-1156

Film censorship, 268-269, 370-371, 420-422, 745-746, 771, 1030-1031

Finley, Karen, 749-753

Firefighters Local Union No. 1784 v. Stotts et al., 402-407

First Amendment balancing, 130, 156, 761

First Amendment guarantees. See *Categorized List of Entries*

First English Evangelical Lutheran Church of Glendale v. County of Los Angeles, 408

First National Bank of Boston v. Bellotti, 409

Fiscal and monetary powers. See *Categorized List of Entries*

Flag desecration, 1019-1022, 1067-1068

Flag Desecration Act of 1968, 1021

Flag Protection Act of 1989, 1067

Flast v. Cohen, 409-410, 424, 1085

Fleeing felon statutes, 1010

Fletcher, Robert, 412

Fletcher v. Peck, 410-415

Florida; *Adderley v. Florida*, 104; *Chambers v. Florida*, 238-239; *Erznoznik v. Jacksonville*, 370-371; *Hoyt v. Florida*, 541; Jacksonville, 370-371; *Seminole Tribe v. Florida*, 944; *Williams v. Florida*, 1157

Florida Bar v. Went for It, 161

Florida v. Bostick, 416-417

Florida v. Royer, 562

Flynt, Larry, 548

Foley v. Connelie, 469

Fong Yue Ting v. United States, 258-260

Foraker Act of 1900, 573-574

Ford, Alvin Bernard, 417-418

Ford v. Wainwright, 140, 417-418, 653, 827, 901

Foreign policy. See *Categorized List of Entries*

Fortas, Abe, 66, 197, 368, 567-568, 714, 1033; career summary, 1203

44 Liquormart, Inc. v. Rhode Island, 172, 418-419

Fourteenth Amendment, 71-73, 98-99, 111, 760, 962-963, 968, 1039, 1184; and civil rights, 272; and equal protection clause, 457, 644, 1189; privileges or immunities clause, 194

Fourth Amendment, 32; search and seizure clause, 559-560, 605-607, 680; and *Whren v. United States*, 1152-1154

Frank v. Mangum, 420, 727

Frankfurter, Felix, 98-99, 106, 147, 220, 285, 293, 318, 458, 552, 596, 610, 661, 666, 737, 859, 888, 930, 1015-1016, 1040, 1080, 1090, 1146-1147, 1169, 1181; career summary, 1204

Fraud, 9-10; voter, 346, 500

Free exercise clause, 316, 364-365, 375, 623, 875, 1248

Free Speech Coalition, 137

Freedman, Ronald, 421

Freedman v. Maryland, 221, 420-422

Freedom Forum, 521

Freeman v. Pitts, 176

Frisking suspects, 561-562, 680, 1017, 1154, 1248

Frohwerk v. United States, 91

Frontiero v. Richardson, 422-423

Frothingham v. Mellon, 410, 423-424, 684, 1085

Fugitive slaves, 89-90, 586, 851

Full faith and credit clause, 1248

Fuller, Lon, 18

Fuller, Melville W., 240, 254, 574, 633, 837, 845, 1061, 1088, 1103, 1121; career summary, 1204

Mutual Film Corp. v. Industrial Commission of Ohio, 221, 745-746
Myers v. United States, 544, 746-747, 1156

Nabrit, James M., xlvi
Napoleon Bonaparte, 1070
Nast, Thomas, cartoon, 710
National Association for the Advancement of Colored People, 216, 502, 512, 779, 950, 999-1000
National Association for the Advancement of Colored People Legal Defense and Educational Fund, 123, 475
National Association for the Advancement of Colored People v. Alabama, 747-748
National Association for the Advancement of Colored People v. Alabama ex rel. Patterson, 907
National Association for the Advancement of Colored People v. Button, 748-749
National Consumers League, 736
National Endowment for the Arts v. Finley, 749-753
National Indian Gaming Commission, 231
National Industrial Recovery Act of 1933, 236, 810, 932
National Labor Relations Act of 1935, 754
National Labor Relations Board v. Jones and Laughlin Steel Corp., 237, 591, 753-754
National League of Cities v. Usery, 432, 755
National Rifle Association, 329
National Socialist Party of America, 1116-1118
National Treasury Employees Union v. Von Raab, 756-757
Nationality Act of 1940, 111

Native American Church, 364
Native American sovereignty. See *Categorized List of Entries*
Native Americans, 32, 62, 248-253, 744; commerce of, 241; and federal government, 248; gaming, 229-232, 944; and Andrew Jackson, 250; land claims, 411, 580, 1172-1174; religious practices, 364-365; removal from Georgia, 249; treaties, 376-377; tribal courts, 1008, 1070-1071
Natural law, 4, 17-18, 131-132, 226-227, 322, 735-739, 887-888, 1251; modern revival of, 18
Natural rights, 1251
Nazi Party, American, 1116-1118
Neagle, David, 568-570
Near v. Minnesota, 757-759, 767
Nebbia v. New York, 740, 759-760, 1040, 1170
Nebraska; *Halter v. Nebraska*, 1021; *Meyer v. Nebraska*, 693-694; and railroads, 968
Nebraska Press Association v. Stuart, 760-761, 882
Necessary and proper clause, 241, 660, 1247
Negligence, 20
Nelson, Samuel, 287; career summary, 1210
Nelson, Steve, 825
New Deal, 108, 219, 236, 348, 510, 631, 754, 1059, 1144
New Hampshire; *Chaplinsky v. New Hampshire*, 245-246; *Cox v. New Hampshire*, 301; same-sex marriage, 465
New Jersey; *Everson v. Board of Education of Ewing Township*, 375-376; *In re Baby M*, 564-565; *Twining v. New Jersey*, 1038-1039; woman suffrage, 708